Praise fo
BEEBE BAH

THE WAY *of the* WILD GOOSE

"A lingering historic mystery and an unexpected personal twist make *The Way of the Wild Goose* an entertaining, thoughtful, and valuable addition to the wonderfully digressive genre of the pilgrimage memoir." **—GIDEON LEWIS-KRAUS, STAFF WRITER FOR *THE NEW YORKER* AND AUTHOR OF *A SENSE OF DIRECTION: PILGRIMAGE FOR THE RESTLESS AND THE HOPEFUL***

"A luminous, heartfelt journey. Beebe Bahrami has produced something unique: not one, but three magical pilgrim walks filled with web-footed Virgin Marys and mother goddesses, eerie coincidences, fairies, and Templar Knights—and with enough Cat Stevens, food poisoning, and scientific backup to keep it all real. Big fun!" **—REBEKAH SCOTT, AUTHOR OF *A FURNACE FULL OF GOD: A HOLY YEAR ON THE CAMINO DE SANTIAGO***

"Beebe Bahrami fills these pages with facts about history, religion, geography, and more. She is a scholar, an anthropologist, and the person you would most like to be seated next to at a dinner party. We can't all have the pleasure of walking across a country with her, but we can enjoy the next best thing: We can read her books.

"*The Way of the Wild Goose* positively shimmers with enthusiasm and wonder. This book will be equally enchanting to the seasoned pilgrim and to those who may pick it up on a whim. Good writing and Beebe's ability to weave together history, mystery, and magic adds up to a fascinating recounting of a remarkable modern pilgrimage. If you are a Camino de Santiago devotee—or are thinking you may be one in the future—you have probably already read some books on the Camino. Prepare to meet your new favorite—you will savor this one!" **—ANNIE O'NEIL, DIRECTOR/PRODUCER OF *PHIL'S CAMINO*, COPRODUCER AND PARTICIPATING PILGRIM FOR *WALKING THE CAMINO: SIX WAYS TO SANTIAGO*, AND AUTHOR OF *EVERYDAY CAMINO WITH ANNIE***

MOON CAMINO DE SANTIAGO

"I have spent several hours going through the book and am amazed at the attention to detail and the amount of work that has gone into it. As an author, I shudder to think of how much fact checking had to happen. And the detailed on-the-ground research is mind-boggling—but in the end that's what made it the incredibly useful book that it is." **–LEIGH MCADAM,** *HIKE, BIKE, TRAVEL* **BLOG**

CAFÉ NEANDERTAL

"We need to understand who we were in order to know where we are headed. In the caves and forests of France's Dordogne region, Beebe Bahrami guides us on a haunting encounter with what may be our earlier selves, a creature whose passions and powers and motives we have only begun to fathom. A fascinating read for anyone who claims to be human." **–PETER STARK, AUTHOR OF** *ASTORIA: JOHN JACOB ASTOR*

"With a pilgrim's reverence and a scientist's exactitude, Bahrami captures the textures, smells, and sounds of the excavation sites and adjacent towns." *–PUBLISHERS WEEKLY*

CAFÉ OC

"Beebe Bahrami gives eloquent voice to a mystical search for belonging. Her rich storytelling, as an observant cultural anthropologist, opens windows into conscious living.... Follow her writings wherever they lead, as her journey aids in our unfoldment." **–KIM GRANT, FOUNDER OF BINDU TRIPS**

THE SPIRITUAL TRAVELER: SPAIN

"Bahrami has tracked down where the sacred ceremonies are still sustained, providing the reader and visitor with an accessible shortcut to living histories and vibrant folkloric traditions and mythologies. The author writes with a felicitous ease, in many ways recalling (in the first person narrative) an earlier tradition of guide books." *–EXPEDITION* **MAGAZINE; REVIEWED BY RICHARD HODGES, FORMER DIRECTOR OF THE PENN MUSEUM**

THE WAY
of the
WILD GOOSE

THREE PILGRIMAGES FOLLOWING
GEESE, STARS, AND HUNCHES
ON THE CAMINO DE SANTIAGO

BEEBE BAHRAMI

Monkfish Book Publishing Company
Rhinebeck, New York

The Way of the Wild Goose: Three Pilgrimages Following Geese, Stars, and Hunches on the Camino de Santiago
© 2022 by Beebe Bahrami

This book is memoir. It reflects the author's present recollections of experiences over time. Some names and characteristics have been changed, some events have been compressed, and some dialogue has been recreated.

Paperback ISBN 978-1-948626-63-7
eBook ISBN 978-1-948626-64-4

Library of Congress Cataloging-in-Publication Data

Names: Bahrami, Beebe, author.
Title: The way of the wild goose : three pilgrimages following geese,
    stars, and hunches on the Camino de Santiago / Beebe Bahrami.
Description: Rhinebeck, New York : Monkfish Book Publishing Company, [2022]
Identifiers: LCCN 2021053104 (print) | LCCN 2021053105 (ebook) | ISBN
    9781948626637 (Paperback) | ISBN 9781948626644 (eBook)
Subjects: LCSH: Pilgrims and pilgrimages.--France. | Pilgrims and
    pilgrimages.--Spain. | Camino de Santiago de Compostela.
Classification: LCC BL619.P5 B34 2022 (print) | LCC BL619.P5 (ebook) |
    DDC 203/.50944--dc23/eng/20220114
LC record available at https://lccn.loc.gov/2021053104
LC ebook record available at https://lccn.loc.gov/2021053105

Book and cover design by Colin Rolfe
Front cover painting "From the Goose to the Girl" by Jane Hammond. Photo courtesy of Pace Prints.
Front cover photo of the duck frieze of the west gate of Morlaàs Church, France by Beebe Bahrami.

Monkfish Book Publishing Company
22 East Market Street, Suite 304
Rhinebeck, NY 12572
(845) 876-4861
monkfishpublishing.com

The author's watercolor and pen-and-ink rendering of the human-scale stone *Juego de la oca del Camino de Santiago* (Game of the Goose of the Camino de Santiago) board game inlaid in the entirety of the Plaza de Santiago in Logroño, La Rioja, on the Camino Francés in Spain.

CONTENTS

PART I:
LA REINE PÉDAUQUE:
A pilgrimage in France

PART II:
THE MISTRESS OF ANIMALS:
A pilgrimage in France and Spain

PART III:
THE SWAN:
A pilgrimage in France and Spain

The author's hand-drawn map of some of the Camino's trails,
showing her three pilgrimages.

MEETING THE GOOSE

A LATE OCTOBER dawn broke soft and low, slowly stretching its rose and purple fingers across the dark horizon as I strode west out of Pamplona. My breath misted in the chilly morning air. A primal sense of freedom pulsed through my limbs. The pack on my back held everything that I needed for several weeks of walking. No one else was on the trail.

A blizzard in the Pyrenees had undone my plans to begin this journey on the French side of the mountains in Saint-Jean-Pied-de-Port, a popular starting point for the most historic pilgrim trail of the Camino de Santiago, the Way of Saint James, known as the Camino Francés, the French Way. But here, in the bowl of the pass on the other side, where the mountains give way to the hills and plains of northern Spain, there was no snow, only arid, tawny-colored wheat fields. The wheat had recently been harvested, leaving behind stubbled shafts that looked like a giant crewcut on the rolling hills.

All I had to do was follow the sun's path throughout the day as it rose behind me in the east, arched overhead by midday, then descended ahead of me in the west by late afternoon, marking my stopping place for the night. Each day was an unknown but held the certainty that each one would end a little farther west. If I followed the sun and the signs, I reasoned, I'd be fine. I moved like the ancient nomads, the way our species journeyed since the beginning, at the pace of feet.

I heard the rhythmic sound of dry earth and pea-sized pebbles crunching underfoot. I breathed in a deep lungful of that cool, dewy air. I felt the weight of my pack, at first comforting but gradually growing irritating. In truth, it held more than I needed, bearing extra weight from a research project requiring several weeks of backpacking across Spain, including notebooks, extra clothes for interviews and archival visits, heavy glossy pamphlets from tourist offices across Spain, and more socks than necessary (though, according to one school of thought, you can never have too many socks). But the heaviest item in my pack was a tight and dense bundle of fear that had made me pack things I might need *just in case*. I vowed that night to shed some of its weight, send home the printed materials, give away extra clothing, and most importantly, release the fear-bundle into the ether with no return address. Resolved, I shouldered the self-inflicted burden more lightly and felt another surge of electricity rush through me—the intoxicating liberation of the open road.

I was heading to the holy city of Santiago de Compostela in Spain's far northwest, where lies the purported tomb of Saint James the Greater. Of the twelve apostles, James the Greater was one of the three closest to Jesus, along with Peter and James's brother John. No historical evidence proves James ever came to Spain, but legends circulating in the sixth century, possibly starting in southern France, mushroomed across Europe. They spread the appealing rumors via stories, songs, poems, and hymns that James had evangelized in Iberia in around AD 40. After James returned in AD 44 to Jerusalem, where Herod Agrippa had him beheaded, later legends relayed how a magical stone boat guided by angels had brought his body back to Galicia to be buried on the ancient funerary hill in Santiago de Compostela. James's tomb was then forgotten. One night, some eight hundred years later, in the early ninth century, a local hermit saw a trail of bright stars and followed them, arriving at the mound and discovering the sarcophagus. The local bishop Theodomir identified it as the tomb of Sant Iago, Spanish for Saint James, which, over time, was condensed to Santiago. As these word-of-mouth fables spread, pilgrims began to flock to northwestern Spain to gather grace. They, along with the locals, wove James's mythic personality intimately into this land. Santiago's presence in Spain became real.

I still had over 700 kilometers (435 miles) left to go, and yet a surprising awareness was already rising up inside me—that the holy goal of this pilgrimage road was not in the far northwest, but also right here, and here, and here.

I heard another crunch of dry earth and stone as my footfall defined this prayer-bead-like engagement with the trail. I felt an ethereal energy emanate from underfoot and all around. I sensed suddenly the cycle that millions before me must have felt, of being reborn each day with the rising and setting sun as it illuminated each rock, tree, stream, and chapel that defined this as a holy landscape. I felt this holiness as profoundly real and also far more ancient than the Christian pilgrimage road's 1,200 years. I could feel them all, the millions of prior footsteps of earlier peoples, from medieval to modern pilgrims, stretching all the way back in time to the first prehistoric hunter-gatherers, herders, and farmers who, thousands of years ago, traversed this same fertile corridor of southern France and northern Spain. The presence of those first peoples was as palpable as Saint James himself. The trail passed through an old geography that included Europe's oldest human remains. Their caves, rivers, mountaintops, and valleys still sang their old songs, which laced the wind and turned concentric circles around the many medieval chapels that lined the path—chapels that had intentionally been built over earlier prehistoric sacred springs, wells, standing stones, groves, and grottos.

From other pilgrims, especially those hailing from France and Spain for whom this road was a birthright, I had heard talk that the Camino was a leyline—a path of energy naturally emitted from the earth itself that could transform you if you walked it. Some said it would initiate you to a deeper state of consciousness and spiritual experience. Others said that signs guided the initiation, especially signs in the shape of a goose or a duck or simply the three-pronged form of their footprint.

Geese and ducks dive, float, swim, and fly—masters of the

lower, middle, and upper realms. They also migrate long distances, especially geese, and in this way they are like nomads and pilgrims. Medieval pilgrims followed many things to navigate their way west to Santiago de Compostela, including watching the flight of geese by day and the splash of stars of the Milky Way by night. In the heyday of the Camino, medieval stonemasons, another itinerant group who surely navigated in similar ways, in their engravings on churches of the eleventh and twelfth centuries often treated geese and ducks as symbolically synonymous. Even modern biologists classify them, along with swans, as close cousins in the same family, *Anatidae*, which includes only these three as members. It was the medieval masons who engraved the Anatidae's images and footprints in stone and wood on select ancient churches. According to some of the pilgrims with whom I spoke, these goose- and duck-marked spots indicated places potent with spiritual experience, places where the energies of heaven and earth met directly, where the veil between the worlds was lifted.

Some of the same French and Spanish pilgrims who told me all this also said that the popular European children's game, the Game of the Goose, was a metaphor and a map to a more esoteric experience of the Camino. The key character in the game was a goose, a lucky figure who aided and abetted throughout the game to help a person reach the winning square, in this case, Santiago de Compostela. I had never heard of the Game of the Goose before stepping onto the Camino, but I soon learned that it was similar to the game of Snakes and Ladders. Both games are played on a labyrinth-like game board with players throwing dice to move their game pieces toward the final winning square. On the way, they land on squares where they endure setbacks or reap rewards, sliding back and forth in an effort to win.

None of these goose ideas made any sense to me. Out here on the Camino, I had yet to see anything remotely related to geese. What did the Anatidae, let alone their footprints, have to do with this path? I dropped that idea and forgot all about it. But I was already feeling the leyline as an undeniable vibratory hum underground that seemed to support me as I stepped along.

I cast my view once more across those taupe-toned and bristled fields that swept all around. They looked different from moments before, stopping me in my tracks. The little cropped wheat shafts in each field seemed as if illuminated from within. The crewcut was aglow.

Prior to beginning the Camino, I had been trekking for several weeks across Iberia—south, north, east, and west, on many varied pilgrim paths. Many months earlier a publishing company had contracted me to write a book on Spain's sacred sites and trails. I had saved the last five weeks of research for walking the Camino from the Pyrenees to Santiago de Compostela to the Atlantic coast. Perhaps because I had already been walking for weeks, I was more susceptible to sense the leyline energy on the Camino. Perhaps this also explained why I began to have vivid dreams, dense with message and meaning. Each night, they came on like a nonstop freight train. I dreamed I attended the funeral of a dear family member who was still living. I dreamed of people I loved who had already passed away, and they came with clear messages for me that I remembered upon waking. I dreamed I was walking the Camino with my husband, brother, parents, and various friends from different stages of my life, and each night we stayed in one of my many childhood homes, which were now all on the Camino. I dreamed I attended my own funeral.

The trail rose and grew more vertical with each step. The numinous wheat fields around me dimmed. I leaned into the hill and made my way slowly up, aware now only of the burn in my legs and the dense weight on my back. Nearing the slope's crest, huge turbine windmills lined the length of the ridge, making it look as if I climbed along the spiky spine of a huge sleeping dragon. With a few dozen more meters to reach the summit, I muscled in again, wondering to myself about the wisdom of making the march the way I was doing it, if it was worth it—and was that a hotspot on the back of my right heel?

"*Buenos días*," I heard from below. A young man suddenly appeared from thin air. He quickly caught up to me. "I'm Javier," he offered cheerfully, "from Argentina." I learned he was a university student in Pamplona, a roadrunner, too, given how swiftly he moved up the steep terrain. I did my best to step into stride with him as he said, "This walk is remarkably worth it."

Trail magic.

"You've done this before?" I asked, puffing for the air that both the hill and Javier had just knocked out of me.

"I've walked the Camino Francés four times," he chirped, "twice from Saint-Jean-Pied-de-Port to Santiago de Compostela in one stretch, and two times in sections. It is a splendid adventure, well worth it," he repeated. "I am now walking it a fifth time, this time also in sections."

He would walk each set of vacation days, be it a weekend, week, or two weeks at a time, and then race back to classes and set out again on his next break, picking up where he'd left off. He was soon far enough ahead of me that we wished each other *buen Camino*, good passage, and I watched him diminish and disappear over the crest.

When I arrived at the top of the dragon's back, I took in a remarkable view: distant chalky mountains to the north, and rugged and scrubby rolling hills all around, some with vineyards, some with wheat, and some with clustered almond trees. I stood near a large monument installed in honor of pilgrims and this place, the Alto del Perdón, the Height of Pardon. A strong wind whipped at me, making the point that this was a place to release things and let the wind carry them away. I stood firm to allow it to lighten my spirit and then continued across the ridge to the other side, where the track plummeted into a steeper climb downhill. It was coated with small, loose river rock.

Stopping to consider a more careful approach, I looked past the hill's base where the trail leveled out and wove in and out of thickets of nut trees and saw that once again I was not alone. This time, a disheveled man paced back and forth in an alcove of shrub and stone. As I looked more closely, I saw that the alcove formed a half-moon shape that wrapped around a glimmering white marble statue of Mary on a pedestal. The man walked to and fro before her, gesticulating violently with his arms, one hand holding a cigarette.

I couldn't tell from where I stood if he was speaking to himself or to Mary or to some invisible entity. There was a shopping cart parked on the other side of the trail's edge and inside it was the man's large backpack. All around the cart's rim he had tied plastic bags filled with food and gear, a modern version of the medieval pilgrim's donkey. Asking Mary for grace, I took a deep breath, and warily began the descent.

Pop! Javier materialized next to me, grinning. I almost skidded down the slope.

"I see you've met our permanent pilgrim," he said.

"Really? He never leaves the trail?"

"Villagers and other pilgrims give him food and help him as they can. He walks back and forth along the path. This," Javier swept his arms indicating the entire pilgrimage road, "is his home. He's perfectly harmless," Javier assured me. He then glided effortlessly down the slope.

I followed, less gracefully, and passed in and out of clusters of almond trees and soon reached the shrine with the permanent pilgrim. Javier was nowhere once again. The pilgrim was still gesticulating and smoking feverishly, seeing only whoever it was to whom he spoke. I tried to slip past unseen, but at the last moment he paused his intense conversation, smiled warmly at me, and called out, "Buen Camino."

"Buen Camino," I returned hesitantly. He smiled and went back to his conversation. I was invisible again. I continued on, but in that brief exchange, wonder replaced worry. My fear bundle was already lightening up and a new reality sank in: that this trail was so generous that it could also become a home for a lost pilgrim who had no other place of belonging. I realized then that everyone here belonged, that the Camino did not judge, it only guided and supported.

By late afternoon I reached Puente la Reina, where I stopped for the night. I showered, rested, enjoyed a celebratory glass of local wine and a hearty dinner cooked with vegetables plucked from the kitchen garden I'd passed on my way into town, and then set to the task of pruning my pack. I kept only what was truly necessary and replaced leaden fear with feather-light trust. If the trail could manifest Javier at will and support a man living entirely and indefinitely on it, surely it would give me what I needed when I needed it.

Javier, in his elfin manner, wove in and out of my walk for another day. My last sighting of him was as we were both making our way towards Estella. It had been a long day and my map told me that the town was right ahead, but each bend in the scrubby and jagged hills through which I walked revealed yet more hills and wild bushes but no view of Estella. I was so tired that I was thinking of just stopping and sleeping under a stand of shrubs when, *pop*, there was Javier.

"Don't worry," he said, without me saying a word as he wheeled along at his usual speed. "Estella is closer than you realize. It always feels like this, as if it will never appear, and then suddenly, you'll round a bend in the hills, and there it is, opening up like a favorite aunt's warm embrace."

"You're heading back to Pamplona today for classes?

"Yes," he replied, "and my bus leaves in an hour!" He picked up his pace but kept talking, words tumbling over his shoulder as he powered on. "Remember that the Camino is what you make of it. It's not linear and it's not about starting in one place and ending in Santiago de Compostela. It's about being where you are and being open to the road, its lessons, and its gifts." He then evaporated into a cloud of dust and disappeared forever around the next turn.

What Javier said slammed into me. I stopped to absorb it. I turned to face the green hill to my left, and in that moment two black horses sauntered towards me. We greeted each other, one horse offering an inquisitive neigh and inviting me to stroke her silken nose. I knew then that I was like Javier—I would continue to return to walk the Camino indefinitely, experiencing its beauty, meeting its challenges, and with luck, receiving its gifts.

I took a deep breath and inhaled the scent of sweet grass, wild mint, and musty horsehair. I turned back to the route invigorated, its dust now settled from Javier's swirling departure. The next bend revealed the town. True to Javier's words, the trail slipped into what looked and felt like open arms, those of a beloved aunt, pulling me into an embrace formed by protective hills around a wide, swiftly flowing river. I wanted to feel this arriving, this magic, over and over.

∨   ∨   ∨

I'D FIRST HEARD of the Camino in 1986 when I was an American college student studying abroad in Sevilla in Andalucía in southern Spain. One early spring day, I sat in the front row, as was my habit, in a chilly, stonewalled classroom to better hear and try to understand the fast-clipped Castilian of my professor in a course on the history of Spain. As I took notes, he paced back and forth, lecturing and chain-smoking, as was his habit. That day, we were thick into the early Middle Ages and the period when Iberia was a rich tapestry of diversity of Jewish, Christian, and Islamic communities, north and south. My professor began to describe a frontier land, a long linear geography that sat between the Christian north and the Muslim south, and just as he passed by my desk, he uttered the name of that geography, *Camino de Santiago,* and also absent-mindedly tapped ash from his cigarette onto my notebook.

It was a fitting gesture, for we were in the old tobacco factory in Seville that had been turned into university classrooms and offices. Like Bizet's Carmen, I flicked aside the unwanted embers and smudged forever a sooty mark around those three words that I had just jotted down, *Camino de Santiago*, making them stand out more and emphasizing the spine-tingling excitement they elicited for reasons I could hardly understand. *One day*, I said to myself as I stared at the ash-smeared page, *I will find a way to go there and walk this.*

When the semester ended, I had a week before needing to return home, and I took a train north to visit cousins in Paris. I sat at a window seat, watching the landscape change from the dry mustard-toned earth and rolling hills of Andalucía and La Mancha, then covered in splashes of pale green spring wheat and sprays of red poppies, to the gray- and cream-toned urban density of Madrid. There, I changed for another train, making for the border with France at Irún and Hendaye in the Pyrenees, where they meet the Atlantic coastline, and then through Aquitaine and onward to Paris.

I sat again at a window seat and watched the rocky landscape of northern Madrid turn to olive tree-carpeted, sand-toned, rolling hills, occasionally catching glimpses of grazing jet-black bulls, their elegant bow-curved horns moving up and down as they chomped on wild herbs and grasses. By late afternoon, the train passed into the rippling green and forested lands of Navarra, and by early evening, into Basque Country, an otherworldly landscape of steep, wild, and velvety moss-toned mountains dotted with red-shuttered, white-stone farmhouses nestled in the nooks of hill and dale. Black-and-cream sheep speckled the high slopes, and a thick and fast-moving mist began to cloak the river valleys whose vertical shoulders stood so near each other that they quickly shut out the rays of the setting sun.

When the train traversed Navarra and Basque Country, it crossed deeply into Camino territory and intersected with that most famous of the Camino routes, the Camino Francés. It was called the French Way because so many Franks helped build the Camino in the Middle Ages as well as walked it as pilgrims. It was in that intersecting geography that I began to experience a strange but beguiling physical sensation I had not felt earlier on the journey or anywhere else in my life. The feeling intensified as we reached the Pyrenean border with France, neither letting up nor dissipating until after the train passed Bordeaux and continued north. It was so strong and intoxicating, awakening all my cells with vibrant energy, that I did not sleep; instead, I stayed glued to the window, trying to pry out of the landscape the reason why it was calling to me. I felt as if I already had a history here, had lived here before, for my spirit seemed to know it well even though my mind and body were experiencing it for the first time.

A week later, I returned from Paris on the same train, now heading south to Madrid to fly home. The same feeling returned with the same intensity as we passed that corridor of southwestern France and north central Spain. When I returned home to Colorado, I never forgot that magnetic pull, nor the magical sensation that the words *Camino de Santiago* elicited when I heard, read, or said them.

But as things worked out, I led my life as a young, just-out-of-college woman with my head, reasoning through everything and rationalizing next steps toward a practical and successful adult future. I worked hard, buckled down, saved money, and ultimately went to graduate school in anthropology. There, as much as I dreamed of doing my doctorate on something having to do with Iberia and its famous road, I heeded my advisor's advice to focus on a non-European society and did the best next thing: I went to Morocco and wrote my dissertation on the persisting cultural and historical connections between Morocco and Spain that were forged in the Middle Ages. Though seemingly far removed from the Camino, that experience serendipitously gave me the essential foundations toward understanding the medieval world that had created the pilgrimage route.

The Camino would very likely never have existed without the competition and creative collaboration of the multiple-faith and highly international Iberian kingdoms and civilizations that arose over the 800 years following the invasion and conquest of Iberia by Berbers and Arabs in AD 711. The not-so-coincidental discovery of Saint James the Greater's tomb around AD 814 gave the fractious and fractured Christian north a common goal around which to rally and fight for power and territory against the largely unified Muslim south. The Camino de Santiago developed as a geographical frontier line between the two competing halves of the Peninsula. By the time of the Camino's peak in popularity, with pilgrims coming from all across Europe in the eleventh and twelfth centuries, the massive building campaigns and development of the pilgrimage road was greatly funded by tribute, especially huge quantities of gold, paid by the then more fractured Muslim south to the still contentious but now more unified Christian north. In this largely collaborative and diverse climate, many Jewish, Muslim, Christian, and even still partially pagan craftsmen and masons from all across Iberia, Europe, and beyond gave their labor and skills to the road's construction, adding layers and nuance to a path that already shimmied through ancient territories that had been occupied by humans for many millennia.

It took me nine years from that spring day in Seville to make my way at last to the north of Spain and walk the Camino. Even then, I had only enough time and means to cover a small part of the trail, but I was finally waking up to the need to let my life be guided as much by my heart as by my head. I did not want to delay any longer. And that first time was enough to confirm that the pull of the Camino and that region of southern France and northern Spain was very real. It also taught me that the path was profound, old, and many layered. And that trail magic was real—a synchronistic flow that breached the barrier between inner and outer worlds and answered all needs.

Like Javier, I kept going back, exploring in sections as time and means allowed. Back home, over the years, I shifted from being a university professor to an ethnographic consultant, to a magazine editor, to a freelance writer. The latter ultimately landed me that contract to write a book about the sacred sites and pilgrim routes of Spain, giving me the chance at long last—twenty-one years since that spring day in Seville—to hike the whole Camino in one season.

∨ ∨ ∨

AFTER ESTELLA AND Javier's departure, trail magic continued.

There were countless kind locals who, unbidden, offered welcoming places to rest along with reviving food and refreshing water.

There was a man weeding his kitchen garden who gave me words of encouragement as I passed when I most needed them.

There was an eighty-five-year-old nun from Montpellier who had walked all the way from her convent in southern France and who, for some reason, kept appearing ahead of me even when I had only just passed her. She never passed me, and yet there she always was, up ahead—and most unnerving of all, by late afternoon already seated at a café and checked in at a local *albergue*, pilgrim's dorm, as I stumbled in. Once, I looked at her in a challenging way, wanting an explanation for this nonlinear reality, but she just smiled, challenging me back to dare to ask how a lifetime dedicated to service, meditation, and prayer could bend space and time.

There was Clara, a chatty English nurse from Norfolk who could talk the legs off an iron kettle, and always appeared when I most wanted silence or felt especially impatient. She taught me about the flaws in my own prejudices and biases, and also about the value of establishing healthy personal boundaries and asking for quiet.

There were two speed walkers from Granada nearing the end of their vacation time and planning to return the next year to finish the Camino. We intersected just as I was arriving at the conclusion—in my head—that an idea obsessively debated by pilgrims in the dorms about whether those who did not walk the whole 500 miles (800 kilometers) in one go were "true pilgrims," was total nonsense. These two struck me very much as true pilgrims.

I matched their pace, and we flew toward Logroño, the capital of La Rioja. At the city's edge, a woman called to us from under a huge fig tree in front of her small roadside home. There was a table with water, figs, and an inkpad and stamp. We gathered around her, and she introduced herself as María. Her mother, Felisa, had begun this tradition in the 1940s and continued it until recently, and now María carried it forward. She invited us to hydrate and feast on the sweet figs from her tree as she stamped each of our passport-sized pilgrim credentials, which gave us access to *albergues*. The two Granadans soon disappeared down the road, but I lingered. The ink stamp on my credential said, *Higos, agua, y amor*—figs, water, and love—which had been Felisa's and was now María's motto and mission on the Camino. María and her mother before her treated us all as true pilgrims, no matter how we walked. I thanked María and continued down the hill.

In Logroño, I met the goose. As I passed into the small square next to the church dedicated to Santiago, I noticed that the entire plaza had been inlaid with a massive Game of the Goose board game of gray- and cream-colored granite and marble squares depicting the different squares of the game, including its gifts and ordeals. Many were inlaid with images of some of the Camino's most famous or enigmatic churches, castles, bridges, and monasteries, along with white geese everywhere, making explicit the connection between game, goose, and trail. Large, sculpted stone dice lay arrayed around the edges, serving as benches on the perimeter, where people could sit and watch as others used their own bodies as game pieces to move along the squares of the winding, serpent-like game. All a player needed was a pair of dice in his or her pocket to throw in order to play.

I froze in place midway across the plaza, realizing that this whole goose business was real—real enough that the city had directed funds to build this metaphoric monument to the pilgrim's spiritual journey. I moved off the board game and sat on a die a long while, watching two little boys run across the squares, in part playing the game and in part playing soccer.

I eventually worked out the rules of the game. The inlaid serpentine game board was divided into sixty-three squares. Square one was the starting point, located at the outer edge of the sinuous path, which wound back and forth to the far end on the sixty-third, winning square. Twenty-three of the squares, a little over one-third of them, had features on them that determined your fate if you landed on them. A goose marked fourteen of those twenty-three squares: thirteen were active in the game, and the fourteenth greeted the winner at the last, winning square.

Suddenly I had a flashback to when I had been in Barcelona a few weeks earlier. There, I'd found thirteen white geese in the heart of the cloister in the heart of the city's cathedral. The birds were kept there by tradition, but no one could explain why. Those thirteen geese matched the number of active geese squares on the game. In Logroño, I learned that goose squares were lucky squares as you made your way forward. If you landed on a goose square, you got to move your game piece again for the same number of times on the original rolled dice that had landed you there.

The other nine marked squares had other adventures encoded into them, some of them obstacles, other ones gifts. Squares six and twelve were bridges, both key medieval sites on the Camino, one on the route beginning in Aragon, farther east, and the second being the famous Queen's Bridge in Puente la Reina in Navarra. Landing on a bridge was good luck, as bridges were indeed good luck in the Middle Ages, making so many river crossings safer. In the game, landing on a bridge let you slide forward another twelve spaces. Two squares, numbers twenty-six and fifty-three, had dice depicted on them. Landing on these allowed you to roll again. Square nineteen was an inn, which forced you to miss a turn. Curiously, in this inlaid game, none other than Logroño's own cityscape with its massive stone bridge holding the foreground represented the inn on square nineteen. Were the town leaders suggesting we pilgrims spend more time there?

Square thirty-one was a well. Landing there halted the journey and you couldn't leave until another player landed there and released you (then they, too, became stuck until another player came along). The same rule held for square fifty-two, which depicted a tower or prison. Square forty-two was a labyrinth that sent you back to square thirty, perhaps providing a lesson in getting distracted on the path or needing to spend more time in reflection and centering one's intentions. Or was it a metaphor for the fact that walking this path was rarely linear, as Javier had said, even if the trail seemed to be?

And most harrowing of all, square fifty-eight landed one on death, which here was depicted by a solitary skeletal figure carrying a sickle. That this square arrived a mere five spaces before reaching the end made it all the more of a gamble to play this game, for anyone who landed on death had to go all the way back to the beginning and start again. Maybe square fifty-eight suggested reincarnation, or perhaps it simply implied a spiritual death before being reborn, or that endings, in many ways, are more dangerous than beginnings and middles, or that life itself is rarely linear and sometimes we have to start all over, even late in the game.

As the boys played, laughed, and competed, I discovered another rule laced with metaphor: If you landed on a square occupied by another player, you had to go back to the square that you occupied before that throw of the dice. This seemed to say that you may be walking this road with others, but you cannot walk another's path, only your own.

And finally, square sixty-three, the winning final square, was inlaid with a replica of the famous twelfth-century image of Saint James that greets arriving pilgrims in Santiago de Compostela at the western entrance gate of the cathedral. It was an elegant depiction of James, who looks you warmly in the eye and sends generous blessings toward you and all the people you love and for whom you have walked. Unlike there, here on the board the image was augmented with a big, fat, white goose—the fourteenth and welcoming goose of the game—who hovered over James's right shoulder. To win the game, you had to land on this goose, but to do so, you also had to roll the exact number dice to land on square sixty-three. If you didn't, you would have to move your piece to the final square and then backward again to complete the full number indicated on the dice. You then kept throwing and moving like this until you finally threw the exact right number to land on square sixty-three, unless someone else did it before you and won the game. Also, if in moving backwards you landed on a goose square, this time it meant you had to move backwards again the same number of spaces you just threw on the dice. So, it seemed that while geese were lucky, they were also teaching us about life. Often, as we strive toward a goal, it unfolds in steps forward and steps backward, but if we persevere, we eventually reach our objective.

Like the Camino, the game is not easy. Now I knew that, in the popular imagination at least, and perhaps in history, the game and the Camino were connected. Yet still, no one had explained the geese to me. How had they come to be on the lucky squares in the game and the guides on the Camino? What did they really mean?

After La Rioja, I sauntered (curiously, *saunter* is an English verb from a French phrase, *saint terre,* holy earth) into Castile and the hilly landscape known as Montes de Oca, hills of the goose. *Oca* came from the name Romans had given this area, *Auca,* which means goose in Latin and later Occitan, the Romance language that evolved from Latin in southern France and northern Spain. Yet, still, no one seemed to know why the Romans named this goose territory.

I forgot all about geese again as I pushed deeper into Castile. I had fallen in love with walking without reservations, not knowing where or when I would eat or sleep, yet each day all my needs were met, nearly all of them in delightful and unexpected ways. I never went without; in fact, I walked in abundance, despite having no itinerary but the plan to walk and to trust. I wrote in my notebook one day, *Trusting in the benevolence of the universe is magic.* My mind had made a significant shift away from fear-thinking to trust-thinking. I hoped I could remember this state of being and practice when I returned home and was no longer in the support network of the Camino.

In Burgos, I met a young pilgrim from Köln, Germany. His Brazilian brother-in-law had walked the Camino that May as a spiritual initiation, guided by a sacred text that was given to him by a spiritual teacher in Switzerland. He was so profoundly transformed by the experience that he encouraged his young German brother-in-law to walk it. The German quit his job in order to fully walk the path, going at his own pace with no set arrival date in Santiago de Compostela. He also planned to continue from there to the coast at Finisterre. As he went, he checked in now and then with his brother-in-law, who now acted as a spiritual guide in the same manner as the Swiss teacher. The young man was also to learn the same sacred text as he walked. He tapped his shirt's breast pocket as he told me this, and I could make out the shape of folded papers tucked inside. I wanted very much to see this mystical document, but already gleaned that it was only for select eyes. Luckily, the young man was willing to share what he could.

"I am also supposed to practice being present as I walk," he said, "and to look for signs."

"Signs?" I asked.

"There are several kinds. One is the goose's footprint." He drew in the air with his finger a three-pronged shape: Ⅴ.

It hardly clarified anything for me—was it the Trinity, or magical things happening in threes, or a threefold path? But I leaned toward him, intrigued, because here it was again: the goose.

"Are the goose signs noted in that text in your pocket?" I inquired, imagining a kind of illuminated manuscript with a colorful, hand-drawn treasure map of the Camino showing thirteen geese waddling across it, or marked along its serpentine back by little waterfowl footprints.

"No," he said patiently to the uninitiated me. "Each pilgrim must find the signs for himself, or it isn't a spiritual initiation. Each person will find different signs in different places along the Camino, ones that are perfect for him and his unique path."

This I understood. And liked. It was less a cultish system or recipe and more a way to truly deepen one's walk in life, to learn to trust one's own intuition and navigate the world, forging a meaningful and original practice. I really wanted to see that text, but the young German man finished his coffee and ambled out of the café. I never saw him again.

Twice after Burgos, I noticed little three-pronged etchings on the stone walls of small churches and wondered if they were signs, but they gave me no hints or insights, so I shrugged them off. Yet, my attitude toward this whole goose mystery had softened. I now knew it was real, even if a modern creation imagining a medieval mystic's path. In that spirit, I sent an email to a friend in Barcelona. "How many geese are in the cathedral's cloister?" I asked her. "Thirteen," she replied a few days later, after she'd had a chance to pass by there and count. She could not find an explanation for why they were there or why there were thirteen of them.

I marched through Castile and into the iron-rich and red-toned mountains of León, then into the green, misty mountains and undulating hills and oak and chestnut forests of Galicia, and at last, into Santiago de Compostela. By the time I strode into the large square before the western entrance to the cathedral and ground zero for the Camino, I had forgotten once again about geese and the Game of the Goose as a metaphor for pilgrimage. All the same, pilgrimage had happened to me. It was very much a real and organic rite of passage—and perhaps even a spiritual initiation—for I had been cracked open, broken down, and built back up. I had replaced fear with trust. I had found faith in myself, in others, and in life. And now, from ample experience, I knew without a doubt that the footpath was indeed a great leyline of potent and transformative energy. I stood before the towering cathedral feeling emotionally raw, physically strong, and completely disoriented. This did not feel like arriving but like being made of mist, a betwixt-and-between creature who could shape-shift into anything at any moment—or evaporate entirely. I stepped into the cathedral, the ultimate pilgrim's goal, hoping it would give me answers and solidify and ground me.

There, just inside, staring beatifically down at me from overhead was the very image of Saint James that had been replicated to depict Santiago in the winning final square of Logroño's Game of the Goose. Had I won? Why, then, did it feel more like the death square, number fifty-eight, than the winning square, number sixty-three?

I continued inside and strolled down the nave to the altar, tears pricking my eyes, triggered by I knew not what. I climbed the stairs to stand behind the large gold and jewel-encrusted statue of Saint James in the center of the high altar. Following those before me, I delivered the ritual hug of gratitude and blessings to his broad, firm back and shoulders. A mix of joy and sorrow surged through me along with the cathartic realization that many people had blessed and supported this walk, this life, this grace, along with the earth herself, who had given me a privileged walk for 500 miles through such immense natural and sacred beauty. I saw everyone's faces, all the beauty, in a lightning-quick flashing procession, from childhood to now. Maybe this was the winning square after all. Maybe I did have to pass death to get here: the death of my old self and the birth of my new, more grateful, and freed self. Tears now streamed down my face.

I stepped down from the altar and sat in a pew long enough to compose myself and dry my tears, and went back outside. I was wondering what to do next when I saw a banner announcing a museum dedicated to all things pilgrimage: *Museo de las Peregrinaciones*. I went inside, seeking answers.

They came in the first gallery. There, a medieval stone engraving of the wheel of fortune was mounted near a classic image of a labyrinth, and next to it, a lithograph print of the Game of the Goose. The display text panels explained that there was a clear historical connection between various spiritual meditative and initiatory techniques that reached back to antiquity and beyond, using circles, spirals, labyrinths, pilgrimage, and more recently, the Game of the Goose. It made a direct connection between the game as a metaphor for the Camino and for a person's life path.

My life path in that moment of arriving in Santiago de Compostela felt amorphous and transitory after so many weeks and months of walking. I stood there staring at the board game and the wheel of fortune and realized that the old person I had been was now a pile of rocks, a cairn out on the trail somewhere. The new person I had become was still being constructed, and it was all too soon to tell who that would be. But the wheel kept turning, we kept moving through life, evolving, and growing. I knew very little then, except two things: that the territories of the Camino's trail had many strata of memory, meaning, and beauty, and that I wanted to sink deeply into it all and uncover its deepest stories. And that what I had felt while crossing the Pyrenees in 1986 had been real. I needed to come back yet again, and with luck, discover what it was all about and why this universe still held me in its orbit. I finally arrived at my tipping point. I began to live my life guided more fully by my heart.

This is what initiation feels like. It comes at the end, not the beginning.

The trick was, how would I do this? How would I address the practical things of living and stay afloat but shift my idea of home and work? I had no answers, but I knew that after weeks of raw walking, meditation, and solitude, it was the right direction. It was worth the risk, wherever on the wheel of fortune I might be right now, and I'd hold on firmly and maybe even, like a goose, learn to float or fly.

PART I

LA REINE PÉDAUQUE

∨

A PILGRIMAGE IN FRANCE

ON A GOOSE-FOOTED THRESHOLD

I **WENT HOME** and dreamed of my return to the trail and that numinous corridor through southwestern France and northern Spain. One year later, I unexpectedly received a windfall that opened the chance to return with more time to live along the corridor, learn, and explore. I began in coastal Atlantic Galicia in Spain's northwest and made my way eastward into Aquitaine, covering the full reach of the Camino's core territory and legacy. I was determined to find the heart center of all this and to go to the source of that original magnetic pull. While in Galicia, I did a late-night internet keyword search for all the things I sought and loved—including rich prehistory, good food and wine, warm society, connection to nature, rich spiritual traditions, and of course, trails of the Camino. That search brought Sarlat-la-Canéda to the top of the list, a town in the Dordogne, the northeast corner of Aquitaine in southwestern France. Without looking anything up about the place except for train schedules, I went.

A hurricane-like winter storm was battering the coast of northern Spain and southwestern France. It took three days, four trains, and one bus to reach Sarlat. At the last minute, I found a place to stay. It all felt as if by luck and chance that I had landed there, very much like a roll of the dice in the Game of the Goose. It also felt preordained, for the town, its people, and my new abode all spoke of home and homecoming, that I had somehow returned there, not arrived there for the first time. I felt this as the train made its way through the craggy limestone hills and dense oak forests that engulfed the town, and even more so as I stepped off the train and ambled down the hill into the golden limestone medieval center of Sarlat.

I felt an even stronger embrace than that of a beloved aunt's as I made my way into the town's square enclosed by amber colored stone and timber buildings with turrets and spiraling stairways, dominated by a towering twelfth-century Romanesque and Gothic cathedral. It all felt familiar. People welcomed me warmly as I passed shops and cafes, despite my bedraggled and rain-soaked appearance—and greeted me as a returning friend, not a stranger. I settled into my rental, a studio called Le Chardon, The Thistle, that nostalgically smelled like both of my grandmothers' homes, mingling the scent of violets, saffron, jasmine, cooking rice, musty linen closets, and rose petals.

I had landed in a town in a region in the midst of the densest concentration of Europe's most important prehistoric sites, including Lascaux. I was also in a geography of the thick crisscrossing weave through France of three of the four main routes and their tributaries of the Camino de Santiago—known as the *Chemin de Saint Jacques* in France—as they made their way south toward the Pyrenees. There, they all merged and became one great road, the most famous Camino route, the Francés, that moved pilgrims and trekkers across the north of Iberia to Santiago de Compostela.

I explored and went for long rambles, tracing those tributary trails that led me not only onto medieval pilgrim paths but deeper into forests, river valleys, and caves where humans have lived for at least 400,000 years. Everywhere I stepped hummed underfoot and felt ancient. It was as if I had just journeyed from the most extreme end of the Camino in northwestern Spain to its most intense beginning in southwestern France. It was not only a part of the region that had magnetically pulled at me in the train in 1986 but was in fact its epicenter, its energetic source, its core, a place where all the influences converged—of geology, prehistory, history, and the natural world, including a traditional economy depending on geese and ducks. With Sarlat as my base, I spent many of my final days afforded by this exploratory windfall trip to delve into the land between the setting sun and the north star, as Julius Caesar described Aquitaine over 2,000 years ago in *De Bello Gallo*.

In my first days there, I made friends who became family. I shopped for all my food at the two weekly markets—on Wednesdays and Saturdays—where all the produce and products were locally grown, gathered, raised, or hunted. I discovered an old subsistence economy at work and a people who existed in an old harmony with the land that gave them all that they needed as long as they took care of it. Tables were piled high with winter vegetables, chestnut chutneys, fruit preserves, walnut oils, truffles, chanterelles, and porcini; and wild boar, venison, and duck sausages sat shoulder to shoulder with the cuisines made from them, especially ones centered on ducks and geese, from confits and cassoulets to foie gras and duck bacon.

I also began to attend the monthly gathering of a group called Café Oc, locals who met to practice Occitan, the original mother tongue of southern France. A Latin-based language with local influences, Occitan was spoken long before French became France's official language, and had survived long centuries of onslaught to snuff it out. It was still the language of the people and the land, and through it I learned about farming, fishing, hunting, working with nature, and cultivating balance and sustainability in one's livelihood. It also gave me deeper access to the culture's folk stories and legends.

So it was that in Sarlat, I met the goose again. Not just the ones out in a farmer's field who ran toward me when I strolled by, or the ones on my plate in a local restaurant, but a mythical one. One day a local casually mentioned a legendary queen, *La Reine Pédauque*, and noted that her name derived from the Occitan *pé d'auca*, meaning goose footed. A fabled queen from Toulouse known to be just and wise, her main physical feature was a goose-like foot.

I began going to the local library, unearthing books containing images of her engraved on a few churches, from Burgundy to the Pyrenees, and stories about her told across southern France as well as in pockets of the north. Some stories held her to be a mythical queen outside of time; others thought she was Bertha, Charlemagne's mother, fabled to have large, grounding, bird-like feet, as well as deep wisdom. Over time, from the early medieval world to the early modern one, La Reine Pédauque may have evolved into *La Mère l'Oie*, Mother Goose, best preserved by folklorist Charles Perrault, who gathered fairytales from across France for his collection, *Contes de ma mère l'Oye*. (*Oye* is another way to spell *oie*.) Perrault's *Stories of My Mother the Goose* was first published in Paris in 1695.

I realized that the goose was chasing me as much as I now chased it. Now, I stood fully on a goose-footed threshold. Intrigued, I entered through the gate and dug deeper, soon learning that there were many other bird-footed women in France and Spain, from the territories of Gascony and Basque Country in the Atlantic Pyrenees, to the springs, caves, and mountains all across northern Iberia. These bird-footed beings predated La Reine Pédauque and were more divine than human. They were known by many names, most commonly as the Basque *lamia* (plural: *lamiak*), fairylike beings with waterfowl feet, always associated with a freshwater spring and cave, who acted as protective guardians of the natural world. At their helm was the top divinity in the pre-Christian Basque pantheon, Mari, the mother earth goddess who oversaw the integrity of both the natural and the human world, implementing protection and justice, rewarding those who lived in balance and kindness, and punishing those who were greedy, destructive, and cold-hearted.

Mari could take many forms—a ram, a goat, a vulture, a bull, or even a shocking bolt of lightning—but she could also appear as a woman with bird feet. Sometimes people would see Mari, like the lamia, combing her long luxuriant hair while seated near a cave opening or a flowing stream. Other times, they saw her there spinning wool or flax into yarn or thread. The same places associated with Mari and the lamia later became associated with Mother Mary, who revealed herself in these places in ways similar to her earlier sisters. Our Lady of Lourdes is the most famous example, but ethnographers and historians have gathered many others.

Among my most intimate friendships forged in Sarlat was with Bernadette. Originally from Paris but a long-time resident of Sarlat, she was in her eighties and had lived in many places and under many circumstances before settling in the Dordogne. After surviving a World War II childhood hidden away by her Parisian family on a remote rustic farm in Burgundy she had lived a fully self-sufficient adult life on a farm in Normandy, perhaps thanks to skills gained during her hard childhood. She had also lived for two years in a caravan in Morocco while being inducted into the shamanic and mystical practices of the Chleuh (Shilha) of the south. And before settling for good in Sarlat, she'd lived for several years in a bungalow on the Mediterranean island of Mallorca. She was a self-taught artist and spent her days painting, drawing, meditating, and reading sacred texts from every religion and spiritual tradition in the world, along with their academic commentaries.

Bernadette and I met one winter's day during the weekly farmer's market. Drawn to each other, perhaps recognizing a fellow nomad who'd found anchoring and sustenance in Sarlat, we sat down in the market café for two hours, swapping tales over coffee and getting to know each other. Therein began a tradition, the first of our many weekly philosophical and existential discussions.

One market day, I confessed to Bernadette my fascination with the goose and finding out why it was so intimately associated with the territories of the Camino de Santiago in France and Spain. And what about all these bird-footed women? She was the perfect person to ask, given all the reading she had done and her life experiences, and also because she was intimately familiar with the Game of the Goose, which had been a popular game from her childhood. She took a sip of coffee, considering this as a loose strand of long silvery hair escaped from her chignon and framed her face and sparkling bright blue eyes, which now fixed intently on me.

"Consider that the goose represents the divine," she said, "especially the feminine aspect of the divine. At root, the divine is neither male nor female, but both, and neither. It's a paradox for us humans because we need to think in terms of both male and female. We create gods in our image. When the dominant god is male, we need a female counterbalance, something to speak to the feminine aspect in each of us. The same is true if reversed. But the original creator was neither."

My mind whirred with the possibility of what she had just said. Ample cultural and archaeological studies around the world have documented how we humans have organized our societies based on all possible variations of gender and power: women in power, men in power, women and men sharing power, and every nuance in between. The gods of a society reflect the world order these societies have created for themselves. No one way has been the natural order of things; instead, the shape of a religion and the relationship with the gods is shaped by a society's particular values and motives, and often driven by who holds power—influence and access to key resources—and wants to keep it.

Could the goose have provided a safe place for an old European goddess to hide in her native lands as they became increasingly dominated by patriarchal societies and religions, including the wholesale conquest by the male-oriented Romans, and then on its heels, the rise of a politically clever, expansionist, and male-centered Christianity? Was this why the cult of Mary also rose in the same places that had thoroughly snuffed out all other earlier expressions of the feminine divine, because whatever the balance of gender power, we humans still needed expressions of both male and female to feel whole?

Soon after that talk with Bernadette, I came upon *Teutonic Mythology* by Jacob Grimm, one of the Brothers Grimm. In this comparative study of European mythologies and folktales published in 1835, Grimm wrote that Bertha, La Reine Pédauque in southern France during the time of Charlemagne and the Franks, was likely a manifestation of the old German mother goddess Perchta, who also had a goosefoot. Moreover, one of Perchta's instruments was the spinning spool, a powerful tool in the ancient world, for spools and spinning gave us the capacity to weave cloth, which protected and warmed us in ways that animal hides alone could not. Spinning also gave us the means to make exquisite fabrics that became status goods to trade and collect. In the ancient worlds of the Bronze and Iron Ages and into classical antiquity, spinning, weaving, were prized skills, and cloth was a valuable commodity—all associated with powerful women and also goddesses, who gifted us these things. Spinning also was symbolic of the turning of the seasons and time, a wheel of fortune of sorts that spoke of life's unalterable cycles. The spinning spool was the perfect tool for the mother goddess who had created the sun, moon, earth, and all of nature and its seasons.

Grimm saw this trail of ancient goose-footed mother goddesses across Europe as later evolving into Mother Goose by the end of the Middle Ages and the beginning of the early modern era in Europe. These were centuries when societies had become even more separated from nature, dominating it rather than living in it. They also were times during which an even wider wedge was driven between the male and female worlds. By then, patriarchal systems were fully operable and dominant, even inventing witch hunts and inquisitions to keep rebels in check. Moreover, with the rise of cities and mass trade (and exploitation) that further separated families from self-sufficiency and the land, women and children, who until then had been equally valued and important in working the life on the farm, suffered most gravely.

As I sat reading Grimm, I closed my eyes to recall the image of Mother Goose from childhood. She was a wise woman seated by a warm fire, spinning wool and telling yarns. I had not known as a child that when I heard the stories of Mother Goose I was sitting at the feet of not just a charming storyteller but also a survivor of patriarchal incursions—that she was from the underground, a mother goddess-turned mother goose. And that she has been biding her time to this day, asking us to sit around her fire and learn through her stories about life and its challenges, transformations, and cycles, and to return again to a state of respect and balance.

After reading Grimm, I began to find many more goose-related goddesses from across Europe. In Dinéault, near Renne in Brittany, archaeologists unearthed a 2,000-year-old Gallic bronze figurine of a young warrior woman wearing a helmet that bore a goose assuming a striking pose on its crown. That goose probably represented a protective Breton goddess. Some think she was the Celtic goddess Brigid. The image is not very different from many Greek images of Athena, holding a spear and shield and either donning a helmet decorated with a protective goose or accompanied by a goose standing beside her, ready for battle. At an archaeological site in Burgundy, excavators unearthed a 2,200-year-old Gallo-Roman bronze sculpture of the goddess of the Seine, Sequana, standing in a duck-shaped boat. This also had Greek parallels to a 2,500-year-old sculpture of Aphrodite standing on the back of a goose-shaped boat and a ceramic of the same era painted with Aphrodite riding on the back of a goose in flight.

I read about the goddess Freyja, the mother goddess of the Norse pantheon and the leader of the Valkyries (also known as swan maidens), who could shape-shift into a bird by wearing her magical feather cloak. And in Lithuania, the folkloric character *Lauma* lives in and near water and has long hair and bird feet. Like the Basque Mari, Lauma can shape-shift into a goat or a horse, and she is mostly benevolent, except when someone disrupts nature or is unjust in human affairs.

I discovered that among Romans, the goose was the mother goddess Juno's sacred animal. The Roman historian Livy recounted that the Gallic Senones' attack on Rome in 390 BCE was averted thanks to Juno's holy geese. One night, the Senones planned a surprise attack on the Capitoline Hill in the center of Rome and made it midway up the hill, still unseen by the Roman guards, when the geese kept on the hill as a part of Juno's temple saw the invaders and raised a loud and raucous alarm. The incident thereafter assured their reputation as fierce and loyal guardians. It also affirmed a direct link between goose and goddess.

I learned from biologists that Europe's wild goose populations have a traditional migratory path they trace in flight every year—a northeast to southwest line from Sweden to southwestern Spain. The line's midpoint and frequent rest stop is exactly where the

Pyrenees meet the Atlantic, near the French and Spanish border. The geese's migratory line intersects midway with all the routes of the Camino from France as they merge and enter Spain, and with the path of the Milky Way as it is traced in the night sky. It was also blaringly obvious to me that this, too, was the very same intersection point of my own first migration across Europe in 1986. The path of stars, the way of wild geese, the routes of the Camino, and my life converged in the same place.

I also understood that perhaps it had nothing to do with me, except that I was ready, my senses wide open, for a great adventure. Perhaps I'd felt a pull that was there for anyone game to take it up, a pull forged by many heaven and earth influences. This intersection of stars, geese, paths, and pilgrims was not by accident. Reinforcing this reality was the fact that in all of Europe, it was this particular territory that also held the highest concentration of goose stories, goose place names, and folklore involving bird-footed beings.

With my eyes at last wide open, I couldn't wait to return again to the trail and follow the sun, stars, geese, and signs. As I said goodbye to Sarlat, the place that had rebirthed me into a fully awake and vibrant life, I knew that I would return. I wanted to launch all future Camino walks from there, to begin from there and return there, gleaning grace and insight from Bernadette, deepening my sense of homecoming to this sacred place, and then folding into the footsteps of medieval Franks who journeyed along those old paths that joined the flight of geese and the way of stars into and across Spain, and who had given the Camino Francés, the French Road, its name.

I saved my pennies, I carved out the space and time, and I made my freelance work even more conducive to nomadic wanderings. Before I could question this strange wild goose hunt on which I'd alighted, the stars aligned, and the signs appeared. I stepped through the threshold and rolled the dice.

THE GAME OF THE GOOSE

PREDAWN, MY BACKPACK at the door, the familiar mixed cocktail of excitement and uncertainty tugged at my ribcage. I was back in the southwest of France, in the Dordogne, in Aquitaine, between the setting sun and the north star, in the medieval town of Sarlat-la-Canéda, the home of my heart and spirit. I had a few days to sink in, see friends, savor this old land and culture that I love so much, and have a few visits with Bernadette before setting off onto the pilgrimage trail once again.

Armed with accumulating goose facts, Camino lore, historical hunches, and a map on which I'd circled places bearing waterfowl stories, names, and migration patterns, I felt ready. Months earlier, a friend from my native Colorado had called with a proposal. Was I interested in hiking with her on one of the four famous Chemin routes in France? She was especially interested in the Voie d'Arles, the southernmost of the four French pilgrim roads that link into the Camino Francés across northern Spain to Santiago de Compostela. I looked at my map. The Arles Route ran through the thickest part of French goose and duck country. "Yes," I said without hesitation. I was already scheduled to be in France then, working on new research projects from my base in Sarlat. The timing of the journey sat perfectly between these projects. As much as it would have served as a restful break from work, I wanted to use the trip to find new material and pitch new stories to editors.

On the day of departure for Europe, my husband Miles drove me to the airport. We were both freelancers, and when not traveling, we worked from neighboring offices at home. We were together all the time, including meals, chores, and food shopping. Despite this—or perhaps in part because of it—I found it harder to say goodbye to him each time, not easier.

We had met in graduate school when we were both already well on our life paths as semi-nomadic researchers and writers. From the start, we had bonded in knowing that each other was an explorer, that often our research would call us to journey alone, and that it did not take away from, but actually added to, our devotion to each other. People often asked Miles, "How do you feel about her going away?" Although he, too, traveled a lot for work, no one ever asked me this question about him. It was such a patriarchal question, but he always handled it honestly and head on, with a positive twist. Once I heard him say, "Better stories find her when she travels alone," something any professional travel writer—or writer, period—would know as a central truth of their craft. Another time I heard him say, "I'm proud of her." No further explanation needed.

I knew in the back of my mind that when I set off on the Arles route, as much as I just wanted to go for a long walk and gather material, that pilgrimage would still happen to me. This was because it never failed: once I set off on a trackway of the Camino, the long days of roaming always brought things up that were long buried deep in the psyche or cell tissue, demanding to be looked at, resolved, released, and put to rest. I usually loved this part of the walk as much as the adventure of being out on wild and historical trails, but this time I wasn't keen on it. Still, I wondered, what might come up this time? I knew it wouldn't be issues about my marriage. Sure, we had stuff, like everyone, but we resolved our stuff pretty quickly as it arose, an essential reality when both people worked from home.

Nor did I think I would process any childhood traumas; I'd already dealt with and done that, largely on prior Caminos. Or problems with my parents. Over the years, as I'd grown up and owned being an adult, I'd had good talks with my folks—two loving, open, and intelligent people—I'd largely cleared any archived issues. If I had any parent issues now, it was worry over their older age and hope that their years would unfold in beauty, peace, wellness, and ease, and that I could be a positive part of their lives.

If I were to be totally honest, any issue that could trip me up right now had to do with my confidence—not my desire, but my confidence in making a living as a writer. The very thing that gave me most life was a hard gig to pull off as an actual living. But I had done many things, worked in many types of jobs and professional situations: as a biochemistry researcher, a European tapestry salesperson, a tenure-track university professor, a magazine editor, a business consultant, an ice-cream maker, a baker, a cheese shop sales clerk, an art frame builder, a musician, a hospital volunteer, a newspaper delivery girl, and even a soda hawker at college football games. I had seen many walks of life and tried on many hats, but at the end and start of any day, ever since I was a child, I wrote. Writing gave me life.

And now, I had finally arrived at the knowing that, despite the financial challenges, my most grounding truth was that I could not *not* write. I knew this was the right path for me, but the more I reflected on the matter, the more I knew that the issue was less my path as a writer than my need to convince others of the legitimacy of my path. My confidence didn't wobble when I had to put nose to grindstone and work. It wobbled when I heard the comments of others, especially, ironically, people I barely knew. Such as a woman I met at a party who wrote me off, saying point blank, after I answered her question about what I did for a living, that I couldn't possibly be a freelance writer because that was impossible. Or another who had said, "Oh, that's nice, but what's your actual job?" Or "Oh, right, I also plan to write a book, when I retire." Why did these comments bother me? They bothered me even more than the patronizingly patriarchal ones others asked Miles about how he felt about my going away for work. Why on earth did I care what others said or thought since I was fully committed to my right livelihood and true path?

Well, I wasn't going to get into it. It was fully foolish to care what others thought. I knew this. I pushed the whole matter aside and instead turned my full focus onto my original reason for saying yes to Sarah—the adventure, the goose, and the potential for new material and photographs for stories to pitch to magazine editors. I was going to prove myself as a writer. For that, this was going to be an epic trip. I ignored the nagging voice inside that reminded me that the Camino always had its own plans—or that the mind, fueled by ego, can be a con artist. Instead, I dove deeply into research on the Voie d'Arles.

The route officially begins in Arles on the Mediterranean coast and moves west across southern France, passing through places such as Carcassonne, Toulouse, and Auch before snaking southwest to the Pyrenean foothill town of Oloron-Sainte-Marie, the staging town for pilgrims preparing to cross the mountains via the Somport Pass into Spain. The Somport Pass is used less by pilgrims because it is more treacherous and higher in altitude compared to the Valcarlos Pass farther west. That pass uses the mountain town of Saint-Jean-Pied-de-Port as its staging point. The two mountain towns are connected by a bridging trail—the Chemin du Piémont, the foothill path, offering last-minute route changes. As such, pilgrims reaching Oloron can opt to take the foothill path to Saint-Jean and cross the Pyrenees there. Sarah and I decided to do just that because the Chemin du Piémont features unusual churches, lesser-known villages, and rugged wilderness—and we didn't want to miss any of that.

"By the way," Sarah added, "we'll be walking the trail in reverse."

"As in going deeper into France, not Spain?"

"Right."

I was delighted. I'd be walking toward Sarlat, my personal Santiago de Compostela.

The plan was to meet in Saint-Jean-Pied-de-Port, hike the Piémont route to Oloron-Sainte-Marie, connect there to the Arles route, and walk toward Toulouse. Sarah had picked this road and direction for a quest of her own, to follow what she called the Celtic Camino, which she had mapped as going the other way, from Santiago de Compostela all the way north to Roselyn in Scotland. This route is based on lore from several writers, mostly French, Spanish, and English, who believed that the original path of the Camino began at the sea in westernmost Iberia and moved into northern Europe, heading east then north.

In Sarlat, with my pack on my back, the day arrived to meet her. I closed the door to Le Chardon and tiptoed down the creaking stairs to the wooden and iron-studded entrance of the building. As I undid the iron latch and pushed the heavy door open, Saint Sacerdos Cathedral, my neighbor across the small street, began ringing out her raucous seven-in-the-morning wake-up bells. I let the deep timbered and oscillating chime pulse through my body as I pulled the door shut and walked into the narrow, medieval cobblestone street. I paused to thank this place for bringing me home and to remember its beauty as I was about to leave it once again. I was thankful that in a few weeks, I'd be back.

In the early October morning, a dark blue sky wrapped itself around Sarlat's amber-toned limestone buildings, with dawn not yet reaching the narrow streets. The grandest of the ancient stones was Saint Sacerdos' sturdy square Romanesque bell tower and Gothic windows. Next to the crumbling flying buttresses of the church sloped the small hill leading up to the cone-shaped tower, the *lanterne des morts*. Midway, a lone pear tree drooped heavy with ripe yellow-green fruit. From its upper branches sang the resident red-breasted European robin, the *rouge-gorge*. I thought of the cat Mr. Stripes. She—for she likes being called "Mr."—often found me along the low stone wall set between the cathedral and the pear tree, just below the enigmatic twelfth-century tower. I heard a pear drop heavily onto the ground, then the rouge-gorge sang once more and flew off. I heard little feet running and then felt a soft bump on my leg. Joy surged. I bent down to give Mr. Stripes a proper greeting and stroked my friend's long, striped, gray-and-black back. Almost as soon as we'd said hello, Mr. Stripes was off again, on to the next demand of the morning. I followed the good example of bird, pear, and cat, and turned to make my own departure toward the train. Just as I was leaving the perimeter of the medieval town, I recalled the suggestion Bernadette had made during our market coffee hour the day before.

"Go look again at the Game of the Goose board game, the

Jeu de l'oie, mounted on the storefront of the shop with the same name." She'd said it while looking up from her coffee as if it were a scrying bowl, her bright eyes and sage smile beaming. "Pay attention to the goose. It's about the goose," she insisted. "*She* is the guide *and* the symbol."

I amended my direction, made a quick right, and went through an arched stone passageway to a lane dead-ending in front of a small shop whose window and door were covered with displays of children's games and toys, especially several cantankerous ceramic geese and ducks in all styles of acrobatic poses, from backbends to handstands. The shop sign, a wooden plank painted ivory and overlaid with burgundy-colored, curly medieval-scroll letters, read *Le jeu de l'oie.* If there was any doubt about the store's name, above the sign lay a giant ceramic sleeping goose, his long neck stretched out and wings dropped down to his side, his eyes closed, and his beak turned up in a dreamy smile. Mounted onto the outer wall over the head of the smiling goose was a large ceramic version of the Game of the Goose board game.

My eyes followed the game's serpentine spiral, which filled the entire rectangle of the board, moving through its sixty-three squares to the center. The spiral traced the classic pattern with key squares marked by geese, a bridge, an inn, a labyrinth, a well, a prison, death, and the winning center. But this one, unlike the Game of the Goose I'd seen in Logroño, which featured Saint James and a white goose on the final winning square, showed a magnificent white goose at the sixty-third square that looked as if it had transformed into a swan. I thought of what Bernadette had said and wondered if the emphasis needed to shift from man to goose, to look for *her* signs more than *his.* While signs for Saint James were evident and in the open, those for the goose goddess were hidden, even if in plain sight.

"I don't know, Bernadette," I whispered. As much as I was now officially obsessed by and committed to tracing goose lore and its connections to the Camino, I insisted that it was just an intellectual fascination, not one with any spiritual underpinning or consequences. If only I could find that young man from Köln whom

I'd met in Burgos years ago. I wanted to ask him how it had played out when he arrived in Santiago de Compostela, and then again, when he had returned home. Had he been changed? And if so, how? Had it been worth it? Had he achieved enlightenment? Or had his life been completely upended without a winning-square reward?

My pack's right strap dug into my shoulder. I adjusted it and turned back toward the train. Sure, I was on a quest, I reasoned, but on *my* terms, as a curious writer looking for a good story. I ignored the words *con artist, con artist, con artist* reeling through my mind. I strode through the medieval town and up the hill to the station and stood on the platform with several others waiting for the early morning train to Bordeaux.

SQUARE ONE

SARAH'S PLANE WAS just landing in Paris as I waited for the train in Sarlat. She and I planned to meet that evening in Saint-Jean-Pied-de-Port, Saint John of the Foot of the Pass, at the base of the Pyrenees. According to the train schedule, I would get there several hours before Sarah, changing trains first in Bordeaux for Bayonne, and then again for Saint-Jean. I looked around and found that there were many more people than usual on Sarlat's platform. A talkative woman chain-smoking to my left explained that most were commuters who usually drove, but that roadwork on the highway to Bordeaux, creating detours through winding country roads, had made the train a better choice today.

As she relit another cigarette, a large American tour group arrived. After two weeks of touring this rich castle, cave, truffle, goose, and wine region, they were returning to Paris to fly home that evening. We all waited in apprehensive silence as the departure hour came and went. A phone rang inside the station, followed by a quick conversation. When the station agent came outside, his face was grim. Due to rail problems, our train was cancelled, but a bus was arriving shortly. He inched toward his office as he told us that the bus would also be doing double duty, serving the villages it usually stopped in, and adding the train stops to its itinerary, along with navigating the highway detours. There was a collective groan. He stepped into the doorway, ready to shut it quickly, as he added that he had no idea exactly when the driver would arrive.

The commuters dispersed and went to their cars and drove away. As one body, the carless among us walked to the front of the station to wait. The sun rose higher. I calculated that by now Sarah was well through passport control in Paris Charles de Gaulle Airport and probably waiting for her own train. The chain-smoker smoked her pack's last cigarette. Dozens of nervous and restless feet shuffled around my own. I knew the *Chemin* had begun and, as Bernadette had told me, it was personal, not intellectual. The game was on, I had cast my dice and made my first move, landing on my first square, recalling too late that pilgrimage likes to deliver ordeals before gifts. *The Camino guides and provides* I repeated in my head, using Sarah's mantra when challenges arise on the path, and to remind myself that ordeals are navigable, and that gifts always arise out of them. A bus suddenly arrived in a frenzied cloud of dust and fumes and screeched to a halt in front of us.

"This was my *one* day off!" the driver shouted as he threw open the door. We hesitantly stepped up and handed him our tickets. "I was just awakened at home," he continued, "and asked to drive the route to Bordeaux. I barely had time for coffee!" Nervously, we quickly took our seats. The tour group filled the back half and grew loud and boisterous, relaxing into their unexpected adventure, which made all the locals take seats closer to the front. I was among the last to board and found one seat left, right behind the driver.

We pulled onto the road and drove the zigzagging country roads too fast, braking and starting and zooming in and out of the villages and then back to the detour markers on and off the highway. All the while, the driver shouted dramatically over the noise of the motor, "*Quel cinema!*" What theater!

"Tomorrow," he turned and looked straight at me over his shoulder, "I am going to hit the reset button and start this week all over again!" *And I am going to hit the reset button*, I thought, *as soon as you return your gaze to the road.* He finally did with a desperate laugh, one that told me he hadn't finished his morning coffee. I began to feel seasick.

By the time we arrived in Bordeaux, I was nauseated and disoriented—not an auspicious start to a long hike. The tour group had departed in Bergerac and many commuters followed their example, finding alternative rides from there. I and another traveler remained the only two passengers on board to Bordeaux, and once there, the driver left us at the back end of the station where trucks dropped off cargo, not the usual, well-marked front entrance for passengers. He'd done his duty and wanted to park the bus and find coffee.

The other passenger departed as I hoisted my pack and climbed down the bus steps on wobbly legs. It took some time of walking around the massive complex before I found the public entrance, and by the time I got there, my train to Bayonne had departed. But then, over the intercom as I stood on the empty platform, I heard that the train from Paris was about to arrive. *I wonder,* I thought, and I waited. The train arrived. I watched carefully as occupants exited each car. As if in a dream, from car seven, a jetlagged but vibrant woman stepped out. Her signature colors of plum, teal, chartreuse, and aqua set her apart from the other passengers, as did her large backpack. She was looking around for the exit when her eyes landed on me. Disbelief turned to joy and laughter. We rushed and hugged each other.

"I can't believe it!" she said. "How is it that you're here?" I told her my sordid tale. "The Camino guides and provides," she said. Of course she did. It was an auspicious start to a trek.

We had a little over an hour before the next train to Bayonne departed and went to grab lunch at a kiosk in the station, each ordering a glass of white wine to celebrate.

"To the Chemin," I said and raised my glass.

"To the Chemin," Sarah said, "and to how can it get any better than this?" Her new mantra, a statement embedded in a question. We clinked and drank. I savored the crisp Bordeaux, drinking it on the land where it was born. How could it get any better than this?

Soon, south to Basque Country and Bayonne we went. In Bayonne we disembarked from a long, multiple-car train and boarded a two-car choo-choo. Sarah and I took seats across from each other and next to a young man who was there with his four friends. The train pulled out of Bayonne and went south and inland, following the Nive River, which leads to Saint-Jean-Pied-de-Port through narrow verdant valleys and increasingly steep and craggy gray-green mountains.

I looked around at the other riders. There were a few commuters among a few dozen pilgrims. The former wore office clothes, had serene faces, and held a purse or briefcase. The latter wore hi-tech hiking shoes, trekking pants, stretch shirts, and mixed expressions of fear and excitement. Locals gazed out the window to the familiar landscape as pilgrims looked at it with awe and anxiety while furtively glancing and smiling at each other. We also scanned each other's packs for size and gear. I fleetingly envied the locals their certainty and routine. But then I reminded myself that this was a voluntary voyage and that I had decided to do this for a reason, for the exact opposite of certainty and routine, to stir things up and see what unknown adventures would meet me on the road, as well as revelations. I heard an inner voice edit this last clause as I looked out the window. *Just adventures. Skip the revelations.* It surprised me. Why was I so resistant to the interior journey that was part and parcel of the outer one?

I looked across at Sarah, a Camino veteran who knew these things as well, and a person with a strong spiritual outlook. I knew if she sniffed my resistance, the gig was up. As I thought this, she suddenly looked over at me, our eyes locked, and she slowly smiled. I knew that smile. It made me feel as if she'd read my mind. I sucked in some air and quickly turned to look out the window again to find that the young man, who had been reading or talking with his friends earlier, was looking back at me.

"I'm Luke," he said. We shook hands. I told him my name.

"And this is my friend Sarah," I said, daring to look back at her, hoping that the inquiring expression was off her face by now. It was not.

I turned back to Luke, who had intrigued me from the moment I'd first sat down. The first thing that caught my eye had been the thick tome on his lap, George R. R. Martin's *Game of Thrones*, not the usual reading material pilgrims took on the Camino. In fact, pilgrims often brought few or no books, trying to keep their pack weight light. Then there was his pack, a teeny-tiny, book-carrying canvas school daypack that was so unstuffed with stuff it collapsed in on itself rather than bulging out like everyone else's. Even his friends had massive packs by comparison. A third thing about him was his bare ankles and feet tucked sockless into canvas sneakers. And last, that all his colors were khaki—his jacket, his trousers, his sneakers, his pack, even the crown of his head covered in thick, long, brown-blond hair.

I had been so proud of how I had winnowed my pack down to fifteen pounds. Sure, it was heavier than usual because we were walking the other way into less supported trails, but it was also light considering that I was heading into said territory where less lodging, water, and food were on hand. The water and food and my sleeping bag, ready for a night in a church vestibule, added to my bulk.

"You must be a spiritual adept," I said to Luke, "a master of minimalist needs." I pointed to his pack.

"No, hardly," he laughed, "but nothing ruins travel more than hauling about too much stuff, and I discovered that I really don't need much." I detected an Australian accent in his speech. He told me he was nineteen years old.

"Is this your walkabout?"

"Yes."

"And you planned to walk the Camino as a part of it?"

"Nope. Nothing has been planned on this four-month trip. My friends and I decided to walk it last night, after too much wine in Biarritz. We have one month left and heard about the Camino, and since it began so close to where we were, and it's cheap, we thought it could be a great last adventure before running out of money and returning home."

"Last night was your first thought to walk the Camino?" I asked, both aghast and in admiration.

"Yup." He smiled casually.

"Do you mind if I ask you what you've got in your pack?"

He smiled more broadly. "Two pairs of socks, a pair of underwear, a sweater, a compact sleeping bag, a toothbrush, a comb, toothpaste, and a thin composition book that I use as a journal.

This," he concluded by heaving up the novel on his lap, "is the heftiest item of all, which, when I finish it, I'll leave at one of the pilgrim dorms and hope to find someone else's cast-off book to pick up and read."

As I appreciated more his idea of needs compared to mine, looking at my suddenly massive pack, his namesake came to mind: another enlightened traveler, Luke the Evangelist. He was considered the most literary author of the gospels, and his symbol, the ox, spoke of his solidity and grounding. He was gentle and soft-spoken. The two Lukes seemed cut from similar cloth.

I applauded Luke's travel style but glanced again at his bare ankles. Rain and dropping temperatures were a guarantee in October and November, not only in the Pyrenees, but all across the windy and expansive hills of Navarra and Rioja, the high plateau, the *meseta,* of Castile, and into the green but rain-sodden mountains of Galicia. I suggested to Luke that he consider getting a pair of warm hiking socks and a rain poncho in Saint-Jean-Pied-de-Port. "At least your shoes will dry out fast," I joked. He took it like an ox.

Just before arriving in Saint-Jean, Luke asked me about my Camino. I detailed the other-way plan and told him that I had walked the Camino a few times.

"Why do you keep coming back?" he asked.

"It called to me a long time before I could walk it. Then when I did, it kept calling me back. I'm hooked. It isn't like normal treks because it combines adventure with nature, culture, and the sacred. I love the mix." I told him that this trip excited me for the challenge of reading the signs in reverse and what new things we might discover. "But my friend Sarah," I added, smiling sweetly at her, "she's on a mission. This was her idea. She's following a road she calls the Celtic Camino and is walking it in seven sections, one for each chakra." I explained that her walk will ultimately end in Roselyn, Scotland, the seventh chakra, and that this section that we would walk together, in her reckoning, was the second chakra. She'd already walked what she considered the first chakra landscape, connected to physical grounding, from Santiago de Compostela to Saint-Jean-de-Port. It was her journey, and I was happy to be along for the ride.

"And the second chakra is about what?" Luke asked, sitting forward.

"Relationships and creativity," I said nervously. All my prior Caminos, except for the very first, I had walked solo. But I also knew, from the times I'd walked with others for portions of the trail, that we fellow travelers become mirrors to each other for what the path is pulling up from inside us each, like mystic Javier or chatty Clara. I now had committed to walk for three weeks intentionally with a good friend, a true and generous spirit as well, but I knew the mirror would be unavoidable. That's the part that made me nervous.

Sarah smiled sweetly. "Beebe has this idea that this is my spiritual adventure, and that she is just here for a very long walk. But I know that the spiritual reason for her being on it will announce itself, and when it does—"

"It will knock me on my butt?" I interrupted.

"It will show you what you need most to learn right now on your life's journey," she said kindly, "but it can be gentle."

I shrugged as nonchalantly as possible and looked back at Luke but saw that he was riveted by what Sarah had just said. That image of Luke's face seared itself in my memory. He reminded me of the young German man from Köln I'd met years earlier in Burgos. Both had the same look of quest and hope. With this added promise of a spiritual adventure, Luke slipped his book into his pack, and gazed out the window, his eyes shining with the limitless possibilities ahead.

The train arrived in Saint-Jean-Pied-de-Port. We hoisted our packs onto our backs as Luke slipped his lithely over one shoulder. We shook hands and wished each other a good pilgrimage and he disappeared with the crowd and his four friends into town, all heading toward its many pilgrim hostels, *auberges*, and *gîtes* in the medieval town center.

It never got old, my fascination with other pilgrims at this beginning point. They always exited the train station with a mix of

excitement and jagged-edged anxiety over finding a bed and starting their walk and disappeared like a cloud of locusts toward the
town center. Many went straight to the pilgrim's welcome office to
get their credential, a stiff passport-sized accordion-folded document with blank squares on which they would gather inked stamps
from the places they stayed to show where they had walked. There,
they also received guidance from experienced volunteers, all locals
who had walked the Camino, many of them several times. The
pilgrims would then disperse to find a place to lay their heads for
the first time on the pilgrimage road, that great leyline forged from
the mix of natural earth energies with the human imagination, all
starting from this mystical location at the foot of the pass in the
Pyrenees.

I was sentimental as Luke disappeared into the pilgrim cloud,
the electric expression still on his face, heartily hoping that what
Sarah had said was true. I knew I would never see him again. I
dearly wanted to know how the path would delight and transform
him.

We followed behind the group and also made our way toward
the walled medieval town built along the banks of the Nive. As
we passed through the Porte de France, an elegant Gothic red and
black stone gate, asphalt gave way to timeworn cobblestones and
narrow lanes; we were transported back to the twelfth century. The
central street, Rue de la Citadelle, was on a steep slope cutting
right up the middle of the old town. It led us to our lodging at
the top, just past another Gothic gate, the Porte de Saint Jacques.
It was through this gate that pilgrims would pass into Saint-Jean-
Pied-de-Port when coming from destinations deeper in France and
Europe.

We'd picked our accommodation for this location, right on
the threshold, to pick up the trail in reverse from where we knew
toward where we'd never been. Standing there with Sarah, I felt
the stones underfoot vibrate with the memory of the millions of
pilgrims who had passed through over many centuries.

We checked in to our lodging, a traditional Basque house of
stone with red window shutters and a heavy carved wooden door

hung with dried protective herbs, then showered and went for dinner at a restaurant along the riverside. On our return, just as I was pushing open the heavy inn door, the innkeeper appeared in the vestibule.

"You speak Spanish, don't you?" he asked while handing me a phone.

I took the phone hesitantly and placed it to my ear. "¿Si?"

At the other end, a sigh of relief. A taxi driver was bringing two American pilgrims up from Pamplona and needed directions to the inn. I did my best and luckily within a few minutes the taxi appeared. Two very tired looking men, a father and son from the Midwest, slipped out from the back seat. As the cab departed, the two told us they were walking the Camino together after seeing the movie, *The Way*, starring Martin Sheen. "It was too weird not to," the father said. "My name is Tom, and my son's name is Daniel."

I felt clammy discomfort creep up my spine. Those were the names of the characters in the movie, Tom and Daniel, father and son, like these two, except in the movie the son was already deceased when the father took up walking the pilgrimage. I could see my feelings written on Sarah's face.

"My son just turned thirty-three," Tom added. The rest of us remained silent. For the religious, which we soon learned these two were, thirty-three was significant as the age Jesus was believed to have been when he was crucified. I wasn't sure I wanted to know how this father-and-son movie would end.

"Are you two also walking The Way?" Daniel asked as we all went inside.

"We are," I said, "but we're walking the other way."

He and his father looked baffled.

"We're walking the opposite direction," I clarified, "along one of the French pilgrim routes. We're going east from here on a bridging route through the foothills and connecting to one of the traditional French pilgrim routes to continue northeast toward Toulouse."

The innkeeper overheard what I'd just said. "Pigeon hunting season has begun a bit early this year," he chimed in. "Be careful."

Pigeon hunting? Sarah and I knew nothing about it and gave little thought to it. How could pigeon hunting affect our pilgrimage? But from the look on Tom and Daniel's faces, it was clear that they also didn't want to know how our movie would end. We said goodnight.

As I fell asleep, I knew I would have to face my resistance: The Way was a spiritual road for everyone, however devout or secular, be it Luke pondering iron thrones and chakras, or Tom and Daniel deepening their father-and-son bond, aided by a strong sense of *carpe diem* mortality.

THE FIRST GOOSE

EARLY THE NEXT morning, Sarah and I slipped out onto the ancient path right outside the heavy wooden door. Mist hung low on the valley. The smell of wood smoke and decaying autumn leaves laced the air. As we plodded east to head deeper into the Pyrenees and France, Tom and Daniel would head south toward the mountains into Spain. I imagined Luke, too, making his way south with his four friends over the Pyrenees and into Spain in his thin canvas sneakers. I hoped he'd picked up a pair of winter socks. As Sarah and I went deeper into the mists and mountains, I sent them all silent blessings. Theirs would be one steep ascent and one murderous descent. Ours, we discovered over the next nine hours, would be murderous ascents and descents all day, plus false turns, retraced steps, lost trails, walks into farmsteads, and careful stepping along narrow goat paths that formed skirt-hem patterns along the sides of nearly vertical slopes above the timberline. We saw no humans all day, but on the mountaintops and slopes we encountered self-herding sheep, horses, and goats. All of them looked at us as if we were lost or mad.

By late afternoon, deep in the folds of mountains and narrow hidden valleys, we stumbled half dead into the village of Saint-Juste-Ibarre, where we planned to stay the night, fantasizing about the reward to come in a regionally celebrated rural inn that we had researched. It was fabled for its three-course meals; large, roaring fireplace; and cozy rooms to retire to after the feast. Having discovered inns like this all along the trail in the planning stage, we had decided to leave our tent and sleeping mats at home and enjoy the local delights offered to pilgrims wending their way through France. We stopped briefly in front of the ancient village church with a small stone vestibule and then, in great anticipation, made for the inn, our inn, next door.

The door was locked, its curtains drawn. Someone had taped a hastily written note to the glass. *Fermée—chasse à la palombe.* Closed—pigeon hunt.

Merde.

The blood drained from my tired limbs. The sun disappeared behind the mountains. A chill set in. We considered our options. The next village with lodging and food was a day's hike. We had apples, cheese, and half a baguette. This would get us through the night. We were now grateful that we'd kept our sleeping bags when we'd jettisoned the tent and mats. We settled on the stone church's vestibule as our best bet for lodging. It was only then that it dawned on me that the innkeeper in Saint-Jean had intended to warn us about this scenario. Pigeons had unexpectedly begun migrating earlier than usual that year. As succulent birds coveted for delicious roasts, the pigeons meant all bets were off as the owners of cafés, inns, restaurants, and pilgrim dorms shut their businesses and disappeared into the woods.

I soon learned that nearly two million pigeons made an annual passage over this part of the Pyrenees every autumn, heading for Morocco, the Canary Islands, or less ambitiously over the mountains into southern Spain. I also soon learned, especially from the prolific publications of Basque ethnologist José Barandiarán, that the pigeon hunt was a far older tradition than the 1,200-year-old pilgrimage route on which we walked. It turned out that it was an important male coming-of-age rite in the Atlantic Pyrenees, in addition to being an annual men's club: six to eight weeks of socially condoned bliss to run off into the woods, live in tree houses, and drink and eat in only the good company of other men. Apparently, it was also a nice break for womenfolk, for they, too, disappeared. In pursuit of geese, I had not anticipated that other birds would crowd the same ancient airways or cause us to be homeless.

Though hunting pigeons in the Pyrenees goes back millennia,

the method hunters use today was devised in the Middle Ages by monks in Roncesvalles, the Pyrenean pilgrim town par excellence in Spain on the other side of the mountains from us, which is where I imagined Luke, his friends, and Tom and Daniel, were snugly lodged and well fed after their hard day. The monks there had observed that pigeons flying high overhead would suddenly make a fast vertical drop to the ground and fly low when pursued by a sparrow hawk, so they built watchtowers in the treetops. As soon as a sentinel up there saw the pigeons approaching, he would launch a clay disk to mimic a hawk, causing the birds to drop low into the forest. There, other monks lay in wait with nets spread out on the forest floor, which they pulled up to capture the birds. Today's hunters communicate between treetop and ground with whistled signals and flags, and otherwise remain silent. The most experienced hunters are in the treetops, while the others wait on the ground. After each capture, they transfer the live birds to little thatch huts, reset the nets, and return to stillness and quiet.

So far, we had seen none of this—or had been oblivious to what to look for—but pigeon hunting was making itself eminently known to us now. Resigned to our fate, we turned toward the church. As we did, we felt eyes upon us. To our left, a small woman in her eighties had appeared in her doorway, dressed from head to toe in black—shoes, socks, skirt, sweater, and shawl. She smiled kindly and gestured for us to approach.

"I've been expecting you," she said.

"You have?"

"Of course. It's the pigeon hunt and everyone is gone. I keep an eye out for pilgrims. I can offer you a place to sleep and eat." She directed us to a door next to hers. Warmth returned to my shivering limbs.

We soon learned that she was the owner of both her small apartment and the massive family compound attached to it. Madame B was her name, and we entered the large house as she explained that she and her husband, who was now deceased, had raised their four children here, who were now all adults living in cities across France. She led us to a large bedroom furnished with two hand-carved wooden beds with bare feather mattresses and instructed us to set our sleeping bags atop these—a form of luxury camping. She showed us the bath and how to operate the shower, and then invited us to return with her to rummage in her kitchen for provisions for our evening meal.

We seemed to have slipped into an old form of pilgrim hospitality where we paid her for what food we took and also made a donation for the beds and shower. We were hesitant to take her food until she assured us that she had someone making daily grocery deliveries, even during pigeon hunting season. "Besides," she said, sweeping her curtain aside so that we could see the backyard garden, "I grow almost everything I need here, and a neighbor brings me milk from his animals." She added, "I will live here like this until I die."

In my head, I began calling her Saint B, *Sainte B* in French. We purchased from her the makings for a simple soup, some bread, a bottle of red wine, and some fruit. All that evening, her last sentence haunted me.

Barandiarán also wrote that Basque culture was largely centered on matriarchy. At the core of the society's structure stood the *etxekoandre*, the top woman (*koandre*), who governed the home (*etxe*) and led with wisdom and authority. This woman-forward worldview was embedded in the idea of the *etxe*, the most sacred center of Basque life—so much so that Barandiarán described the household as part of a larger physical placement with footpaths from it connecting it to the church in the middle of the village. He went further to describe invisible footpaths below the earth that the ancestors of each *etxe* used to journey between home and the churchyard, where they now lived.

At Sainte B's home, I realized that we had walked deeply that day into the realm of the Basque mother goddess Mari and the *lamiak*, those divine beings with waterfowl feet—a place whose worldview upends the patriarchal one and gives women their own power and autonomy. And that there before us was an *etxekoandre*, Mari's mortal representative.

Sainte B left us to settle in, adding that she would make us breakfast and set it on the dining table early the next morning. Before cooking our soup, we put down our packs and went to wander the village and visit the church once more before the sunlight faded. We noticed as we went that Sainte B's two domiciles' doors faced east, looking right across at the church and the rising sun, and that beneath our feet were the well-worn grooves of what seemed to be an oft-used footpath leading to the church cemetery where the ancestors now resided. In the moment of that realization I could feel that all of Sainte B's family—past, present, and future—were there with her and with us. As Barandiarán explains, all these paths, above and below ground, merge at the surface of the central hearth inside the home, the true center of the universe, the place of cooking, gathering, and warming fires. The entire village was arranged in a sunburst pattern of these radiating roads from each hearth to church and tomb—invisible and underground soul roads that were active to the inhabitants. Even with pigeon hunting season, things were bustling there in the little village in the Pyrenees. We returned to Sainte B's home, made our soup, uncorked the wine, tore off chunks of bread, and ate with gusto.

"We were really tested today," Sarah said as we slurped down the reviving broth. I nodded. "Let's see what's possible," she added, attempting to rally our spirits with her new mantra.

We unfurled our sleeping bags atop the plump feather beds, and then climbed inside them. Embraced in this ancestral warmth and comfort, and feeling the unbelievable fatigue of the day's efforts, I sank swiftly into sleep. As I did, I heard Bernadette's reminder wafting through my quickly departing consciousness: *It's about the goose. She is the guide* and *the symbol.*

She's real, I answered dreamily back, surprising myself. *And her name is Sainte B and she and the other etxekoandres bring luck to dicey circumstances.* A smile came to my lips. I bid Bernadette a good night.

In that bed that night, I slept heavily while also tossing and turning for the throbbing ache in my tired limbs, a dynamic that created a nightlong sine wave of waking and sleeping that made it possible for me to recall three dreams, all incredibly vivid.

In the first dream, I was at Harvard walking up inordinately steep and polished sanctified hallways crowded with professors. It appeared I was one of them as well. All my colleagues wore impractical high heels, men and women alike, but I looked at my feet and saw I was wearing my trusty hiking shoes. I thought to myself in the dream, *Why are they making the climb harder than necessary with those ridiculous shoes?* In the moment of that thought, I knew that I did not belong there. The dream seemed to harken back to years earlier and my decision to leave academia; it simply had not felt like my life path, the shoes didn't fit. But my training in how to do quality research, uncover solid sources, and sort fact from fiction was golden. I took that with me and ran onto the road I began to forge as a writer. Now, though fully on that trajectory, I was still striving to make the path more stable, stronger, and more robust.

In the second dream, I was with a friend who in real life had died tragically a few years earlier, along with her infant daughter. She was a gifted historian and someone I had met when we were both in graduate school. In the dream, we were at her college, and she was showing me around. I marveled at how wonderful it was to see her again, but I was also aware that this was not my place. Yes, I had been a university professor, but I had left that world many years earlier.

Why was I having these purging dreams now? Perhaps I hadn't fully expelled the debris from my system? Perhaps I still felt I had to prove myself, to show the world that leaving the promise of security and success for the dream of writing was panning out. But what if it never did—could I face others, let alone myself? Why did I care so much what others thought?

Right after these two dreams about the past, a third dream took me into the future. In it, I saw Sarah and me walking into Barran, a village that was over two weeks away on the trail, in the Gers region of Gascony. Ever since I'd seen that name on the map, I'd felt an affinity because *baran* in Persian means rain, and rain is always considered a gift of grace and abundance. I began to imagine that the village of Barran in the Gers in southwestern France was going to be a place of grace and abundance. In the dream,

Sarah and I had arrived there, and as soon as we reached the village church, we were surrounded and greeted by the town's elders. It was festive and heartwarming. It felt as if we were longtime residents returning home.

With this odd trinity of dreams swirling in my head, I woke up in the early morning and pushed myself onto my elbow from the deep folds of the old drooping feather bed to tell Sarah about the dreams. She listened carefully and confirmed that the first two had to have been purging dreams, sloughing off any remaining residue from my past life. "Let's pay attention to what Barran holds for us once we get there," she said about the third dream.

Excited by the prospects before us, I climbed out of bed and opened my map to locate Barran once again. It is a tiny village deep in Gascony and the last stop before Auch. Its name on the map held even more magic after the dream. *Barran, barran, barran,* I thought, and then worried that thinking so might evoke a rain dance that would drench our path. So I restrained myself, noted the dream in my journal, and left it at that. I had not noticed in that moment of glancing at the map that Auch itself was also a sign, a more obvious one, for the name comes from the word for goose in the Occitan dialect of Gascony.

5

PIGEON, BOAR, RABBIT

FOLDING UP THE map, I went over to the window and threw
open the shutters in time to see the sun pushing its rays up and
between the narrow peaks, casting soft light into the valley, where
a low fog hovered and blanketed the earth. The mist masked the
field of wild grasses and Sainte B's backyard garden with its rows
of kale, staked tomatoes, and lettuces. I heard the door below and
went downstairs to find that Sainte B had slipped in quickly and
departed, leaving a large breakfast tray on the kitchen table. Sarah
and I sat down and poured hot coffee and steaming milk into our
drinking bowls and spread soft butter and homemade plum jam
over fresh, chewy baguettes. After cleaning up, we packed and
left, casting grateful backward glances toward the ancestors at the
church and Sainte B and her abode.

The morning hike resumed on steep and narrow ascents and
descents. Toward midday, we reached a plateau, and by afternoon
we had plunged into a dense oak, chestnut, and pine forest. The
trackway narrowed. Fern tips from the undergrowth brushed our
legs as we passed. Midway, a horizontal metal bar appeared across
the path. A makeshift gate, its sole purpose was to stop trekkers
and make us read the sign secured to its center.

"*S'il vous plaît, Amis Randonneurs,*" the note read, "Please, Hiker
Friends, *Pas de bruit.* No noise. *Chasse à la palombe du 1er octobre
au 15 novembre.* Pigeon hunting from October 1 to November 15.
Merci."

"Really?" I said. "It's nice, though, how polite they are." I heard
a snort behind me as Sarah read over my shoulder. Snorting is her

signature response to things in life that are really amusing or positively contradictory, or both.

We slipped around the barrier and continued, quietly, but trying to make ourselves as visible as possible. We came upon a second sign, on a post on the trail's edge, reinforcing the request for silence. Two hundred meters later, a third sign appeared, nailed to a tree at eye level. "Oh, come on, this is overkill," I grumbled. But we stopped dutifully and read.

"Dear Walker, *Chasse au sanglier*. Boar hunting. *Faire bruit SVP.* Make noise, please. *Merci.*" A robust snort escaped from Sarah.

"It looks like we have a fifty-fifty chance of getting shot," she said.

Before we could discuss whether to make noise or remain silent, a man appeared on the trail, a foot-long, fang-shaped dagger tucked under his leather belt and a rifle in one hand pointing to the ground. In his other hand he held a ram's horn fitted with a mouthpiece at the narrow end. His ancient leather fedora had been softened by time to conform to the shape of his head, and it sat draped at an angle over one eye and ear.

"I don't want to shoot you accidentally," he said, "you're too quiet. I came out from hiding to tell you that you need to make more noise."

I heard a soft snort next to me. "How should we balance that out with the pigeon hunters?" I asked.

He thought a bit and shrugged. "Just be careful. Pilgrimage has its risks." He then disappeared into the thicket.

Pilgrimage certainly does have its risks, and it especially did in the Middle Ages, when people left home knowing that the odds of returning were as good as ours of getting shot. We were at least comforted by the idea that once we passed through Oloron-Sainte-Marie and veered farther north and away from the mountains, we would be leaving the thickest hunting territory.

But that encounter with the boar sign and then the boar hunter increased our anticipation of adventure. Sarah and I whispered to each other that we hoped to see a wild boar on our trek. We knew it was foolish. Boars were dangerous and powerful and had sharp tusks. But oh, how splendid it would be to see such a beautiful creature, one held sacred by the many ancient peoples of these very hills! In this wistfulness, we fully forgot about the dangers of being shot.

Carrying on, we soon discovered that pigeon and boar hunters weren't the only ones leaving notes. It was *cèpes* season and these porcini mushrooms were popping up quickly after a recent rain, so property owners began leaving signs indicating where in the forest mushroom hunters could or could not seek their quarry. We saw a mushroom hunter make his way into the woods with a basket covered with a red-checkered cloth. Soon after we passed him, the trail veered to the right, away from the forest and into a field of corn that grew well over our heads.

We plowed along through the dense stalks so heavy with plump ears that they leaned in and formed organic Gothic arches above us, making the trail feel like a natural church—that is, until midway, when a sudden and painful high-pitched screech rent the air, paralyzing us on the spot. In the same moment, a rabbit crashed through the lower stems and tumbled to a halt near our feet. We three remained that way as someone approached. A man appeared wearing a tiny brass horn around his neck. His rifle was pressed firmly against his shoulder with the business end pointing right at us, and his finger was on the trigger.

He quickly lowered the gun. The rabbit took off. We remained in place and tried to act calm, though our heartbeats were thumping like rabbits. Not all hunters left notes; rabbit hunters were surlier than the others and seemed to like to tell you stuff to your face.

"It was for the rabbit," he said while pointing at his horn, "but then I heard feet that were too big for a rabbit's. I'm glad I held my fire." He slipped his rifle's safety catch on and continued, speaking slowly so we could understand his thick Gascogne Occitan dialect. "You're lucky. Didn't anyone tell you? Walk only in corn that is shoulder high *e non plus.*"

No, I had to admit, that was a new one.

"Let this stand as a warning," he added, then began to chuckle, probably at the looks on our faces, which were drained of blood. This drew his hunting partner out from behind the next row of corn, which nearly paralyzed us all over again. We were grateful that he, too, had his safety catch on and that both men now slung their rifles over their shoulders. The first one cracked a joke, one intended only for his friend, for he now spoke in rapid bursts of the local dialect. I understood not much except that it had something to do with rabbits and us and maybe that stunted little horn. As they erupted into belly laughter, we quickly followed the rabbit and slipped away. The track soon exited the cornfield, and we went back into the safety of the forest with its gentle notes.

Just before sunset we passed through an ancient forest on a hillside thick with chestnut and walnut trees that were dropping their nuts. With the cadence of nuts falling and bouncing onto the loamy forest floor, which sounded like soft rain, we descended toward Mauléon. We passed homesteads overgrown with lush vegetable gardens and orchards heavy with fruit. Upon reaching the bottom of the slope, we entered a cheerful gray-rose stone town huddled along the sinuous banks of the river Saison. Fuchsia, lavender, and orange flowers in flowerboxes on the bridge and the fronts of the riverside houses were reflected on the river's surface, and the sky held the same colors as the sun sank below the horizon. Relieved to be in a small town that seemed active and open, even during pigeon-hunting season, Sarah and I felt renewing energy surge into our flagging limbs. We bounded toward the town center to look for lodging.

A young woman heading for her car saw us. "The pilgrim's gîte is open but is very basic," she offered, reading our minds. "There is also a hotel," she added, "that offers pilgrim prices and includes breakfast." Magical words. She kindly took us there and we soon found ourselves in a spacious corner room with ample light and a large balcony that looked out onto a backyard vegetable garden and the forest.

We washed up and then wandered through the medieval heart of the town and along its river, giddily stocking up on groceries when we found an open store, and then enjoying an early dinner and turning in. The next morning, we returned to the route as the sun rose to illuminate our way.

THE BRIDGE

SOON AFTERWARD, AS we climbed up the rising slope through dense chestnut forest, we met three Canadian pilgrims, two from Quebec and one from Ottawa. They were the first pilgrims we'd met since Saint-Jean-Pied-de-Port. We swapped information, a boon since we were heading toward where they had spent the night and vice versa. The Ottawan added a warning.

"I saw a boar run across a mist-covered cornfield yesterday morning, close enough for me to see the size of its tusks and think better about getting any closer. Be careful." Her warning only fanned Sarah's and my desire to see one, but we kept that to ourselves.

As we said goodbye, I thought of Luke again. By now he would be in Pamplona. The autumn had been dry and warm, good for his sockless feet in their thin canvas shoes. I wondered if he had yet found his path into the spiritual quest that had been ignited in him. I could still see his expression of hope mingled with excitement. It made me realize that I no longer felt as much resistance as I had on that first day. But as I felt around with my inner antenna, what I found was radio silence, no spiritual anything, neither resistance nor longing. It seemed that I really was out for a long walk, *e non plus*. But I also noticed that I was taking more and more photos, obsessively, of everything around me. I kept falling behind Sarah, but with each click I told myself it was my way of taking notes, of remembering smells, textures, and experiences for later on, when I came to write about all this. And then the darker side appeared, and I saw what was really under this compulsive behavior: although I was documenting every detail with my camera, I myself was less present.

I ran to catch up with Sarah and began making an effort to be more fully present, to not think of past or future. We walked on in silence. The only sounds around us came from nature and the soft footfall of our steps on the fertile forest loam that padded the path. It lulled me into a meditative state, and I could feel thoughts from deep down bubble up, each one more demanding than the one before it. These thoughts told me why I took so many photos: to prove I'd been there on the Chemin, to ensure that I had something to show for it, and to impress those glossy magazine editors. My thoughts revealed homesickness, for Miles, for our home, and for Sarlat, where I had a strong desire to be. They made me face the fact that I was growing older and dealing with new physical and emotional sensations and issues as well as identities. They told me I hungered inordinately to be a success and prove my worth. After each thought I asked myself why, but could not, or would not, answer. Resistance was back.

The path turned softer, and it was now entirely covered in emerald-green moss. We went through oak, beech, and chestnut forest, down a steep ravine, and into L'Hôpital Saint Blaise. The hamlet's stone houses radiated out from a sturdy, square, twelfth-century Romanesque church with an octagonal tower in its center that formed into a rounded dome. I recalled Bruno, my medievalist friend in the Dordogne, telling me about this combination that stone masons built with principals both of physics as much as metaphysics, where geometry was both solid and sacred. The square symbolized the earth and its cardinal directions, while the circle represented heaven. The two together, called "squaring the circle," marked where heaven and earth came into direct contact. In this tradition, a church's placement was never by accident but was chosen for special qualities implying that the veil that separated the realms was entirely lifted. This was one reason medieval churches were almost always built over earlier sacred sites, ones venerated by prior peoples who had identified these special energy spots. The church form—acoustically harmonious walls and dome formed by the circle and square—served to amplify the special energy of the place. To sit, sing, or pray there was strong magic.

I was excited to step inside, but the sight of four geese at the west gate jolted me to a halt. Situated on the left capital of the doorway's arch, each engraved goose had an elegant curving neck and was preening and smoothing its feathers. Why were these four here and why were they depicted in this way? Did it have anything to do with the joining of heaven and earth? Perhaps they were there as beings who are as comfortable on the earth and in water as they are in the sky.

Sarah was already inside the church. I went in and joined her where she stood in the center, looking up. I held my breath. Overhead was an entrancing geometric octagon with elegant cross ribbing that formed an eight-pointed star. It was an identical replica of the prayer niche dome in Córdoba's mosque, now a cathedral, in Andalucía in southern Spain. I had stood many years before underneath the mosque's dome and had felt an uncanny surge of electricity, as if energy flowed from the dome's center down its ribs into the earth. I now felt that sensation again: electricity rushed up and down the stone spines as well as my own. And yet, despite the majesty of the moment, I pulled my camera out and manically took photos, first of the dome, then of practically every engraved stone, including returning to shoot photos of the geese outside. I wanted to show this to everyone. I also wondered if I could some-how capture those pulses of energy in my images, like jarring fire-flies. So caught up in preserving the future and not being fully here and now, I jumped like a startled mouse when a voice called out from the periphery.

"Can I help you?" asked a man in his forties who had just stepped out from a small side door. "Pilgrims?"

"Yes," Sarah said. I slipped my camera in my pocket, feeling as if it contained precious cargo now, more precious even than before. My life force, my worth, seemed to have shifted from me to it. I joined my friend at the small table where the man now sat.

He welcomed us warmly and took our pilgrim passports and

stamped them with the image of the church surrounded by twelve scallop shells.

"This little place was long forgotten by time," he said, "until the Abbot Haristoy rediscovered it in 1880 and was astounded that such a church, of Islamic-Iberian style, was this far north on French soil."

The abbot knew it was something rare and remarkable, hard evidence of a medieval world that mingled more than it warred. The Camino, a force of both pilgrimage and trade, was a great webwork of roads that opened up seemingly isolated places and cross-fertilized them, interweaving diverse peoples from across the Mediterranean, Africa, Europe, and Asia. Abbot Haristoy launched an effort to restore the church, including historical research that revealed this church was a sister to a handful of other churches in southwestern France and northern Spain, especially in Oloron-Sainte-Marie, Eunate, and Torres del Río. The masons themselves who built the churches also came from diverse backgrounds—Christian, Jewish, Muslim, and pagan—and imbued the stones with stories from diverse religious and folk traditions. This manifested here in L'Hôpital Saint Blaise in the twelfth century, when canons from the abbey of Saint-Catherine at the Somport Pass just south of the church founded and built the church to care for pilgrims making the journey to Santiago de Compostela. The church survived many onslaughts, from the Wars of Religion to the French Revolution. Shortly after 1880, it was declared a historical monument and restored in 1903.

As the man finished, he called to two girls, ages seven and three, who were just outside playing in the garden, to show us to our pilgrim dorm. The eldest picked up a slip of paper and led us out of the church.

Midway through the village, the seven-year-old handed me the piece of paper. It had a code written on it. She explained that it was how we would unlock the lodge's door. "It is self-catering," she said expertly, a very mature seven. "You just need to close the door, so it locks as you leave in the morning." Business over, she added, "I know Basque as well as French, but she doesn't." She jeered at her little sister. The girl's childish seven-year-old side was back.

The younger scowled. "I know how to say, 'yes' and 'no' in Basque," she retorted proudly.

"Puh," mocked the elder.

"They are good words!" defended the younger.

"I think those are very good words too," I stepped in, "and that knowing when and how to say no is as, if not more important than yes." The three-year-old busted out a triumphant smile at her sister and then they both went quiet, considering these two words of power as we stood in Mari's ancestral lands. Maybe this, too, was the way of the wild goose?

"Would you like to know some Basque?" the younger girl suddenly blurted out.

"I would," I said. With that, she stepped ahead of us and sang, "*Oui* is *bai, bai, bai*, and *non* is *ez, ez, ez*!"

"Ez!" said I.

"Ez!" said the younger.

"Ez!" said the elder.

"Bai!" we four said with a shout that ended in gleeful laughter.

At the gîte door, the two made sure we could open the door and knew how to use the appliances in the kitchenette before saying goodbye. As the door closed behind them, I could hear them heading down the road singing, "*Ez, ez, ez, ez, bai!*" Heaven and earth indeed intersected in L'Hôpital Saint Blaise—its goose footprints were everywhere, great and small.

Our mobile home-style pilgrim dorm was clean and well organized, with a few bunk beds on one side and a dining table and counter and sink on the other. Vending machines offered packaged foods. But, miracle of miracles, we discovered that the village restaurant was opening up for dinner. After taking hot, reviving showers, we went for a stroll through the village and to dinner.

A young chef welcomed us and led us to a table. "You can pick from here," she said, handing us a menu "or, I can make you anything you desire, as long as I have the ingredients."

"A steak and salad?" I asked.

"Easily done."

"The same for me," Sarah chimed.

The chef returned with a generous carafe of local wine, followed by just-plucked salads, thick grilled steaks, and pan-crisped fingerling potatoes. We devoured the feast and lingered over the remaining wine to study our topographical map. Tomorrow we would reach Oloron-Sainte-Marie, ending our leg on the Chemin du Piémont. From there, we would pick up the Arles route and head northeast and out of the mountains.

Walking back to our gîte, the Milky Way splashed above us in the pitch-black sky, marking our earthly path in stars and stardust. I felt a strong visceral kinship with pilgrims before me. I was a tiny player in a grand adventure. We unlocked our door, stepped inside, and swiftly fell asleep.

7

THE SECOND GOOSE

SUNRISE SLIPPED ITS fingers through the spaces in the blinds over our bunks and gently woke us from our deep sleep. I was having a vivid dream about being with friends, including two who had recently died. It was both joyous and strange to be with them and then wake up and mourn anew their absence. I felt the weight of nostalgia for times past, and also the pull of homesickness for Sarlat and for my family and friends. Sarah, in contrast, was all sunshine and cheer. Not wanting to dampen her mood, I said nothing about the dream and hoped my heavy feelings would be lifted with coffee and hitting the trail.

We left the village and immediately plunged back into an extensive beech and oak forest and down into a ravine, and then trudged up the other side and down into another, and then another; this undulating terrain would define the entire day's hike. As we trudged along, my dream did not evaporate but instead hovered over each rise and fall of the landscape and began to weigh me down even more. I countered the anxiety rising in my chest by returning to manically taking photos. Each shot set me farther behind Sarah. As much as I tried to catch up, I felt the cumulative fatigue of prior days building, and I resisted any forward efforts.

We were now deep in impenetrable woods with dark brown earth, an opaque canopy, and thick undergrowth. I could no longer see Sarah or hear her footfalls. Damp air hung low to the ground. Moss dripped from the towering beech, oak, pine, and chestnut branches where a soft mist hovered. The otherworldly atmosphere halted me, suspended time, and sent a rush of emotions through me, the most dominant being my love for my parents, even beyond my ever-present worry for their well-being as they grew older. I basked in this warmth and love until I realized I could really lose Sarah, and I willed myself to continue. But just as I raised my foot and leaned forward, I spied a slow movement below me on the forest floor. It gave off an ethereal glow. I caught myself and pulled my foot back.

Bending down slowly, I came eye to eye with a hazelnut-sized frog. His little body was the color of dark-roast coffee, and he had chestnut and red racer stripes along his sides. Overall, he emitted an amber glow. He seemed unperturbed by my presence and continued his very slow ramble across the dark chocolate soil. I watched, frozen with enchantment. I heard a voice inside, an answer to the dream, to my heavy thoughts. *Just think of today. Focus on right now. The things of tomorrow will be taken care of tomorrow. The things of the past are past. Love your parents but do not spill life force on worry.*

I shifted back to give the frog ample room. The cloud that had fogged my head all morning evaporated. I slipped off my pack and carefully shifted from a squat to lying belly-down on the earth. Watching the little prophet's progress, my heart grew a thousand-fold, and thumped into the dark, soft, forest floor. The frog's big, soulful brown eyes seared themselves into my soul.

I eventually willed myself to move back farther still, then slowly pulled out my camera, grateful for its robust zoom lens. I clicked away from afar as the little fellow's five-minute journey across the path ended with him disappearing into the undergrowth of feathery ferns and moss. Then I rolled over onto my back and looked up at the ancient beech trees towering above me, seemingly wrapping me in their grandmotherly arms. I took a photo of them, too, enamored with the forest's tiniest and grandest creatures. I could have stayed there like that for an eternity, but I snapped out of it, realizing Sarah would be wondering by now if I had gotten lost. Grateful that my dreary mood had lifted, I strode swiftly but carefully, effervescence flooding every step. Two kilometers later, I found Sarah and gushed to her about the frog.

"I got it all on camera," I told her. "I can't wait to show you the pictures." As I said this, I felt it was all wrong, as if in that moment of transcendence, I had missed the full gift of just being. Instead, I had committed a theft—from the frog by making it an object, not respecting it for the full miracle it offered, and from time and myself by letting my ego negotiate away full presence once again. Frog joy and ego demons tangoed the rest of the morning, and I felt often in my pocket to be sure the camera with its precious cargo was still there. By afternoon, the demons slumbered and joy dominated. I had a new realization that pilgrimage was indeed happening to me, despite my resistance and imperfections, and it had just announced itself in a holy experience. Later, I learned that the Lilliputian frog I'd met was *Rana pyrenaica*, an endangered species of the Pyrenees. To see one is a rare event.

As we neared Oloron-Sainte-Marie in late afternoon, we left forested ravines and sauntered through riverside hamlets and fields heavy with corn, their backdrop the dramatic purple folds of the Pyrenees. We needed to find lodging in the medium-sized town, but we were sure that options in Oloron would be abundant. However, we had not anticipated that pigeon-hunting season would be coupled with a large annual reunion gathering of Portuguese immigrant families. A kind innkeeper took pity upon us and, after many calls, found the one spare room in town at a hotel near the train station. The owners had not wanted to rent it out, in hopes of reducing their workload, but when we asked to stay for two nights, they agreed.

Everything dated to 1940: the inn itself; its eccentric couple wearing a beehive chignon and candy red lipstick (Madame) and Perry Mason cardigan and slicked-back, black-dyed hair (Monsieur); and the old-timers smoking and drinking at the hotel bar while shouting at the rugby match overhead on the television. After taking quick showers and having a pizza dinner in the only place in town available for diners without reservations, we returned to our room, and in minutes were out cold for the night.

8

THE THIRD GOOSE

I **WOKE EARLY** and wandered out into a quiet Sunday morning, leaving Sarah to sleep in. After enjoying a tomb-like sleep, the excitement of exploring Oloron had roused me out of bed. Oloron has two historic Romanesque churches, each on its own historic hill, which have been welcoming pilgrims for over a millennium. I crossed to the other side of the Gave d'Oloron River, which cuts the town in two, and hiked to the tallest hill, atop which towers Oloron's oldest church, Sainte Croix.

As I climbed, a strange weight pressed down the nearer I got to the summit. Excitement drained away and heavy homesickness returned. I just wanted to turn back, roll downhill, and catch the next train to Sarlat. I was fretting that, of the little time I had in France, too little was allotted to Sarlat. My mood confused me. What was my problem? I loved exploring and these long-haul hikes. I was exhilarated over the chance to follow this strange goose mystery in France and Spain. For goodness's sake, I was already in southwestern France. Was my problem greed, wanting it all? Or was it not having enough of any of it for long enough to feel sated? Losing perspective of the sacrifices and graces that had made it possible to even be there, I felt like an ungrateful idiot. I also felt bad for Sarah, who had picked such a shabby walking companion.

Sainte Croix was open early, preparing for late-morning mass, but it was empty at the moment of any other people. Two newly lit candles flickering in a small chapel near the altar told me someone had just been there for their private devotions. I decided to follow suit, light a candle, allow whatever this was inside me to pass, and submit to higher powers. I dropped two euros in the donation box, lit a taper candle and set it next to the other two, then sat in the nearby pew, closed my eyes, took a deep breath, and worked to empty my mind of its chatter.

Several breaths in, the oddest impression flitted before my mind's eye: the image of an old wild man, like an aged John the Baptist, living in the forest and dressed in furs. He appeared this way and then, in a flash, transformed into a great old bear of the Pyrenees who was hibernating and in retreat. He would reemerge in a future time when the world returned to a state of harmony and balance. My eyes flashed open. Pulling in another deep breath, I looked up. I stopped inhaling.

Overhead was another dome like the mosque in Cordoba and the church in L'Hôpital Saint Blaise. This one was even larger and towered at greater heights, making it easier to see the crisp symmetrical lines of the octagon and cross-ribbing forming an eight-pointed star. And here, too, it sent pulses of energy up and down its ribs and adjoining pillars, joining heaven and earth. The bear, the star, the goose—all spoke about union and balance. It was creation, it was harmony, it was Bernadette's message spoken again.

The weight lifted. I forgot what it was that seemed so pressing, why I had been so unreasonably discontent. I let my eyes follow the lines of the star and pillars, and before long they landed on one of the pillar's capitals, where four engraved geese stared back. I laughed. The sound boomed through a perfectly calibrated acoustic chamber. Standing to take a closer look, I found the carved stones had retained the original pigments that had been painted on them in the twelfth century: these geese were creamy white with feathers shimmering in gold and they were kindred spirits to those on L'Hôpital Saint Blaise's entrance, each one craning its neck elegantly over its back. Here, they did not preen feathers, but instead nibbled on a gold-painted disk that looked like a Eucharist wafer. I felt myself return to the game, landing on a lucky goose square. They seemed to tell me to be patient, that I had made this journey for a reason.

I sat a while longer. I lit another candle of gratitude. I then rambled down the hill to the other side of the river and toward the other Romanesque church, the cathedral of Sainte-Marie-d'Oloron. Unlike the serenity of Sainte Croix, its west entrance was dizzying and crowded with scenes and beings from many worlds, all colliding in one place. Stories in stone filled nearly every inch of the wall, pillars, capitals, and five-arched gateway.

Begun in 1102, the dominant theme in the masons' carvings showed a chronicle of local life in the early twelfth century, all of it governed by the seasons. One stone was engraved with a hunter pursuing a boar, another with a fisherman filleting a salmon. On a third, a man was shown seated on a stool sacrificing a goose or a duck. Sainte B figures were up there, too, one with a massive wheel of cheese, another with fresh baked bread, another with wine barrels. At any moment, I expected also to see pigeon hunters hidden in the trees and rabbit hunters behind stalks of corn. Like a private letter sent a millennium ago, the stones conveyed that pilgrimage might be an old pursuit but that hunting and gathering and living by the seasons were even older and celebrated here in Oloron. Taking a closer look at their faces, I found the exact same joy, humor, and effort as in the faces of people Sarah and I had encountered in the forest, town, and village.

But what about that man sacrificing a waterfowl? Folklorist Joan-Marc Bertucci, a member the French Society for Mythological Study, offers an answer in the Society's *Guide de la France merveilleuse*. He says that the goose, or duck, represented a sacrifice made in honor of Oloron's local saint, Saint Grat, the town's first bishop in the sixth century. It was not simply an animal sacrifice, Bertucci added, but the sacrifice of an animal symbolic of a native goddess who protected people and land. The engraving delivered a double punch, as both a sacrifice made in honor of Saint Grat, and as a sacrifice made of the goddess to the new patriarchal faith.

A look at the remaining engravings on the doorway reinforced this double meaning and competition between two vastly different orientations in sacred space. To the right, on the entrance's innermost arch, was a squatting naked woman with weblike feet and long flowing hair, standing in a flowing river. Bertucci identified her as Mari, the Basque mother goddess. She had strong muscular legs and big aquatic toes pointing straight into wavy lines depicting water. Near her, another ancient being appeared: a *Basajaun*, an ancient and mythic Basque wild man of the forest. Here, men hunted him, another sacrifice to the new patriarchy that wanted control over nature, not harmony with her. To achieve this, the patriarchy needed to reign over both women and non-compliant men.

Even the tympanum held pre-Christian secrets. Its half circle form was made up of several vertical panels of stone, first engraved and then inlaid overhead. One panel held the scene of Christ's Deposition, when Jesus was taken down from the cross. Another, to the left of where I stood, depicted Mother Mary holding Christ's right hand. The color of Mary's stone was different enough from those used in the other panels that the restorers of the church had taken it down to investigate and found that medieval masons had repurposed a Roman stone to make this one. They discovered that the other side of the stone holds the image of a nude man with Roman inscriptions identifying him as Mars. He is a thousand years older than the Mary image on the other side, and the choice of this stone by masons was probably not a simple accident of reusing available stone. Had they picked it for its symbolic power as much as its physical dimensions, or because they wished to offer a deeply feminine and divine counterpoint to the most masculine of the Roman gods? Moreover, only this panel had been reused; the other tympanum panels were blank on the back sides. The whole doorway was a study in balances even as the male-driven Catholic Church was beginning to gain greater control over people's lives. But people, especially rural people living so closely to the land and nature, quietly pushed back, demanding some acknowledgement of the old, the female, the wild.

I stepped through the threshold and went inside, hoping to clear my head and return to the inn soon to have breakfast with Sarah. Instead, I saw something that boggled my mind even more, something I'd never seen in a church: a separate holy water font for lepers.

The regular holy water font was just below it, to the right, its large, round bowl and sturdy, tall pedestal reaching to hip level. But the leper's font was a rectangular bowl engraved out of the side of one of the church's supporting pillars and it stood head high. To dip one's finger into it was an act of faith, for you could not see the water inside. It was further decorated with the scene of a dog chasing a rabbit. And it had an even more nuanced and segregationist past. Before being called a leper's font, it was known as a Cagot font. *Cagot*, in French, and *Agotes* in Spanish, were the names given to a minority people in the Pyrenees who were viewed as being of an untouchable caste.

Treated like lepers and kept separate, the Cagots' first firm historical reference comes from the early eleventh century. Over the centuries, they were seen more and more as dangerous and contagion-carrying people. Semi-nomadic and itinerant, they were allowed only to make a living through ropemaking and carpentry. They were banned from touching non-Cagots, had to wear shoes so as not to touch the earth with their feet, and could not share public items, such as fountains, or the penalty could be severe, including having one's hand cut off. Some churches in parts of southern France and northern Spain built side doors expressly for the use of the Cagots/Agotes. No one but they could pass through those side doors, and they were forbidden to enter through the main entrance. At the height of this prejudice, Cagots were required to wear a symbol on their clothing to mark them out and keep others from touching them: a goosefoot.

No one knows for sure who the Cagots were originally. They may have been families formed by a guild of itinerant stonemasons trained not only in construction techniques but also in esoteric traditions, and who identified themselves with a goosefoot. They could be among the diverse peoples who infused churches along the Camino with many layers of diverse traditions and meanings. Because the Cagots were nomadic, independent, and practiced more heterodox Christian ideas, it is possible that townsfolk held them at arm's length. Another theory posits that the Cagots were descendants of the Goths, who expanded and conquered parts of France after Roman decline and who converted to Christianity but still wove their more ancient pagan ideas—including that of the goose and goddess—into their veneration practices. Another possible theory is that Cagots might have been Berber settlers who came from North Africa soon after the eighth-century invasion to make a new life in the remote Pyrenees. Some documents even claim that whomever the Cagots were, they also had webbed feet and hands, a possible reason why they later had to embroider a goosefoot on their clothing.

Archaeologists in Denmark recently unearthed a series of graves with whole geese buried with the people. These graves date to the time when Scandinavians first came into contact with the Roman world, around two thousand and one hundred and fifty years ago. One of the excavators theorized that the geese represented a newly introduced Danish affinity for the Roman goddess Juno, whose animal is a goose.

Another grave, found in Fyrkat, also in Denmark, dating much later to the late tenth century and contemporary to the time of the Cagots, contained a woman who the investigators consider a shaman. She was buried with several amulets, the most striking of which were three silver pieces the shape of webbed duck or goose feet considered to offer protective powers as well as the ability to plant one's feet in many realms: upper, middle, and lower.

Northern Goths, southern Berbers, nomadic stonemasons, and natives living close to the land in remote, wild Pyrenean places all brought their older extra-Christian beliefs into the mix—and most astoundingly, a goose-associated goddess and her three-pronged footprint appeared in them all.

All of the theories and historical details also point to the fact that whomever the Cagots were, they were seen as outsiders, so much so that even though they looked like many of the European peoples around them, others began insisting they looked different. The descriptions are befuddling: people reported that Cagots had pale skin, dark hair, blue eyes, and webbed feet. It seemed a case of seeing a group as being so "other" that even traits that were common, other than the webbed feet, were considered exotic.

Until the mid-twelfth century, the Church's influence in the countryside was patchy, and pagan practices persisted, especially those associated with assuring the health of herds and crops. But the rising control of the Catholic Church, even in the countryside, coincided with the Cagots being forced to wear the goosefoot on their clothing (and European Jews and Muslims also, to wear distinguishing symbols on their clothing to set them apart). This period was also when orthodox beliefs promoted a wider separation between humans and nature, diminishing the sacredness of the earth and promoting the divinity of the sky—and when the goose goddess began to go underground in earnest only to reappear in public as a less threatening figure like a kind grandmother seated near a cave or stream or hearth fire, spinning wool, flax, and tales.

Hungry, and feeling down for reasons that were entirely different from when I'd started out that morning, I returned quickly to the inn and found Sarah out on the terrace catching up on her journal notes and enjoying a leisurely breakfast of hot coffee and fresh baguette slathered with butter and jam. I went inside to order the same. All the usual suspects from the day before were gathered at the bar, plus a troubadour in a full leather vest, billowing poet shirt, and velvet cape coming from an all-night gig. His leaned his lute against the bar and regaled Madame—Oloron's Sainte B, as it turned out—about his long night of poetry, *amour*, and song. Everyone was there for his or her daily coffee, wine, and gossip, and to enjoy Madame's cooking and Monsieur's jokes. Fragrant butterscotch-colored roses sat on the bar in a large vase. I pressed my nose into them and inhaled.

"They are from my garden," Madame said proudly, pulling away from the troubadour and placing my coffee and baguette on the counter before me. She leaned forward and whispered, "My rose garden and my fruit orchard are what keep me sane." She cast a glance at the jovial madness around us, and then pushed a jar of preserves toward me. "Try my apricot jam." I thanked her, sheepishly eyeing the others, and was about to join Sarah when I noticed the newspaper on the counter with a story about bears in the Pyrenees.

"There are still bears here?" I asked.

"Of course," Madame said.

"They will always be there," the troubadour said. He leaned over and added, "protected by the spirit of Hartza."

"Hartza?"

"An ancestral spirit and wild guardian," he offered before return- ing to lobbing jests at the other regulars. I gathered my breakfast and went outside, wondering if it was Hartza I had met in Sainte Croix's church, hibernating until we humans got our act together. I was thrilled that the bears were making a comeback.

Sarah had another pot of jam, made from Madame's plums. We swapped and tried both, savoring the fruits, the land, and the sun in Hartza's special realm. I filled my friend in on my morning adventure and apologized for being so resistant at times to this journey. "I finally realized why I've resisted," I said. "All this long- ing and effort to be here in France, both in Sarlat and here on the trail, have made me feel like it can all be taken away before I've even begun. I fear I'll never get enough, that I'll never get to really be here long enough to find out all that is here for me. It makes me feel how finite time and money are. It's a selfish problem—I want it all…"

"Why not let the walk be the process where you resolve this?" Sarah said without judgment or pause. "Why not let it all be a mystery?" I let that sink in. "I think your purpose on this hike," she continued, "is just to experience being here. Let each day guide you. And, if it helps, I'll be fine with it if you decide to stop early and return to Sarlat. We began this together, but we each need to walk our own path."

"Just hearing that makes me know I want to stay," I laughed. I did want it all, this walk, that belonging. I needed to balance it and always be grateful for the fact that I was there. I also liked the idea of resting in a mystery. Wasn't that the whole point of this quest?

"And how about you?" I asked Sarah. "Is this trek fulfilling your hopes?"

"Yes," she said. "To me, this journey is just about seeing what's possible. But these first days really tested us." I realized then that she too had had doubts about continuing. It had been an ordeal all along.

After breakfast, we leisurely explored the town, walking along its riverbanks lined with colorful flowerboxes and rainbow-colored slate-and-stone homes. We found the one shop that was open on a Sunday and bought provisions for the next day. Early in the evening, we thanked Madame for her hospitality, paid up, and turned in.

9

AMBER WINE

DAWN LIT OUR route as we left Oloron and entered a forest of loamy dark earth and dense native beech trees. Lightness flooded my limbs, making me feel as if I were floating, even with my provision-laden pack. I let myself walk in mystery. I didn't need to have all the answers. My resistance loosened even though my manic photographing did not. Despite my attitude adjustment, my photo taking added edginess to the day, making me constantly fall behind and run to catch up.

We climbed down and deeper into the woods toward a center inhabited by older, towering, pale-gray, and thick-trunked trees, which radiated limitlessly around us and raised their arms protectively, weaving an intricate, sheltering canopy. Mist pushed in from the forest's edge and all I could see after a while was within a radius of twenty feet around me. The lightness I'd first felt shifted into a deeper energy, a pure and clear sensation of entering a wildness untouched by humans. The earth hummed, announcing without a doubt that we walked along a leyline. My senses grew more alert. I could feel other living beings, even if I could not see them. Nearby, deer nibbled on moss, bark, and leaves. An aloof but observant badger trundled along. Ferns nodded their leaf tips to the gentle breeze. Cèpes pushed up through decaying leaves layered on the forest floor. Chestnut trees rustled their leaves and dropped their nuts with soft thumps onto the spongy earth. Somewhere, I knew, an elusive wild boar nuzzled the soil for grubs, worms, and roots. The Mother Goddess walked here softly with webbed feet, as did the wild spirit of the forest, the Basajaun, both of them overseeing this wild world's well-being.

After several kilometers, the footpath ascended, leaving the forest and mists and opening into rolling hills alternating between farmsteads and vineyards. The soft autumn sun cast a lens of shimmering golden light onto everything. I halted before a row of vines as the honey light passed through their thin, orange-yellow grape leaves and translucent, pale-yellow clusters of Jurançon grapes hanging heavily near the dark earth. I took out my camera and captured it, feeling a rush similar to the one I had felt with that ethereal frog days before. I felt joyous and anxious. I double checked to be sure my camera was safe. It had become inordinately precious.

We arrived in the hamlet of Lacommande as the sun dropped below the hills. Village children were running home to help with dinner. A massive wine cooperative next to a fortress-like eleventh-century Romanesque church dominated the tiny place. Old round sun-disk tombstones leaned askew in the church cemetery like stone lollipops, announcing the place's ancient foundations. We made straight for the pilgrim's dorm next door, a tiny building with two bunk beds. Expecting it to be empty, we found all four beds already claimed by a couple from the nearby city of Pau, a young German from Munich, and a taciturn French recluse from somewhere we never learned. He had already turned in and was quietly reading in his bunk, ignoring us all. Sarah and I went to find the villager in charge of the dorm to ask for her help. We found her home across from the cemetery, its door facing east, the church, and the rising sun.

An enthusiastic woman in her late thirties greeted us, and two young children peeked from behind her at the door. She told us not to worry and grabbed a set of keys from the wall, leading us back toward the pilgrim gîte. Next to it was the village Red Cross building, used primarily by the village school. She unlocked it and we went inside. It was a concrete room lined with metal counters and two army cots.

"It's not as comfortable as the pilgrim's beds," Lacommande's Sainte B apologized, "but it's a shelter. Best of all," she guided us into a cul-de-sac to the left, "it has plumbing." We peered into a bathroom with three sinks and two toilets.

Before she left to let us settle in, I asked about the local vintage. "Is it possible to purchase a bottle of wine from someone in the village, since the wine co-op is closed?"

"We have several bottles in our cellar," she offered, "and can sell one for the price we paid." This revived our flagging energy. We procured the bottle and carried the golden elixir over to the pilgrim gîte. The other pilgrims were intrigued—even the recluse. We popped the cork, poured, toasted, and tasted the semi-sweet wine with flavors of sunlight, saffron, and nectar. As soon as he took one sip, the recluse accordioned again like a caterpillar into his cocoon, wrapping his sleeping sack around himself and ignoring us once again.

The rest of us remained, drank, and bonded. We shared stories, pooled our provisions into a makeshift dinner, and finished the bottle. One pilgrim was Matthias from Munich, a twenty-five-year-old who had just finished his studies in sustainable development and hoped to make the world a better place. But he needed a break, so here he was. He had begun in Arles and planned to go as far as Puente la Reina in Spain before returning home to start a new job. The couple from Pau were both office workers, also in need of a break. They had begun their trek that morning, simply by stepping out their front door and marching on. They had two weeks and expected to get as far as the Somport Pass in the Pyrenees. The following year, they hoped to return and continue from there to Santiago de Compostela. We all confessed our curiosity about the recluse. Who was he? Why was he walking? From where in France had he come? He hadn't spoken to any of the others, not even in such close quarters.

Sarah and I said good night and returned to our shelter. It had no heat and had become a refrigerator with the setting sun. We kept all our clothes on, adding layers, and sank gratefully into our sleeping bags atop the canvas cots and fell asleep right away. Half an hour later, I woke, feeling as if I was trapped inside a vice or a block of ice. In the half hour I had lain on the cot, its canvas had loosened and I'd sunk deeper into the fabric with the metal frame enclosing on all sides. I looked over at Sarah and saw she, too, was awake, her face ashen and grim. She looked like a creature in the closing jaws of a Venus flytrap. We inelegantly wrenched ourselves free, threw our sleeping bags onto the icy floor, and shivered our way through a long, sleepless night; the church vestibule would have been warmer. At predawn, we stood, shook our limbs, hoisted our packs, and went outside. We glanced at the gîte's door, hoping to see our fellow pilgrims emerge.

"Maybe we can find out who the recluse is," I added, hopeful. Matthias stepped out as I spoke.

"Not happening," he said. "He was up three hours before dawn and parted. The others just left." We hugged Matthias and wished him a *bon Chemin*. We watched as he marched south, then turned ourselves north and wove through Lacommande's pretty limestone houses, well-tended grape vines, rose gardens, and pumpkin patches. A warm autumn day dawned and thawed our frozen marrow. We ambled into oak forests and soft rolling hills dotted with more farm-steads, vineyards, and fields of sorghum, pumpkin, and corn.

It was a serene day but our lack of sleep slowed us down. Arriving in the early afternoon at the medieval hilltop village of Lescar on the outskirts of the city of Pau, we declared it our stop for the night. We climbed up the summit to the town center, passing gingerbread cottages with overgrown flower gardens. At the top, the original site of Lescar's Gallic Iron Age oppidum, we found the pale-yellow, limestone, twelfth-century Romanesque Église de Sainte-Marie. Entering it was like stepping into a forest. There were towering pillar trunks capped with carved capitals showing birds as heavenly messengers and humorous baboons making faces at those of us down below—a reminder of our flawed humanity. I took dozens of photos, and a greedy thrill rushed through my tired bones. Simultaneously, so did that gnawing anxiety over how very important these photos had become. They now included not only rare gems of the Romanesque but also sacred landscapes and experiences, and fellows met along the way, from pilgrims to all the Sainte Bs of the route.

A woman on the church square told us that the basic pilgrim gîte was open but also that a business hotel on the road to Pau offered pilgrim discounts if we wanted a private room with hot water. We walked straight over there and entered to see people in crisp and starched business attire milling about. We looked and felt like bedraggled medieval pilgrims in a time warp, but the elegant young woman at the reception desk didn't flinch.

"*Bienvenues, pèlerines!*" she enthused. She offered us a great room at a highly discounted rate and checked us in swiftly so that we could shower, nap, and make a leisurely walk to a roadside diner for dinner. Coming from the death grip of icy cots the night before to warm quilts and firm mattresses, we plunged into a heady, long sleep and did not rise until midmorning.

From Lescar we footed our way through oak woods, grassy meadows, and small farmsteads, landing in the small town of Morlaàs just as school let out at mid-afternoon. It seemed the whole town milled about the one large central square, with neighbors visiting as liberated children ran and played. Bordered on three sides by flowerboxes overflowing with marigolds and cosmos, the fourth side of the plaza featured a towering, majestic, cream-toned stone church. Sarah was already standing at its west gate when I ambled into town.

"You have to see this," she called to me, a huge grin on her face. "I think you just hit the goose lottery."

Its heavy, brass-studded wooden door was framed by a stone, five-rung Romanesque arch, with the middle rung displaying twenty-six ducks marching in a row. My jaw hung open. They were two sets of thirteen, two times the number of geese in the Game of the Goose. Thirteen waddled in a line up one side, and thirteen up the other. At the center, the two groups met, the lead duck of each group giving the other a big beaky kiss. It seemed that there were two goose games at play here. I stepped closer and tried to close my mouth.

TWENTY-SIX DUCKS

THE DUCKS MARCHED with plucky confidence, chests puffed, backs straight, and cheeky smiles. Several blew curling streams of water from puckered beaks. Three grasped wiggly snakes in their bills. One duck held a frog, another gulped down a fish, and yet another nipped at a round biscuit, possibly the Eucharist host. At the center, the kissing pair made it clear that the two groups were joining as one merry, possibly amorous, band.

"Stone is hard to sculpt," I recalled a lithographer friend once telling me. "Nothing the mason would commit to engrave in stone is there by accident, nor is the choice of the stone." What then, was the intended message behind these birds? As medieval scholarship documents, to the average medieval European, everything visible was a symbol and sign, an outward manifestation of an invisible and divine world at work. Moreover, these church stone images were largely intended for the nonliterate majority of the population, everyday people who labored in field and forest, believing in and working with entities that were invisible, hidden, and made of spirit.

"This is the church of Sainte-Foy," a man said. I jumped. He stood so close that I felt the warm air from his breath on my neck. So transfixed by ducks, I had not noticed the stranger approaching, or that Sarah was now across the street at a café. I turned to see a middle-aged man smiling broadly, with a small group of people standing behind him, waiting for him to continue his exposition. He was a local guide who was showing the church to two couples from the Loire Valley, and he invited me to join them. *What's possible*, I thought, glancing across the way at Sarah.

"Sainte-Foy was built in the eleventh century," he said. "It is among the earlier Romanesque churches in France and also related to the church of the same name in Conques. Both are dedicated to Sainte-Foy, a powerful saint who imbues both places with a strong feminine energy."

I almost jiggled my ears to be sure I had heard correctly. Only the year before I had made the pilgrimage to Sainte-Foy's church in the southcentral French town of Conques, in the Massif Central region, a wild and isolated volcanic mountain range. I had gone there with my medievalist friend Bruno. After exploring the church, we visited the museum that contained Sainte-Foy's reliquary, a stunning gold sculpture encrusted with gems all around her crown and body that came from both the Gallic and Roman worlds as much as they did the Carolingian Empire, during which the reliquary had been commissioned. The reliquary depicted a powerful woman seated on a golden throne, the four corners of which were topped with large orbs of rock that looked like fortunetelling crystal balls.

Bruno, a decidedly rational and secular person, and I took turns visiting the special room holding the reliquary. Though we always have something to say to each other, we went strangely silent and said nothing until half an hour after leaving the space and going to sit in the sunshine on a stone wall that looked out over Conques' narrow, oak-covered, volcanic valley.

"Did you feel that?" Bruno finally said.

"I did." I knew exactly what he was talking about. As soon as I stood before Sainte-Foy's image, I'd felt a definite energy waft toward me, one that was warm, loving, and potent. It felt like a real presence, one that was gentle but fiercely strong, and was devoted to high integrity and well-being for both the earth and us. Bruno described the same sensation.

Sainte-Foy was a Gascogne girl from third-century Agen—a town 150 kilometers (93 miles) northeast of Morlaàs—who at a young age converted to Christianity and refused to observe the pagan rites that were popular in Agen. The Roman authorities martyred her, and the locals buried her in Agen. But in AD 866 a monk stole Sainte-Foy's relics away to Conques, justifying his theft by saying that he was protecting it from Viking raids and taking Sainte-Foy to safer ground in remote and rocky Conques. There, she offered healing and protective miracles, and pilgrims flocked to her.

"What about the ducks?" I asked the man in Morlaàs, coming back to the present. "What do they represent?"

The two couples had already lost interest and were wandering toward the café where Sarah sat. The man pulled a pamphlet from his pocket. "Begin here," he said. "You need to study the ducks, and all the other images in stone, and see how they tell you their story." He sounded like the young man from Köln I'd met in Burgos. The guide caught up with the two couples. I saw that Sarah had ordered two glasses of amber wine. I joined her and we lifted our glasses in a toast to Sainte-Foy and then studied the pamphlet. It offered some brief history and included a black-and-white photo of the church's western arch with a key that identified each element of the five arches and capitals. But all it said of the middle arch, the one with the ducks, was that it was a row of ducks. As the man had said, I had to work it out for myself.

From where we sat, we could see the ducks and ponder them. The longer I looked at them, the more the ducks appeared to somehow represent us pilgrims parading into town, full of both serious aspirations and human folly—preening, praying, kissing, feasting, wandering, and wondering. They seemed to act and plod about like pilgrims, an idea confirmed by a publication from 1865 by Abbé Laplace, a local priest from the neighboring village of Bassillon. He theorized that the most plausible explanation for Sainte-Foy's twenty-six ducks was to represent pilgrims to Santiago de Compostela, many of whom plodded through Morlaàs to pay respects to the very popular Sainte-Foy. They were represented as waterfowl because they also were on the move as a group following the flight of geese and path of stars to map their way. But what about the snakes, frogs, and wafers? Were they symbols of earthly and heavenly concerns? Could the wriggling snakes perhaps represent the earthly leyline and sinuous star trail they followed? No answer to this seemed forthcoming, but it was clear that there were two sets of thirteen. Maybe they were two groups journeying together, or, it occurred to me, the same group going to Compostela and then returning back home. The kiss in the middle marked their midpoint, their arrival in Santiago, and the turn-around point to head back home.

With no answers but deeper impressions, we paid for our wine and located the pilgrim's lodging, which we were grateful to find open despite the pigeon hunt. After we showered and rested, we returned to the church. It was early evening, and the doors were unlocked. We went inside.

While its exterior is Romanesque, the church's interior is Gothic. Looking up at its pale-blue, wood-planked ceiling, which resembles an overturned boat, was like gazing up into the sky, with one's eyes drawn toward the altar where the sky gives way to the cosmos, a dark blue mandorla speckled with stars in whose center stands a celestial Sainte-Foy. She has long flowing tresses and holds a generous bundle of wheat, looking very much like a harvest goddess. I fell in love with her all over again since Conques and plunked myself down right in front of her in the front-row pew.

The air was perfumed with lilies and roses from massive bouquets on the altar. I inhaled and closed my eyes. Instantaneously, a fountain of light erupted as if gushing up from the earth before my feet. I traced the path of light in my mind's eye. It bathed everything in arching and radiating rays, some pouring back onto the ground, some shooting all across the earth, and yet others reaching deep into the heavens. Entranced, I sat in this glow and asked for guidance.

As instantaneously, my question was answered, and I saw myself before a keyhole in a door. It grew larger, became a cave mouth, and then morphed again into an ornately engraved door. I stepped through, and as I did, I heard someone whisper, "You are walking in."

My eyes flew open. I suddenly understood the ducks. Like the goose, they were gatekeepers and guides, guardians of thresholds to worlds hidden right before our eyes. I looked over to see Sarah settled in the pew next to mine. Her eyes were closed, and she was in a deep meditation. I quietly slipped out and went outside to visit the ducks with new eyes.

A few moments later, Sarah joined me. Without a word, we went back to the café from that afternoon and ordered two more glasses of golden wine. After her first sip, Sarah told me about the fountain of light she witnessed in her meditation, describing much the same image I had seen. It was déjà vu, like my time with Bruno at Sainte-Foy's temple in Conques. How was this possible? Even though it happened behind my eyes and was something I felt but could not explain, it was real and was universally accessible.

That night I dreamt I was back in my hometown in Colorado. I was in the backyard of a dear childhood friend's home and she was helping me extract with a trowel and shovel the pieces of my life buried there. Under the dirt, we found clothes, shoes, and other belongings—things I had forgotten and left in her care that I now needed to bring to the surface. I woke up realizing I was excavating my past and pulling to the surface of my awareness forgotten resources that might serve me now. I was also aided by a friend who had acted as guardian of my forgotten treasure. I wondered if the simple and seemingly silly act of following ducks and geese, and the mystery of the goose game, was activating these dreams and bringing about some form of initiation.

THE INN

THE SUN WAS bright and soft as we left Morlaàs. We now pointed almost due east and into more open hills, large, harvested fields, and tiny hamlets. By midday, clouds rolled in, and the remainder of the day was gray and overcast with a light drizzle. The damp brought out the intense orange, red, and brown tones of the autumnal oak and beech forest. I was feeling lighthearted, thinking of ducks and dreams, leylines and stars, and I walked with ease. At the same time, I was still clicking away, incessantly taking photos, a dozen at a time, and falling once again far behind my friend. I had also developed a new tick: each time I pocketed my camera, I had to pat it several times to be sure it was still there, safely zipped away in my pocket. A few moments later, I would begin the whole cycle again: photographing, pocketing, and patting.

When we reached Anoye, a hamlet of some twenty homes, we decided to stop for the night. Midway along its central street we found the pilgrim gîte, a stately two-story stonehouse with pale blue shutters. Up the hefty stone steps we went to the heavy wooden door on which someone had taped a note in French, German, and English welcoming pilgrims and saying that during the day the door was open so please enter and claim a bed. Furthermore, the gîte volunteers would arrive at 5:30 p.m. to greet us, open the grocery store until 6:00 p.m., collect money, and depart.

"Grocery store?" I said, looking around and seeing nothing.

"All will be revealed at 5:30," Sarah said with a jovial snort. She turned the handle and entered.

Every upright surface of the vestibule was plastered with taped notes directing us where to hang our coats, store our boots, and wash and dry our laundry. Notes then continued up the wooden stairway to a door leading to the dorm rooms and kitchen. There, notes told us to keep the door closed and lock it at night, how to use the kitchen, and to be sure to clean the bathrooms after use. The kitchen was large and centered around a massive, rustic wooden dining table. Off to the side were two dorm rooms fitted with brand-new bunk beds. We were the only ones there. We each claimed a bunk and then returned to the kitchen, where we saw a note on the small refrigerator door advertising an interior filled with one-euro beers. I dropped two euros into the tin box on the counter and handed a beer to Sarah. "I love this place," I declared. We plunked down at the table and savored our reward after a long but beautiful day.

At 5:29 p.m., like a squad of cops arriving at a bank robbery, four cars appeared and screeched to a halt outside. From the stirred-up dust emerged four men, all attired in trekking shirts and pants. They rushed toward us and enthusiastically shook our hands. One went inside and threw open a side door off the vestibule to reveal a makeshift grocery store expressly for pilgrims in a village with no shops or cafés.

"*Voulez-vous faire le shopPING?!*" he called out, with the last half of the last word sounding like an arrow being released from a bow.

We went inside. The entourage followed. We made selections for dinner from shelves filled with tinned prepared foods, dried beans, pasta, rice, and canned vegetables. A special shelf held bottles of the regional Madiran wine and small jars of local jams. A refrigerated case guarded cheeses, butter, and milk, while the freezer held only baguettes. We paid for our provisions and our bunks, had our passports stamped, and returned outside to chat before the four men zoomed off at precisely 6:00 p.m.

"When did you each walk the Camino?" I asked, curious about how these four came to devote a half hour each day, all year round, to pilgrims.

They looked at each other and laughed. "We drove it together," one said, "for a week, a few years ago. We just wanted to sample the experience and see the sights; we've never dreamed of walking the whole thing." The others nodded in accord. He saw my surprise. "We just dress like this," he added, "because it's practical when working in the field and garden."

More laughter and banter continued until they simultaneously looked at their watches just as six o'clock arrived. Like a film going in reverse, they vigorously shook our hands, jumped into their cars, and now, like bank robbers escaping, jetted off in four directions, another dust cloud erupting in their wake. We went upstairs, uncorked the wine, set the bread in the oven, laid out the cheese, warmed the vegetables, and lingered at the table, savoring the peaceful village life, our warm welcome, and being temporary masters of a lovely abode—all the while sipping excellent wine.

I woke that night from a jumble of strange dreams. In all of them, I was half nomadic and half seeking home, half a man and half a woman, half in France and half somewhere else—at times I was in my native Colorado, at other times my current home in New Jersey, at still other times in Spain. I loved the experience of being in a man's body and the liberation it offered. But as I woke up, what lingered most potently was a muddy feeling that came from being swung like a pendulum in a dualistic world, half in, half out. As the fog of sleep cleared, the feeling morphed into a deep-rooted sensation that I had fallen short of the mark of being accomplished in any of those areas, feeling successful in neither the male nor the female world, but wanting desperately to prove I was worthy of both.

I pushed past my doubts and got out of bed, gazing out the window to see a gray dawn and drizzle. We had breakfast, cleaned the place up, pulled on our rain ponchos, and departed. Out in the elements, the weight of the dreams returned. I swept them aside again and resumed my default coping method, pulling out my camera to photograph practically everything in my path despite the precipitation. Soon, Sarah was far ahead. I walked alone in my stormy mental cloud.

I saw Sarah waiting for me in the hamlet of Momy, standing under a rain shelter with a bench that a kind local resident had built for just such a day. I went to join her but first stopped to photograph the lacy rust-red October hops growing against a dilapidated, dark-brown wooden barn. The overcast and wet day had made their colors saturated and brilliant. The shot came out blurry, so I took it again. I then went back to delete the prior image, concerned that my camera's memory card was filling up before I could buy another, given how remote we were. I felt under control, my mood lifting, when a mind-numbing message flashed on the camera screen: *Deleting all 1,001 images.* Instead of selecting the "Erase current image" option, I'd accidentally pressed the line below it: "Erase all photos."

A sick, sticky feeling spread like glue in my gut. I rushed to stop the command, but before I could do anything, *No memory* flashed on the screen. One-thousand-and-one stories—weird that this was the actual number—all gone. All physical sensations ceased. I began to cry as snapshots of the loss flitted through my memory. The precious little frog, the kind locals, the quirky pilgrims, the sun glistening through golden grapes, the enigmatic churches, the twenty-six ducks of Morlaàs, the four volunteers of Anoye, the Ottawan, Matthias from Munich, the dog who had followed us for five kilometers, the boar hunter. Then I plunged more darkly as I realized that now I had nothing to show for this journey, no glossy color photos to publish with my glossy magazine stories. In that moment, I realized I had truly given over too much to the idea that to be a successful writer I had to be published in the gatekeeper magazines, almost all of them publications that chased fleeting trends with little interest in the deeper, longer stories of peoples and places. Worst of all, I realized that in this shallow ambition of mine, I had committed a thousand and one minor thefts, commodifying beauty, places, and people. I had committed as many thefts of my own integrity as I had forgotten to be present, to savor the beauty around me, and to listen to what stories the earth wanted to tell me. I was the culprit in a classic northern Iberian story of the mother goddess sitting near her abode of a cave or stream and testing each person she met for motive and character. Those pure of soul received true gold; those falling short, got gold that turned to charcoal as soon as it hit his or her hands. I looked at the charcoal in my hands and began to cry even harder, not caring about making a spectacle or the increasing rain, when I recalled again the ephemeral moment on the forest floor with the tiniest frog of the Pyrenees. Gone.

Sarah saw my meltdown and left the shelter to join me in the downpour. I told her what had happened. She put a consoling arm around me and let me sob as we got royally soaked. When at last I could lift my leaden feet and return to walking, I didn't have the heart to retake the photo of the barn door with amber hops. We left the village. The rain thickened. I tightened my poncho and relived with each step the shock of what had just happened. I just wanted to crawl under a bush and go to sleep.

WILD BOAR, PIGS, AND PUGS

AFTER A FEW kilometers, we reached the village of Lucarné. The rain lightened. A tiny sliver of hope-laced light wedged into my sealed-off heart. *Those photos are in you*, I heard inside me. With each footstep, I relived more fully each moment, person, and place now lost on the camera. I mourned each one, every little death, but I also celebrated them, and slowly realized that all these experiences had registered more deeply inside me than just my camera. *Write*, the same interior voice said, now more loudly: *Write, and do it now.*

I called ahead to Sarah that I would catch up to her and stopped under the eave of a stonehouse, pulled out my notebook, and wrote with a rushing flow of consciousness every image, memory, smell, color, taste, emotion that gushed forth. I wrote and wrote until I was spent of any more images, words, sensations, or feelings. In that moment, I knew that I had recaptured what I had lost, but this time more honestly and deeply by listening to them tell me what I needed to share rather than the other way around. Relief washed over me. I dried my last tears, tucked my notebook into my pocket, and practically skipped like a child to reach Sarah. As I went, a sense of ownership and empowerment came over me: I was owning my own life as I wanted it to be, not as what others thought it ought to look like. Joy, love, connection, beauty, experience, and writing meant more to me than the socially condoned ideas of success. The wedge in my heart widened. More light poured in. I skipped past a fig tree so plump with heavy purple fruit and massive Edenic leaves with dew-drop orbs of rainwater gathered in their centers that I felt compelled, just by their beauty, to take a photo, first testing myself for the motive. A heavy branch leaned over the public road, one plump juicy fig hanging right at nose level. I plucked it, thanked the tree, and stuffed it into my mouth, letting the juice run down my chin.

"I'd still love to see a wild boar," I told Sarah as I came into stride with her, wiping my chin.

"Me, too," she answered, cheered to see I had turned my mood.

The rain stopped, but the atmosphere remained gray and over-cast, and it amplified sounds. The path turned into a large, spa-cious cornfield. We looked at each other and grinned. The corn was high overhead, but the rows were wide and we were sure that no one, not even the surliest bunny hunter, would mistake us for rabbits. Midway in, we came upon a kindly placed picnic bench under a large oak on the side of the corn-lined trail and stopped for lunch. I unpacked our provisions. Sarah spread out our topograph-ical map. We ate in silence and gazed at the map.

Auch was five to six days away. I wondered if I would encounter any more goose or duck clues. As I thought this, the sharp pang of shame over losing my photos jabbed me in the gut. I hadn't said anything more about it to Sarah since Momy, but she was now giv-ing me her piercing gaze. I thought of when I'd last seen that look on my friend's face, of Luke and his hopefulness and my resistance.

"Speak truth from your heart," Sarah said succinctly. "Write the deeper stories." She went back to eating and map gazing.

That was the very truth I'd discovered, and briefly forgotten, out there in the soaking rain. My heart reopened to light and my remorse slithered away.

Five minutes after returning to the trail, we both heard the corn and the precipitation amplifying the sounds of snorting and rustling coming toward us from a few meters away on our right. Adrenalin shot through my bloodstream. Sarah stopped and looked back at me, silently mouthing, *boar*.

We heard more snorting along with rooting that was causing the dry stalks to rustle. There had to be at least three boars. What a very bad idea it was to be so close to boars—magnificent beasts with spring-loaded thighs, meaty forward-thrusting shoulders, and sharp tusks. There was no way out now, for the trail went thick through corn and all around us was simply more corn. I took up my trekking poles in both hands and held them low and horizontal. The snorting grew louder. I could almost feel hot breath on my ungloved hands. More adrenalin surged, my muscles warmed, my senses grew unbelievably acute. There were five, six, maybe even seven tusked creatures on the other side of the stalks. I began to panic. We slipped along, bracing ourselves.

At a parting in the corn, several porcine faces appeared, their eyes locking on ours. We almost peed ourselves. Some were pink and some were smoky gray. All had higgly-wiggly curly tails and no tusks. One belted a loud squeal and they all charged gleefully toward us. We had fallen into a flattened field in the center of the corn that was the residence of a large band of small pink and gray free-ranging pigs. A dozen inquisitive, playful, and rambunctious faces surrounded us, looking expectantly—but did they want us to play with them, offer them something good to eat, offer words of endearment? Sarah and I doubled over into uncontrollable laughter only to be met with the pigs' sweet gray-and-pink faces looking befuddled and bemused. We laughed even harder. We stayed a few moments to talk to our new friends, managing to contain ourselves until a new porcine group came trotting over the next hill to greet us. It seemed word had gotten out. As with the frog, I knew that this was what pilgrimage and this walk was about, this rich and deep connection with all beings and with *being*. At last I was more fully present.

Finally the rain ceased but the day remained gray. We passed through chestnut forests, meadows grazed by herds of black-and-white goats and cream-colored sheep, a farm with pheasants and curious geese, a homestead where a dozen large hunting hounds baled loudly as we passed, and field upon field of *potimaron,* tiny, agate-toned pumpkins that go into silky rich winter soups.

Footfall, presence, beauty, and porcine humor healed the day's bruises and lifted my spirits. Just before nightfall, we crossed the flower-strewn bridge over the river l'Adour into Maubourguet.

Larger than most settlements on the trail, we nevertheless found its inns largely shuttered for the season. Just as we were about to give up, after pacing through the little town's streets twice, we passed a place with beautiful French-blue shutters that stopped us simply to admire its elegance. At the base of a window, in engraved words on a brass plaque so small it was easy to miss, we read: *Chambre d'hôtes.*

"What's possible," chirped Sarah as she knocked on the door, which elicited a fever pitch of barking on the other side. A woman opened the door, three dancing and wriggling black pugs clamoring at her feet and rushing to greet us. The woman told us they were indeed open and had a room. This was a bed and breakfast, she added, and included an English breakfast.

"You're English?" Sarah asked. She herself is originally from England.

"We left England a few years ago," our host affirmed, "to give it a go in the south of France."

"What's possible," I said to Sarah as we were invited in. The woman's husband came out from the kitchen, launching the pugs into another jumping dance. The couple and their pugs showed us to our room, a spacious Renaissance suite with a high molded ceiling, velvet and taffeta drapes and furnishings, and dark lavender walls with oil paintings and musical instruments hung on them.

After a rest and a reviving shower, we went to dinner at a packed café across from the market square. Everyone welcomed us warmly, and we were seated at the one remaining table. The waitress brought us a carafe of local rosé; we filled our glasses and toasted. It had been a rollercoaster day, a hard start but a beautiful finish with a lot of bumpy emotions and jolly pigs in between. Even before I took a sip, Sarah had that look again, for the third time on this trek. I set my glass down and waited.

"I think today's lesson is that you need to write the stories that have depth and truth and long life. It's what you do best. And so," she grinned, "your *new* mantra, should you choose to accept it, is: *What's possible if you have nothing to prove to anyone, not even yourself.*"

A seismic shift, a loud *yes*, and the feeling of a weight being lifted rocked through me. The mantra encapsulated my own epiphany from earlier in the day. Why had it taken me so long to arrive at this point? I raised my glass again and this time took a sip. Then and there, I began the practice of giving up worrying about what others thought. I was ready to own my life without needing to explain or validate it. I was ready to savor the presence of a dear little frog simply for being there with him. I was ready to take on the old craft of deep stories that lived long past passing trends. I was ready to own whatever it was that was in my soul desiring to express itself in this one unique life, the only one I have.

THE TEMPEST

AFTER AN ENORMOUS English breakfast, we departed
Maubourguet. The town's eleventh-century church stood
on the edge of town. Though dark clouds gathered, we quickly
explored it. Its boldly engraved ducks and geese over the entrance
and their brass heads forming spigots on the church fountain
reminded me of the Morlaàs church and the fact that the goose
quest was intimately bound to this pilgrimage. The sky grew even
darker, and we hastened across a quilt-patterned landscape of corn,
sorghum, and sunflower fields into rolling hills and dark chestnut
groves paved with knobby nuts. A few hours later, just beating the
rain, we walked with high spirits into Marciac, a fortified thirteenth-century bastide town, which was like entering a maze; we
wove in and made for the well-protected central square. All the
services were gathered there. We easily found lodging, a grocery
store, several cafes, and welcoming locals at every place. We forgot
all about the hardships of pigeon-hunting season, now a distant
memory.

That night, I slept deeply but had no dreams, as if wiping my
camera's memory card clean had done the same to my subconscious. We woke to a rosy-pink and mandarin pastel sunrise that
gave way to a powder blue sky with benevolent cottony clouds.
But the air smelled different. It carried a metallic note that said
autumn was surrendering to winter. I put on all my layers, and
we continued our northeast march, with our aim and sentinel in
the distance being the medieval monastery hilltop ruins of Saint-
Christaud. All the way there, it felt as if we were walking on a

leyline, and we knew we were on the ancient pilgrim path with each throbbing pulse of energy underfoot.

Just before climbing to Saint-Christaud at midday, we met a French pilgrim going the other way. He had begun in Arles and planned to go as far as the Somport Pass before the first snows arrived. He looked up at the sky and dug into his pocket, pulling out a dog-eared guidebook.

"I think it's a good idea for you to jot down this number." He pointed to a handwritten name and number on the cover for one Monsieur and Madame P. in Montesquieu, our roost for the night. "They are a wonderful couple who help pilgrims," he said. We noted the number as he looked anxiously at the sky. He quickly parted. When we turned back to the northeast, we saw the source of his anxiety. As if blown by Zeus's strong lungs, a dark slate cloud bank was moving quickly toward us, swallowing all the fluffy clouds and pale-blue sky. Montesquieu was still a half-day's plod. The clouds would meet us in less than an hour, but we didn't worry because we knew from our research that Montesquieu had two good lodging choices: a basic pilgrim's gîte and a highly acclaimed country inn celebrated for serving sumptuous dinners at tables set around a well-stoked fire in a large, walk-in stone fireplace. On Saint-Christaud's hill, we ate a quick lunch, put on our rain gear, and pressed on into the steamrolling storm front that now fully swallowed the sun, turned the day to night, and engulfed forest and field. We picked up our pace.

Half an hour later, swollen drops of cold rain began to fall, growing larger and heavier as we advanced. We stopped once under a protective church vestibule in an abandoned village to put on any layers of clothing that we hadn't already been wearing, reposition our rain jackets, and tie down our ponchos, which had been strewn askew by the strong winds. We still had over ten kilometers to go as true nightfall threatened, and the temperature had dropped below freezing. My fingers numbed and my shoes squished with water, their waterproof capacity breeched. But just then, as my spirits were plummeting with the temperature, I heard honking and looked up in time to see two wild ducks flying like fighter jets just over my head, the strong muscles of their wings and necks powering against the wind and rain. An ancient feeling of consolation came over me; I knew now why medieval pilgrims found comfort in following ducks and geese—they were in the same exact boat and offered guidance and company in their daring, faith, and homelessness. Like the pilgrims of old, I drew courage from knowing that I was not alone.

An hour later, in the frigid dark, we arrived at last in Montesquieu. We found the promising inn with its warm fire and sumptuous dinner. With frozen knuckles we knocked on a polished wooden door. I looked up and saw a warm light pouring out from the upper floor, already feeling the warmth, tasting the food, coveting the dry and plush bedding against my cold and aching limbs. The door opened to a waft of pine resin, wood fire, and caramelized onions that escaped over the shoulders of a very handsome man regarding us from his vestibule. But if I smelled pleasure, his face told me he smelled dog feces. He looked us up and down, his nose pinched, his eyes narrow, his lips tight.

"*Bonsoir*," I said as cheerfully as I could.

"I am sorry," he blurted, "all the rooms are…taken."

"Not even one small room we could share," I begged. Behind him I saw the large stone entrance, draped in tapestries and set with a Classical marble sculpture on a pedestal. I knew then the only answer was no: There was no way in hell he was going to let a couple of wet, dirty pilgrims into his perfect place.

"Go find a bed at the pilgrim's gîte," he said brusquely and slammed the door, the derisive tone from when he'd said *pilgrim* ringing like tinnitus in my ear. Anger and bile rose in my throat and then collapsed into powerlessness and misery. I had lost all feeling in my fingers and toes. We walked quickly into the village center and found the gîte on the main square. No lights glowed out from inside. A rain sodden sign drooped on its window: *Closed for the season*. We looked at each other and said, "Pigeon." Our breath frosted in the air.

Now what? It was after dark, the rain unrelenting, and we were frozen and soaked. Where was our Sainte B of Montesquieu? We looked around and saw a makeshift shelter with a community bulletin board on which was posted one lone business card, miraculously, for the local taxi. I pulled out my cell phone and dialed, with great effort using my icicle fingers, the phone number for Mr. and Mrs. P that the Frenchman had given us. The phone rang four times then went to a recording machine. I left a message without much hope and then dialed the taxi.

"*Bonsoir, Carlos Taxi*," answered a man.

"*Bonsoir!*" I screamed with joy, almost dropping the phone. "We're in Montesquieu with no place to stay and need to get to the nearest hotel. Can you help us?"

"You're stuck in *that* village in *this* weather?" I heard horror in his voice and began to feel better. "*Mon dieu!*" He cried. "*C'est terrible!* I'll be right there!" I heard frantic movement. "I'm turning off my stove," he said, keeping us on the line as if we were sailors lost at sea who had finally radioed in with coordinates. "Hang on!" More shuffling and a clank. "I'm feeding the dog! I'm putting on my trousers! Hang on!" he repeated. "I'm grabbing my keys…" I felt terrible for disturbing his cozy evening, but I was ever so grateful. His kindness obliterated any remaining residue of the innkeeper's disdain.

The big-hearted Carlos was almost out his door when a car drove past us and stopped. The driver rolled the window down; inside were a middle-aged man and woman. "Are you pilgrims?" the man said. "Do you need a place to stay?" the woman added.

"Mr. and Mrs. P?" Sarah asked.

"Yes. We went food shopping in Pau. Have you been trying to reach us?" We nodded. I quickly returned to the phone. "Monsieur, we may have another option." I could hear relief, but he said, "Stay on the phone until you are sure." What a dear man.

"You had a French pilgrim stay with you last night?" I asked the couple.

"Yes," Madame replied, "plus a couple on their honeymoon walking to Lourdes on the same trail." The French pilgrim had told us about the honeymooners. "Would you like to stay with us and have dinner?" Mrs. P. added.

"*Oui!*" Sarah and I said together.

"*Oui!*" Carlos shouted over the receiver. I told him we would stay and thanked him profusely.

"*C'est normal,*" he said. "*Bon Chemin!*"

We followed our rescuing angels back to where we had first entered the village and stepped into a fifteenth-century home adjoined to a fourteenth-century building. The former was where we would dine with Mr. and Mrs. P, and the latter was where we would sleep. Mr. P remained in the kitchen to build a roaring fire in a beautiful stone walk-in fireplace, and Mrs. P led us through an interior courtyard to the other building where the couple's now adult children had their childhood rooms, all now vacant and open for pilgrims. She gave us the warmest and most spacious room, which had its own bath and was lined with radiators puffing out plumes of heat. A Bart Simpson poster hung on the timbered stone and stucco walls over a queen-sized futon with heavy wool blankets.

"Dinner is at seven," she said and left. We took reviving hot showers, laid our clothes and shoes next to the radiators to dry, and walked across the courtyard to find the fire of my earlier fantasies blazing away. Our hosts invited us to take a seat at the already set table.

"I'm sorry that all we have right now are leftovers and simple fare," Mrs. P said as she ladled fragrant pumpkin, ginger, and sage soup into bowls. Roasted chicken and a garden salad followed. We were invited to polish off the rest of Mr. P's Alsatian beer, left by a visiting relative, and then devour generous slices of Mrs. P's plum tart with a splash of cream for dessert, accompanied by a plum after-dinner wine. It had to be the best meal we had eaten so far on the trek, and I wondered what less simple fare looked like.

We learned that Mr. and Mrs. P had taken over the village duty of caring for pilgrims in need when another couple in the village, who had done this for decades, had both passed away. It was a service that villagers had rendered to pilgrims since the Middle Ages and our hosts were called to step in and take up this long tradition, especially now with all their children grown up and living elsewhere.

The next morning, we left a donation in a guestbook in our room and went down to breakfast. When we readied to depart, Mrs. P advised us not to follow the modern pilgrimage trail, which traced the valley, for it would be rain-sodden, and instead follow the medieval route that traced a high and dry ridge.

I was surprised. "Not all the Chemin follows the medieval route?"

"Some of the medieval route was diverted," she said, "due to modern roads and construction, or to satisfy modern walkers' desires to hike in nature. But medieval pilgrims were practical; better to walk a little farther and stay dry and healthy."

We hugged our hosts and stepped into the street. "Also," Mrs. P called out to us, "there's an enchanting chapel on the old trail that only locals know about. Be sure to visit it."

It was a cloudless sunny morning, in high contrast to the prior day. We took the ridge route and saw the modern muddy trail below. Our track took us straight to the tiny chapel of Brétous, tucked in a pleasant grove of trees. Arriving in time for a picnic lunch, we stretched out over the dry grassy slope. Afterward, we visited the ivory-toned limestone church.

The vestibule was framed with heavy wood beams engraved with royal medieval faces. Inside was a long, narrow, stone room with a few pews stacked against the walls and an apse engraved with several unusual figures. One figure was a crown-wearing man with a fish body—a fisher king?—on whose back sat a bird who whispered secrets or celestial messages into the fish-man's ear. Another was a green man—a wild man and guardian of the forest—with intricately detailed vines growing out of his mouth and ears. Opposite him, another sculpture revealed twin stags, their horns intertwined like interlacing fingers. Though not explicitly geese or ducks, these figures harkened to images of old earth magic and the honoring of nature spirits; the whole chapel and its location felt like the pure joining of heaven and earth.

I forgot photos, I forgot editors, I forgot ego. I forgot my shortcomings, my grievances, my hurts, my regrets, and even my very tiny bank balance. I was pulled instead into an embrace that transcended all that, and only beauty and generosity existed, as well as oneness with all of creation and spirit. There, I had nothing to prove, not even to myself, for I knew I had enough, and always would have enough, especially if I carried forth this energy, this knowing, and this beauty.

So caught up in rainstorms and transcendence, I had not realized until we were two hours away that we were walking to Barran, the village I'd dreamed about on our first night on the trail in Saint-Juste-Ibarre, nearly three weeks and a lifetime earlier. I wondered what, if anything, Barran might hold for us as we strolled across rippling hills covered in golden wheat and red sorghum. I turned every now and then to take in the now snow-capped Pyrenees that still towered nearby but grew smaller by the step. Rising out of the hills ahead of us was a strange, twisting, slate steeple that looked like a giant, spiraling soft-serve ice-cream cone piercing the sky. It belonged to Barran's church and grew larger and larger as we neared.

Before long we stood at the village's edge, where we found the one and only pilgrim gîte. It was boarded up, a sign on its door explaining an early closing due to migratory pigeons. For the first time, this didn't distress us. We, too, had become migratory birds who knew that no matter what happened, our needs would be met. We took the small road into Barran's center and walked to the church, hoping to find a local to ask about lodging, or at the very least, a church bulletin board that might offer guidance.

14

THE RECLUSE

THE CHURCH ENTRANCE under the elegantly twisted tower had a bulletin board toward which we walked just as six gregarious locals in their seventies and eighties rounded a corner and quickly surrounded us. "We saw you coming and ran to meet you," said a very tall man with gray sideburns and a black beret worn at a slant.

"We hope you're planning to stay in Barran," a woman to the man's left added as she reached to my shoulder and gently straightened the twist on my pack's strap.

Before I could ask where, another woman, her rainbow-striped hand-knit cap pulled low over wild and thick snow-white locks, said, "Don't worry, we will show you to Marie and Jacques's place."

"They have spare rooms for pilgrims," chimed another, a portly man with paint-stained hands and a striped scarf, also covered with paint smudges, tossed casually over one shoulder.

"You will eat and sleep well, for they also serve an excellent dinner and breakfast," finished a third woman. She had short-cropped gray hair and wore a teal tracksuit.

"It is settled," said the man next to her, who was dressed in a matching running suit, his in navy.

"*Voilà*," they said as one, the Greek chorus of Barran. My dream from three weeks earlier in Saint-Juste-Ibarre had just come true. Here were the welcoming elders of Barran.

They led us to Marie and Jacques's house, explaining that they were members of the village afternoon walker's club, which was what they were returning from when they saw us arrive. There was also a chess club and a painter's club. The man with paint-stained hands and scarf was an artist and invited us to stop by his studio after we settled in. They then left us in front of a house with a large fenced-in garden that had been overtaken by ceramic gnomes, pigs, and roosters; scallop shells were everywhere, on stones, fence posts, and hanging from trees. A large vegetable garden bordered by a fruit orchard tumbled down the slope next to the house. The elders bid us *à bientôt* and nudged us toward the entrance, which was also hung with a large scallop shell. We knocked. In three breaths, a woman opened the door. Marie.

"*Oui?*" she asked. I heard doubt.

"We learned from the villagers that you let pilgrims stay with you…" I began.

"*Oui,*" she said, still hesitant. "Let me ask my husband. He just came back from a long trip." She disappeared inside, leaving the door ajar.

"Jacques?" we heard. "There are two pilgrims here. Can they stay the night?" Sarah and I held our breath, waiting for the verdict. If Jacques said no, our next lodging option was Auch, the place we hoped to reach at a leisurely pace tomorrow, our last day of walking together. Today, it would make for a long trek. But we heard no answer. Instead, we heard heavy footsteps approaching and soon a tall and stern man appeared, looking ready to adamantly say *non* to our faces. He stopped before being able to utter a single word. We couldn't believe it. Nor could he.

"You two!" he cried when he found his tongue. "What does it take to get away from you! Shouldn't you be halfway across Spain by now?! My god, Marie, these two are really lost."

Marie was taken aback. Little did she know that before us was the Recluse of Lacommande. He looked at his wife's shocked face and for the first time we'd ever witnessed any mirth from the man, he began to laugh. "We have to let them stay," he finally said. "It's the only way to get rid of them." He looked at us and laughed some more. "I was sure you were slow—probably the wine—but I never imagined you would get so turned around to walk the wrong way."

You share your wine, I thought, and this is the thanks you get. We filled Marie in. "If he had actually talked to us," I jested, "instead of just drinking our wine and ignoring us, he would have learned that we were intentionally walking the other way." Marie rolled her eyes at Jacques, pushed past him, and invited us in to their stone farmhouse. They both led us up ancient wooden steps to the next floor and a room fitted with two hand-carved wooden box beds surrounded by Renaissance lamps and chairs and East Asian tapestries. We learned that Jacques had returned from his pilgrimage just the previous night: he had gone as far as Jaca on the other side of the pass. Next year, he planned to return and continue from there.

"He's walked the Camino every year, ever since his first," Marie explained, "which led us to give up our demanding jobs and stressful life in Paris." They had wanted to live on the Camino, to be woven into it year-round. They found this old house to fix up, sold everything, and moved here. Like Mr. and Mrs. P, they wanted also to offer hospitality to pilgrims in need, such as when the gîte was closed or filled. They also wanted to plant a more sustainable life and had installed a kitchen garden, kept chickens, and ate only locally produced foods, if not from their garden, from neighbors and farmers whom they now called friends. We would indeed eat and sleep well here.

"I walk a stretch of the Chemin each year to hit a reset button on my life," Jacques said, "and to stay clear about what matters in life. I also use it to cleanse my body, mind, and spirit of junk, which is why I eat and drink little when I walk." His sip of our wine had been a concession.

Showered and settled in, we went to see if we could help with dinner preparations. Other than setting the table, everything else was already done. Marie gave us a tour of the restored church and its cemetery, then returned home. Sarah and I wandered in the village center and soon saw the same six people who had greeted us: one from her open window, another weeding his garden, three gathered on the church square chatting, and the sixth, the painter, in his studio. Paintings leaned in stacks along every inch of wall space. Most were landscapes of the Gers, but also of Paris cityscapes and a series of the "most beautiful villages" of France. One popped out at me, an intimate familiar, the cathedral square in Sarlat showing my special patch of earth there, St-Sacerdos, the street on which I stayed that led to the tower, and the building in which Le Chardon existed. It was so realistic that I squinted to see if my cat friend Mr. Stripes was sauntering about. Sharp pangs of homesickness hit me, mixed with excitement that I would soon be there. But I also felt sadness that this splendid adventure was about to end. What a mixed bag we humans are, I thought, always longing for something but sad to leave what we have.

We returned to Marie and Jacques's home and sat down to what turned out to be truly the best meal of the whole trek: herb butter-roasted chicken; ratatouille robust with late autumn tomatoes, peppers, and garlic; rice and green lentils; and a just-picked garden salad. Midway through the meal, we heard a knock on the kitchen's sliding glass door and saw a young man with a massive pack. He peered in at us with a drawn and reticent face, looking beyond exhausted. Jacques jumped up and welcomed him in, taking his pack off him and setting it down as the youth staggered in. Hanging off the side of the pack were heavy leather ankle-high hiking boots. On his feet, quite the opposite, were deeply worn neoprene finger-toe barefoot runners.

"I just ran into a group of villagers on the road," he said, stunned, "who seemed to appear out of nowhere and led me here." His name was Yann.

Jacques carried Yann's pack and showed the young man his room. Five minutes later, the young man joined us, looking better for having splashed water on his face and put on warm socks. "This looks so good," he said. "I haven't eaten all day."

"Where did you walk from?" I asked.

"From Auch, but I started early this morning hitchhiking from Paris." His face resumed the haunted look he'd had when he'd first knocked.

We let him eat before plying him with more questions. After Marie brought out dessert—homemade full-cream yogurt with jars of plum jam, quince jelly, and wildflower honey from a neighbor who kept bees—I couldn't resist any longer.

"From Paris?" I asked. "And what made you decide to walk?"

"I'm twenty-one," he began. "I suddenly jolted awake to all the illusions of my life, and I want to become more authentic." He was wise and remarkable in my mind; it had taken me twice as long to jolt awake. "Until recently, I was a sports coach at a very exclusive gym in Paris," he continued. "I made good money because my clients were wealthy and determined to look their best."

I could see why. Yann looked like a Greek Adonis, with firm, marble sculpted muscles; a dancer's build; thick, curly, black hair; sparkling, dark-brown eyes; and a chiseled jawline. He was a walking advertisement for looking one's best.

"But that was exactly the cause of my breaking point," he explained. "All my clients were concerned only with looking good, staying young, and impressing and staying within their circles of influence, money, and power. It all started to feel more and more superficial—no, soulless, that's the word. I felt incredibly empty around people like that: Everyone looked good but said nothing of interest; they consumed life but didn't contribute to it. Two weeks ago I quit my job. I gave up my apartment. I reduced all that I needed to fit into my pack, and then I left for a ten-day meditation retreat at a Zen monastery just outside of Paris, recommended by a friend. Midway, in the middle of a day-long meditation, the idea came to me to walk the Chemin. It excited me like no other idea I'd ever had. I knew it would help me sort out my life and find what mattered." After the retreat ended, he had written "Toulouse" with black marker on a piece of cardboard and stood holding his sign on a road on the outskirts of Paris.

As Yann finished, I knew this was also why I walked and that my sense of urgency to track the goose and step into this quest was also about claiming my real life and my connections to others and, as essential, to the beloved mother earth. This walking for us all was a quiet and peaceful revolution to reconnect and become more real. As Yann finished, I saw his face was relaxed and glowing. I also saw Yann's dreams and hopes in Jacques' face, reaffirming the same truth, the same reason for walking I had felt. Sarah's and Marie's faces mirrored this too.

"How did you pick this route?" I asked.

"Someone at the monastery had mentioned that the Arles route was less populated than the other three main routes in France. And as soon as I stuck out my thumb, a person stopped and offered me a ride all the way to Toulouse. But there, it didn't feel like the starting point for me, and I had a hunch about Auch."

I looked at Sarah. Hadn't we had the same feeling even though it cut three days of walking off our trek? She gave me a knowing look back.

"Like magic, the first car that picked me up outside of Toulouse was going to Auch," Yann said. "There, it felt like the natural starting point." What was the likelihood of meeting someone on the eve of our last day of walking who confirmed our choice of holy goal in Auch? The same likelihood of having a dream come true or meeting the recluse of Lacommande. Sheer trail magic.

We cleared the dishes and Marie shooed us all off to bed, including Jacques, who was still recovering from his own trek. When I returned from brushing my teeth in the shared bath, I saw that Yann was sound asleep in the neighboring room, his face cherubic and at peace.

Early the next morning, he rose before the dawn and slipped out quietly. Over one thousand kilometers (621 miles) lay ahead of him. We had just twenty left. We lingered over breakfast, then packed up and hugged Marie and Jacques goodbye. As we stepped out into their garden, the walking club came out in force to send us off, hugging us and doting over us and then bellowing cheerful *bonne route et bon Chemin* as we plodded down the main street, through Barran's medieval stone gate, and into the wild forest. I knew I had just passed through more than a physical threshold. I was not the same person I had been three weeks earlier; I liked the new direction of my growth and transformation and felt more comfortable in my own skin. I sent a quiet prayer out to Yann at the beginning of his transformative journey, and another to Luke, who by then would be nearing the end of his.

THE FOURTH GOOSE

WE CLIMBED UP the first ridge above Barran and I turned to see the twisting church steeple piercing a stunning blue sky over the huddled village and rolling golden hills of Gers, a solid wall of purple and snow-capped Pyrenees standing guard on the far horizon. We traversed the ridge through wheat fields and then entered the Forêt d'Armagnac to be engulfed by wind-rustled oak trees and a forest floor entirely carpeted with shimmering pink flowers that looked like lit fairy lamps. Leaving the tree cover, Auch emerged from across several folds of emerald-green hills, the cathedral's symmetrical twin towers rising above the land and marking our final destination on the town's highest hill. It was there that the Auscii, Aquitainian Gauls, had built their fortified hilltop town 2,600 years ago, calling it Elimberris, a Basque word meaning "new city."

We approached it as if in a dream, walking through the lush green valley surrounding the hilltop settlement, passing quince trees heavy with fruit, rose bushes bursting with fragrant white blooms, and more pink fairy-lamp flowers interwoven with autumn crocuses cupping their faces to the sky. I felt a wildness stir inside me, an ancient knowing coded in my cell tissue and bones that I and all of us are one and woven with all this beauty. This, here, was the way of the wild goose.

We entered the city with the orchards and gardens giving way to sturdy stone walls and ancient homes. A sculpture of the musketeer D'Artagnan, his arm raised in noble gesture, welcomed us to his native town. Soon afterward, we landed on the Auscii's central hilltop, on top of which the twin-towered Basilique Cathédrale de Sainte Marie d'Auch was constructed. The first church was built in the eleventh century, but a fire destroyed most of it in 1171. Locals rebuilt it in the fifteenth to seventeenth centuries, so it largely reflects late Gothic and early Baroque styles.

We easily found a place to stay on the square—a nice end to pigeon-hunting season—and returned to explore the cathedral. I lingered beneath the twin towers at the cathedral's western entrance, searching for signs as Sarah went inside. I saw none— the older Romanesque engravings had either been lost or were obscured—but I picked up a strong feeling of peace and wellbeing there, as if the cathedral's current form intended to hide and pro- tect some older beauty and presence, to shield it from belligerent outsiders. Though it was just a feeling, after weeks of walking in nature and clearing my mind of its detritus, my senses, including that less tangible knowing sense, had been honed, polished, and sharpened. I was willing to go with it and see what I might learn with all my receptors open. I went in.

The wide, three-nave church was intersected in the middle by a choir stall of dark carved-oak seats that had the effect of cutting the church in half, and its main altar at the apse end was hidden from view. But from where I stood, I could see another, more informal, altar sitting right in front of the choir, which seemed to be the central hub of local activity. People milled in and out, making a direct line there, and a number of them gathered around a pedestal holding something to the right. Unable to see what it was, I took a seat in a row of wooden chairs and waited. The group thinned after a while so that I could see a modest statue on the pedestal, which was referred to as Our Lady of Auch. I watched as more locals came in, each approaching her like a friend, uttering a prayer or request, lighting a candle, and heading back out to shopping and errands. I peered around at the many chapels and statues in the grand Gothic church and found this one to be the most modest in size but the most potent in spirit. I rose and walked to the statue. I felt something there, a sweet energy that the locals seemed to understand and engage, but also something invisible but hinted at: Mary's lips held a soft, playful, upturned smile. She seemed to hold a secret.

I walked around the church to find Sarah on the other side of the choir stall at the semi-circular chapels built around the apse. "Each chapel in this church is magical," she said when I stood next to her. "It's as if the people who care for this place know the deeper spiritual mysteries of their faith and are protecting them."

"That's also the sensation I get," I confessed, but we didn't say any more. As we walked around to the last chapel in the apse, we saw an open door in a section of the back wall of the choir installation. Inside was a small room and a priest reading a book at a tiny desk covered with pamphlets, postcards, rosaries, and a big ink stamp. We pulled out our pilgrim passports.

"*Bonjour!*" he boomed, setting aside his book. He gestured to us to hand him our credentials.

"Where did you begin walking?" he asked.

"Saint-Jean-Pied-de-Port," Sarah said.

He gave us a quizzical look. I explained we had walked in reverse and had chosen Auch as our holy goal for this walk. This delighted him. He stamped our passports, then opened a drawer and pulled out two postcards and handed one to us each with our credentials. It was an image of the cathedral's stained-glass window showing Saint James, which the priest pointed to on the north side. It showed James as a pilgrim, his hat and cape fixed with scallop shells and a walking staff in his hand.

"He has clearly guided you here," the priest said, "and Auch is a fine final goal; this is a very special cathedral in a very special place." As if he had fulfilled his service for the day, he stood, picked up his book, locked the door, and rushed off. I wanted to ask what it was that made the place so special, but he had already disappeared. We visited the original of the image on our postcard, finding the window even more dazzling in person, glimmering with saturated jewel tones in red, yellow, blue, and green. I paid one more visit to Our Lady of Auch and then we went out onto the square and joined the locals in a crowded bistro for a final festive dinner.

That night, sleeping there at our place on the edge of the

cathedral square, I had a dream. I walked inside the cathedral and stood before Our Lady of Auch and asked her what she hid. She quickly answered with a nearly blinding flash of light that emanated from her and formed an almond-shaped doorway with her in its center. She invited me to enter. As I did, I saw she had magnificent wings and stood in a fertile forest surrounded by myriad animals—stags, deer, wolves, boar, fox, hedgehogs, rabbits, frogs, snakes, and hundreds of varieties of birds, butterflies, and dragonflies. I understood as I looked at them all that they, and I, and all of us, were the interwoven web of all life, coming and returning to her—she who made and sustained us all. In that reckoning, I woke up. It was still the middle of the night and pitch dark, but I basked in the warm glow of the dream vision, the shock and beauty of it shimmering in the night air. I could feel the soft sponge of the forest floor still pressing up and cushioning my feet. I knew I had beheld the Great Mother of many names—Mistress of Animals, Reine Pédauque, Mother Goose, Mary, the Earth—the oldest being we have known and revered as humans walking the earth, long before we waged a war against nature and separated ourselves from the web. I had felt for a moment the ecstasy of being rewoven back into the web and it sent me into a profound and peaceful sleep. Three hours later, just before the dawn, I woke with unusual energy and clarity. Sarah and I dressed quickly, packed, and left to make our early departing trains.

LA REINE PÉDAUQUE

AS WE WALKED past the cathedral, I recalled my dream. The doors were locked, and I dearly wished I could visit Our Lady of Auch once more. I now felt sure that the cathedral, and Mary inside, had another layer that hid some ancient secret, but I could only bank this knowing on a dream and a deep sense of communion forged from walking in nature and rich history for three weeks.

Sarah's train arrived first. We hugged, speechless to sum up what this journey had meant to each of us. As Sarah boarded her car, she turned and mouthed the words, *What's possible,* smiled, and then disappeared behind the closing door. In less than an hour she would arrive in Toulouse for a few days of rest and exploration before flying home. My train was arriving in another half hour. After two more trains and several hours, I would be back in my favorite foothold of Sarlat. I sat on a bench. *What's possible?* One, the station had WiFi. Two, I pulled out my tablet and found digitized historical documents online detailing Auch's history.

After the Romans conquered the Auscii in 56 BCE, they renamed the settlement Augusta-Ascorum and extended the fortified hilltop town downhill and along the river, pretty much where I now sat. Over, or next to, Auscii veneration sites, Romans built temples to Hercules, Bacchus, and Venus, all very likely under or in the vicinity of the present cathedral. In fact, one Abbé Caneto, writing a monograph on the cathedral's history in 1850, reported that within the church's foundation builders found a pagan idol, Venus's head. Venus was depicted at times in Greek art with a goose, much like her wilder sister, Artemis, who was among the most popular goddesses worshiped in Roman sites in France and Spain, followed close behind by Venus. I then came upon historians' proposed etymologies for the name Auch, the vast majority saying it came from Auscii. But one historian claimed it came instead from the Latin-based Occitan word, "auca," which like the Spanish "oca," means goose. Just as my train arrived, it hit me, the final leg of our journey had landed us on a lucky goose square.

I grabbed up my pack and jumped aboard, knowing in my gut that La Reine Pédauque in some form of mother goddess—be it Venus or Mary, or some older Auscii goddess, or all of the above—had been venerated there in Auch. I heard again the priest say that it is "a very special place."

Hours later, Nadiya greeted me at the door of Le Chardon with a bottle of wine to toast my pilgrimage and return to Sarlat. After we caught up on each other's news, she left me to settle in, reminding me to turn in early because the next day was market day and the fishmonger would be waking me at 5:30 a.m. with her shoveling of ice. Joy shot through me. I was home.

I was so excited that I woke before the fishmonger appeared. I dressed and was out on the street just as she arrived, along with the bread baker, cheese seller, sausage maker, wineseller, and Occitan-speaking lettuce grower—all of them pulling in and unloading their goods. I wandered the medieval streets, returned to do my shopping early, and wandered some more, pinching myself to be sure this was no dream; and then at mid-morning I found Bernadette. She was already installed at our table at the market café, her full pannier at her feet overflowing with leeks, lettuce, beets, turnips, and radishes.

"Did you find the goose," she asked in greeting, as usual cutting the chitchat.

"In more ways than one," I said, "but I think there is more. I've only just scraped the surface. At least I now understand that this is both an inner and an outer journey and that the goose path is different for each person but very real and that the goose really does guide us."

I told her all about all the lucky geese and the goose footprints I'd discovered all along the way, the Sainte Bs and pigeon hunting, the engravings of waterfowl on myriad churches, the place names and etymologies, the ancient forests and their native nature-spirit inhabitants, and the electric landscape and throbbing leyline path. I also confessed my grungier interior wild-goose chase, my resistance, my false gods, my misled ego, how the Chemin slapped me good, and at last, about the lesson and my new mantra.

She listened, nodded, and smiled. "Now you see how it is about the goose as both guide and symbol of many things," she said, offering almost the same words she'd uttered before I'd left, but now she reached across the table and touched her fingers to my heart, and added, "And all of it is right here."

"All of it?"

"All of it. The mistress of everything, our most fundamental nature, what is real, what we most need, our oneness with everything. It is all right here." She tapped again. "We are the goose, and the goose is us. It's all interconnected and has never been separated except in our own minds. We are La Reine Pédauque, and simultaneously, we are guided by her grounded, webbed, and wise footsteps."

"Yet I had to go for a long walk to learn this?" I laughed.

"Absolutely," she said. "That's the call to the quest. It can wake us up much better than staying in the routine and comfort of home."

As she said this, I found wholeness and also the missing piece toward fully understanding those pesky twenty-six ducks of Morlaàs: They represented pilgrims, yes, and also the mother goddess and her ways, but they also told us we got the best results by undertaking both the inner and the outer journeys, by feeling the divine and being the divine, by casting the road before us as simultaneously the door and path opened and made inroads inside of us. There is no more powerful way to unearth the interior world than to meet the unknown out there. One must step up to the first square, roll the dice, and follow geese, stars, and hunches into deepening understanding and experience.

I savored those last days in Sarlat, with market-day coffees with Bernadette, visits with friends, hikes into the prehistoric landscape, sessions on the wall with Mr. Stripes, meditations in St-Sacerdos, and soaking up every aspect of life of this deeply rooted and grounding land and its people. When I flew home to the States, I felt full and grateful for it all, but I also knew that the goose journey was not done. Now that I had tracked the goose deep into the core of its traditional country, I knew I had to return to pick it up from there and track it as it expanded out along the most goose-embedded path of them all: the Camino Francés. This is the path that was born in Aquitainian goose country that then conveyed her ways and message all across the north of Spain, the most historic and most trodden route to Santiago de Compostela. I would wait for the next roll of the dice and the next chance to walk. When it came, I would seize it and go—this time, with no resistance, with my heart and mind fully open from the start, ready to follow La Reine Pédauque and her goose-footed signs.

PART II

THE MISTRESS OF ANIMALS

V

A PILGRIMAGE IN FRANCE AND SPAIN

THE DICE

PASSED THROUGH a spacious red brick hall with neon-rose and cobalt-starburst chandeliers dangling on wires overhead, making it feel as if I walked under a psychedelic starlit sky. Stone pillars, radiating in rows all around me, were crowned with intricately carved capitals, creating a forest of Romanesque church engravings—the survivors of destroyed medieval churches across southwestern France now preserved here in the Musée des Augustins in Toulouse. Yet despite the diverse and quirky array of engravings, my focus was on an installation held in a small room at the end of this ballroom-sized expanse, through a doorway where a guard stood. I whisked past stone carvings of running stags, a row of wolves holding each other's paws, acrobatic flying fish, birds pulling at an owl's ears, handsome knights on horseback, head-butting rams, and tiny fairy people hidden amidst Celtic-style knotted vines. It was a fitting modern use of a fourteenth-century Augustinian monastery devoted to Aquitaine's medieval art.

The guard smiled as I approached, and she stepped aside. I slowed and entered and caught my breath as I faced a four-foot slab of gray marble mounted onto the wall, its lower edge meeting me at eye level with carved aquatic but human toes. I followed them up muscular and sturdy legs to the being's well-defined labia, where she was giving birth to a sinuous serpent that emerged and slid across her belly to suckle at her left breast. One arm was resting on her belly, and the other, with her legs and body, floated on the surface of what appeared to be a river. Her hair merged with water and seemed long and flowing, her eyes partially closed as if dreaming the world into being, and her mouth almost nonexistent. Despite the shocking birth scene before me, the whole countenance of the woman was of regal nobility and self-governance. When I could finally take my eyes off of the stone, I read the small text panel next to it.

La femme aux serpents was the text panel's title, followed by the description, stating that this motif of the woman with snakes long predated any Biblical ideas and came from ancient images used to depict the Mother Earth, La Terre-Mère. But by the high Middle Ages, the image shifted to represent vice and lust because of strong Christian ideas about women and snakes as being Eve in the Garden with the cunning snake. The image depicted in Romanesque engravings came to mean sin and lust but earlier sculptural work still captured the older meaning of Mother Earth. This, to me, was as exciting as it was shocking. The truth was being printed at last—that the Mother Goddess had been perverted from her earlier meaning to suit a foreign faith. Like the goose goddess who went underground to be reincarnated as Mother Goose, so Mother Earth, the source of all life and creation, was defiled to represent sin, and in so doing, propagated an already inaccurate idea of what really happened in Eden between Eve, Adam, the Serpent, and God.

Until recently, common interpretations of women with snakes in Western medieval art defaulted to the all-too-easy idea of lust and sin, conveniently using the Biblical account in the Garden of Eden to justify increasingly hostile attitudes towards women in European society. Yet that very source—the Old Testament, in which the Edenic events are recounted—does not make evil either snake or woman. That twist is only present in certain strains of Christian interpretations.

This perversion was most strikingly investigated and set straight by contemporary Princeton Theological Seminary New Testament scholar James H. Charlesworth. He began questioning the popular default idea that the snake in the Bible was evil after looking more deeply into the Gospel passage from John 3:14–15, which stated that as Moses raised up the serpent in the wilderness, so, too, must Jesus thus be lifted up.

Why, Charlesworth asked, if the snake represents sin and evil, would John refer to Christ as the serpent? Furthermore, Charlesworth knew that neither here, nor anywhere in the Old Testament, was the snake ever referred to as expressly evil, not even in Genesis after the events in the Garden of Eden. There, the snake was pitied, demoted, and cursed, but never called evil. In fact, some Biblical commentaries argue that the snake was set up, as were Adam and Eve. In this reasoning, God actually wanted them to eat of the fruit of the Tree of Knowledge in order to see his creation animated into action and drama by opening its awareness to the fields of time, space, and duality; God actually wanted this to happen in order to experience his creation and see it evolve. In the timeless eternal Garden, these things just couldn't happen. Every day was the same and paradise never changed—it was beautiful but ho-hum. Moreover, that tree had been there all along, and Adam and Eve didn't think about it until the day when God said, oh, and by the way, don't eat from that tree. After that, the two couldn't stop thinking about it. Finally, God granted guardianship to this tree, one of the two most precious trees in the eternal garden (the other being the Tree of Life), to none other than the serpent. Genesis 3 describes the snake as more subtle than any other animal that God had created. The Creator had spent a long time in his workshop on this one and was especially proud of it.

Charlesworth, whose work, *The Good and Evil Serpent: How a Universal Symbol Became Christianized,* on ancient and Biblical serpent images and lore is over 700 pages long, tallies the many attributes ancient Biblical-era cultures gave to snakes and finds that they were almost all positive. The most common associations cast the snake as a source of healing, fertility, regeneration, resurrection, and eternal life. He also discovered that the problem was not the serpent, but was we humans who, since the middle of the Middle Ages, began to lose our ability to think symbolically. Up until the past five hundred to six hundred years, humans were more gifted at complex and nuanced thinking that allowed them to see the many layers of a thing. Since then, we have become more literal and two-dimensional, especially in our reading of ancient symbols, texts, stories, and the Earth herself. No longer are we a part of the earth, living in a way that requires finesse and nuance, but we consider the earth to be a commodity to be exploited for financial gain, and our way of living is blind to balance, let alone the interconnectedness of all things. In ironic contrast, the vastly nonliterate ancient and medieval masses understood the many symbols of a thing and saw everything as symbolic of something that was less evident when using just the five senses.

The form and phrase of *femme aux serpents* was a new one that I had recently encountered through reading the work of medieval art historians. From them I discovered the *femmes aux serpents* engraved on numerous eleventh- and twelfth-century Romanesque churches on the Camino, the highest concentration of these engravings being on pilgrim churches in Aquitaine and northern Spain—a perfect overlap with the highest concentration of goose lore as well. In these churches, a few *femme aux serpents*, like the one in the Musée des Augustins in Toulouse, show the mother birthing a snake but all, without exception, present her breastfeeding a creature, most often a snake, but at times a goose, frog, lion, or stag. Art historians, like the ones who had written the text panel before me in Toulouse, have established that these *femmes aux serpents* were older pagan ideas that had been slowly woven into newer Christian ones. In looking at the series of them across Aquitaine and northern Spain, I also discovered that they show the progression of their slow weave from early to later forms. The older *femme aux serpents* engravings show women with faces like the one in Toulouse: regal, commanding, serene, and life-giving. In contrast, the later ones have distorted, grimacing faces that convey only the taint of lust and sin. This hundred-year progression reflects a historical reality, that it was only in the late twelfth century that the Church finally gained full centralized power over all of Europe's people—not only those in towns and cities where an urban faith was easy to establish and control but also throughout the farthest reaches of the remotest countrysides, places where people still lived close to nature and its protective divinities.

The decisive turning point in all this took place at the Fourth

Lateran Council in 1215, convened by Pope Innocent III. He called together the largest number of clergy and representatives of royal houses of any prior papal council meeting, a massive men-only club whose sole purpose was to define, formalize, and make into law central edicts of the Western Christian world. The Council codified practices in every area of life and set down rules for monitoring and punishing anyone who fell outside the straight and narrow, which included clergy who did not practice absolute celibacy, a matter which, up until then, had been loosely interpreted and not entirely observed. The Council also enforced that European Jews, Muslims, and other marginalized peoples like the Cagots, had to wear special markings on their clothes to set them apart from Christians, and it focused on eradicating pagan worship, such as setting up an altar in a field or forest. Guidelines were established for unearthing heretics and putting them on trial. These procedures would evolve in later centuries under such a male-centered absolute power into witch hunts, largely directed at women, but also at men who did not conform.

The 1100s provided the last free-flowing chance for older ideas to circulate, and yet, even with greater restrictions to erase them, they persisted because they still gave life to people. French art historian Jacqueline Kadaner-Leclerq writes that the older pagan images and their ideas migrated over time into new meanings, even as their forms stayed the same. For instance, a woman could still be depicted with a snake, but instead of this being Mother Earth, the figure became Eve, and instead of being life-giving, she represented sin.

The stone before me in Toulouse had been carved sometime in the twelfth century and originally came from the village of Oô, a remote mountain valley in the center of the Pyrenees near the source of the Garonne River. In the early nineteenth century, an eccentric antiquarian, Alexandre du Mège, found this Lady of Oô in a dusty corner of a neighboring village church, presumably set there to protect it after Oô's church had been destroyed. Du Mège sensed that this stone needed even better protection, that the modern viewer would entirely miss its meaning and possibly destroy it. He oversaw its transport to Toulouse and its installation in the museum there. He was sure, and recent art historians have confirmed this, that medieval masons were still deeply versed and influenced by Gallo-Roman mythologies about the spirits and divinities of the Pyrenees and had included these older ideas when they carved this stone.

But why depict the creator goddess birthing a snake? There are many explanations. One is that the snake, confirmed by Charlesworth's painstaking documentation, has been one of the most common ancient animals depicted in human art throughout the ages. This is very likely because the snake is so distinctly itself but is also very much a basic model of all multicelled animal life—with its mouth, tube, and anus, the snake has a beginning, middle, and end. Because of this, no other creature caresses the earth with its whole body or as intimately than the snake.

Like birds, the other most commonly depicted animals in human art—especially geese, ducks, and swans—the snake also has a wide association across cultures and times as a symbol of regeneration and rebirth. Snakes shed their skin and hibernate, while birds molt their feathers and migrate. Both lay eggs, blatant expressions of fertility, unlike us mammals who hold our fertility inside.

In all that, I also sensed that the goose and the *femme aux serpent* were somehow interconnected and ancient expressions of the same primordial mother goddess.

"She's something, isn't she?" the guard said over my shoulder.

"She sure is," I said. The guard flashed me a conspiratorial smile and told me that she was proud of the work art historians had done in researching and correcting the earlier misinterpretations of the *femme aux serpents*, and restoring this Pyrenean goddess to her original status.

La Terre-Mère, Mother Earth, had since at least the Neolithic, if not earlier, been represented as a woman using her body to feed all life forms, an image that persisted into the Bronze and Iron ages, as well as Greek and Roman eras where she was often depicted as a commanding woman birthing life forms from her body and nourishing them at her breasts. Sometimes the painted and sculpted life forms appeared as deer, bears, lions, wolves, and frogs, but among the most common animals were geese, swans, and serpents. In Greece, she was called the Mistress of Animals, *Potnia Theron*, often identified as Artemis, who many scholars now see as among the oldest gods in the pantheon, one probably born of a prehistoric goddess of regeneration, creation, and nature. She became Diana to the Romans and continued to protect and defend life, justice, and nature, not unlike Mari and the lamiak. The Greeks often showed her with large wings on a strong body, standing in a forested setting, her arms out and surrounded by and holding animals close to her flanks and chest. In the early Middle Ages, especially under the Carolingian Franks, these classical images were replicated and still represented Mother Earth. In several Carolingian works of religious art, Mother Earth is there below the cross or in another Biblical scene, holding a serpent to her breast, not to represent sin but to include nature as an essential part of the picture.

The guard stepped out of the room for a few moments, and I briefly had the space to myself. I stepped back to regard *La Terre-Mère* before me. There was very little about her that felt sexual, as we now objectify female sexuality, but there was the very sexual serpent as phallus that gave the woman a self-sufficient, hermaphroditic quality: she could beget life on her own, a prehistoric immaculate conception, for she was the creator birthing life from her own body—something a male god cannot do. (Except, of course, for Zeus, who sews the baby Dionysus in a slit made in his thigh and carries him to term, or gives birth to a fully grown Athena through a split in his skull—both very unnatural acts.)

But this Lady of Oô was beyond sexual. The more I looked at her, the more she appeared as a mother with child: serene, a bit exhausted, and giving her all to her newborn. The serpent on her body did not appear evil, just hungry, a newborn reaching for sustenance.

A man entered the room. He passed uncomfortably behind me, then whispered, his hot breath on my neck, "*C'est dégueulasse*"—"It's disgusting"—which sent a sickening chill down my spine. I quickly exited the room into the great hall. The guard was nowhere. Anger rose inside me, and I knew, then and there, that the old power war still raged. Du Mège had been enlightened to know over a hundred years ago that he needed to protect this stone from modern minds stunted by more limited and less imaginative thinking. I went out into the sunshine in the monastery's cloister and sat on a bench. The aromatic medieval herb and rose garden there surrounded and calmed me.

I had not had an easy time upon returning from my last pilgrimage, and the most recent winter had been especially hard. My parents had serious challenges and transitions. I'd had a health scare. Several certain writing projects had suddenly been canceled, entirely from circumstances outside of my control. I had two book projects with my agent, but the publishing industry was more in flux than usual. I returned to teaching to bridge the gap. As much as I loved my students and sharing rich material with them, I was reminded of why I had originally left academia: I discovered that its outrageous politics, stifling attitude toward creativity, and over-enrolled courses had changed very little and, in some ways, had become more entrenched and looked to be the trend of the future. It didn't feel right in my bones and reminded me that my path was as a writer.

And yet, there were gifts. Despite the trials and tribulations of recent months or the demands of daily life since my return two and a half years earlier from the trek I made with Sarah, no matter what work I took on to pay the bills, I held true to two practices each day: in the dark hours of early morning, before life demanded anything else of me, I wrote; and in the early evening after work, I went for long treks to stay in hiking shape. And I dreamed of returning to France, to Spain, to the Camino, to the goose. I knew if I could find my way back, it would return me to my center—and with luck, help me reclaim my life.

After the spring semester finished, I boarded a flight to Madrid, then another to Toulouse. That morning, before I left, when I had gone for a quick run on the beach, two old friends greeted me: a mallard duck pair. I had begun to notice their appearance every spring and autumn, as they headed north or south and landed on this beach like clockwork to rest and refuel. That I saw them return on their spring migration, which was also the day I was flying, felt like a profound sign.

Miles drove me to the airport, as encouraging as always for me to go and find out what all this was about and to resume my much-desired long walk. The mystery of the goose and my own life felt urgently bound together, as if it held a secret that could free me and possibly others. Yet, despite the adventure and the absolute belief and support backing me, I found it harder to say goodbye than ever before. I knew I was stepping through a significant threshold: it was all or nothing now to claim my right life and livelihood, to see what would happen when I threw every ounce into it without resistance.

In that cloister in Toulouse, the warm sun revived me like a newborn sucking at Mother Earth's teat. I left the cloister garden to visit *La Terre-Mère* once more, seeing the guard back at her post, order and justice restored. I then stepped out into Toulouse to explore before alighting upon the pilgrim path the next day.

18

THE FIFTH GOOSE

BECAUSE MY TIME and budget were tight, I planned to visit Sarlat after the Camino and just before flying home from Toulouse. While it was a tremendous dream to be back in southwestern France and walk the sacred road again, I keened at being so close to Sarlat but not there. Bernadette had anticipated this, and two weeks before my flight, a letter arrived from her for me in New Jersey. "Recall the language of the birds," she advised for my forthcoming Camino. *What?*

I found the answer a week later, with one week left before departure, when I came upon Parisian alchemist Bernard Roger's book, *The Initiatory Path: The Alchemical Secrets of Mother Goose*, written over half a century ago. Roger had been a student of a famous and elusive, and possibly fictitious, alchemist Fulcanelli. Roger wrote that Mother Goose tales contained esoteric wisdom born from a mythic time when animals spoke and humans could understand them. This was a far deeper language than what we speak or understand today; it was the language of nature, of animals, of the birds. As if directed by Bernadette, Roger next launched into a meditation on the goose, a bird who had a lot to tell us and hence why Mother Goose was thus. *L'oie*, the goose in French, Roger points out, is a play on words and has a double meaning, *l'oie* and *loi*, goose and law. The ultimate law is the first law, the same thing in his reckoning as "mother law." If we really listen to the stories and meanings conveyed by Mother Goose, we might just reclaim our primal capacity to hear the first languages of nature and tap into nature's wisdom. This was similar to what Charlesworth had said, that the modern mind has declined in its capacity to understand the language of symbolism, which was also the language of nature, of the birds, and of a way of seeing below the surface to the many layers of meanings in any one thing.

I remembered Bernadette's directive to seek this lost language as I exited the Musée des Augustins and meandered along the medieval streets of Toulouse's historic center, easily finding myself on old pilgrim paths that led to the city's many pilgrim churches. I visited them all, looking for geese. No more the wiser, as the sun set and jetlag descended in full force, I arrived at the last church, the Église Notre-Dame du Taur, church of the bull. I had fifteen minutes before it closed for the night.

Inside was a sturdy square church with high and thick Roman-style columns, clove and sandalwood perfuming the air. Smaller and less ornate than the other churches, everything there led the eye to the altar and a Black Madonna, one I had never heard about. Toulouse had another more famous and miraculous medieval icon carved of darkened wood. It was down the street by the river in the Basilique Notre-Dame de la Daurade, from which I'd just come. Black Madonnas were popular in the Middle Ages and imbued with power and mystery. Some scholars think the Black Madonna represented wisdom; others believe it was Isis; some, the true face and features of a Palestinian Mary; and yet others, the dark, rich Mother Earth herself.

"Is this your first time here?" a man asked. I turned to see him smiling warmly and standing next to a table to the side of the nave, pamphlets and postcards arrayed across the surface.

"It is," I answered. He stepped forward and extended his hand.

"I'm Richard. I'm a volunteer dedicated to this church. Would you like a tour?"

"Please."

He led me down the nave. "Saint Saturnin," he began, referring to Toulouse's top patron saint, "also called Saint Sernin, was martyred right here on this spot in the fourth century when Toulouse was Tolosa and under Roman rule. Roman authorities didn't like his influence and dispatched a bull, tied Saint Sernin to its hindquarters and made the animal drag him through town. The rope finally snapped here, freeing the saint's dead body from further humiliation. Devoted locals built this church in his honor."

That was grim but explained the prominent painting of a bull on the altar. We arrived at the Madonna and Richard explained that she was a powerful patroness. "Do you know what Mother Theresa told Dan Rather," he said out of the blue, "when he interviewed her and asked her, 'What do you say when you pray to God?'"

I shook my head.

"'*I listen*,' she said. And then Dan Rather asked her, 'And what does God say?' She replied, '*He listens.*'"

I laughed. This was the secret to understanding the language of the birds. Bernadette was with me after all, in the form of her ally, Richard of Toulouse. The goose isn't always female.

"People talk too much and don't listen enough," Richard continued. "I recommend that, as you walk the Chemin, listen."

"How did you know I was walking?"

He chuckled. "You have the look."

Before bidding me a good evening and locking the church for the night, Richard gave me a small, printed image of Saint-Saturnin to take with me. "It will remind you to listen." It was the perfect blessing—and new mantra—to launch my second goose journey.

THE WELL

THE MORNING TRAIN left Toulouse and shimmied along the northern foothills of the Pyrenees the entire way west to Bayonne, where I arrived in the early afternoon to wait for the familiar two-car train to Saint-Jean-Pied-de-Port. My friend Cédric from neighboring Biarritz came to give me a proper pilgrim send-off. We had met and become friends years back in Sarlat, but since then he had been relocated to the Basque coast as a part of his work for the national rail system. He informed me after we greeted each other that, due to rail works, my train to Saint-Jean was now a bus. It was due to arrive any moment in the station's parking lot. We went out together, alerting other pilgrims as we went. I looked behind us to see that Cédric had become a Pied Piper figure: a flock of far-flung pilgrim geese from South Korea, Australia, the Americas, and northern Europe all gratefully followed his lead. Many were so heavily jetlagged that they could hardly walk, let alone think straight. I could see my friend was overwhelmed by so many people, all heading to walk the Camino, and he queried me about how a wild walk could be so populated.

"Maybe I should just skip the Camino and go straight to Biarritz with you and spend my time surfing," I joked. We both knew I had waited too long to get to this point to turn back now, but I too was overwhelmed by the crowds.

"*Non.* Maybe after forty days of walking," my friend said, "you'll come back wiser."

"Maybe," I laughed. "Maybe I'll achieve Nirvana and become

the Buddha, or maybe I'll just come back tanned, thinner, and really muscular."

"That, to me, *is* Nirvana."

"A very temporary one."

"Okay," he said, holding out his hand, "let's see after forty days what happens." We shook.

No sooner had the bus arrived then the group clustered around its door like iron filings to a magnet. I said goodbye to my friend, who wished me well on my path to enlightenment. The last to board, I took the only remaining seat, next to an older Korean woman who was already fast asleep, her head leaning against the window.

The bus departed, and soon its lulling cadences and vibrating motor put many of the remaining jetlagged occupants to sleep. I watched as the green countryside folded and wrinkled into lush forests and steep hills, then mountains. Still in deep slumber, the woman next to me shifted her head from the window to my shoulder. I felt kinship and sat still so as to not disturb her. Each time the bus hit a bump, she jolted awake and shouted at me in rapid-fire Korean. Each time, I shrugged and tried English, French, and Spanish, and she would shrug back, laugh, and go back to sleep. The last time this happened—by which point I was sure I had learned a few Korean expletives—she patted my arm dotingly and lay her head on my shoulder and slept all the way to Saint-Jean-Pied-de-Port. The bus stopped in front of the train station, and everyone poured out, anxiously reaching for their backpacks from the storage compartment. I woke the grandmother. She smiled and gave my arm a squeeze in thanks. "*Buen Camino,*" I returned, which she understood. We hugged and went to grab our packs.

Like a school of fish, the whole group surged as one body down the road to the town center. I lost sight of the grandmother and missed her already. I went more slowly, having reserved a place to stay ahead of time, wanting to start this trek with a sense of continuity by staying in the same inn from which Sarah and I had begun our trek. I passed through the gate into the medieval walled town and climbed the historic street marking the path of the Camino. Midway up, the pilgrim welcome office had a long line winding out from it where all my companions from the bus waited to get their credentials and advice on where to stay. I continued up to the top of the street.

"I had a last-minute cancellation," the innkeeper told me when he opened the door. It was for the room in which Sarah and I had stayed. He had remembered this and switched rooms so that I could stay there again. It felt like the first hit of trail magic, boding well for the trek. Leaving my pack, I returned to the street and went back down to the pilgrim office. Four volunteers stood around chatting and all the pilgrims dispatched to their gîtes. One, a local woman in her early seventies, invited me to sit at the table. She told me she had walked the Camino three times, from Saint-Jean-Pied-de-Port to Santiago de Compostela and Finisterre.

"I hope to walk it once more," she added.

"When did you walk the Camino the other three times?"

"The first time I walked it was when I got engaged. I made it as a solo journey to deepen my connection to myself before my life became bound to another's and to starting a family. The second time, I walked in celebration with my husband when he retired. And the third time," she chocked up and paused, "I walked when my husband was very sick. I walked for both of us." That had not been too long ago, and since then, her husband had passed. "My fourth Camino," she added, "should grace shine upon me and let me walk it once more, will be a celebration of a long and rich life lived fully and in love." She leaned in. "And to be honest, as wonderful as it is to share the journey with another, it is far more powerful, for you and your loved ones, if you make this journey alone." I thought of Miles. He had said the same as we hugged goodbye.

The volunteer handed me two pieces of paper. One was a topographical chart showing the altitude of each day of walking from there to Santiago de Compostela. The other was a list of all the pilgrim albergues along the way.

"Crossing the Pyrenees is not to be taken lightly," she said, pointing to the chart, "and we have a cold front coming in. Tomorrow morning be sure to check the weather report before setting off." She stamped my credential, wished me a safe journey, and ushered me back out into the cobbled street and town that has been greeting pilgrims for over a thousand years. I wandered to the bank of the Nive river and found a crowded place for dinner. The waiter led me to a large dining area and sat me at a table next to another solo pilgrim. He was just finishing his last course when he looked over and smiled. I learned he was at the end of his trek. From Köln, he had taken the train to Paris and started walking from there, a four-to-five-week trek.

"I miss my family and am ready to go back," he said. "But even if I wanted to keep going, I don't think I would want to continue from here."

"Why?"

"I'm in shock over all these pilgrims. For most of my weeks of walking, it's been peaceful and sparse. I slept in places no one had ever heard of, and finding a place to sleep was not a problem. But on the last two days of walking, the number of walkers began to swell, and chipper and chatty new pilgrims constantly interrupted the solitude I'd enjoyed before. It was tiring. I did not like it. And then, I could not find a place to sleep; they were all booked up."

I was amazed he was even talking to me. I listened, thanks to Richard, and decided not to challenge or join his diatribe.

"*Bon Chemin,*" he said a few moments later and stood to pay his bill and leave.

"And to a good return," I replied. A smile actually broke across his grim face.

After dinner, I walked back up the steep cobblestone street to my inn, feeling a bit of trepidation. The German's words had muddied my resolve to trust the path and not resist it. It had been easy to trust the road years earlier when the Camino wasn't so well known, but it had been a few years since I'd walked this most popular historic path, the Camino Francés, and in those few years, it truly had been discovered. I took a deep breath and resolved to trust anyhow. Wasn't the Camino's popularity a good way to test the extent to which it guides and provides?

I distracted my mind from worry by focusing on the beauty around me, and soon I was taken by how many doorways on the stone-paved street had dried herbs nailed to them. A thorny-looking plant resembling a sunflower was especially frequent, along with bundles of rosemary and laurel. The thorny flower was a dwarf thistle common in the Pyrenees and known as *Carlina acaulis*, or in Euskera, the Basque language, as *eguzkilore*. It was a deep symbol of Basque identity because it represented an ancient Basque story, which had been passed on orally and then was finally written down in more recent decades, about the Creator, Amalur.

Ama means mother, and *lur* means earth. Amalur created everything, and she is very much the equivalent of the Bible's creator god of Genesis. She formed the earth and the heavens, and all of life, including the animals, plants, and the first humans. But at the beginning of human existence, the earth was still in darkness, and the first people lived in caves and subterranean caverns, which they had to share with other beings, some of them very frightening. So the people petitioned Amalur.

"Please help us," they said, "we are frightened. We never know if we are going to run into something frightening in the dark."

The goddess responded by making the moon. "To illuminate your way in the dark," she told them.

People rejoiced and were grateful, but soon they found that it did not quite solve their problem. Though the moon shone with the same intensity all the time, the scary monsters of the dark soon got used to the moon's light and returned to trouble the people, so they went back to Amalur. "Can you make a stronger light?"

She made the sun and set it into motion in the sky with the moon, creating the cycles of day and night. The people rejoiced and thanked her. The sun lit their path and completely dispelled the frightening creatures and their shadows. It also set into motion a great flowering of plant life and animal migrations on earth. Yet nights brought the shadows and monsters back to the edges of their homes.

"Amalur," they petitioned a third time, "we love the moon and the sun, but is there something else you can do to make our nights safer?" Amalur responded by creating *Carlina acaulis*, a flower that shone like the rays of the sun day and night and planted it everywhere in the mountains and fields. This made night as pleasant and safe as the day; the humans rejoiced.

While the Biblical sky god would have smoted these demanding people of little faith by now, Amalur was patient, loving, and tolerant. Her flower hung on the doors was a reminder of this gentler creator god and persisted as a protective talisman. Her way was surely one and the same as the way of the goose, the stars, and *La Terre-Mère*.

I forgot all about the German's anxiety-provoking words. I thought about the Korean grandmother and her comfort in sleeping on my shoulder, and I began wondering where she was that night and if I would see her again. I returned to my inn and fell into a contented sleep in the bosom of Amalur's creation.

THE SIXTH GOOSE

BRIGHT RAYS FILTERED through the shutters and woke me from a lucid dream: I was sitting at a café table in Paris across from a man who looked like Cat Stevens when he was in his twenties. We were talking breezily about nothing I could recall, but as I woke up, he leaned forward and very clearly said, "Follow Mary, follow the Neandertals, and follow French folklore."

I reached for my notebook and jotted this sentence before the dream message faded, despite how absolutely wacky it sounded. I was sure it was just subconscious gibberish. After all, I had long been obsessed with Mary and both French and Spanish folklore. Neandertals had also entered the picture most likely because one of the two book projects that my agent was pitching to publishers was about several previous summers when I had worked with archaeologists on excavating a Neandertal site in the Dordogne. It was always on my mind because if my agent landed a publishing contract for that book, I would need to visit several other Neandertal sites and conduct a few dozen more interviews with archaeologists in order to write it. The other book, also on the Dordogne, was a travel narrative, and I had recently finished writing the manuscript. It gave me less worry, but still, the fact that no book deals were yet forthcoming was a part of why I'd felt so compelled to leave home and go on a long walk. On the surface, the trip returned me to the goose, but deeper down, I hoped it would give me a new perspective or fresh start for my work, come what may, whether book deals or lucrative writing projects were or were not forthcoming. But why on earth would Cat Stevens come to tell me to focus on Mary, the Neandertals, and French folklore, as if they were all related?

I dressed quickly and went downstairs, anxious to learn about the day's weather. By the time the innkeeper peeked out from behind the stove, a pot of hot coffee and a pitcher of steamed milk in hand, I entirely forgot the enigmatic dream message. He invited me to take a seat at a table set with fresh breads, creamy butter, Basque cheeses, thin slices of Bayonne ham, fresh fruit, and jars of apricot and plum jams.

"Rain will arrive by this afternoon," the innkeeper told me, "but it will be light, and tomorrow looks to be all clear skies. But be careful," he told me again, the way he'd told me on my last trip about pigeon hunting. "Weather can change quickly here." This time, I listened. Thank you, Richard of Toulouse. As it stood, my plan for the day was flexible and suited the forecast: I was hiking only as far as Orisson, a third of the way up the mountain. I planned to sleep at the refuge there, enjoy a communal dinner around a large walk-in stone fireplace, and finish the mountain crossing under sunny skies the following day.

After breakfast, I sent an email to my family on the small tablet and keyboard I had brought along for writing and staying in touch with family and work colleagues. I told my family I had landed well and was about to head over the Pyrenees along a section of the trail that had no connectivity. I had no incoming emails. I packed up and stepped out onto the worn cobblestone street, feeling once again the scintillating energy underfoot of so much history and so many feet having gone before mine. I also had the eerie feeling that my prior footsteps were now a part of the fabric of this place. I walked slowly, savoring each step.

Just before the stone bridge over the Nive River and up the mountain, I stopped at the pilgrim church devoted to Mary and visited her altar. Morning visitors had already lit candles. The light, like Amalur's flower, flickered all around and the air was fragrant with honey-sweet beeswax and sandalwood. A basket of notes sat on the stone. I scrawled my petition on a small slip of paper and set it with the others, thanking Mary for this new chance "to see what's possible, in gratitude and grace."

I crossed the bridge, left the walled town, and followed the signs pointing left for the Napoleon Route, the higher of two paths crossing the mountains, the one taken by Napoleon's invading armies in the nineteenth century (and also the Romans, many centuries earlier). The other route, the Valcarlos (Valley of Carlos, Charles) or Charlemagne Route, wended to the right through the Nive's river valley and marked the mountain passage where Charlemagne had camped with his army in AD 778. It was at that same moment, near Roncesvalles in Spain, that Basques and Navarrans attacked Charlemagne's rear guard led by his favorite officer, Roland, in retaliation for Charlemagne's sacking of Pamplona just days before. Today, more peaceful, the valley route was used during winter or poor weather conditions. In good weather, like that day's, the Napoleon route, named for another imperialist with designs on Spain, with its high mountain views, was the advised path to take.

Amalur's sun warmed my limbs. The mountains radiated a thousand shades of lush green, and herds of curly-horned black and cream sheep and thick-furred chestnut horses dotted the slopes. Despite the steepening vertical slant, enchantment arrived at every turn. Rain arrived, too, as I was midway to Orisson. I stopped to pull on my poncho when a young woman from Leipzig approached. She dug out her rain gear and we helped each other drape ourselves and adjust our packs and resumed the climb together. She had just finished writing her university exams and was waiting for the results, which would determine her job prospects and future career. Rather than sit around anxiously waiting, she had decided to walk. "The Camino is a rite of passage for many Europeans," she said, "because it's a part of our history and legacy." My friend Béa in Sarlat had said much the same.

Four engineers from Madrid caught up to us and joined the conversation. Their rite of passage was an annual three-day event to meet on the Camino and walk for one long weekend a year, picking up each year where they had left off.

"We'll be lucky if we finish walking the Camino in the next twelve years," one jested.

"We're in no hurry to see this end," another added, and everyone laughed.

Soon, a woman from Arkansas caught up with us and we learned she had walked away from her life as a nurse and was traveling and blogging her way around the world, a professional nomad. She was strong and unstoppable under a pack twice her size, now covered by a plastic trash bag, and her dreamy idealism was infectious. I could see the young German realize that this rite-of-passage business was everyone's birth rite: just by stepping onto the path, we stepped into the footprints of all our ancestors.

She stopped at a farmhouse just before Orisson. The engineers and Arkansan were already like goats up the mountain, soon passing through Orisson. I continued more slowly, stopping for a breather under a dense ancient oak grove to take in the dramatic rolling vista radiating around me.

"Shi-iii-it," I heard, a sharp curse piercing the air from below. It was followed by a petite muscular woman emerging from a hidden bend, a shock of snow-white hair cropped and formed into sea-urchin spikes. She looked straight at me and after a few more expletives added, "If this is the whole Camino, I am *fucked*." She doubled over in laughter and then stayed there from a sudden side cramp. Her accent had the musical lilt of someone from the American South. Behind her appeared a tall blond man with a Turkish-style curled and waxed mustache.

"I'm from Georgia," the woman said, extending her hand toward me from her toppled pose, "and this is my Viking husband," she waved her hand toward the man.

"What, again," the Viking said to his wife, "are they doing this for?"

She stood straight and gave him a searing gaze. "You know." I heard no humor, just foreboding. He nodded and climbed on. "Are you heading to Orisson?" the woman asked, massaging her side.

"I am," I said.

"Is it far?"

"I don't think so?"

"What are you doing?"

"Taking in this amazing view."

She turned. "Oh, god. I totally forgot to look. I need to remember to do that." She continued up. I heard colorful expletives long after I could see her no more. I lingered to take one last look at the huddled warm houses of Saint-Jean-Pied-de-Port tucked far below in the protective foot and valley of the mountain. I heard wind and then saw steely clouds coming nearer. Just before they fully covered the sky, I watched black vultures floating high up on air pockets, unhindered by the coming storm. The language of the birds was one of calm, grace, and command. With both Richard and Bernadette as my invisible companions, I returned to climbing and found cover in Orisson just as the clouds dropped their torrential contents, grateful that the next day called for clear skies.

The gîte's host showed me my bunk in a squat and claustrophobic bunkhouse for ten. The front door practically opened to the sheer drop of the mountain slope into which it was built. The gray clouds parted long enough to give a brief view of the Pyrenees spread all around us, expanding to infinity. Though cramped, I found warm fellowship in my room with pilgrims hailing from New Zealand, Wales, Ireland, Canada, and the Georgian Viking couple I'd met on the way up. A dour Italian man tucked himself into a corner bunk, rolling over on his back to make it clear he had no desire to interact with any of us.

We took turns taking showers in the small, shared bath and then retreated uphill to the large dining room, which was arrayed with several long wooden tables. We helped set the tables while enjoying the blazing fire in the central stone fireplace. Over forty pilgrims from across Europe, the Americas, East Asia, and the South Pacific took seats at the tables. We helped ourselves from large serving dishes loaded with coq au vin, buttered noodles, roasted vegetables, and endless thickly sliced rustic bread, jugs of water, and carafes of red wine.

"This is why I am walking," the New Zealander next to me said as he poured wine for everyone. *I'm looking for goose signs,* I replied, in my head, *and for direction in case all my efforts in the writing department go south.* We clinked our glasses and tucked in.

After dinner our host invited us each to stand and tell the group why we were here. The Italian, who had still not spoken to anyone, even over dinner, stood first and said he sought a long walk of silence and solitude. The Brazilians stood together and clarified that they were not here for a mystical quest despite their compatriot Paolo Coelho's book *The Pilgrimage*, but to party. A German said he wanted to take a break from ordinary life. A Catalan father and his three grown daughters and two grandchildren were taking a meaningful family vacation together. Two French couples just wanted to walk and enjoy nature, food, and wine. The couple I'd met earlier stood next. They walked to give thanks, they said, for the Viking surviving a life-threatening illness. They also hinted, but never divulged, that they also walked to honor overcoming a make-or-break challenge to their marriage. After they sat, a young Australian woman with thick, long, below-the-waist black hair and haunted eyes stood. "This is my walkabout," she said softly and sat back down. There was more there, guarded under her surface. I liked her and was also intrigued. As we set off to our bunks, our host informed us that tomorrow's weather forecast was shifting and still unclear and to check in with him before departing in the morning.

After I climbed into my sleeping bag, it did not take long for the snoring to begin coming from five different companions. I slept poorly. At dawn, I dressed and slipped out and looked across the mountain vista, seeing even less than the day before, the gray cloud cover now thicker and hovering lower. Precipitation gathered on my face. I went to breakfast in the great dining hall, which was warmed with a roaring fire and steaming bowls of coffee. I learned that the day's forecast was for constant cloud cover. The spectacular view of the mountains would be occulted, but the temperatures would remain pleasant. By the time I set off, all my dorm companions had already departed. The air was warm and humid. I donned a short-sleeved t-shirt and rain jacket and hoisted my pack. Within minutes, it felt like a sauna under my parka. I climbed to the shepherd's outdoor shrine of La Vierge de Biakorri, a ceramic Mary set atop a pile of boulders, but not even her feet were visible in the mist and drizzle. I was about to take off my rain jacket when the drizzle turned to rain. I instead scrambled for my poncho and pulled it on to protect my pack. By the time I resumed climbing, only two feet before me on the path were visible, and the temperature began dropping, one degree per step it seemed. The rain increased. I began to shiver and picked up my pace to a jog, keeping my eyes closely on the trail so as to not misstep over a rock or hidden drop.

THE ICE STORM

EVERY NOW AND then I heard another person behind or ahead of me, but otherwise I walked in the rain and an opaque fog that intensified as warm air collided with plunging temperatures. I sensed I'd reached the mountain's apex at the top of Col de Lepoeder peak, but its usual eagle-eye view of the entire Pyrenees below one's feet was erased by white mist and the pinpricks of rain now turning to ice. After an unrelenting ascent, I faced an even more relentless and sheer descent on a wet slate-coated mountainside in freezing rain. I went as carefully but as swiftly as possible, using my hiking poles to steady my effort. Stinging, then numbness, worked across my tightly gripping fingers and I lost feeling. I picked up my speed, at times sliding, my pant hems often catching rocks and roots. Seven kilometers to Roncesvalles, four Guardia Civil officers climbed toward me, telling me to get off the mountain quickly and safely. They had just closed the trail.

"The weather's getting even worse?"

"Temperatures are descending quickly," one answered as all four kept moving up the mountain. His face was grim. "Two pilgrims are missing, and we may have a fatality." A shock rocked through me. I flew down the mountain, miraculously without injury. The one thing I recall was landing on the valley floor and entering another world, a native beech forest so elegant and ethereal in the thick mists that I forgot my numb fingers and frozen body. Pale white and gray trunks swayed like dancers—the branches, their arms bejeweled with emerald leaves, reached in reverence toward the sky. I went deeper and the air warmed, the mist lightened, and I wove in and out in pockets of trees and ferns, the strong untainted presence of wholeness and nature caressing me.

All physical discomfort returned in a flash the moment I crossed the arched gate into Roncesvalles. Rather than offering its promised relief, everywhere I went—the monastery's albergue, the village inn, restaurant, or café—the whole place was overtaken by wet pilgrims clambering for every inch of warmth on any dry floor. Beds were filling fast, and I was at a loss, as frozen as my fingers in indecision. Unable to grip my zipper to open my jacket, let alone open my pack for more clothing or to pull out my list of nearby villages and accommodations, I pushed my hands in my damp pockets and left for the only place free of mayhem, the monastery church of Our Lady of Roncesvalles.

I pressed the door open and entered a thirteenth-century temple of peace, calm, and, best of all, dry stones and warm candle-scented air. I shrugged off my pack and poncho, left them to the side of the vestibule, and, blowing on my fingers to reanimate them, walked down the aisle toward the altar and to the statue of Nuestra Señora de Roncesvalles set high up under a filigree silver canopy. A crafts-person from Toulouse had sculpted her image from cedarwood, then coated it in silver, gems, and gold and carried her here in the thirteenth century. Her gaze pierced mine. She seemed to smile.

Spanish writer Juan G. Atienza recounts a legend about her from the ninth century. Over several nights, a beautiful stag approached two shepherds as they watched over their sheep on this hillside. On the final night, the stag led the two into the forest, where it stopped at an earth mound and began to scratch at it. The two men helped and discovered an ancient dolmen in whose center was hidden a statue of Mary. Soon after, people built a church in her honor, calling this lady of the forest, this mistress of animals, Our Lady of Roncesvalles, but also, over the centuries and with her great popularity, La Reina de los Pirineos, the Queen of the Pyrenees.

I no longer felt cold but instead basked in the radiance of the mother of this mountain and the enchanted forest. I uttered grat-itude to her for being here, for meeting her face to face, for this journey. And if she wouldn't mind, could she also return warmth to my hands and give me guidance on what to do next? *Keep walking,* came the answer. Enough life returned to my digits to dig out a coin, light a candle, put on a sweater, and hoist my pack. Outside, the sun appeared for the first time all day and was burning off the gray and cold. I visited the chapel of Saint James, then the cloister-like structure marking tombs of medieval pilgrims and possibly Charlemagne's fallen men. I went to the village bar to order a warm drink before setting off onto the trail once again.

The bar was still packed to the gills with wet pilgrims. In the center I spied my Orisson bunkhouse friends huddled at a table, along with the long-haired Australian with haunted eyes. After a long wait, and being no nearer to a warm drink, I told my friends I was heading off. They wished me *buen Camino* and we promised we'd see each other soon. The Australian said nothing but met my eyes and seemed to convey that she would have preferred to join me but was already committed.

No one else was on the path, which narrowed quickly after leaving the village and entered a tight native oak forest. The canopy draped low, just above my crown, and let in scant light, giving the effect of walking in a green tunnel with light at the far end, a path into another universe, a wormhole on the trail of the Milky Way. All was silent but for the occasional bird song. At times I hit pockets of air scented with honeysuckle and wild herbs. It had to be the woods where the shepherds followed the stag and unearthed Our Lady.

THE SEVENTH GOOSE

IN THE DEPTHS of the forest I came upon a large white cross in a clearing to the left of the trail. A plaque near it identified this as an old and magical forest where women healers would gather to perform protective and healing spells for their community. In later centuries, from the late fifteenth into the early nineteenth, women healers became the target of witch trials. By then, church and state were fully in cahoots with each other in their joint effort to dominate, expand, and exploit the world, nature and humans alike. Anyone dedicated to the old ways of revering the earth were suspect, especially women. Such misogyny was not only meant to suppress women but also anyone who stood in the way of the male elite who wielded their toxic brand of patriarchy, including egalitarian men and the earth herself.

From queen to witch, I now felt the day's fatigue overwhelm me. I willed myself to plod on and at last alighted upon the village of Burguete. The Camino became the village's main street, lined on both sides with tightly huddled, sturdy, square homes of stone with thick wooden doors and shutters, many with shields, names, and centuries-old dates engraved over their lintels. I stopped at the first one with the signs of life, a whitewashed and green-shuttered traditional house where a few locals had gathered around a table in the side courtyard playing a game of cards. I went closer to find that it was a small bar and the attached building was an inn. I went inside to the reception desk at the end of the long wood-paneled vestibule. A man entered from the bar through a side door and cautiously welcomed me.

"Do you happen to have a room for tonight?" I asked, doing my best to project respectability. A glance down at my mud-caked trousers and the feel of my wind-whipped hair drying in tangles around my rain-stung face probably undid any effort. He looked at me, face grim, rubbing his chin, then opened his ledger.

"Let me see," he said slowly. He caught a glimpse of my crest-fallen face and suddenly burst into laughter. "Of course, *Señora*, I have a room for you. Take your pick. Today, a Monday and with all the pilgrims staying in Roncesvalles, all my rooms are available." He scanned his book and selected a room. "I think this will do nicely," he said handing me the key. The price was not too much more than I would have paid in Roncesvalles, but I had my own hot shower and no one to wake me with their snoring. He went back to his card game in the bar, and I went upstairs to an old-fashioned room with a wooden writing desk, bureau, and hunter-green quilt over a sturdy bed. The window offered a spectacular view of the Pyrenees, the first glimpse I'd had of the mountains all day. I stripped out of my wet clothes and stepped into a blissfully hot shower.

Dressed and warm, I went back downstairs to inquire about WiFi, as I was anxious for news from home and to let my family know I'd made the crossing well. I hadn't seen it the first time, but now I noticed a portrait hanging in the vestibule.

"Is that Ernest Hemingway?" I asked when the owner came in through the side door.

"It is," he answered. "Hemingway used to come here to go trout fishing. Sometimes he came alone, and sometimes he came with friends. I remember him well. I was a boy. My family liked him a lot."

"This is where he stayed to go trout fishing in the Pyrenees, as in *The Sun Also Rises*?" I stammered. Hemingway was one of my favorite authors, but I hadn't made the connection with Burguete.

"Yes," the innkeeper said casually, handing me a slip of paper with the WiFi code on it. "And," he added with a smile, "I've given you his favorite room." He disappeared through the door to the bar as electricity seared through me. I clutched the room key and skipped up to the room, Hemingway's room, sat at the desk, his desk, and after considerable effort to calm myself, first caught up on my journal (something I enjoyed imagining him doing right there), and then checked emails (something I was sure he'd find alien and antithetical to being in such a place, when one should be getting away from it all).

There were three messages from Miles, two from my parents, and most unexpectedly, two from my agent. The first from my agent had been sent around the time I'd woken up that morning in Orisson. It read that a publisher was interested in my travel narrative on the Dordogne and to stay tuned as my agent commenced negotiations. The second email she had sent hours later, as I slid down the mountain into Roncesvalles: Another publisher had just expressed interest in the Neandertal book. The two publishers were entirely independent of each other, but after months of waiting, it was weird how both their responses arrived mere hours apart. Something had to be in the air.

Disbelief mingled with joy and wonder. I stood and paced the room and hooted a few times. I finally sat and sent my agent my excited reply, and also told her about where I was sitting to write. What were the odds of all this? Had it been the candle I'd lit before leaving Saint-Jean-Pied-de-Port? Or Hemingway's mojo? Or walking the Camino with intention? Or all of the above? And should I keep walking? I mean, hadn't I just landed on the winning square in the goose game? Didn't I have two books to get cracking on, one with a lot of research still left?

"But wait," I told myself, "we still have to get a sure deal, with signed contracts and deadlines." And that could be another period of waiting. No, I would keep walking until I knew differently. I sent my emails, threw on my jacket, and went to celebrate over a glass in Hemingway's bar next door, plunking down at the table next to the card players. The sun slipped behind the mountains and streetlights came on. I asked the innkeeper's wife manning the bar for a glass of local white wine. She pulled a bottle and showed me the label. *Nirviana Chardonnay.*

"It's perfect," I smiled. She gave me a generous Hemingway-sized glass, which I raised to toast my companions, who did the same with their beers, brandies, and wine. When they went back to their game, I pulled my French fliptop phone out and sent Cédric a text.

"Nirv(i)ana achieved. The extra 'i' is for inspiration," I wrote. I then told him my news and hit send.

A few moments later, my phone vibrated. "(I)ncroyable," he wrote. "And remember, you have a place to stay here if you need it." I thanked him but knew I would continue deeper into the north of Spain, excited for the adventures to come. I sauntered into town and found a pilgrim dinner at a nearby inn where a group of Japanese pilgrims was gathered. They pulled me to their table and into their celebration of getting this far. We toasted our journey with more local wine, which was another reason Hemingway loved this part of Spain. That night the stars shined brightly in a now fully clear sky. I fell into a deep restful sleep in Hemingway's room, folded into the arms of the tribe to which I most wanted to belong—writers and pilgrims. I vowed to listen, to see what was possible, to be open and continue my walk of total submission to the path. And what a miraculous path it had already been.

23

AN ANGEL AND A SAINT

O VER AN EARLY breakfast in the dining room, where an upright piano played by Hemingway stood against the central wall, the innkeeper told me that it was the day of the annual local pilgrimage to Roncesvalles. Every May, villages in the area took turns making a procession in honor of Our Lady of Roncesvalles; today was Burguete's turn. I decided to stay to see it even though it would mean I would arrive late in Zubiri and risk not finding a bed. My mission was to go where the road guided, and it felt important to stay.

At mid-morning, the whole village, dressed in their best, began a heartfelt march down the central street, going toward Roncesvalles on the same path I'd used to get there the day before. Some were dressed in robes and carried crosses and standards. I followed them as far as the healers' woods in their celebration of the Queen of the Pyrenees and the Lady of the Forest, a beautiful melding of Mary's manifestations as the feminine divine to both old and newer faiths. When they disappeared into the trees and continued to Roncesvalles, I turned back toward Burguete, whose church, because of the festival day, was open. A small, sturdy Romanesque-to-Baroque-style chapel, it has few surviving stone engravings, but nevertheless possessed a beautiful stained-glass window, which was lit up by the morning sun to highlight its central image, Mother Mary. The window's design showed Mary seated on a stack of stones on a riverside; behind her was a lush forest like the one the villagers had just entered. In her left arm she held her son, who pressed his hand to her heart. In her right arm, she held a bouquet of sunny, daisy-like flowers that, on closer inspection, looked more and more like Amalur's flower, the *eguzkilore*. Mary's being in a deep wild wood, seated near water, holding the goddess's flower—all these symbols to me pointed to a fusion of old and new mother goddess. And maybe I was hallucinating, but the dark charcoal and misty gray stone just behind Mary and Jesus looked to me very much like a goose tucking its head under its wings. The window was beautifully syncretic and reanimated my sense of the initiatory, testing goose quest that had invited me to see beyond surface stories, images, and ideas to find deeper and truer tellings of sacred earthly life and existence.

Back outside, midway down the village street, yellow arrow markers pointed to a sharp right turn off the pavement and through a local farmstead toward a dirt path into hills and forest. I had to bypass the caramel-colored cows who roamed freely across the open yard. Ahead of me were two other late-starting pilgrims dressed like twins in matching orange rain jackets, black rain pants, and blue backpacks—one tall and lean, and the other, who stopped often to take photos, more compact and robust. Given how often the compact one paused with his camera, I quickly caught up to them. We exchanged names: Gabriel was the photographer, and Santiago, his taller friend.

"An angel and a saint," I said. "That's perfect on the Camino."

"I don't know," Gabriel replied, "we are just humble pilgrims, and possibly the slowest. I like to take photos. I'm also giving up smoking. Once you pass us, you may never see us again."

"We're in no rush," Santiago chimed in, "we're so happy just to be here." I could feel their mirth and kindness to each other and understood the matching clothes were just the surface of a deep and supportive friendship. Gabriel spied a purple orchid on the trail edge and turned his lens to capture it. "See you in Zubiri," Santiago said as I wished them *buen Camino* and continued on.

The trail ribboned along undulating green hills and meadows exploding with wildflowers and tumbled deeply into an oak and holly forest. Sometimes the path was of smooth, packed dirt, but then it would turn quickly to rough, uneven, jutting layers of striated rock. I meandered, roamed, savored, and felt giddy over the beauty all around me, not to mention the bolstering news from my agent, which was making me walk on air.

I turned a bend to find a group of pilgrims gathered around a woman seated in agony on the edge of a creek. She had just slipped on a slick stone and broken her wrist and asked someone to call for help. I pulled out my phone and dialed 112, connecting to an emergency operator who assured me she knew where we were. I told the injured pilgrim help was on the way, and learned she was from New York.

"I wanted to finish this walk," she cried. "I can't believe it's over now."

"Maybe it is, but maybe it isn't," I offered. The Camino had its ways, didn't it? "Maybe once you get your wrist set, new possibilities will arise?" She grabbed my hand with her good hand and smiled, a glimmer of hope. I squeezed back and waited until the medical team had guided her to the back of the ambulance and she disappeared down the road with her friend riding by her side. Despite what I had told her, I too was shaken by how abruptly events can turn. It was the Game-of-the-Goose, Wheel-of-Fortune, Camino as life-path metaphor once again: sometimes you're up, and sometimes you're down. I took a deep breath and stepped cautiously around the slippery rocks and over the creek.

I arrived late in Zubiri and every bed in all the albergues were taken. Even in the large municipal albergue, pilgrims had claimed all the remaining floor space. Bone tired and with early evening already having arrived, I was weighing whether I should keep walking when five nurses from Barcelona told me they had just booked a place in Akerreta, a village some seven kilometers away, and had called a taxi to pick them up.

"Come with us," one said. The cab came. I hopped in. Five minutes later we pulled up to a seventeenth-century farmhouse. On the way, the driver had learned of my predicament and taken it upon himself to call the innkeeper to ask if he had a spare room. He did, with dinner included. I calculated my budget and knew it would be tight, but I was there not to resist. When I went to pay my share of the cab ride, the driver waved me off. "The nurses already paid for you. *Buen Camino!*" He drove away. The day's gifts had far outweighed its challenges. I thought about the American pilgrim and hoped by now she was cooking up a new way to keep walking. I thought of the angel and the saint and the five fairy-godmother nurses. I thought of the procession and the Lady of the Forest with which the day had begun after I'd slept in Hemingway's room. I thought of the news of the day before following on the heels of an ice storm. I went and hugged all five nurses and thanked them. As we were heading to our respective rooms, another pilgrim arrived, a doctor from Tarragona, and she claimed the last bed. I slept well that night, knowing that if anything went wrong, I had all the medical help under the sun sleeping under the same roof.

My room's window opened to a sweeping green meadow covered in wildflowers with steep green mountains beyond. I left the window open a crack as I drifted off to sleep, inhaling the sweet grassy evening scent of the burgeoning spring. But I tossed and turned all night, my limbs growing stiff and painful. By the time I woke, they felt like hardened cement. I set off early but slowly. In the next hamlet of Zuráin, I ran into my Orisson bunkmates at the village's riverside café. They jumped up and hugged me.

"We lost you! What happened?" the Georgian demanded. Before I could answer, she grew more animated about getting to Pamplona today. "We've booked ahead and are staying in Hemingway's hotel in the city. And you, where are you staying?"

"I don't know," I said, feeling anxious. Was this to be the story of this walk, to either book ahead or hunt daily for beds on arrival? I didn't want to be locked into a set plan, nor to resist. The young Australian woman was standing behind the woman from Georgia and she gave me a look that told me she knew how I felt. She also looked as if she wanted to flee. Why didn't she? They all set off. I stayed for a much-desired coffee and breakfast.

From Zuráin to Pamplona the track went down the center of a widening valley, following the bank of the Arga River, which flows straight into Pamplona, sitting atop a bluff overlooking expansive rolling hills and open plains. Wild scrub, flowers, and dozens of butterflies in orange and black, yellow and white, and purple and blue, fluttered and carpeted the hills. Pamplona grew larger as I approached, and it towered overhead by the time I reached its ancient walls and climbed the rampart through a stone gate and entered the medieval town center. Contrary to my worry in Zuráin, I found a bed in the first place where I asked. I showered, did some laundry, hung my clothes on the line, and left to visit the cathedral before it closed.

Although the cathedral's exterior is an uninteresting Baroque façade, inside I found a breathtaking Gothic vault from the thirteenth century, all harmony and grace with pillars soaring high and merging with a celestial ceiling of painted polychrome stars, planets, and celestial beings. A pilgrim stood next to me in the nave, tears streaming down her face. "Don't worry," she said, "I just feel so overwhelmed by the beauty. It's been a hard road to get here, and I just didn't expect to walk into a church and feel this good." Me, too, I thought, as she walked on, needing no reply. The pain in my legs diminished and I felt rejuvenated.

But soon, as I sat to a pilgrim's dinner in Café Iruña—one of Hemingway's haunts on Pamplona's large central square—all my muscles seized up, especially around my knees. Gripped in pain, I watched as other pilgrims came in and grabbed tables. I could see the same grimace on many of their faces as I felt on mine. My dinner arrived and somehow, I ate, paid, and limped to my bed.

In the morning, I felt fully recovered and walked with excitement, weaving west through the city toward the countryside. Now and then I felt a slow, at times painful, throb in my left knee. I was sure it would stop once I warmed up. Another perfect day had dawned, and I was going to return after many years to the chapel of Santa Maria de Eunate, sure that this enigmatic octagonal chapel devoted to Mary contained goose-related clues. The last time I had been there, I'd walked with a pilgrim who hadn't stopped talking from the moment we began stepping into stride with each other and who hadn't let up even in the echoing prayer dome of the chapel. I was excited to return this time alone, hoping to sit in the chapel and listen well to what it had to say.

On Pamplona's outskirts, I lost the trail markers and stopped on a suburban sidewalk, searching every surface. A man in a nearby café stepped out and pointed to a faint and scuffed-up painted shell icon on the sidewalk. "It's there," he said. I noticed he was dressed as many elderly men are in Spain—in formal trousers, a pressed shirt, and a knit cardigan, but on his feet were metallic gold running shoes.

"You should know," I jested, "with those shoes surely you are on the trail every day."

"I am," he laughed. "I walk the Camino every day, the same section, and then I end my walk here for my morning coffee. It's a good life."

"It is."

"But just the same," he added, "when you get to Burgos, say a prayer for me in the cathedral."

"Why Burgos and not Santiago de Compostela?"

"I'm practical. These days, most pilgrims walk in sections and many never make it all the way. But Burgos, that's a good bet."

"Burgos, then," I said, "and if I make it to Santiago, I'll pray for you there too." This elicited another hearty laugh from him. I felt a tug inside. I hoped I would make it to Santiago.

I left the city. The concrete track became dirt and stone and plunged into rippling meadows of new, pale green wheat, speckled here and there with red poppies. The view was spectacular, but as the path began to slope up, the throbbing in my knee increased. Midway up, a mind-numbing jolt of pain shot into my knee, and I toppled, fully paralyzed in its unrelenting grip.

In all my years trekking, I'd never experienced anything like this. Another shot of pain ripped into me and fully flattened me onto the trail. I whimpered out of my pack and watched it roll to a stop a few feet below me as I curled like an injured pup into a tight ball. And I panicked. Had I torn something? What was I going to do? I hadn't seen any other pilgrims on the trail. As usual, I had started a little later than most and almost everyone was up ahead and long gone. Tears flowed down my face. I forced myself to take deep breaths and focus on the cerulean, cloud-free sky instead of the pain. "Please, help," I uttered, to no one and to everything. In answer, I heard footsteps. Two sets of feet crunched up the trail. I managed to lift my head just as the angel and the saint approached. I hadn't seen them since that first meeting outside Burguete. When they saw me, they rushed over.

"What's wrong?" Gabriel asked, shrugging off his pack and kneeling next to me. I explained as best as I could.

"Show me exactly where it hurts," he said. I did and I saw a relieved smile wash across his face. "It's not your knee, and you haven't torn anything. It's your quadriceps. A lot of pilgrims who crossed the Pyrenees in the ice storm are having the same problem. They all hurried down that steep descent into Roncesvalles, muscles cold, and then, I am guessing, you didn't stretch right after." No, I hadn't.

"That's why your quads are so tight," Santiago interjected, "and now they are pulling the tendons attached to your knee and causing excruciating pain."

I managed to prop myself up. "How do you two know this?"

"We're emergency room doctors," Gabriel said. "We work together in the same hospital in Buenos Aires." Not only did the Camino guide and provide, but it was well staffed with medically trained pilgrims. I would have laughed, but I was in too much pain.

Gabriel gave me his hand and helped me stand as Santiago picked up my pack and hoisted it onto the front of his body. "Let's get you to the next village," he said, "After that, you shouldn't walk anymore today. You need to rest and to stretch." Gabriel nodded and helped me take my first steps. We walked slowly up the hill toward the village of Zariquiegui. The two kept talking and asking questions to take my mind off the pain. I asked them why they were walking the Camino.

"One day at the hospital," Gabriel answered, "I said to Santiago, 'Let's walk to your namesake's tomb in Spain.' After that, he wouldn't let me off the hook, reminding me it would be a good way to lose weight and to stop smoking. And saying it out loud also made it more real to me, more possible." It had taken a lot of finagling for them to take time from work and away from families in Argentina to travel across the world, then walk for several weeks. "But we realized," he continued, "that we just had to do it. We picked a date and before I knew it, here we are, plunging in." They also asked me about my reasons for walking. I gave them the full story, as best as I could, of my outer quest for goose signs and medieval lore, and my inner quest for trust and guidance for my desired walk in life.

Reaching Zariquiegui, we stopped at the village café where Santiago set my pack down and went to the counter to order us all an orange juice. The two also took a closer look at my knee and confirmed their diagnosis. Santiago opened his pack, pulled out a full medical kit, and offered me some ibuprofen. He then taught me stretches to do every day, before and after walking. One of the locals at the cafe offered to give me a ride to Obanos, a village near Eunate. I hugged my saviors goodbye, feeling all raw with deep gratitude and strong emotions. "Don't worry," Gabriel whispered, "we'll see you again."

In the blink of an eye, I was in Obanos, limping toward a place to stay. I lay a long while on my bed before willing myself to get up, stretch, shower, and stretch some more. My muscles slowly began to release their grip. My vision and thinking grew clearer, as did my appetite. I walked into the village to find a late lunch. Feeling better, and free of my pack, I located where the trail of the Camino entered Obanos, and in a slow, cautious amble traced it in reverse heading east.

24

THE EIGHTH GOOSE

"**PERO NIÑA, BUT** child, you're going the wrong way," an elderly man called to me from his front stoop on the outskirts of Obanos. He was seated in a wooden chair just outside his front door, taking in the sun.

"It's okay," I called back, "I'm going to Eunate."

"Ah, Eunate, a powerful place with good energy. *Buen Camino*, then," he said. He readjusted his slanting black beret higher on his forehead and closed his eyes, facing the strong late-afternoon sun. I plodded on, noting how easily people living on the Camino spoke of energy and without feeling the need to explain it in more rational, five-senses terms. For them, it simply exists. Even if you can't see it, you can feel it, and likely, measure it, for the earth does have its weave of electromagnetic energy.

The walk warmed my limbs. Though the sharp stabs of pain were everpresent, they became duller. I continued down a hillside into scrubby hills covered in thistles, wildflowers, and grazing sheep. The trackway rippled down to a final descent that revealed the cone-shaped, rounded roof of Eunate poking up between two slopes whose edges acted like theater curtains. The closer I drew, the more those curtains opened to reveal greater details of roof, walls, corbels, and most dramatically, the enigmatic thirty-three-arch cloister that circles the church like Saturn's rings. The Iglesia de Santa María de Eunate was built out in the middle of wild, rolling countryside—a singular sentinel to guide medieval pilgrims.

Most churches with cloisters have them set to one side of the structure in the form of a square surrounding a central garden. No one knows why this one was built around the church. What were the builders saying by doing this? Was it to identify the church as a high holy site or a garden in stone? Excavators have found burials around the arches of people with scallop shells, so one idea is that this was a funerary chapel for pilgrims, though it still doesn't explain the ring. A key to that, though, comes from "excavating" the Basque name. Eunate means "place of one hundred doors."

Years earlier, when I had first visited the church, I had wondered if the numbers thirty-three and one hundred were random, but then I remembered what medieval scholars often say: Nothing is an accident in medieval sacred art, let alone a work that takes so much effort to create. Thirty-three could be symbolic of many things. First and foremost, in Christianity it is believed to be Christ's age at the time of his crucifixion. Many convents in Spain traditionally limited the number of nuns to thirty-three for this reason. Thirty-three is also the number of prayer beads on Muslim rosaries and some Christian ones. Among Sufis (the mystics of Islam) and Anglicans, there is a similar practice of using a thirty-three-bead rosary to recite a meditation on the ninety-nine names of God, each bead a name or an attribute. One circles the rosary three times, with each circling taking one a layer deeper into the qualities and experiences of God to reach the full ninety-nine. Moreover, once a person arrives at the ninety-ninth attribute, he or she then touches a larger bead hanging off the strand, to which is attached an amulet—in the Christian tradition, this is most often a cross. This offset bead concludes the meditation by symbolizing one's arrival at the center—the hundredth door—finding paradise, union, and communion with God.

I also considered that in Judaism, the number thirty-three represents two threes next to each other, another code for the Seal of Solomon, the two intersecting triangles that form a six-pointed star representing wisdom as well as the merging of heaven and earth in harmonious union. Places on earth that are believed to be in direct contact with the heavens, and considered places of transformative power, are where sacred temples of many faiths tended to be built. Finally, in Hebrew, the system of *gematria*—assigning the alphabet's letters numeric values, and those numbers, in turn, sacred attributes—some say Jesus's Hebrew name, Yeshua, numerically translates to 888.

Every arrow seemed to point to this eight-sided church being circled three times. As if we pilgrims needed to be hit over the head with this idea, the two capitals flanking the main entrance door were also engraved with two men's faces, each man in possession of a spiraling beard that wrapped around itself three times. Eunate had been built by a mixed group of masons and their etched mason marks, signatures in the stones, indicated at least nine builders worked here to construct this church, a lot of masons for such a small place.

Was Eunate's church a large rosary inviting such a three-circuit meditation, the hundredth door being the west entrance that opened to the nave and led to Mary on the altar? Was she in the heart of the garden, paradise? Every stone said yes, and from a multifaith perspective. All these signs together seemed to direct me to walk around the church, treat each arch as a rosary bead, contemplate the many qualities of the divine, and then enter the hundredth door to paradise and divine union.

I began my first loop on the outside of a low, circling wall that enclosed the whole complex, the second between the encircling wall and the arches, and the third circuit between the arches and the chapel. On each turn, as I passed by, I studied the stone engravings on the arches and the chapel, which make a parade of humans and animals: a man's face contorting between pain and pleasure; a woman standing on a giant's head; a smiling, toothy dragon; a pair of wolves; a goose-like bird preening its feathers; a coiling and shimmying snake; a subtly grimacing woman breastfeeding a snake. *Wait.* I stopped. Here was a *femme aux serpent*, but unlike the one I'd seen in the museum in Toulouse: she was a later one whose symbolic migration was almost complete, not so much *La Terre-Mère* but more the face of sin. But in her contorted face I saw the faint vestiges of the older meaning hanging on. Somehow this temple, with Mary inside at its heart, still acknowledged the Mother Creator.

I finished my third turn, passing the ninety-ninth bead, and stood before the hundredth door. I was taking a deep breath and preparing to step in when a large bus pulled up and forty Spanish tourists climbed out. As soon as I pushed the door open and went inside, communion took place with the many others. I'd had only enough time to catch a glimpse of Mary. Fresh lilies surrounded her and filled the small, round chapel with a honey perfume. The tour group flooded past me, and I hung back, taking a seat in the last pew. The sun filtered in across the nave from the door, lit up the alabaster windows on the dome, and most spectacularly, illuminated the twelfth-century polychrome wooden statue of Mary on the altar. Despite the crowd, or perhaps aided by their good company, I felt myself merge with the place and with her. Harmony and grace bounced off the walls. I felt whole, well, and loved.

In the Middle Ages, one of Mary's names was *hortus conclusus,* enclosed garden. It referred to her purity, a garden free of the blemish of sin. It could also be that the hidden garden could only be reached through prayer and devotion, such as a walking meditation through ninety-nine doors while contemplating the divine, and arriving at the hundredth door within, the place of communion. So focused on the doors was I that I had overlooked the fact that this place was called *Saint Mary* of One Hundred Doors. *She meets us here in the center of an enclosed paradise,* I thought. Could this also be the message of the swan in the center of the Game of the Goose, that other spiral walk toward a garden of transcendence? All this seemed reinforced by the fact that medieval cloisters surrounded gardens enclosed within. Was this the implied garden of this unusually arrayed cloister and chapel?

Whatever it was, it felt good to be here. I whispered gratitude and I closed my eyes, taking in several deep breaths. It dawned on me then that I had been pain free since around the time of the third circuit outside. I looked up to see a star pattern radiating all around the chapel as if it were a vessel of the Milky Way. After the crowd left, I remained a while longer. When I slipped outside to return to Obanos before nightfall, I passed an information board about the chapel that recounted a local legend.

A stonemason who had been commissioned in the twelfth century to build Eunate's main doorway arrived to find that a giant using supernatural powers had already built it. The local abbot challenged the mason to build another door and gave him a mere three days to do it. Because that was an impossible task, the mason enlisted the help of witches, serpents, and spells and accomplished the feat, making a mirror image gateway to that of the giant. When the giant saw this, he kicked the new gate with such a force that it flew high into the air and landed in the village of Olcoz, six kilometers (3.7 miles) to the east. There it is today, at that village's church. Any way you slice it, both churches were built by supernatural forces. The legend is another piece of evidence that older beliefs persisted even when the Catholic Church tried to banish them from people's minds.

The scent of wild herbs and the fluttering of blue and white butterflies on thistles and roses guided me back to Obanos as the setting sun lit their colors afire. My legs remained pain free.

THE SERPENT

I ALTERNATED BETWEEN deep sleep and restlessness, both of which were governed by the cadence of a low throb returning to my knee. I woke before dawn, massaged my muscles, stretched, and slowly shuffled out of Obanos, anxious. But as I moved more and passed the robust, patchwork-patterned gardens with staked rows of tomatoes, beans, artichokes, lettuces, and peppers, I forgot my worry. In a blink, I was in Puente la Reina. Its eleventh-century Queen's Bridge, which spared pilgrims from making an otherwise treacherous crossing over the Arga River, is Puente la Reina's most famous feature, but close on its heels are the town's three churches. One of these, the first I passed, was the Iglesia del Crucifijo, the Church of the Cross, which houses an unusual crucifix showing Jesus on a goose footprint-shaped cross. An unknown German pilgrim brought it there in the fourteenth century. The church's door was ajar, its mixed Romanesque-Gothic arch flanked by two long-necked and intertwining birds—one could justify that they were geese if that was what one was looking for. I went inside to find a double-nave church with two altars. The oldest nave, from the twelfth century, led to the original altar that held Santa Maria de las Huertas, Saint Mary of the Gardens and Orchards. The nave and altar beyond the first were added in the fourteenth century to house the human-scale crucified Christ, his cross unmistakably the shape of a three-pronged goose footprint. Taking in the whole of the two naves and their altars to the Mother and Son, it seemed clear that both held equal sway here—another Solomon's Seal of two intersecting triangles harmonizing heaven and earth and god and goddess. What if long ago the story had gone, *And Goddess so loved the world, She gave it Her only Son?*

Midway down the street into the center of Puente la Reina I came to the second church, which is devoted to Santiago. Its scalloped archway was a threshold of diversity, the work of builders schooled in Iberian, Persian, Byzantine, North African, and French styles, who created a menagerie of fantastic creatures and testimony of the remarkable crossroads of people moving along the medieval route. Inside I found the fourteenth-century statue of Saint James, which was fabled to possess potent miracle-working powers. I asked for safe passage and full recovery for my knee. As I crossed the famous bridge on the way out of town, I learned that once there had been a little sparrow-like bird called a *txori* in Basque, who had lived there centuries before in a tower on the bridge that held a statue of Mary, which had been destroyed. Every day, without fail, the *txori* would carry water from the river and wash dust and cobwebs off the sculpture. After the tower's destruction, in the nineteenth century that sculpture was relocated to Puente la Reina's third church, the Iglesia de San Pedro, which was to the left of the bridge where I stood. But that church's door was firmly locked. As much as I would have liked to see the bird's beloved Mary, the language of the local birds spoke loud and clear that this place still listened to and revered nature, and was above all, devoted to the Lady.

I climbed up the elegant, bowed arch of the bridge, its thousand-year-old stones humming with the marks of millions of pilgrims. It led me over and out into tight craggy hills that tested my knee, but I held on and passed into a smoother more open vista of vine-covered hills radiating in all directions. Straight ahead arose the hilltop village of Cirauqui, once a Roman town and later an important pilgrim stop. One of its two churches was a sister to Puente la Reina's Santiago church, possessing a scalloped doorway that could have been forged by the same worldly band of itinerant masons who built the church devoted to Santiago. But the gate there held one more enigma, a *chi-ro*, the oldest symbol used for Christ before the cross became the faith's emblem. (It is noted that

Emperor Constantine had a dream of Jesus wherein the chi-ro, also called a *chrismon*, was shown as the Messiah's symbol: a circle enclosing two overlapping letters, the first two letters—*chi* and *ro*—of Jesus's Greek name, Christos, which, to the Western eye, look like a P and an X. Overlapped like this, the letters form a six-armed star, another Seal of Solomon of sorts—or, for esoteric goose devotees, two geese footprints joined at the heel end. On the upper arms of the X, from many engraved depictions of the chi-ro, hung the Greek letters *alpha* and *omega*, the first and last letters of the alphabet, to convey that Jesus was the beginning and the end. Most commonly, the alpha was hung on the left upper arm of the X and the omega was on the right to suit the direction in which Greek and Latin speakers would read. But sometimes, and most often on churches on the Camino, the alpha and omega are reversed, going from right to left, the way Hebrew, Aramaic, and Arabic speakers would read—like the one here. My knee gave a pull, and I felt a numbing shot of pain that shook my concentration. I found a bench and sat down to massage the ache.

Some art historians speculate that the letter order could have reflected the mixed heritages of the masons who built these churches. Others think they were accidental, that a mason may not have been literate and could have made a mirror image of the original. Echoes of the giant and the spell-working mason of Eunate come to mind. Others speculate that the reversed order could actually signal to the person paying attention to see things beyond the conventional way, to see below the surface. This is an idea perfectly in line with the goose game as an initiation process on the Camino where these reverse chi-ro are more common.

I stretched and decided to log a few more kilometers before calling it a day, leaving Cirauqui along its surviving Roman road and bridge whose grooves and high polish reflect two thousand years of footfall and cartwheels. The trail took me over irregular limestone hills with stunted oak and hazelnut forests and up a ravine into the tiny hamlet of Lorca on the edge of a vast meadow. A cheerful *hospitalera* greeted me at the door of the albergue and, seeing the grimace on my face, handed me a glass of refreshing cold water and invited me to sit. As I rested, she stamped my passport and set me up with a bed.

"You will sleep well here," she said as she led me to it, insisting on carrying my pack and setting it next to my perch for the night. She pointed to the head of the bunk. "When you lie here tonight, you will lay your head right on the leyline of the Camino's energy. Be sure to note your dreams." She left me to rest.

I showered, stretched, and handwashed my clothes, thinking again of how many locals spoke of the Camino and its telluric energy. At dinner I met the six other pilgrims staying in Lorca. Two were older women, friends for over forty years, one of them living in Utrecht, the Netherlands, and the other in Calgary, Canada. They had decided to meet on the Camino to have a month to walk and catch up on each other's lives. There was also a chipper newly-wed couple from Mallorca who had decided to walk for their honeymoon and to deepen their knowledge of each other. Another was a woman from Dusseldorf who said little but listened and nodded to all that we said. A man in his mid-forties from Barcelona skipped preliminary details and simply said, "I think this walk is a dream." We all nodded to that. When we turned in, I lay my notebook open near me, a pen at the ready. I just hoped laying my head on the leyline wouldn't be like sleeping in a railway station.

It was. My dreams came on like freight trains all night. In the most vivid one, I was at my grandmother's deathbed. In waking reality, she had died nine years earlier. I had been very close to her. In the dream, I began to clean her room. As I did, other female relatives arrived, one by one, to help. Soon, all the women on my mother's side of the family were there, helping clear passage not only for my grandmother in her ultimate transition, but mine and everyone's as well, as if all our female ancestors were there, midwifing our next steps in life. When I woke, I could still feel them all around me, the profound presence of all the women from the very beginning of my lineage on whose shoulders I stood.

I walked that morning to Estella, light of heart and with only occasional stabs of pain. I crossed the sweeping meadow into hills that enshrouded the town I sought, the same hills where I'd last seen Javier from Argentina many years earlier. I heard him remind me that Estella would eventually appear as a beloved, embracing aunt. Only now, for me, the embrace of that beloved aunt would be that of all the aunts of the world. A soft rain fell, leaving in its wake a brilliant rainbow arching across the valley floor.

I entered Estella's embrace to find the weekly Thursday market in full swing on its medieval squares, a happening ever since a royal decree in 1164 that made Estella a market town. I ambled past colorful produce stands, household goods, and clothing ranging from women's lingerie to thermal hiking socks. The town was built on a cluster of hills, each hill crowned with a church, the oldest hill and church of Le Puy being the reason Estella, which means star, was given its name.

Legend recounts that one night in 1085, shepherds saw a bright and unusual star that led them to a hidden place on the hill where they unearthed a wood sculpture of Mary (not too unlike the one found by shepherds in Roncesvalles). This one, however, was recognized as another image, that of Our Lady of Le Puy, a Black Madonna. Le Puy was one of the important pilgrimage towns in south-central France, drawing people to its powerful healing Mary. With the rise of the pilgrimage to Santiago de Compostela, Le Puy also became a stopping place or, for many, a starting place from which to set off for Spain and Santiago. Many Franks from southern France also settled along the Camino to help build up the road, and some among them were devoted to Our Lady of Le Puy, so to find a Madonna of French origins in Estella was a natural progression. Soon after the shepherds discovered her on the ancient hill, Estellans built a church there in her honor. On my first visit to Estella, a local had told me that Venus had been venerated on that same hill long before Christianity arrived. As in Auch and many other Marian places, Venus or her sister Diana were often prior occupants of these same places.

It was a steep climb to reach the church so I first went to the market to shop for food and then found a place to stay. Rested, and with my muscles dutifully stretched, I went out in the early evening and climbed up Estella's oldest hill. It lifted me above the town and gave me a view of the many protective surrounding hills that radiated outward in purple, green, and blue layers. The church itself was ordinary looking on the outside and quite modern, having been rebuilt in the 1950s after the older temple's destruction. But entering it was like stepping into an exploding kaleidoscope of sunburst prisms. The modern architect wanted to honor Estella's diverse medieval population of Jews, Muslims, and Christians, so he designed the building around an eight-pointed Mudéjar star, a pattern honed by Muslim craftsmen working in Christian Spain. Geometric rays of light poured down from the ceiling and also led my eyes to the center of the star, where Our Lady of Le Puy, both mother and queen, sat on her throne, her smile warm and commanding. She was a replica of the original, which I found later in a protective clear case at the start of the nave. The original statue radiated the same sunburst pattern of the building and emitted festivity and well-being, as if saying, *Welcome to the party, have fun, be present, be happy.*

I sat a long while, enjoying her light. I then climbed down the hill and visited the next holy hill, a less daunting climb but still a high place, to the Iglesia de San Miguel, Saint Michael's church. As archangel of high places and dragon slayer, Michael's churches are almost always built on summits. "He's not slaying the dragon, which is not evil," I remembered my medievalist friend Bruno telling me once when we were visiting another chapel devoted to Michael. "He's actually cleaving the earth open and the dragon represents the earth; Michael represents heaven." Michael's was not a fight but rather the joining together of heaven and earth. Yet many people shift the meaning and see it as a battle to force the earth into submission rather than to achieve harmonious union. Here, the fight was on, for on San Miguel's west entrance I found another *femme aux serpents*. This engraving, even more so than the one at Eunate, showed her full decay and symbolic migration from Mother Earth to pure sin: she was a grotesque, haggard-faced woman with an emaciated body and nothing of the pre-Christian

Creator remaining. The patriarchy had fully taken over here: sure enough, I learned that the church was built on the cusp of Romanesque transiting to Gothic, when the Catholic Church had gained full control over the lives of all of the people of Europe. Both the *femme* and the dragon represented an earth we once revered and now oppressed. I shuddered and left, turning toward a third hilltop. This church was my favorite of all Estella's temples, the Iglesia de San Pedro, located on the other side of the Ega River. The approach was a steep stone stairway up the hill to the church's scalloped arch gateway, which was almost identical to the scalloped gates in Puente la Reina and Cirauqui. Like Cirauqui's, it had a reverse chi-ro medallion with the alpha and omega reading right to left. If I looked beneath the surface, searched for hidden clues here, what would I find?

I cast an eye at the elaborately engraved Persian and Byzantine-style griffins and other fantastical hybrid creatures and went inside. It was another round church, only visible from within. The half-moon apse had three chapels, the center one devoted to Jesus, the one to his left and my right featuring Peter, and the one to Jesus's right, a polychrome Mother Mary similar to the one in Eunate. To her right was a pillar formed from the braided bodies of three snakes, their tails at the base and their heads holding up the capital. They were the work of a nineteenth-century local mason, Cayetano Echauri, whom the town commissioned to carry out restorations due to his training in medieval techniques and his immersion in its worldview. The three serpents were a theme already present in the older church, representing not sin or evil but wisdom in action. The middle snake was wisdom weaving into balance and harmony the polar opposites of good and bad—the duality and tensions of living—symbolized by the other two snakes. Like Solomon, the king of wisdom, the braided-snake column showed a merging middle solution for a troubling world pulled by extremes. It also reflected what New Testament scholar James Charlesworth uncovered about the serpent being mostly a symbol of good. Like the goose, the serpent was about union and balance, not dominion.

That night I feasted on my market purchases and checked email, catching up with Miles and my family but finding no new news from my agent. I would keep walking, then, until the signs told me otherwise. I felt anxiety return. I felt throbbing in my knee. I stretched, readied for bed, and tried to put the worries aside. I was here, wasn't I? And that was splendid.

Early the next morning, I passed the stone gate leading out of Estella as a sprightly older woman stepped out from her vegetable garden to chat. She was curious about where I was from and why I was walking. "Remember," she said before I continued, "though this road is long and can at times seem to defeat you, *todo es ánimo y fé y nada más,* all is courage and faith and nothing more. Remember this and it will help you." She hugged me as if she were the aunt incarnate.

"Courage and faith," I repeated with each footstep as I left Estella, heading up yet another hill. At the top, I could see the monastery of Irache nestled in a sea of grapevines, home to a famous fountain that flowed with both water and wine. Footsteps approached and a German pilgrim, Tomas from Frankfort, introduced himself. Together, we approached the magical fountain. He carried a thick birch staff carved to look like a great snake, the sort of staff Moses might raise up in the wilderness or turn into a live serpent. Tomas said he had carved it over several months as he dreamed of walking the Camino. He still couldn't believe he was there; it had been a feat to take four weeks off from work as a municipal administrator. And now that he was there, he suddenly confessed, he feared that he might not be able to finish because of problems with his right knee.

"Ever since crossing the Pyrenees in the ice rain," he said, "it's been killing me."

"Are you stretching?" I asked.

"No."

I told him about my left knee and the angel-and-saint saviors and their prognosis, and then I assured him that he and I would both probably be fine. But I sounded more certain than I felt. My knee was already throbbing.

"Maybe I will get to Compostela after all," he said with relief.

"But doesn't it strike you as funny that you have the same problem, but the other knee, a mirror image of mine?" Here was the mirror image theme again.

"Maybe," I offered cautiously. "The Camino certainly has a sense of humor."

"Think about it," he pressed. "The left is symbolic of the rational and male side of us, and right is symbolic of the intuitive and female side. I definitely have issues with my female side that I need to balance more." He was turning Jungian by the second. "How about you? Do you have issues with the masculine aspects of your personality?

"Maybe," I evaded. "What's your issue that needs balancing?"

"I am recently divorced," Tomas answered easily, not minding that I'd dodged his question. "I'm raising two children, and now I'm in a new relationship, one that has more potential for sharing and equality than my prior one. I am learning new things that I like but my old conditioning is hard to rewire. I'm doing my best but I'm not sure I can rise to the challenge. I want to be a better partner, more nourishing and supportive. That is a reason why I am walking, to work on myself and sort these things out. And you?" I fessed up and let it roll as it came.

"I want to release my anger over past injustices, especially in the workplace, as a woman. I want to be strong enough to build a whole way of living and working for myself, free of all that. Mostly, I want to stand on my own two feet, firm and strong, and be a successful writer, partner, daughter, aunt, and earth resident in general."

He laughed and cocked his head. "Your hopes are like a mirror image to mine."

We walked in companionable silence. We reached the wine fountain and took turns taking a ritual sip of the red vintage from our scallop shells. We continued to walk together until we neared the hilltop town of Villamayor de Monjardín, a castle ruin on its peak, and vineyards everywhere. Tomas suddenly grew anxious about getting a bed and picked up his pace. With my knee growing more tender, I said goodbye as we reached the hamlet of Azqueta, just before Monjardín. I sat to rest, and had my lunch next to a green meadow speckled with lipstick-red poppies. As I stood, I saw Azqueta's village albergue across the street, its door wide open and its white-plastered vestibule walls visible. On them were vibrant paintings of bold, swirling, and multicolored serpents. I went over.

The hospitalera, who was also the artist, appeared in the doorway. With her was a young man from France who was staying with her and helping in the albergue. The woman, originally from Estella, had walked the Camino a few years earlier. When she returned home, she knew her calling was to open a place offering hospitality to pilgrims in a less-served village. She loved Aboriginal art, and to her, it captured what the Camino's energy, its leyline, looked and felt like. The two led me upstairs and gave me a bed in a small room next to the larger dormitory. As in Lorca, my host mentioned when I lay down that night, my head would be right on the leyline of the Camino.

I settled in and stretched before taking a quick shower. By then a few other pilgrims had arrived. Six of us gathered for a communal dinner of a lentil casserole, garden salad, and homemade flan. My companions were a computer scientist from Arizona on indefinite leave from her work, two just-retired engineers from Brittany, and another engineer, a young woman from Mexico who was about to begin a new job. At the last moment, a man in his thirties arrived just after dark. He dropped his pack, took a seat, and without preliminaries stated he was from Denmark and "running away from home and from everything." At present of no profession, he said he was "happy just to walk," though the haunted look in his eyes said he was anything but happy. He never told us from what he was running, even after a good three-course communal dinner with plenty of wine.

In the morning, the Dane was gone and soon the others were too. I lingered, worried over my knee, which had given me trouble through the night. I didn't remember any dreams. As I prepared to leave, the hospitalera sensed my worry and invited me to sit in her kitchen where she pulled a jar of a green balm from her shelf. Made by an herbalist friend, it was for just my issue. Except I hadn't told her or anyone else about my knee. Nevertheless, she pointed to my left knee and asked if she might rub the ointment on it. I acquiesced.

"The Camino is a great energy line," she said as she rubbed in the ointment. "If you attune to it, you learn many things, among them, to sense and read energy in general, not only in the earth but in others." The ointment gave off a pleasing aromatic scent and the rubbing relaxed my sore and tired muscles.

"I feel as if I am walking on the back of a great serpent," I admitted, "and it is hard to deny the reality of the energy you feel when walking."

"The Camino is the kundalini of the Earth," she said. "The best way we can walk it is to be open to it and also be clear about why we walk." She finished applying the ointment and then placed her hand over my knee. I felt a sudden warmth radiate through it and a great sense of wellness.

"I don't think you need to worry," she said. "Your walk will be strong, just listen to yourself, the road, and your reasons for being here."

"Why did you walk?" I asked.

"For love," she said without elaboration.

"I walked to find joy," the Frenchman said as he came into the kitchen. "I was too serious before, but on the Camino, I relaxed and found the great fiesta that is life. That now is my goal, to make a fiesta wherever I go, inside me and for others." He handed me a small bottle of children's soap bubbles with bubble-blowing wand. "For you, to spread joy as you go."

I hugged them and parted, blowing bubbles as I passed along the serpent back of the Camino, watching each glistening orb rise and pop above meadows of poppies and wheat, all of it a fiesta. I passed into Villamayor de Monjardín and onward to Los Arcos, arriving there by midday. A matter-of-fact woman crossed the church square, her high heels clicking in snaps against the stone.

She unlocked the heavy church doors and pulled them open with a heave. I scampered toward her and entered. The calm stone plaza gave way to dizzying Baroque. The walls, ceiling, and even the floor heaved with gilded, colorfully painted, and minutely sculpted forms. Before I knew it, the woman was by my side.

THE NINTH GOOSE

"**W**OULD YOU LIKE me to stamp your pilgrim passport?"

"Please," I said, reaching into my pocket and feeling for my credential as I looked up at the ceiling, every inch of it writhing with repeating swirls. "That's lot of spirals."

"They are not mere decorative trifles," she replied, "but mark the energy of this road, a flowing vibrant energy that comes to the surface in the churches."

"Where earth and heaven meet?" I ventured.

"Exactly," she said triumphantly. She stamped and dated my passport with a flourish, adding, "these are the places that honor the Madonna." She pointed to a sculpture I'd not seen, right in the center of the high altar, another Black Madonna. "Stay a while," the woman said, "and look at her closely, especially her face and smile."

I went down the nave and craned my head up. From the fourteenth century and made of oak, Mary held the infant Jesus on her knee, both of them seated in regal, straight-backed poses. Both also had plucky bow-shaped eyebrows that made their gazes penetrate like released arrows. I peered into Mary's eyes and she seemed to issue a challenge: *Will you embrace trust and joy over despair?* Try it, she seemed to goad, her mouth puckering into a dare. *Trust and joy, for sure,* I replied in my mind. I was sure she and the baby Jesus winked back at me. If the woman who had opened up the church was right, that these potent places where heaven and earth met honored Mary, then they aligned with old idea of this very land about the primacy of the mother goddess and her sacred places as marked by the goose's footprint. I turned to thank the woman, but she was gone. I returned to the trail.

The earth grew drier and more open, and vineyards gave way to flowing meadows of wheat and wild plains dotted with fluffy ivory sheep. Going slowly to go easy on my knee, I descended the ravine by late afternoon and crossed the Linares River to reach Torres del Rio. A towering twelfth-century church, the Iglesia de Santo Sepulcro, Church of the Holy Sepulcher, crowned the hilltop village. Named after the original church in Jerusalem, the site of Jesus's tomb, it was another round, octagonal church, like Eunate and like Le Puy in Estella, but with an extra-tall domed ceiling that was a replica of the dome in Cordoba's mosque and a sibling to the domes in L'Hôpital Saint Blaise and Oloron-Sainte-Marie on the other side of the Pyrenees in France. I noticed swallows flying around its octagonal tower in frenzied circles, but they were nowhere else—they left all the other buildings alone, including the neighboring sixteenth-century parish church of San Andrés, which had a jutting bell tower.

Santo Sepulcro was locked. I turned and found a bed in the first place I asked. I thought of Tomas—there was no bed race here. I wondered where he was and how he was faring. I found no familiar faces among the few pilgrims in the village, and all of them were keeping to themselves. Some were clearly fatigued and unable to talk, some were glued to their phones, and still others just seemed sullen and nursed a beer or blister, or wrote moodily in their journals. I went back outside to shake off the dark mood. Santo Sepulcro was still locked, but a taped note on its door said that a volunteer would open the church in the morning. I looked up its tall eight-sided tower and saw the swallows still flying around the church as if caught in a swirling vortex. I circled, too, studying the engravings on the outer wall's stone capitals and corbels. Most were vegetal decorations of leaves and vines—but one was of birds intertwining their necks; another, of two serpent-like dragons with wings facing each other; a third, of two snake-tailed birds staring at each other; and a fourth, a woman with a long snake body twisting around itself. The theme of snakes, birds, and women once again intertwined.

The sun slipped below the horizon, sending ripples of orange and rose across the ochre village stones and surrounding hillside covered in vineyards and orchards. As the sky turned dark cobalt, the swallows abruptly stopped their flight and disappeared into the night. I, too, turned in early after a light dinner of whatever food I had left in my pack. In the morning, any lingering twinge of knee pain was gone. I felt strong and whole as I shouldered my pack. I walked back to the Church of the Holy Sepulcher and found its door open; inside, an older woman sat at a small wooden table.

Her short, hennaed hair and big glasses framed a face like that of a stern army sergeant. Despite the early hour, she showed strong irritation toward the many pilgrims who whisked by, demanding a stamp for their passports but not stopping to see inside. She kept telling them that a stamp came with a visit and a one-euro donation for the church's upkeep. I hovered a while outside, growing astonished at the majority of my fellow pilgrims, who demanded a lot from the locals but gave little back. During a lull in their visits, I stepped inside and said good morning to the woman. She threw me a poisonous look, but when she realized I might speak Spanish, she ordered me to sit on a chair next to hers.

"I have a euro and I'd like to visit the church and to get a stamp," I began.

"Sit!" she barked. I almost resisted, but then remembered I had made a vow not to resist, plus I realized I could learn things from this woman. *Listen,* I heard Richard of Toulouse whisper. I sat down.

"I have things to tell you," the woman said suddenly, smiling sweetly and completely shifting gears like a stage crew changes scenes, "and don't tell me you're in a hurry like these tourists." She waved her hand at the pilgrims fluttering past, many anxiously poking a head in, taking a quick peek, with some even taking a hit-and-run photograph, then running off despite the large, inked sign right at eye level that asked for one euro for such privilege. "All they do is rush from one bed to the next, without really being here. Pilgrimage is as much about exploring and learning as it is about walking to a sacred place. It's *absolutamente* barbarous. And you, *hija*," she said, looking piercingly at me, "I've decided are a pilgrim, *una peregrina*, not a tourist. Therefore, you have time to hear what I have to tell you."

I didn't dare argue. I listened.

"This church," she began, stamping and taking euros from the few pilgrims willing to contribute as she spoke, "is the yang of the yin of the octagonal church of Eunate."

My eyebrows shot up in surprise. Only the day before, Tomas had mentioned the Taoist duality of male and female striking balance and wholeness in us. Now, the caretaker was suggesting that the same thing happened for the body of the earth, too. Then there was what the *hospitalera* in Azqueta had said, that the Camino was the earth's *kundalini*, the energetic mechanism of striking balance in all its parts. The caretaker ignored my rising eyebrows, though she did study my face and soften a bit, as if she were deciding that maybe I wasn't as dense as she had originally thought.

"Eunate," she continued, "is the feminine half. You made sure to stop there, yes?" I nodded. "Good. So you noticed that there was only a statue of Mary there, right?" I nodded again and looked toward the altar before us. It held a wood statue of similar size and style of Jesus on the cross. I cast about the whole church but saw no image of Mary, an unusual thing in a Spanish church where hers was the most frequently present icon. The caretaker followed my eyes. "Exactly, this is the masculine half," she said. "The two churches share energy currents that flow like a closed circuit, the yin of Eunate and the yang of Torres del Río." I wished Tomas were there with me to hear this.

"Let me tell you something else," she said. "After living here all my life and working here as a volunteer in this church, I decided it was time for me to visit Eunate—it is so close, yet I had never gone there—to experience the full circuit of energy for myself. So

I went. But I felt such a tingling, then a jolt of electricity all across my skin, just from walking around the arches on the outside of Eunate, I knew I couldn't enter the chapel."

"But why?"

"Because as a guardian of Torres del Río, Eunate's counterbalance in the circuit, I was too committed to being *here* in this place of the opposite energy. If I went into Eunate's chapel, where the energy, like here, is most concentrated, I knew it would simply be too much for me to withstand."

I didn't really fully understand what she was saying, and she knew it.

"Listen, you don't connect two live wires, do you?" she asked. "No, you ground them. I am aligned with this place. Now, let me tell you about this place." She gestured for me to look all around the octagonal space, the dome overhead, that replica of Cordoba's mosque, an eight-pointed star with eight pillars that ran down the sides of the walls from each point.

"Each of those eight columns that support the eight-sided dome overhead is channeling energy from the earth here. It runs up from the ground via the stones, meets at the center, a concentration eight times more powerful than the energy in each column. That energy surges into the sky at the dome's highest point, forging a full connection with earth and heaven." She suddenly stopped and grew impatient once again as a new line of gawkers formed, demanding a stamp but making no offering, grabbing shotgun photos and running off. She yelled at them. A few thought better and stepped forward to drop in a coin and receive a stamp. The caretaker then employed me to tell them the church's history in English. The group left.

"Do you know now what I am talking about, *hija?*" she said more sweetly than I thought possible, returning to the lesson she had been giving me before the latest tourist inundation.

"I think so. But it's not easy to reconcile with the modern mindset."

"I know. There is a local politician who tells me that he can't believe or think that any of this stuff that I talk about is real. I tell him, and I'm telling you, that it's energy, it's physics," she said, gently jabbing my shoulder, "How much more real can anything be than energy and matter? But he doesn't get it. He uses words like 'think' and 'believe.' It has nothing to do with thinking or believing, it has to do with feeling. But what do you expect of a politician? They don't feel, and they certainly don't want the rest of us to, or there would be no need for them."

I laughed out loud. My laughter boomed as a magnified echo all along the walls of the high-octane cylinder. It stunned and silenced me. She looked at me sternly, then demanded, "Sing!"

"Sing?"

"Sing! Sing for me, sing for yourself, sing for this church," she insisted. "Sing to experience—*to feel*—the power of this place."

"But I don't sing well."

"Excuses. Sing!"

I knew one medieval song, a simple Gregorian chant. What the heck. I stood and hesitantly began. The more I sang, the more confident I grew: no matter the voice, this place made it sound sublime. I closed my eyes and sang the chant once more. When I opened my eyes, everything was more brilliant and in fine relief: the images on the capitals, the lines of the pillars, the movement of light and sound along them. I turned back to the caretaker. She looked triumphant.

"Thank you," she said, and stood. "Now, I have to close the church up briefly to go home and get more candies to hand out to the pilgrims." The army sergeant was really a mother hen, I realized. I suspected she even liked lambasting pilgrims into being better ones. She gave me a massive grandmotherly hug and scooted me out. "Remember to remain a pilgrim, she said as she rushed off, "and not become a tourist." She disappeared around a bend in the road.

As I left Torres del Río, the last building I passed was an albergue by the name Pata de la Oca, Footprint of the Goose. The church surely was such a footprint, even if it was deemed the masculine counterpart to Eunate. It was the gander's footprint, and ganders had their place on the Camino as well. I knew then that I definitely wasn't imagining any of this. How long had locals been telling me about energy and pagan survivals on the road to Compostela? For centuries, perhaps millennia.

I moved forward, trying not to think too hard, but simply to walk and feel. What I felt right then was ease in my steps and the total absence of discomfort or pain. Even in my knee. Sometimes, indeed, my feet felt jet propelled, as if I wore Mercury's winged sandals. I flew through an oasis, a small public park, small tree groves, and large meadows of swaying grasses. I neared the town of Viana and walked along the border of a vast vineyard, the head of each row of vines planted with a rose bush, some flush with pink blooms and others with pale yellow flowers. At the end of two rows I also found Tomas, holding his Moses staff, with a fellow pilgrim—a robust German woman with cropped military-style hair, an army rucksack, boots, and fatigues. She was bent down sniffing a rose.

"The yellow roses are planted with rows of white wine grapes," the Valkyrie woman told me authoritatively when I stopped to say hello, "and the pink roses with the red wine grapes." She then hastened off, a look on her face like that of the Dane's, as if her steps were haunted. Tomas told me his knee was better, that it had seemed to improve as he worked on his issues and entirely and miraculously healed soon after passing through Torres del Río. His news boded well for us both. He then rushed off, still feeling the urgency of the bed race, hoping to get to Logroño early in order to be among the first at the albergue.

At a slower pace I entered Viana, took a rest on the animated central square, then returned to rolling fields, vineyards, kitchen gardens, and orchards. On the outskirts of Logroño, there was Felisa and her daughter María's homestead on the hillside overlooking the city, the grand old fig tree standing as strong as ever. Though it was not fig season, the table under its shade still bore the jug of water, inkpad, and stamp as it had years before when I'd first passed by with the two speed-walking Granadans. No one was there now, but a note invited pilgrims to rest, hydrate, and stamp their own passports. Heartened, I glided down the road, across the stone bridge over the Ebro River, and into the heart of historic Logroño. I realized that all day my knee had felt good. Had the yin-yang of the Eunate-Torres del Río circuit healed me? Had it helped me find my inner balance?

Before I could answer this thought, I ran into my Orisson friends. We rushed over to each other and hugged and laughed. The Georgian and her Viking seemed acclimated and in good form. The Irish woman and the New Zealander man talked boisterously and also were in good spirits. The Canadian, too, was happy to go with the flow. The long-haired Australian was there as well, but she appeared distant and perplexed. They had already settled in and performed the daily ritual of showering and washing clothes and were now on the prowl for an early dinner. I agreed to find them later. I had a few missions to accomplish first.

After checking in and washing up, I sent quick emails to my parents, then to Miles, whose advice I asked: What should I do if things moved in a sure direction for the two book projects? Leave or stay on and finish the Camino? It had taken so much to get there, but it also had taken so much to get those two books off the ground. It all mattered, but my thinking was muddied, and Miles always had a good sense of things and how to help me direct my compass toward my true north. I next went to the Game of the Goose inlaid on the Plaza de Santiago.

A boisterous soccer game of girls and boys knocked across the board as other children zoomed their bikes around its border, with happy screams and laughter everywhere. Despite the cacophony and chaos, I could trace under all the running feet and spinning wheels the massive board game and its sixty-three squares. The last time I'd stood there I'd had my first real encounter with the goose, and I had felt utterly unconvinced and in the dark. Now, with goose themes repeating through so many avenues, I knew this thing was real and that the game before me was indeed a metaphor for the Camino and for life. I also knew it held more information than I was able to fathom, something to do with a very real mystery encoded in the pilgrimage to Santiago de Compostela.

A soccer ball shot toward me. I stopped it at the last minute and kicked it back, watching the ball slice diagonally across the plaza, rolling over several inlaid squares and then slipping right to square sixty-three, where a gleeful little girl halted it with her foot and cheered. Score! She ran off with the ball, but I stood stock still, hoping that, indeed, I had landed on the winning square. If so, it had been a lucky shot, a true random casting of dice. There still had been no news from my agent.

I had one more thing to do before looking for my friends. I walked back toward the albergue and straight to the church of Santa María del Palacio and the illuminated side chapel holding the medieval wood and jewel-toned sculpture of Our Lady of the Ebro, one of my favorite Marys on the Camino. She had a kind, gentle, and ancient face, and hers was a classic Mother Goose tale.

Some centuries back, a washerwoman on the banks of the Ebro saw a sculpture floating down the river. It got caught in the reeds near the woman, and she waded in to retrieve it. People surmised that it had been hidden in some cave or underground spot but had come loose during a recent flood and gotten pulled into the river. This was one of many stories on the Camino, and all throughout Spain, of miraculously discovered images of Mother and Child unearthed from a cave or river, those deep dwelling places of pre-Christian goddesses. It wasn't a coincidence because it happened too often. Old goddess places had been appropriated by the Church to transplant them and let the new faith take root.

I had fallen in love with this Mary when I'd first stood before her and witnessed how the locals came and went, not only to pray but to chat and visit with each other around her, as if she were one of the townsfolk. No sooner had I gotten there then a gaggle of women arrived and did just that. It was much the same as what I had seen at the altar of Our Lady in Auch. People connected to her, gave her their woes, visited with each other in community, and found comfort in her gentle love, witness, and generosity—her archetypal river and washerwoman magic.

The Ebro itself was held as the mythic birthplace of Iberia, which gave its name to the Iberian Peninsula. Born in the Cantabrian Mountains near Reinosa in the north, the river flows east and decants in the Mediterranean in Tortosa just south of Tarragona. Logroño is located near the midpoint of the river's flow. Moreover, the Ebro to the south and the Garonne River to the north in France, with the Pyrenees in the middle, form a natural geographical territory, one predating any divisive national boundaries, that contains interconnected rich and fertile influences, which drew ancient humans to it for a long time. It is a place of diverse wildlife, both plant and animal, of myriad fresh water sources, and of abundant natural shelter. Those ancient peoples had also followed the flight of geese to this place and forged the first footpaths that we pilgrims now followed to Santiago de Compostela.

Curious, I pulled out my map and saw that the Ebro's birthplace near Reinosa was exactly due north of Frómista, a Camino town I would reach on the trail in eight or nine days. I felt a pull in my gut. Or would I? I folded and put the map away and went to find my friends.

MELUSINE

EARLY THE NEXT morning, as most of Logroño slept, I followed the Camino through quiet streets, past the Game of the Goose square, and off to the industrial edges of town. I hadn't found my Orisson friends the night before and I walked alone once again. Logroño's concrete and industrial edges gave way to a green oasis of shady groves and curvy, striped, vine-covered hills. Spring flowers and fresh grass perfumed the cool morning air. I meandered, then climbed up into Navarrete, a hilltop town of stone homes spiraling from base to crown with a church near the top.

The Camino cut up and through the middle of the hill on a central cobbled street. Midway, a tiger-striped cat, just like Sarlat's Mr. Stripes, jumped out of the shadows and bounded toward me, bumping into my legs just like her sister in France. Overjoyed, I bent to pet her, feeling the prick of homesickness that extended to Sarlat, to Miles, to family and friends far away, possibly accentuated by so much time walking alone.

"I see you've met my little friend," someone said. I stood and came face to face with a woman in her early eighties dressed in a colorful cotton housedress pulled like an apron over her sweater and wool skirt, her feet in striped wool socks and pushed into velvet slippers. Her eyes sparkled and her smile welcomed. She was the Sainte B of Navarrete.

"Come, come," she gestured, toward her doorway as the cat slipped inside. "Let me show you something." She pointed to a stone in the foundation of her house; on it was an engraved mark: two circles enclosing each other, with a line drawn through them.

"Is that the signature of a medieval mason?" I asked.

"My home is that old, but it has since been restored. This signature is from a modern mason trained in medieval techniques. It is possible, thanks to the recent revival of the Camino. Before this, our village was dying. Fewer people worked the fields and young people left to find work in the cities. But lately, there is little work in the cities as well. Thanks to the rising popularity of the Camino, my daughter and her family returned here, and we all live and work in service of pilgrims, as was the way of our ancestors in the Middle Ages."

"Have you lived here all your life?"

"I have. My parents, too, and my grandparents, all the way back to the founding stones of this house. Be sure to stop at the cemetery when you leave Navarrete," she added, "and look at its gate. It is what survived of the town's monastery of San Juan de Acre." She wished me *buen Camino* and disappeared behind her door.

On the edge of town, I stopped at the cemetery, where the buried inhabitants are younger than the gate. It was carried from the other side of Navarrete, taken from the ruins of the transitional Romanesque-to-Gothic monastery and repurposed here as an elegant gateway to the beyond. Three arches displayed well-preserved engravings on the capitals atop their pillars: there were two angels embracing, another blowing an oliphant, a dragon blowing wisps of smoke, and another dragon being speared by Saint Michael. But the latter image to me looked more as if Saint Michael was spoon-feeding the dragon something tasty, which reminded me again of what my medievalist friend had said about Saint Michael really being about cleaving open the earth to mingle in communion with heaven.

The image on the capital next to Saint Michael and the dragon was the most unusual of them all, showing two people dressed in medieval hooded capes, their faces human, their upper bodies bird-like, and their lower bodies featuring long serpent tails. Their tails were intertwined around each other, and they pressed their faces together in an embrace of very close friends.

In both French and Spanish folklore, these two figures could represent two of the many children begotten through the union of a nobleman and a fairy queen who was also a *femme aux serpents*. The most famous story of these snake women rose in popularity in the Middle Ages, sometime in the late twelfth century, the same age as this gate was made. It is still told to this day—a Mother Goose-worthy fairytale about a forest fairy known as Melusine in France, and Melusina in Spain. Melusine's most famous telling was written down in 1392 by Jean d'Arras, a French scribe who served in the court of the Duke de Berry.

Once upon a time, Arras wrote, the Duke of Lusignan in the Poitou region went out riding near his castle. Deep in an enchanted forest he heard a beautiful voice and followed it. It led him to a glade in which stood Melusine, the lady of the forest, guardian of animals, plants, and the natural elements. He fell instantly in love and proposed marriage on the spot, which Melusine accepted on one condition: that one day a week, he would leave her alone to her rooms and never disturb her solitude. If he broke this one promise, she would leave him. Easily done, the duke proclaimed. The two married, both deeply in love and devoted to the other. They had three children—Urien, Guion, and Geoffrey—two of whom are actual historical figures, one who ruled in Cyprus and the other in Armenia. The marriage also founded the noble house of Lusignan, a historical line and territory in western France, which to this day claims this magical merging of human and otherworldly worlds, a heaven-and-earth marriage in its own right but fully pagan and older than the church.

After many years of bliss, curiosity won over the duke's resolve to honor his one promise to his wife. On the next day that Melusine isolated herself in her rooms, he snuck in and found her in the bath, her whole body that of a massive serpent. In shock, he stumbled and gave himself away. Melusine swiftly grew wings and flew out the window. The last thing the duke saw was her tail slip out and whip into the air. She returned to the forest, and no matter how the duke tried, he could not find her again. Two of their children went with her into the forest and continued the half-human/half-magical lineage. It is said that Melusine and her descendants still inhabit the earth, such as the two depicted on the capital before me. Melusine, like La Reine Pédauque, was a hybrid being, a merging of heaven and earth who inhabited this world—unlike the distant sky god of Jews, Christians, and Muslims—to protect, nourish, and grace the world here and now, even if we could not see her.

The central arch of the gate displayed a six-petaled rose window, another version of the six-pointed star, Solomon's Seal, also called the seed of life, that repeated symbolically the message of a harmonious merging of heaven with earth, just in case a visitor misses that message from the other capitals.

I walked on, the color of the earth taking on darker shades of iron-rich dark red as I went, the hills striped with emerald-green vines as far as the eye could see. The trail led me to the red sandstone cliffside town of Nájera, built along the Najerilla River, which cuts the town in half and is lined on both sides by promenades, cafes, and a velvety green park. I found all the albergues full, but I located a room in a pension where I shared the bath down the hall with a group of bikers from Madrid. Once I'd showered and hung my wash on a clothesline, I walked across the bridge to the oldest part of Nájera, which was built right into the red sandstone cliff, the site of the town's monastery and miracle.

In 1044, King Garcia III of Navarra was out hunting along the Najerilla with his falcon, when the bird suddenly took off in pursuit of a dove, disappearing into the thicket of trees where I now stood. Garcia followed his falcon to find a long, narrow tunnel hidden behind the trees. It led to a cavern where he found his falcon peaceably perched with the dove, the two birds flanking a luminous image of Mary, at whose feet lay a bell, a lit candle, and a vase of lilies. Garcia knew a miracle when he saw one and he recognized, from the symbolism of his time, that the bell represented the voice of God; the candle, divine light; and the lilies, Mary's purity and grace. He wasted little time in founding a monastery there, building a church in Mary's honor in a place where feminine divinity appeared yet again with birds, a river, and a cave.

I went in, passing through the cloister to the church and walking past the tombs of Navarra's kings into the tunnel and cave in the back wall, which houses the old cavern Garcia had entered before the church was built over it. There I found Mary, candle-light warming the amber cave walls, a bell and lilies at her feet, and calm and peace everywhere, including within my little human heart.

Back at my pension, I checked email: nothing had come from my agent but there was an email from Miles and another from my mother. "The description you wrote of the guardian at the church in Torres del Río," my mother wrote, "fits the guardians of the saints' shrines in Iran." These shrine keepers, she explained, served as archetypal stewards of the gateway between heaven and earth—the theme, it seemed, of that day and the road. "Pay close attention to your dreams," she continued, "because I think when you are on the road by yourself, you are more connected with your inner self and its messages than at other times." It felt good to feel my moth-er's support fully behind me. It also gave me comfort not to know what might happen next, and to embrace this precious time alone, even when at times it felt too solitary, even for me.

"My sense of your way?" Miles's email began. "I say, put the next foot in front of the other and the Way will show you. The Goose will show you, and the showing may not be in the form of a goose." I could hear him chuckle and it made me laugh. He was right. The goose could shape-shift. After all, it had done so to go from goddess to bird to snake. It could be Melusine. Or a lady in velvet slippers in a doorway with her cat.

The red-gold light of the setting sun reflected in my room's win-dow, beckoning me toward it to watch it set behind the cliff, cave, and river. Then movement below my window drew my eyes down, and for the first time I noticed a rustic yard covered in tall, wild grasses that began to wiggle and shake. Before I knew it, a menag-erie of creatures came walking out from the edge of the tall growth. No less stunning than Garcia's birds and the Madonna, there was a big fat white goose followed by two ducks, two turkeys, a hen and a rooster, and last but not least, a miniature white goat. They looked just like the twenty-six ducks on Morlaàs' church, a merry band of eclectic pilgrims, a perfect sign.

THE ROOSTER AND THE HEN

THE ROOSTER WOKE me early with a screeching crow mixed with brittle yip-yip sounds. Any dreams I'd had slipped forgotten into a fog except for the vague recollection that they had to do with walking and looking for food and places to sleep. My lumpy bed and aching legs had contributed to a beleaguered night of sleep. I looked out the window to see the white goose parading about again, pulling everyone in her wake, the little goat weaving to and fro with the birds. The rooster crowed again, and this time everyone answered: the turkeys fanned their tail feathers and belted abrasive metallic sounds, the ducks waddled and quacked, the goose let loose a loud honk, and the tiny goat bleated. A dog down the street kicked in, barking emphatically. I dressed quickly, thinking of the old stories coming from a time when people lived close to the land and its creatures, a time when animals talked, and we understood the language of the birds.

A soft fog lay on the red sandstone cliffs and the river as the sun rose behind me, and I marched ever west and into even deeper red earth and rolling vineyards toward Santo Domingo de la Calzada. As I grew close to the town, La Riojas' vineyards gave way to wheat fields under a partly cloudy sky.

Santo Domingo de la Calzada—Saint Dominic of the Road— was named after the celebrated medieval engineer, monk, and saint, who, along with his student San Juan de Ortega, built roads, bridges, shelters, and churches to make safe this once unruly stretch of the Camino. One of the most famous miracles on the Camino also occurred here, recounted in the *Codex Calixtinus*, the first pilgrim's guide about the road, written in the twelfth century. It involved a young German pilgrim, traveling with his parents, who was unjustly accused of stealing a piece of silver from the inn where they stayed. He was tried and hanged, but the parents saw that their son still lived. They rushed to the town judge, saying their son was both innocent and still alive. The judge was just then sitting down to a dinner of a roasted rooster and hen, and he declared that no more could the two birds on his plate rise and sing than their son could be alive. But suddenly, the two birds rose and sang, and the judge had the son brought down from the gallows and released. Though God, Santo Domingo, and Santiago all leaned in to keep the boy safe and assure justice, it took two amazing birds—a male and a female at that, reinforcing holy harmony—to seal the deal and reunite him with his family. Duck, duck, goose, and gander.

I walked down the Camino path that turned into the main street and led to the cathedral, and arrived in a smaller square where the cathedral's bell tower stood, separate from the rest of the building, along with a tiny chapel that was intimate and humble in full contrast to its massive Gothic neighbor. Dedicated to Nuestra Señora de la Huerta, Our Lady of the Harvest, this site of devotion to the health of the harvest, abundance, and fertility was where Santo Domingo used to hold outdoor services. It was humble but holy ground. Inside the small chapel were two modest but potent stained-glass windows, one of the six-petaled seed of life, and the other, a rare image of a very pregnant Mary.

I crossed the square and was passing under the arcaded passageway leading to the cathedral square when someone called my name. I turned to see the jovial faces of my Orisson Camino family, all of whom ran over to hug me. Everyone was still walking together after all these kilometers, including the Australian woman, and they were in a rush to get to Grañon, hoping to stay at the church's pilgrim's dorm inside the church and bell tower of San Juan, Saint John the Baptist. "Will you join us?" the Georgian asked. Again, I was tempted, but my desire to see more in Santa Domingo and visit the cathedral won out.

"But you might not get a space there," she said.

I only shrugged in reply but was thinking how I would regret even more not taking time to visit the cathedral. I saw a subtle covert smile form on the Australian's lips, as if she had sensed my thoughts. We said goodbye. As my friends walked west, I stepped inside Santo Domingo's temple, the Romanesque and Gothic cathedral where his tomb lay. It was also home, to this day, of descendants of the miraculous hen and rooster. They clucked daily from on high in a gilded chicken coop inset into the wall near the tomb.

I wandered through a sea of columns and capitals, all engraved with intricate images that reinforced the ones found in other Camino churches I'd seen so far—hybrid animals, Biblical and moral themes, stumbling characters who remind us of our flawed humanity, and many, many birds. I paid my respects at the foot of Santo Domingo's tomb and also to the rooster and the hen. I had learned that there were many descendant pairs of the original bird couple, and these were rotated from the coop often so that no one pair had to be there too long. The off-duty birds roamed freely in a nearby yard.

As I was parting, I saw a special exhibit installed on one side of the cathedral, a large collection of medieval carved wood and poly-chrome-painted statues of Mary. It was extraordinary to wander among so many images of the Mother in many manifestations and postures, each with a unique face and attitude. One, Santa Maria de la Leche, Saint Mary of the Milk, held her breast firmly to the baby Jesus's mouth, so similar to earlier images of the Mistress of Animals offering her breasts and body to sustain all the life she had created.

I walked quickly toward Grañon, hoping to catch up to my friends. The clouds dispersed, the sun sparkled in a robin's-egg-blue sky, and the air was sweet and mild. Vineyards gave way more and more to wheat fields splashed with crimson poppies. The rolling hills shifted to broad, expanding horizons.

On the outskirts of Grañon, I passed an elderly man wearing a black beret at a slant and sitting in the shade of his garage with the door flung open, watching the world go by. He called out *buen Camino*. I returned the goodwill and waved. As I did, a hawk took off from a nearby tree and flew over my left shoulder, low enough that I could feel the wind from his striated cream and brown wings. A sudden chorus of frogs rang out from the irrigation ditch near the path and erupted into quick slip, slip, slip, and splashes to take cover under water. In that sudden stillness and unnatural silence, I went up the slope into Grañon. The albergue was already full. My Orisson friends were nowhere to be seen. I visited the old church devoted to Saint John the Baptist, then kept walking. A little terrier sat next to the trail marker leading out of Grañon and woofed softly at me. I bent and rubbed his ears. When I stood up, a throbbing mirage moved toward me, halting me in my tracks.

29

THE DEER

AT FIRST APPEARING small and then growing larger and nearer, a herd of shaggy black, brown, and tan sheep trotted up the hill that I was about to climb down. Their long, clumped, wool bounced on their backs in thick dreadlocks. A ram hurried ahead of the ewes and came right up to me to investigate. He was quickly pushed aside by a few inquisitive goats, also members of this peripatetic society. Next, two herd dogs jogged up to keep the group moving, followed by a shepherd whose face was both ancient and ageless, as old as the sun and as vibrant as the wind. His dark, tanned face and sunbaked wrinkles held luminous eyes that had absorbed decades of sun and starlight. He passed me slowly, tipping his cap, and continued onward, his herd wrapped tightly all around him. Enchanted and forgetting time, I watched them as one body move up and over the bluff into the town behind me. I waited until the pleasing sounds of the shepherd's tapping staff and animals' clip-clipping hooves dispersed before continuing down the ridge and into a vast, sweeping meadow rippling with wheat and wildflowers. A village in the far distance became my aim, and I even considered it might be a good place to stop for the night.

By the time I arrived there, it hit me that I had not seen a trail marker for many kilometers, in fact, not since meeting the terrier in Grañon. I drew up to a large communal garden on the village outskirts, where an older man in a blue cardigan and dress pants was stooping in the middle of a lettuce row, cutting a leafy head with a large kitchen knife. I waited until he had sheathed the knife, slipped the lettuce into a cloth bag, and set it in the basket of a bike leaning against the garden fence before asking about my whereabouts.

"If you are a pilgrim," he said, "I am sorry to inform you, you are lost."

"I am indeed both," I laughed. "Where am I then?"

"In Quintana," he said proudly, "the last village in La Rioja before crossing the border into Castile." He explained that soon after leaving Grañon, the Camino veered right and off the road. I realized that the turn had been right where I had met the shepherd and his flock. I groaned audibly.

"You have three options from here," he offered. "You can go back and pick up the trail, but that will take you an hour. You can go back partway and look for a footpath that leads up the hill," he pointed to a ridge that lay between us and Grañon, "and take it up and over to the road that goes into Redecilla del Camino. Or I can show you the third way, the shortcut we villagers take to go to Redecilla, through that oak forest," he pointed behind him and the village to a ridge covered in a thick, dark canopy. "Footpaths through it are hard to discern and the ferns quickly cover them, which is why I should take you."

I weighed the options, including a mixed worry over inconveniencing this man as well as trusting him. My instinct told me he was both trustworthy and sincere, and the third option was the most interesting. "As long as I'm not taking you away from getting home in time for lunch, I'd like to take the forest path." It was mid-afternoon, exactly the hour most Spaniards sat to eat.

"Don't worry," he said, "my wife is still preparing the stew. We won't need to make the salad until the last minute. Besides," he jested, "she knows I always get caught up in talking with someone in the village, and here, there are eyes everywhere. Word will get back to her that I am helping a lost pilgrim. It's no trouble, *hija*." He rolled his bike to a hedge to hide it and then led the way up the hill toward the woods. "*Y quien sabe*, who knows," he called back to me as we climbed, "maybe this is your true path on the Camino, and you are not really lost?" I heard him chuckle. He was like the archetypal witchdoctor who's met at the fork in the road.

The right path, deary, is sure but boring. The left one, however, is anything but.

The dark forest closed around us. The trees grew so close to one another that their branches interwove into a compact tapestry, letting in only narrow slivers of light. Ferns and bowed grasses brushed against my knees and covered the forest floor. I saw only here and there a slight pencil thin line that hinted at a footpath. I asked my guide about himself, his wife, and family.

"I'm seventy-eight," he answered over his shoulder. "I am lucky, I am married to a lovely woman, and we have three grown children—two daughters who now live and work in Burgos, and a son who is in Logroño. I'm also a grandfather to two twenty-one-year-olds!" He told me more about them all as he bounded like a much younger man through the trees and to the ridge. At the summit we made a soft descent to the other side. Light increased and trees thinned. Within moments, we stood at the border of a wild meadow sloping gently downhill. Midway down was a ribbon road that tumbled all the way into Redecilla del Camino, where I also could see the path of the Camino entering the village. There was no way I would have gotten here without my kind guide. I was about to thank him when I felt a presence and looked to the left. It was a deer who had been watching us while grazing on succulent spring grasses on the forest rim. She lifted her head and stared.

"I told you, this was your right path," my guide said. "That is very unusual behavior for deer here. They are very shy and usually don't show themselves to people, but here she is, unafraid of you."

"Or you," I added.

"No, I am sure she is here for you," he said definitively. "Listen to her. She offers you a message."

With that, the lettuce picker and wizened shaman of Quintana turned back toward the forest. The deer lifted her head again and watched him go but did not depart. I thanked him for everything. Just before stepping into the forest, he called back to me. "Remember, *hija*, walk your own path. *That* is the Camino, not the physical trail. Perhaps that is the deer's message, to trust the unmarked path. You'll still be a pilgrim if you step off the known trail." Then he disappeared into the woods. The deer held my gaze for a few more seconds and then, like the old man, entered and dissolved into the forest. I felt a charge in the air and lingered.

When I climbed down to Redecilla del Camino, I found a town absent of life. Even the albergue looked like an abandoned construction site. I visited the church, celebrated for its intricately engraved medieval stone baptismal font depicting the celestial Jerusalem, the ideal city. Even more stunning to my eye was the stone sculpture of Mary in a niche next to the font, as beautiful as the ones I'd seen in Santo Domingo de la Calzada. This really was a road devoted to Mary, the most represented holy figure on the whole route. Gothic and stately, Redecilla's Mary sat Isis-like on a throne, the edges of her mouth upturned into a subtle smile, like the ones in Estella and Los Arcos, inviting us to embrace joy, not wade in grief and sorrow.

Hungry and tired, and with the Spanish lunch hour come and gone, the afternoon late and hot and still no one around, I moved on to the next settlement along rippling plains and an open horizon, walking parallel to the local highway where more cargo trucks passed than cars. It led me to a roadside motel across the street from the hamlet of Castildelgado, a handful of houses clustered around a church, no albergue or other open business in sight. I crossed to the trucker's inn to find a hopping place run by two sprightly and engaging women. In the dining room were a few pilgrims and a dozen truckers all tucking into fragrant and tempting dishes as one big family.

"Do you need a room?" asked one of the women greeting me.

"Yes, please," I said, "and lunch, too, if possible."

All was possible in this celestial city. I was settled into a room of my own—clean, basic, and restful, just what a trucker needs and a pilgrim fantasizes about—and then offered a seat at a table with four other peregrinos. Two hailed from Normandy, and two from Valencia. We exchanged notes of the day as our hostess brought out the first of three courses of the fixed-price trucker's menu: robust mixed salad; grilled trout stuffed with cured ham with roasted peppers, carrots, and zucchini from the outside garden; a hefty spaghetti tossed with chorizo, garlic, and herbs; and a whiskey tart for dessert—all served along with generous bottles of local red wine. We all seemed obsessed with the fact that no matter what we had planned for the Camino, nothing of the sort unfolded. Instead, there were surprises at every bend.

"I think the Camino teaches that we need to let go of our old ideas and embrace the new possibilities as they arise and adapt to them," said one of the Valencians. It seemed to be the theme of the day.

I asked our hostesses for the WiFi code before I retired to my room. It had now been many days since I'd had any news from home. To my surprise, there was an email from my agent. We had a firm contract for the first book, she wrote, and an almost sure thing for the second one.

The herd, the path, the deer, the lettuce-picking shaman, the messages, the signs. My head spun. *Remember,* hija*, walk your own path. That is the Camino, not the physical trail.*

I couldn't believe it. I now knew that once there was a firm contract for the second book, I would need to get cracking on it and leave the Camino. I would do so when and if that time came. For now, not resisting, listening, trusting, had served me well. And my life path as a writer also was getting a serious confirmation. I determined that I would surely go as far as Atapuerca, which would serve all my purposes: it is not only on the Camino but is also one of the most important Neandertal sites in Europe. Soon after it, I would land in Burgos, and from there, I would remain on the Camino until it became clear it was time to get off. As if the day weren't weird enough, in thinking about Atapuerca, I recalled the odd dream message I'd had at the start of this pilgrimage, delivered in the Cat Steven's voice in my head: *Follow Mary, follow the Neandertals, follow French folklore.* It now made sense. So, this was my path? What a strange and glimmering day.

It took some time to calm my excited nerves and fall asleep. Once I did, my aching muscles and throbbing feet interrupted my slumber, and I tossed and turned all night. When I woke, I realized that soon, just before Atapuerca, I would walk through the Montes de Oca, the Hills of the Goose. There, I hoped, some deeper insight into the goose would arise, some key clue before I had to veer off the path of the marked and goose-footed Camino.

THE TENTH GOOSE

DEW FLICKED OFF grasses that rippled like silk in the soft morning wind. I ambled over hill and dale toward Belorado and beyond. The sun rose and warmed the day. My mind wandered far, casting across the open expanse, wondering what the tree-laden Montes de Oca looming on the horizon might hold. By mid-morning, my mood shifted. There was a sudden influx of new walkers on the trail, especially large groups in matching t-shirts and day packs marching to loud clapping, singing, and shouting, often pushing solo trekkers off the trail without notice as they passed. Then came the dirt bikers, who careened past without warning and knocked several full-pack hikers off kilter; one almost fell face first into a ditch before a fellow walker pulled him back.

I had lost track of the days and not noticed the approach of the weekend. But with the warming temperatures and the coming of summer, Spaniards were taking every moment away from work to escape to the countryside. Overnight, the trail had gone from a quiet trek to a busy parade. Spanish weekend pilgrims and trekkers—friends, couples, whole families, church groups, and hiking clubs—jostled along the path with the growing numbers of pilgrims coming from abroad.

When I saw that the groups and bikers were stopping in Belorado, I kept going, leaving its river valley and rising up into a vast, dry plateau edged with towering limestone ridges. As shocking, I found myself suddenly alone again on the trail after hours of constant onslaught. It took a few kilometers, as I neared the hamlet of Tosantos, tucked at the foot of a sheer limestone ridge and on the edge of Montes de Oca, for my thoughts to relax again and at times return to the goose. Though the village nestled at the base of the cliff, two-thirds up was a cave-turned-shrine. Its origin story was similar, with a twist, to the one about Nájera's magical Marian cave, but this one was devoted to Nuestra Señora de la Peña, Our Lady of the Rock.

In the eighth century, following mystical signs, locals discovered an image of Jesus deep in the cave. They integrated the icon into the town's cyclical tradition with their town patroness, Mary of the Rock, something that has continued to the present. I was told that in the fall and winter, the icons of Mother and Child are kept in the cave from which they overlook and protect the settlement. Then, in the spring and summer, the young men of Tosantos carry Mary down to the central village church, in whose yard I now stood. There they keep Mary through the growing and harvesting seasons, leaving her son to protect from on high while she guards from the soil and earth. In the autumn, Mary is carried to the cave, but this time by the older women of the village.

It was hard to overlook the earth-based symbolism, which follows and honors life's cycles—fertility and growth, harvest and rest, young and old, male and female, spring and autumn—which is reenacted to this day every year by a people who still live by the old rhythms. This was indeed Mother Goose country.

The cave above was closed, as was the church below, but on the church's grounds grew an ancient and massive chestnut tree, its canopy stretching wide across the holy ground, mirroring the fertility and sustenance of Mary of the Rock inside the church. I noticed swallows circling around the church and recalled the same behavior in Torres del Rio. What did the swallows know?

As I left Tosantos, I saw four pilgrims seated outside the village albergue, shoes off, airing their toes and soaking up the warm sun. Three of them I knew, from the Orisson group. We hugged again as they related that two others of the Orisson contingent were inside napping. The Australian woman, they told me, had mysteriously disappeared somewhere before Belorado. They urged me to join them. Again, I was tempted, but again, I felt a stronger pull to keep going.

The path rose along a plateau of pale-yellow limestone with crunchy cornflake-like pebbles underfoot. The intense high sun bore down, as did my hunger, and soon, having forgotten to refill my water bottle in Tosantos, so did thirst. With the repetitive sound of footfall, it all played games with my head. A green forest appeared on the horizon and, as I neared, it gave me another sense of déjà-vu, as if I were back on the trail with Sarah and about to walk into Auch. Maybe in my addled thoughts I was connecting the two geese, Auch to Oca, both Romance variants from Latin meaning goose.

But there was more. As I neared the forest, a strange feeling also descended, the very physical presence of my friend Irene. I felt her on my left, walking with me, smiling her serene smile. She had died two years earlier at age fifty-five, which was nearly my age now. We had met in graduate school, she a kind soul and gifted archaeologist. I still had not really gotten over the grief of her loss. But here her presence was almost as visceral as the last time I had seen her, sitting across from her in a Denver pub, sipping beer and laughing.

Just as suddenly, my maternal grandfather appeared, then my maternal grandmother, and these two were on my right. I next sensed that my paternal grandmother, a person more introverted than myself and very quiet, was also with us and walking just to the other side of my other grandparents. As much as I was sure I needed to get out of the sun and hydrate soon and get something to eat, I also basked in what was very real warmth, like a protective cloak of energy from these four loved ones. Tears unbidden flowed down my face. I kept walking, feeling that if I stopped, this chain might be broken, that it was somehow connected to the rhythmic crunching of the ground beneath my feet.

I walked through a swaying meadow of wheat toward the forest, passing a beehive-shaped ruin, the only standing remains of an extensive ninth-century Mozárabic monastery named for San

Felices de Oca. He was a famous hermit-turned-saint from La Rioja who had performed many miracles, the best of which were healing the sick and feeding the hungry. The whole place felt pure, free, and exceedingly beautiful as sweet air arrived with the wind, making the fallow field's multicolored wildflowers bob and dance. I crossed a small wooden bridge over the Oca River and walked into the village of Villafranca Montes de Oca, French Town of the Goose Hills. This curious name was emphasized on the first sign that greeted me on the edge of town; it was for the local grocery store and depicted a cartoonish white goose with a pilgrim staff and scallop shell next to the words "Alimentación Oca," or Goose Grocery. The whole place was dominated by a massive building in the center—the recently restored monastery and hospice of San Antón Abad, now a pilgrim albergue and luxury hotel, something for both prince and pauper. It had been the project and gift of a local man who had returned from walking the Camino inspired to do something to make this section of the trail more hospitable. I pulled open the heavy door and went in, heading straight to the reception desk near a sitting area outfitted with plush velvet high-back chairs.

I wiped at my face and pressed down my flyaway hair in a futile effort. The young woman behind the desk greeted me warmly and offered a price hard to refuse for a night on the princely side of things. I took it. All the pilgrims, she told me, in either form of accommodation, took dinner together in the shared dining room. With my key in my hand, thinking of hot baths, copious water, and good food, I was turning toward the wide stairway when someone called my name. The voice had come from the behind one of the high plush chairs. It was the long-haired Australian woman. She jumped up and gave me a big hug.

"After Belorado, I booked it," she said. "I needed to walk alone. And the crowds today…"

"…were a real shock to the system," I finished. I was about to suggest we have dinner together but hesitated, given her desire to go solo.

"Want to have dinner together?" she asked.

We agreed to meet later on, and I went upstairs to a huge room adorned in velvet furniture, with velvet curtains framing a large picture window looking out over the church. After hydrating, snacking on nuts, and taking a hot shower and drying myself luxuriously with thick, soft towels, I went into the village to buy provisions for the next day from the Goose Grocery. A local informed me that running south out of the village was a small road that led to the healing fountain and shrine dedicated to both San Felices and Nuestra Señora de Oca—Our Lady Goose. I definitely wanted to meet her.

The shrine was closed but set within an enchanted grove of trees on the banks of the Oca River, and the healing fountain cascaded in tiers beside it. The air was ion-rich and refreshing. A soft wind rose and gently caressed my brow. I found myself crying for the second time that day.

Back at my room in the grand medieval monastery, and now endowed with WiFi, I pulled out my tablet and found Villafranca's municipal website. On the page dedicated to local history, the text referred to the Mary of the shrine as Nuestra Madre La Oca, Our Mother the Goose. I read it again to be sure. Yes. That's what it said. I continued reading. It spoke of the Montes de Oca as an ancient and wild place and a place inhabited by ancient Celtiberians and later traversed by medieval pilgrims, all crossing the Oca River, a tributary of the river of rivers, the Ebro. The Oca River, it added, was also a place where duck-footed river fairies lived.

For a second time, I reread the website copy to be sure, and found that, yes, it really did speak about duck-footed fairies. It continued in explaining that Villafranca Montes de Oca got its name from the Roman name, Auca, and that this had been a sacred place long before the pilgrimage, that the goose was a sacred animal highly revered by the Celts, and more, the goose represented the old mother goddess, herself possessing aquatic bird feet. Moreover, the chapel on the Oca River here had been built to venerate Our Lady in the same place that the pagan goddess had been worshiped. Mary was the living embodiment of the old mother goddess, right down to her holy webbed feet.

It was almost time to go down to dinner, but a hunch struck me that I had to follow. Was it pure whimsy that had made me feel as if I were walking toward Auch today? I pulled up topographical maps online to find that the contours of the approach to Auch were similar to those toward Villafranca, fanning vertical north-south ridges coated with oak and pine and forged by rivers making deep valleys—there the Gers, and here the Oca. The two places looked almost equidistant from the watershed of the Col de Lepoeder at the Pyrenees, crossing from Saint-Jean-Pied-de-Port to Roncesvalles. I typed in directions for walking to each goose point from the Col, along the path Sarah and I took to get to Auch, and the one I had treaded to arrive here. The Col to Auch was 214 kilometers (133 miles), and the Col to Villafranca Montes de Oca was 215 kilometers (134 miles). Okay, I thought, is that weird?

I could feel my heart beating harder and faster as I considered the odds of hitting it so exactly equidistant on a hunch. I also considered the evidence: both places had a Lady Goose to which they were wholeheartedly devoted, both had been heavily occupied by Romans and given goose names. I also suspected a third possibility, so I did a quick search. I pulled up an historical map based on Roman accounts of the native tribes they encountered in the western Pyrenees: Auch and Oca sat on the outermost edges of the territories of the ancient Aquitainian tribes. It also was a northeast to southwest territory that marked where wild geese crossed the Pyrenees on their migrations north and south. Prehistoric peoples surely had long witnessed and benefitted from geese crossing into these territories, and the Romans too. Perhaps they named these places in a magical pact with the animal that was as loyal and protective as it was delicious?

Overwhelmed by overlapping goose associations, and that I had now walked entirely across the old Aquitainian territories, core lands of goose and goddess, I suddenly realized that I was late for dinner and rushed down.

The Australian assured me she had only just arrived. We sat at a table for two. Clusters of other pilgrims occupied a few tables around us, interspersed with tables of elegantly dressed posh guests who were probably driving the Camino. It was the first time I'd seen the Australian looking relaxed and happy.

"I feel like an escapee," she said and laughed. "Tomorrow, my plan is to walk all the way to Burgos, just to make up for lost time." That was 39 kilometers (24 miles), almost double the distance of an average day. "The irony is that I came here to sort through my life, to process old stuff, childhood stuff—unwieldy, unsettling, and unassimilated stuff that is harming my marriage. But I haven't had a chance to even to hear myself think since Orisson."

I told her she was right on schedule, according to old pilgrim lore—sometimes the first lesson is about boundaries and claiming them—and that she hadn't wasted any time.

"I liked you from the moment we met," she blurted. "I just felt something."

"Me, too," I confessed, "and I could feel that you needed to book it." I raised my glass. "To owning your path." She raised hers and clinked. We drank and paused to savor the good wine. She then sat back in her chair and looked at me for a long moment, as if she were wondering whether to say what was on her mind.

"At the risk of sounding nuts," she finally said, "I need to tell you something more."

"Go ahead," I smiled encouragingly and took another sip.

"They were there that night in Orisson," she began, "and they're here now, too, I see them all around you." I almost spit my wine out. She continued.

"Both grandmothers, your maternal grandfather, and three friends. All except for two are deceased. The two friends who are living are still with you almost all the time in spirit, cheering you on."

I set my glass down, my hand slightly jittery. "Go on."

"Your maternal grandmother keeps telling me to tell you to remember the turquoise, a color that will bring you luck, to remember something she gave you as a child that is connected to her and to turquoise." Just before turning thirteen, my grandmother had given me a ring and earrings set with a Persian turquoise the color of a bright-blue, cloudless sky. They were treasures to me, ones I wore only on special occasions.

"She says you should get these out and wear them all the time, not only for special events. You should also know that all three grandparents are always with you," the Australian continued, "cheering you on, surrounding you, alongside your friends." Before I could ask her to describe the three friends, she described them to me. "The one who died had long blond hair and beautiful eyes. She died from breast cancer not long ago. Is that right?"

I nodded. Tears began to well in my eyes.

"And the two living friends have both hiked the Camino with you, at different times. Both are trekkers—you've walked a part of the Camino with both of them—and they get what you are doing, not only as a pilgrim, but as a writer; they really believe in you. One has brown hair and the other has copper-colored hair. Every day they cheer you on from where they are." I knew exactly who she was referring to. One was Sarah and the other a close friend in New Jersey.

"These six people," the Australian added, "are around you as you walk, pushing you gently to do the work you've come here to do, and to trust your own sense of where to go next. And now that I have your attention," she said with a lilt of humor in her voice, knowing her words had hit their target, "the most important message I need to deliver to you is this: walk your own Camino. Don't feel pulled by the ideas of others. Events might take you off this trail—and I think they will, and soon. Trust your instinct about what to do and where to go. In fact," she concluded, "I don't think the marked Camino is in the cards for you right now."

My jaw dropped. No one knew this was a concern for me, no one but my husband and my parents.

Our food arrived. We devoured it and drank more wine. Between mouthfuls I told her that everything she told me was spot on. "How do you know these things?" I asked.

It was a talent she'd had since childhood, she told me, and it was the reason she was walking. "I came to walk the Camino to sort out for myself how much to reveal or incorporate this skill in my life

and with others. I hadn't anticipated being around so many people
from the start, and they come with their people, both deceased and
living, who stand around them and walk with them. When I see a
group of five pilgrims, I'm also seeing their entourage."

"Like our Orisson family?"

"Exactly. Those five become twenty, sometimes thirty."

"I'm guessing you never told them about this."

"Oh heavens, no. I think it would freak them out. But I also
realize I can't hide this. I'm hoping the Camino will offer me some
answers for how I can integrate all this and create better balance in
my life back home. Maybe I have to accept the fact that I'll never
be what other people call 'normal.'"

"Maybe 'normal' isn't really so great, anyway," I offered. "You
just delivered a message to me to embrace my unique path. Maybe
that wisdom applies to you too?"

She laughed. She relaxed more and we sat a long time, draining
the last of our wine, before climbing up the massive stone stairway
to our rooms. I saw her to her door, and she asked me if I wanted
to draw a few runes to guide my next steps.

"Sure," I said. Why not? It's not every day you meet someone
carrying runes.

Of the twenty-five runes in the little velvet sack she pulled from
her pocket, I pulled the one called *algiz*, the rune letter that looks
exactly like a goose's footprint. For Goddess's sake.

"It's the rune of divine guidance and protection," the Australian
said. "It means that there is a higher plan unfolding before you
and your walk right now." It was true guidance. I thanked her
and hugged her. When we said good night, we both knew that
we would not see each other again. At least not on this particular
Camino. "One more thing," she said. "I just got this. Sometime
in the near future you're going to meet someone connected to the
Inca Trail, to Machu Pichu. I can't say if it means you are going to
go there yourself or if this person will be key in helping you make
sense of things."

"Machu Pichu?" I said, incredulous.

"Yeah, I know. I have no idea. I only report what I'm given." We laughed and wished one another *buen Camino*. Then I returned to my room with my grandparents and three friends and thanked them all, and all my family and friends who love me and supported this walk too, before drifting off to sleep in my massive and very comfortable bed.

RED ROSES AND WHITE HONEYBEES

THE TRAIL ROSE vertically through Villafranca Montes de Oca and along an oak- and pine-covered ridge with exhilarating first views of the tightly layered mountains ahead. Then it went back down into dense, dark woods—reminders of why, centuries before these more peaceful times, this was a notorious hideout where bandits preyed on passing pilgrims. A soft wind rushed through the trees as did acrobatic titmice tumbling in the branches and the melodious song of the European robin. In the undergrowth, pink foxgloves, white orchids, and ferns swayed their heads. My leaping ahead to Villafranca the day before seemed to have put me ahead of the hoards who had bedded in Belorado. I climbed over one final ridge and saw the welcoming monastery and church of San Juan de Ortega clustered in the valley below. Named after Santo Domingo de la Calzada's disciple, San Juan was a fellow engineer who had chosen this desolate spot to offer greater support to pilgrims making their way through the treacherous hills. I picked up my pace, drawn like a bee to honey to the pale yellow stone church glowing in the saturated light of the late afternoon sun. When I got there, I saw where all the hoards had been—far ahead of me and now crowding into the one café in the hamlet and all across the main square, leaving their bikes parked anywhere backpacks were not. A long line snaked out of the café, with many waiting to put in a takeout order or wrangle a liberated seat at a table inside. I took a quick right turn into the church, the first building on the square. Strangely, it was empty of people but for San Juan de Ortega in his tomb.

He had built this church and dedicated it to San Nicolás de Barí in thanks to the saint who had saved his life during a treacherous ship journey returning from his pilgrimage to Jerusalem. *Ortega* means nettle and San Juan had settled on this remote place that was covered in stinging nettles and riddled with bandits and cleared it of both, offering a safe harbor to pilgrims. Though the church appears stocky and square on the outside, inside, it felt airy and round. I smelled roses and looked for the source but saw no flowers, oils, or incense, and yet it wafted around me with such intensity that I felt as if I were in a rose garden. Like a hunting dog, I sniffed around more earnestly and decided to try the Gothic marble tomb in the church's center. I went to its right side, an inviting meditation space arrayed with cushions on the floor before candles set in a large stone bowl. Nothing. Next, I went to the altar, taking in its sculpted capitals with vivid scenes from Jesus's life, the most expressive one showing the Visitation with the pregnant Mary receiving her cousin Elizabeth's news of also being pregnant with John the Baptist. The two are shown hugging and rejoicing in the good news. But the source of the rose scent still eluded me.

To my left I saw a simple roughhewn stone sarcophagus, and as I approached, the strong rose scent came straight from it. It was San Juan's first and true tomb, the first stone in which his body had been laid upon his death. Thick pillar candles flickering with flames covered the floor before the sarcophagus, and scattered around them on the floor were many prayers scribbled on slips of paper that visitors had left. I sat on the floor, the rose perfume wrapping around me.

Medieval accounts detail that one day, many years after San Juan's death, people smelled roses coming from his tomb. They slid off the lid to find not only the fragrance's source but also thousands of white honeybees milling about, adding to the perfume a heavenly ambrosial note. Where his teacher Santo Domingo had a special affiliation with hens and roosters, San Juan was thereafter associated with roses and honeybees. To the medieval mind, roses represented purity and divine grace, and white honeybees were luck, fertility, and the souls of unborn children waiting to incarnate. His tomb became a pilgrimage center among women and couples desiring children. As a servant of God who preferred nature to the company of people, it seemed fitting that his symbols would be so wedded to the fertility of the earth and mother.

I went back outside to see that the crowd had died down and found a spare seat at a table in the café with three pilgrims: a ship captain from Madrid seeking space for reflection, a young man from Kyoto seeking a pilgrimage experience outside of Japan after having walked Japan's Shikoku island's 88 Temple Pilgrimage, and a woman from Helsinki searching for life direction. As we waited for our omelets, we gave the sea captain grief. How was it that the sailor made a living in land-locked Madrid? The jest was on us: he was hired by wealthy clients all over the world to fly to their private boats and man them. "But it's not all as glamorous as it sounds," he added. "That is why I am walking, to enjoy a solid time planted firmly in the beauty of the solid earth." Three older men at a neighboring table overheard our conversation. They hailed from Tarragona and were all wearing dress trousers, dress shirts, and Mister Rogers-style cardigans tied around their shoulders, yet on their feet, state of the art hiking boots. They said they were grandfathers from Tarragona now walking their fourth Camino together.

"Walking?" the sea captain asked

"Of course," one said. "A landlocked sea captain can hardly judge our attire," he quipped. "You wear what works, and for me, these threads hold their shape better, are more comfortable than those industrial trekking fabrics, and also have deeper pockets."

We laughed. Our food arrived as the three Tarragonans turned to flirt with the Finn and me and nudged the Kyotan to do the same. "This, too, is pilgrimage," one said to him, which made him blush crimson. Everyone was staying in San Juan and waiting for the albergue in the old monastery next door to open. As much as I wanted to stay, I was a few kilometers from Atapuerca. I had been following Mary and French folklore so far, and now came the Neandertals. Atapuerca had four-hundred-thousand-year-old remains that belonged to them, and much earlier than even they:

Atapuerca's deeper strata also harbored Europe's oldest human remains, ones predating Neandertals by almost a million years. I wanted to slumber tonight in the bosom of the cradle of Europe's earliest humanity.

I reluctantly said goodbye to my companions and returned to the oak and pine forest that gave way to sweeping yellow fields and bright blue sky. The far horizon was formed by the limestone ridge of the Sierra de Atapuerca. Underfoot was a subterranean world of Swiss cheese created by thousands of years of water flow through soft stone that carved out tunnels and caverns. Every now and then, a cavern opened to the surface, making this ridge a place to which humans and wild animals had been drawn for its natural shelter, water, and food. At the foot of the bluff I could just make out the rooftops of the village of Atapuerca.

Just before reaching it, I passed through another village, Agés, where I ran into the Orisson group, all lounging in the sun at a village cafe, barefoot and nursing cold beers. Again, they urged me to stay. Again, our timing didn't align. Atapuerca beckoned. Had I seen the Australian, they asked? I told them yes but offered nothing more. We said we would see each other in Burgos, and I continued on across the vast meadow that connected the two villages.

In Atapuerca I found all the inns and albergues full, every bed and floor space in town taken. Pilgrims teamed everywhere. As a last-ditch effort, hoping there had been a last-minute cancellation, I returned to an inn with a large flower garden in the center of the village, but still there was no such luck. The innkeeper invited me to take a seat at the bar and consider my options. I ordered a beer and mulled things over. The hour was late. If I kept walking, I could find the same situation in the next places between here and Burgos. But maybe, like the Australian, I could book it to Burgos and arrive there after dark. But it was a twenty-one-kilometer stretch. I looked up as I considered all this and noticed a series of photos on the wall that I'd missed seeing upon entering. Several showed the innkeeper standing with three others, faces I knew for some vague reason. Then it came to me: I'd read an article about Atapuerca, and these were the lead archaeologists at the neighboring dig site. I rushed out to the garden to find the innkeeper.

"Those are photos of you with the archaeologists?"

She smiled, pleased. "They come here a lot, but how do you know who they are?"

I told her about my time in southwestern France and having recently worked on a Neandertal site there, and about my, I hoped, forthcoming book. She grinned and laughed.

"There are no accidents on the Camino," she said. "I'm from Bordeaux, and listen to this, my grandparents were from Sarlat. That is where I spent all my summers as a child. I met and married a man from Atapuerca. We decided to make our married life here with its double legacy of prehistory and the Camino. And where do you stay when you are in southwestern France?"

"Sarlat."

Her face registered shock. What were the chances? "There are no accidents on the Camino," she said finally, this time more seriously. I told her why I so desperately wanted to sleep in Atapuerca tonight. She considered everything then said, "It is ironic, but it is easier to sign up for and get to the archaeological site here from Burgos. Reserve your ticket there at the Human Evolution Museum, where a bus will take you directly to the site with an expert guide, which is the only way to enter." She paused and looked long at me then added, "Here is what I think you should do: Go to Burgos tonight. It is too late to walk. I'll call you a taxi. You will need a whole day to visit Atapuerca, time better spent than walking through the industrial outskirts of Burgos." I felt torn, but also saw the hand of grace and accepted.

Ten minutes later, a taxi pulled up. My new Bordelaise friend walked with me to the cab door. "This just struck me. Given the research you have ahead of you for your new book, you might consider leaving the Camino after Burgos and taking the train north to Santander. From there, you can reach Spain's truly most famous Neandertal site of El Sidrón."

That indeed was one of the sites I needed to visit, a cave where the archaeologists had recently discovered the remains of thirteen

Neandertals who had lived 49,000 years ago. Most strikingly, with the new strides in genetic analysis of fossil remains, those thirteen appeared to have all been members of the same small group, a truly rare and remarkable find. But I wasn't sure I was ready to leave the Camino so soon, despite her optimism, until I had a signed contract. "*Bon courage,*" she whispered in my ear as she gave me a hug, "and remember, there are no accidents on the Camino. Let it guide you."

In less than fifteen minutes, I was on the Plaza de San Juan, the first historic square that pilgrims reach in Burgos, near the banks of the Arlanzón River that sliced through the city. A stone's throw from there, the Camino passes through the gate of San Juan into the walls of the medieval town. I crossed the square, passing the church of San Juan and a municipal library, aiming for an adjacent pilgrim's hostel. When I entered, the owner acted as if he had been expecting me.

32

CALL ME ISHMAEL

"**L**LAMAME **ISMAEL,**" **HE** said as he scanned his ledger and reached for a set of keys.

"Ismael," I repeated, taking in his long, salt-and-pepper hair and thick beard that framed his intense, dark-brown eyes, "what can you offer a pilgrim for three nights?" Between Atapuerca, uncertainty, and the library, I had a lot of work and soul-searching to do in Burgos.

"This," he handed me a key. "It is my last room—you will have to share the bathroom down the hall—but tomorrow," he scanned the ledger once more, "I can move you to a private room with a magnificent view. I'll charge you the shared room's price for all three nights." I accepted. "Just leave your pack by your bed tomorrow morning," he instructed, "and we'll transfer it to the other room when it's ready."

An hour later, clean and refreshed, I bounded down the stairs to get to the Human Evolution Museum before it closed for the night and reserve my spot on the morning tour. Ismael was in the lobby and about to head home, going in the same direction, and walked with me. It was a soft mild evening. The dark rose of the setting sun reflected in the calm waters of the Arlanzón River as we crossed on a footbridge to the other side. A Burgos native, Ismael had only recently shifted gears and opened a pilgrim hostel, a dream and gamble that was paying off with fully booked rooms most nights. "I love meeting people from around the world and making them feel at home. I especially love pilgrims because they're not your typical tourist—they're on a quest."

"What do you think if a pilgrim's quest tells him or her that he or she may need to leave the road to Compostela and head in another direction?"

"The true seeker," he replied without hesitation, "must listen to what feels right and follow it. The Camino in truth is everywhere. Each pilgrim must find his or her path on it."

Call me Ismael. I heard his advice more deeply than I had heard similar messages only days, and hours, before. Perhaps it was time to take this pilgrim quest off-road and find my own life-giving spring in the unknown?

At the museum, the prophet of Burgos bid me a good evening. I rushed inside and reserved my ticket with five minutes to spare and then relaxed into an aimless ramble along the riverside, eventually crossing back to the other side and walking into the walled historic center to stand before the formidable cathedral with its wedding-cake-icing towers and elaborate engravings parading long lines of Spanish nobility and saints. The cathedral impressed me as being as much a political biography of Spain in stone as it was a sacred temple built in high French Gothic style. It was closed for the night, so I walked circles around it—no swallows were there— and paused along the way in a caravan-sized tapas bar to sample the local specialties and patch together a peripatetic dinner. I also passed the café where, years earlier, I had met the young man from Köln who had opened my eyes to the goose. I raised a glass to him, wondering where his quest had led him and what he thought of it now. Little did he know the door he had opened to me that day.

When I returned to my lodging, Ismael was at the desk.

"I thought you went home."

"I did," he smiled, "but we had another last-minute cancellation and I walked back to make sure my staff prepared your room and moved your things. We have already moved you into the private room, yours for all three nights." No extra charge, and he had also put some complementary beer and fruit in the refrigerator that came with the room. More gifts of the Camino.

Ismael said good night again and was gone before I could properly thank him. I went up to find my pack and things laid out carefully on the bed in a spacious room with a high ceiling and crystal chandelier—a honeymoon suite of sorts. But it was all forgotten when I went to the large picture window looking out over the square and rooftop of the library and church of San Juan. Peering eye-level at the church's bell tower, I discovered I was not alone: A mother and father stork were taking turns guarding the nest and flying off for fish from the river as two awkward and leggy babies scuffled about in the woven depths of twigs and leaves. As soon as one parent returned, all elegance and helicopter-landing precision, the other took off in flight for the next round, their squawking, inelegant young jostling each other for first dibs. No matter how early I had to rise the next day for my tour, I had to kneel on my bed watching until the feathered family settled for the night and the sky turned a deep dark blue speckled with diamond-like stars. What a gift Ismael had given me: my own high-altitude perch nested near intense beauty.

I slept deeply and woke early. Already, the mother and father stork were up and deep into the morning's task of feeding their quickly growing chicks. I opened the window to hear the clack clacking of their bills and take in the fresh morning air, and I was hanging my head out for a deep breath when, out of nowhere, a large form flapped toward my head. I ducked in as the creature did a doubletake and flapped, honked, and quacked indignantly, losing some altitude, and then lifting and flying on with added speed. A duck. *A duck!* I still heard its startled honking as it disappeared, heading dead northwest, and flapping hard to catch up to a companion farther ahead, also going due northwest. I watched in disbelief—since when did ducks almost strafe people leaning out high windows in cities? I began to laugh the more I thought about it. And then I considered, if this were a bizarre sign, how should I read it? Looking at my map and drawing a northwest trajectory from Burgos in the flight line of the two *Anatidae,* as the bird flies, they were heading straight to El Sidrón in Asturias and near the Atlantic Ocean. How very, very funny, and odd. But I had no time to consider more. I rushed off to the Human Evolution Museum before I missed the bus.

The group was just boarding when I got there and consisted of several Spanish couples, a family with two young children, and two other pilgrims, one from Chile and the other from Mexico. I sat next to the pilgrims as the bus departed. Like me, they both had decided to take a rest day. They also grumbled about the growing crowds on the Camino and wondered if they would finish; the bed race was getting to be too stressful, and it no longer felt like the pilgrimage they had envisioned. Yet we had all come a long way to be there, so the decision to leave felt epic. I shared Ismael's words of wisdom. The idea of being a seeker seemed to relax them and infuse trust that the right path would announce itself. But it did less for me as I wondered—and simultaneously resisted deciding—whether I should follow the ducks heading northwest or walk farther due west on the arrow-marked Camino. Then our bus slipped out of the city and into the arid landscape of the Atapuerca hills, and with it my worry turned to excitement and time-traveling enchantment as we followed the footsteps of the Camino's oldest pilgrims and the oldest human footprints in all of Europe.

Twenty minutes later we entered the archaeological site, a deep groove in the ridge that revealed complex layer-cake strata with several caverns chock full of prehistoric remains, both human and animal, as well as the stone tools people had used to hunt and process their food. The Neandertals of Atapuerca were Europe's oldest, having been there some 400,000 years ago. Even older were human fossils discovered there dating to 1.2 million years ago—the European Homo erectus that excavators gave its own name, *Homo antecessor*. It was mindboggling to stand where they had stood, Europe's first people. Everyone in the group was speechless and contemplative as the visit progressed, even the young children.

At lunch I sat with the two pilgrims. We were overwhelmed by time, and more, that we felt a deep sacredness here that was far older than anything we'd ever touched.

"Wherever we walk is sacred," said the woman from Mexico.

This deep sense of the earthbound sacredness only intensified in the afternoon when we revisited Atapuerca's ancient landscape and then had time on our return to Burgos to take in the rich and layered prehistory displays in the museum that lay out human existence from over the past three million years. Up until the last ten to twelve thousand years, we humans were nomads, moving along the earth, reading her body, knowing her intimate secrets, following her signs, and living by her laws. The last few thousand years had changed all that, with wandering less and cultivating and domesticating more. I was sure a great part of the appeal of the Camino was how it returned us to our nomadic roots and tapped into the deeper wiring of our bodies and minds, all of which had evolved over the three million years as wandering beings. The stories were still there, in the landscape, in the footworn paths, and in the old stories that hung on, like Mother Goose, migrating with the times. Now I knew what I needed to do with my remaining two days and nights in Burgos.

The next morning I woke with the storks, and after a good breakfast I went across the sidewalk to the library and I perused the prehistory stacks and then the folklore section, all organized by each Spanish region, with an especially dense collection for Castile and its neighbors of León, La Rioja, Basque Country, Cantabria, and Asturias. I pulled every relevant tome off the shelves and read until I was bleary-eyed. Around me, teens did homework, elders sank into a good novel, and parents with children read stories aloud in a colorful sunlit corner. They all kept me going as I saturated my brain with archaeological, historical, and ethnographic accounts of ancient Iberia, much of it reinforcing what I had learned so far: the Pyrenees has its own unique cultures, the territory from Auch to Auca is a region in its own right; and almost all regions have central stories of a fierce, just, and beautiful mother goddess, often with aquatic bird feet. Moreover, a great snake is almost always the form of her powerful male consort, the two working together to protect and defend nature and justice. I understood that the way of the goose and goddess was deeply encoded in this landscape of the Camino since long before the Middle Ages and preserved in stories and stone sculptures. I understood that I should trust my own experience here that on some uncanny level, the landscape and its ancient leyline energy would guide me and anyone who tuned to it.

In the late afternoon, I broke for lunch and strolled along the river to rest my eyes and stretched my legs. Before the cathedral closed, I went inside to find the late-afternoon light piercing the stained glass and coloring the cream walls and ceiling. I returned to the library and stayed until it closed. The next day, I returned for a morning of more library research, and an afternoon of lingering in the Human Evolution Museum, learning everything it had to teach me about Neandertals, including their cousins up north in El Sidrón. That evening, my last in Burgos, I ran into Ismael as he crossed the square. We made chitchat, and then, before I parted, he told me, "Trust your instinct on what to do next, and always pick magic and adventure over following the crowd."

The next morning, satiated with research and with no news yet from my agent, I departed early and rejoined the Camino heading west. Until something clearly pushed me off the trail, I determined to take it a day at a time. I knew I was resisting, the thing I had said I would not do. How many guides, how many ducks, needed to fly into my path before I went north?

33

THE LABYRINTH

I **PARTED BURGOS'** heavily fortified walls through the western gate of San Martin. It was a pleasant jaunt through parks and suburban gardens and onto straw-colored low hills splashed with bright red poppies. Beehive swarms of pilgrims had overtaken a village café in Tardajos, and as much as I hungered for strong coffee and a filling breakfast, I felt compelled to flee. But bacon and eggs fried in olive oil filled the airwaves along with strong hits of espresso. I ordered a hot egg, ham, and cheese sandwich from the enterprising chef inside and carried my fortifying breakfast to an outside table, finding one seat open and taking it, sharing the table with two German girls who kept to themselves and a couple from New Zealand who chatted up a storm in quick bursts. The husband was especially sardonic and seemed to speak aloud whatever was in his thoughts.

"It's more a circus, than a contemplative walk," he groused. I had to admit, it felt that way right then, but, man, was this a good sandwich. I nodded but said nothing, occupying my mouth with the delayed joy of filling my empty belly.

No matter how one paced it, we all walked as a procession of pilgrims. In the next village of Rabé de las Calzadas, I took my turn filling my water bottle at the fountain before crossing a long stretch of open terrain without shade or village. The rippling landscape spread people out. Soon, I was walking alone. I climbed a high hill at whose summit I had my first true view of the *meseta*, a patchwork quilt unfurling to the endless horizon in green and yellow with dots of red, all of it capped with a cloudless,

robin's-egg-blue sky. Who cared if it was crowded—this was magnificent! Feeling high, I dashed downhill and into the village of
Hornillos del Camino. All the albergues were full except for one,
where I took one of the three last beds. The albergue was run by
four women and their grandfather in his ancestral home. The sisters welcomed all their guests warmly and the grandfather pro-
ceeded to treat us all as if we were his grandchildren. I felt I had
rolled lucky dice and landed on a goose square.

Seeking dinner in the only bar in town, I ran into the Georgian
and her Viking. They told me that the Orisson family was no
more, it finally had scattered to the wind, with some people rushing ahead to keep to their schedule before having to return home,
others finding the crowds too much and departing, and still others
needing to take some rest days after so much walking. We shared
a table with a business administrator from Catalonia and a spe-
cial-needs teacher from Ireland. Both men admitted that they were
walking to take a break from the intensity of their respective jobs,
but that they hadn't expected the Camino to be so stressful. We all
laughed to keep anxiety from gobbling us up. It seemed that, in
recent days, this was all we pilgrims could talk about: no more trail
magic, synchronicity, and "the Camino guides and provides," just
a lack of trust and angst over finding a bed. The seeker had been
replaced with the survivor. Even I was having a hard time remembering the goose, let alone to listen well and not resist.

After dinner, agreeing with my Orisson friends as usual that
we'd see each other down the trail, I walked back to the grandfather's house, passing a row of villagers seated on a bench. They
were amused by us pilgrims and watched us with humor, their
evening's entertainment. I joined them for a few minutes to learn
that they and their ancestors had been living in Hornillos for two
reasons only, agriculture and serving pilgrims, all the way back to
its heyday in the eleventh and twelfth centuries. I enjoyed their
kind but funny observations of our limps and blisters, our panic
over beds, and our constant hunger and thirst. We indeed were the
quirky ducks of Morlaàs church, waddling this way and that with
myriad antics. Even at the survival level, this peregrinating was

intoxicating and hard to give up. I just wanted to keep walking and be pulled along this great river road.

I fell asleep fast and hard and would have stayed like that, were it not for three young Frenchwomen who turned on the lights in the kitchen across the hall from my bed at three in the morning and began banging pots and rustling silverware to make their coffee and buttered toast. Fuming, I rose and was about to rip into them when I realized it was a losing battle. I dressed, packed, and left, slipping out onto the village's one road in pitch dark and utter silence. No chatter, no rushing bodies to get the first beds, no pavement-clicking trekking poles, a total novelty in recent days. The French girls, who were still back in the albergue, who by then were probably rustling plastic bags as they repacked their packs, had given me a gift.

I climbed over the ridge beyond Hornillos and up onto rippling, chalk-toned plains, which were covered in jagged white stones. At the summit the sun began to emerge behind me, kissing the sky gently from the horizon and then spreading pale pink into the dark blue expanse, which in a blink exploded into an orgasmic psychedelic rainbow with large, tufted, fluffy clouds reflecting rose, deep lavender, and tangerine back onto the earth. The light show illuminated a busy, wild world at work all around the seemingly barren meseta: lizards scurrying, frogs hopping from ditches, birds clinging to fat wheat stems pilfering plump seed heads, bees fussing about in blossoms, and clusters of still sleeping white butterflies clinging in vertical rows to purple thistle blooms. It also released the sweet fragrance of dew mixed with ripe grains and wild grasses. A mist blanketed the crowns of the low hills, at times dipping to touch the path, it, too, reflecting the burst of color and life all around. In this delirious beauty, I walked more deeply into the meseta. In the village of Hontanas I breakfasted in an open café with the company of a rescue greyhound greedily eyeing my egg tortilla. Then I marched across more expanse toward the ghostly ruins of the fourteenth-century monastery of San Antón, its freestanding Gothic walls and arches overgrown with vines. As I passed beneath what had once been the arch of its vestibule, I found a nook set into the wall where pilgrims had left dozens of notes and small offerings. At the monastery's peak, the monks of San Antón, famous for healing and feeding ailing pilgrims, would use the very same nook to leave food, bread, and wine for anyone who arrived at the monastery after it had locked its gates for the night. Modern pilgrims had turned it into a place of petition and offering. I wrote a note of gratitude, asking also for guidance in the decisions up ahead, and tucked it under the other requests.

Only when I turned to go did I see a goose footprint right at eye level etched into the wall behind me, set right on the joint where two Gothic arches intersected. It was clearly a work of modern graffiti, left by a recent seeker on a bit of reinforcing plaster that had been applied to that joint in the deteriorating wall. Had it been the young man from Köln, or his Brazilian brother-in-law, or the Swiss master teacher, or someone else on the esoteric initiate's journey? Did seeing it make me an initiate, too? And why had they left it here?

The answer to the last pondering came when I turned the corner to explore the ruin from the inside: One of the crumbling Gothic walls held the Y-shaped Tau cross, a symbol of the Antonine order of monks. It was also seen as a magical talisman: the monks decorated the tops of the loaves of healing bread they baked with the Tau. But the Tau cross was also connected to the Templars, yet other devoted protectors of pilgrims on the Camino. This connection between the Templars and the Tau had been alluded to back in Puente la Reina with the goosefoot-shaped cross in the Iglesia del Crucifijo. In fact, of late, there was another modern trend on the Camino, some pilgrims taking up the Templar history on the Way and turning it into a knightly quest to find hidden clues leading to hidden treasure left by those warrior monks. (But was the treasure material or spiritual? That was the question. Not surprisingly, pretty much all of these modern Templar treasure seekers were men.) Try as I did to puzzle out the meaning of the goosefoot sign, I couldn't find any clue. But I did find the place elegantly beautiful in how its walls were merging with nature and how they exuded a fresh, healing energy.

I continued toward the castle and town of Castrojeriz, built on an unusually high hill popping up in the midst of flat, open plains and appearing like a ship on calm waters sailing right toward me. At the hill's outer skirt lay the Romanesque church of Nuestra Señora del Manzano, Our Lady of the Apple Tree, a Marian place of so many medieval miracles that they made their way into troubadour songs sung across Europe. Many of the miracles concerned stonemasons saved by the Lady from fatal falls off scaffolding or high walls. Other miracles involved curing pilgrims of all manner of illnesses, especially the blind and the crippled. In my opinion, here was the goose of this stretch of the Camino.

The church door was open, but a locked metal grill barred entry. Inside, several women were busily cleaning the nave and setting fresh flowers in vases on the altar. As my eyes adjusted to the muted interior, I could just make out the sculpture of Mary. According to legend, Saint James had been riding his great white horse across the sky when he saw Mary in the apple tree. So astonished, he landed with his horse in a screeching halt, and the horse's hoof left a deep impression on a stone that is now in the church's foundation. Once again, Mary appeared via a natural channel, this time an apple tree. If you were to cut an apple in half along its horizontal midsection, the seed pattern revealed is a five-petaled flower, called in the ancient world the Star of Venus. I wondered if Castrojeriz, like Estella and so many other Marian sites in France and Spain, had once been a veneration place for Venus, or her other goose-associated sister, Diana, a.k.a. Artemis, a.k.a. Mistress of Animals.

I climbed along a central terraced road leading into the town built into the side of the hill below its castle. Though the castle was in ruins, it was no less impressive. By then it was late afternoon, and locals began streaming out of their houses to exercise, run errands, and gather on the squares for their daily visits with each other. Despite the late hour for walking and my enjoyment of the town, I wanted to keep going. I left Castrojeriz and continued into a broad ravine and up another, steeper hill. I slowed and flagged and wished I were back in Castrojeriz. But a flutter of finches, sparrows, and small black-and-white birds I couldn't identify jetted across my path, some landing on flower stalks, all playfully restoring my energy. At the summit I saw flowing fields of wheat and sunflowers fanning into the distance. Just visible at the farthest reach was a sturdy rectangular stone building in a tree grove near a riverbank, the old monastery church of San Nícolas that had been converted into a pilgrim's albergue by the Italian association of pilgrims. Excitedly, I made my way there to find numerous pilgrims and two hospitaleros milling about, preparing for the evening. The albergue was full but beautiful, and I stayed long enough to see inside, a high ceiling with Romanesque arches. Beds were arranged on one side and the altar with a circle of chairs on the other. In the center was a large wooden table for communal, candlelit meals. The place had no electricity. One of the Italian hospitaleros stamped my passport and advised me to cross the river, where he was sure I would find a place to sleep in the farming hamlet of Itero de la Vega.

Sweaty, thirsty, and no longer hungry, I crossed the Pisuerga River as the day grew late. I felt as if I walked in a maze, circling around over and over, going from bed to meal to drink but not moving forward, so much like both the inn and labyrinth squares in the Game of the Goose. Soon after passing Itero's village church, I found a pilgrim inn. All the bunks were taken, but several single private rooms remained. Their day's chores done, fellow pilgrims were lounging in the inn's large backyard, feet up, sipping cold beers. Chickens clucked and pecked at the earth around them.

I washed up and joined the communal dinner in a large dining room. The innkeeper led me to a table with six pilgrims and sat me near a quiet brother and sister from Dusseldorf who were "walking for fun," and a Norwegian psychiatrist on Camino for "a mental cleanse." Farther down the table sat a taciturn Frenchman on holiday who preferred to speak to no one. Next to him was a retired couple from Chicago who told us that they opted out of their usual luxury cruise vacation because they had just seen the movie *The Way* and wanted to follow in Martin Sheen's footsteps. After these preliminary introductions, the Europeans ignored us

Americans, apparently deeming us people without culture. But when our host came to take our order and it became clear that I was the only person present who spoke Spanish, I saw some about the table eating crow as I helped sort out everyone's choices. Our host left and the Norwegian sheepishly filled my glass to the rim with red wine.

"Tell me more about your mental cleanse," I asked.

"I walk the Camino every year, the same route, the familiarity, the long days of walking, the simple food and accommodations all discarding a year's worth of accumulated psychic trash from my mind, most of it from the demands of my work, but some also from my family. It's good to take a break from both."

"Do you return home free of all the unwanted debris?" I thought about the long-haired Australian woman and so many others coming to the Camino to come to terms with something difficult in their lives. This was hardly a cruise or a holiday.

"With proper personal boundaries so you don't pick up more detritus, yes," he answered.

"How about judgment of others?" I asked as sweetly as possible. Wasn't that a can of crap, too? He raised his eyebrows and then let out a barking laugh.

"Touché. You are right. Sometimes the boundaries should be with ourselves, and we should not mind what others think, or waste our energy pushing our ideas on others. We must honor our own walk and listen to what comes up each day and deal with it." He reached the carafe across the table and poured wine for the Chicagoans and the Frenchman.

Early the next morning, after a quick coffee and toast in the bar, I walked into the dawn and infinite flat wheat fields as far as the eye could see; the trail cut straight through, a direct line to eternity and Kansas. A snail with a pale yellow shell and dark brown spiral pattern slid slowly across the path. I stopped and watched the whole surging universe in and of himself. When I returned to walking, I let myself slow it down, take my time, even if it was all monotony up ahead. This was where the cleanse could be most potent, where few distractions kept us from the work. Going at my own snail's pace, I arrived in Boadilla del Camino well after my companions from Itero had passed through. After a second breakfast in an albergue with an oasis-like garden, I followed an irrigation canal that was flush with birdsong coming from its reeds and wild yellow irises growing on the water's edge. A white heron waded in and froze still, waiting for its breakfast to swim past. Countless frogs harmonized in a boisterous chorus, their tune in rhythm with the flowing eddies on the water's surface. Enchantment took me all the way into Frómista.

Last to arrive once again, I found the albergues were full. Yet luck remained with me, and I found a modest place on the square of the church of San Martín. After a late lunch, I went straight to the church. Swallows circled it with the same fervor as those in Torres del Río and Tosantos, turning round and round the many-towered church with engraved corbels on its three levels, over 300 of them, depicting animals and humans over 800 years old. The birds made it feel like living theater.

I looked at each corbel using the zoom function on my camera lens to go in close, turning like the birds, and photographed the face of a jeering, toothy, giant; bibulous men with wine barrels and immodest, swollen members; laughing dogs; grinning wolves; flippant rabbits; wisecracking donkeys; friendly lions; snorting pigs; and whimsical horses. All of the images seemed to poke fun at us humans down below. It took me two more circuits before I discovered that here, too, were ducks and geese, three of them, each one located on a different side of the church. One tucked its head under a wing. Another looked out to the horizon. The third waddled aimlessly about. All three appeared as both guardians and pilgrims, much like the ducks of Morlaàs—good-luck creatures and loyal companions.

A caretaker arrived at the church and opened it up. Just as I stepped inside, I saw a carved capital depicting a gathering of swallow-like birds, all of them swarming around one bird holding a Eucharist host in its beak and offering it to another. The air and energy inside the church changed from motion and drama to stillness and harmony. I could feel it penetrate my cells. The church's proportions were based on sacred geometry and were meant to elicit balance in every way, from physical wellbeing to acoustic perfection. One sung note would echo like celestial music across the walls. Built in AD 1066, it was early and pure French Romanesque, which also promised that the sculptures held older stories and ideas than later churches that came under more vigilant Catholic Church control. I found a pamphlet on a side table that detailed the corbels, reinforcing this idea, right down to the church's restoration in the early twentieth century, when more risqué corbels had been removed and stored away and replaced with safer floral or geometric themes. Many were vivid depictions of the facts of life, as any medieval person living on a farm would know.

As we are no longer in the prudish early-twentieth century, the booklet's writer happily detailed the scenes no longer here: all of which depicted humans in various states of sexual exploration, from self-pleasuring to mutual pleasuring and the many positions one could assume to do it. These were similar to another church in Spain, the booklet noted, located just north of here, which had preserved its corbels without removal and censure. It was in the remote off-the-beaten-track village of Cervatos, near Reinosa, as it happened, which was at the source of the Ebro River, the same gateway to the north that the Bordelaise in Atapuerca had suggested I take. And now, here I was, in Frómista, which was right on the train line going to Reinosa. Heading west from there, as the flying ducks of Burgos had mapped, would land me square in El Sidrón. It seemed too perfect, and with too many coincidences to not be a sure sign. But I had no firm book contract yet, even if prospects were good. If I went north now, I risked abandoning a walk I had worked hard to make happen, and with no guarantees. Nagging resistance tugged at my solar plexus. I grew stubborn. I then bargained, a fatal move with both God/dess and the Camino: I'd wait for another sign, and if it was clear and sure, I'd leap.

Feeling foolish but light, I went back outside into the golden, sunlit square. A group of pilgrims sipping wine and beer under colorful umbrellas at an outdoor café invited me to join them. I went into the bar to order a glass of wine and saw a sulky pilgrim at the bar staring at his beer. He looked over to me as I placed my order with the bartender, but I couldn't tell if his expression was angry or depressed, or both.

"I'm Rohan from Ireland," he said, extending his hand, then pulling it back before I could shake it. "And please don't tell me you're a fucking hippie pilgrim."

"A what?"

"A *fucking hippie pilgrim*," he said loudly and emphatically, pointing toward the table outside. "People who are here for fulfillment and meaning and some sort of *fucking enlightenment*. Well, fuck that!" He pounded his fist on the bar, jostling his glass and mine, which the bartender had just set down. He gave Rohan a stern look. I paid quickly and took my glass up, about to make a fast retreat, when Rohan continued, his tone suddenly soft. "Look, I just want to say to them, just walk, just *fucking* walk. What's wrong with being here just to walk?"

"Why can't one person just walk, and another seek fulfillment or enlightenment?" I asked, knowing it could be a trap.

"You really don't get it," he said, patient but exasperated. "They are the problem; they say they are here for enlightenment, but they do anything but. They walk through nature but do not see it, and worse, they keep to themselves, get caught up in each other's dramas, don't notice the local villages they walk through or talk to the villagers. They drop litter, demand things of people without a thank you, relieve themselves in a farmer's field, and at night seek physical pleasure but say they're here to find enlightenment. Well, fuck them." He took a swig of beer. I was beginning to understand what troubled him, but then he took an unexpected turn.

"As long as we still live in the fucking patriarchy that has overtaken all of Europe and all of the world, until we buck that system of exploitation, we're all fucked! There will be no enlightenment until everyone has a fighting and fair chance. We need to stop thinking so much of ourselves and more about others and the earth. We need…" he trailed off. I saw tears welling in his eyes and wondered how many beers he'd nursed to arrive at this point. "We need kindness," he whispered. I actually liked him. He was honest, even if kind of messed up. I also felt that part of his anger was from being left out.

"Come join us," I gambled.

"Fuck that," he said, wiping his eyes with the back of his hand.

I let him be and went out. At the table now gathered three Dutch cousins looking to party, a young German entirely focused on a beautiful Italian woman, and her two walking companions from France who acted aloof and looked miffed by the German. They talked about others, about who was walking how far from where, how much or how little they carried, who had hooked up with whom, how to win the bed race, why were Spanish towns so quiet in the afternoon, and on and on, caught up in a bubble. I understood Rohan, heard his warning, and also realized that right now, he was the most honest and interesting pilgrim among us. Just walk and lay all the babble aside. *Just*, however, had deeper meaning than I'd first heard. It meant to make the walk while being fully present and to see and feel and revere and honor—and cut the bullshit. Rohan was like Sa'di, my mother's favorite Persian poet, a mystic from the thirteenth century who was also an avid pilgrim, heading off to a holy site at the drop of a hat for the power of pilgrimage to completely change one's life and perspective. In his verse, Sa'di rails against pilgrims who act holy and better than others but who return home unchanged by the pilgrimage. Pilgrimage is supposed to change you, knock the dust off, throw you together with people from far-flung places, open your eyes. Sa'di wondered, how could a person walk and return and not be changed? How could people continue to judge, act holier than thou, and close themselves off from the unknown?

I quickly finished my wine. My stomach was rumbling, surely from hunger even though I'd had a late lunch. I returned to San Martín's church *just* to be there. It had a stunning sculpture of a Black Madonna, a twentieth-century modern rendering of the twelfth-century style, that I had only quickly glanced at on my first pass. I sat at her feet and let the peace and perfect harmonies of San Martín's stones wash over me. On the central altar was Jesus on the cross and, to his side, Saint James the pilgrim. Good company, all.

It was only here that I recognized the sign. It had definitely been loud and clear: the shouting Irishman. Rohan was doubtless an official spokesman for the Mistress of Animals, La Reine Pédauque, the Mother Earth, the goose and the goddess, and all that was just and fair. He had the courage to say the emperor had no clothes. I laughed, then took deep breaths and lingered more in the cool calm. In the pause between breaths I heard the message as if Mary had whispered it into my ear: *Go north.* My gut rumbled again, but there was no pull of resistance this time. North it was to be, then, like the two ducks of Burgos, following Mary, French folklore, and the Neandertals. I had a light dinner and turned in.

At midnight I woke to sudden pain, as if someone had punched me in the stomach. I managed to reach the bathroom in time and spent the remainder of the night there, purging an invisible invader from both ends. By five in the morning I was able to crawl back into bed and grab two hours of rest before rising and gingerly walking to the station, my body sore and my head full of fog. I stopped at a small grocery for sparkling water, yogurt, and a banana, and then limped to a bench to wait for the train. Somehow, I managed to dig out my French cell phone, which I had not used since calling for help for the pilgrim who had slipped and broken her wrist weeks back in Navarra. I found a place to stay in Reinosa, hung up, and prayed I would get there soon, without incident.

I had asked for a sign and gotten two, both explosive: Rohan and food poisoning. The Camino gave gifts. The Camino gave gut punches. A renewed wave of nausea engulfed me, and a new and unexpected path opened before me. I was now on another mythic path, one to see the older Romanesque folklore that once inhabited Frómista, one to the source waters of the Ebro, one to the Neandertals. And though all of it still pursued the goose, I still felt deep sadness to leave the Camino, especially like this.

THE EBRO

THE TRAIN THREADED through Castile's arid hills and into the steeper and greener slopes of Cantabria. The farther it went from the Camino, the more I realized how stressful the crowds and the heat had been. I disembarked in the softly sloping green mountains of Reinosa, a pragmatic but pretty agrarian, industrial, and skiing town. The air was humid and mineral scented from the nearby source and reservoir of the Ebro. I walked to the center and found my inn; I was one of only two guests, the other one a farm-equipment salesman. I was definitely off the Camino. The inn was peaceful, restful, and inexpensive. I asked to stay four nights.

The young owner, a woman in her twenties, greeted me brightly as her infant daughter slept in a crib behind the reception desk. She, along with her child, husband, parents, and grandparents, lived in a family apartment on the third and fourth floors of the inn, which had been founded by her great-grandparents. The family also ran a dairy farm in the hills nearby, she told me as she led me to my room, and I could enjoy their butter and milk with my breakfast in the morning. We passed a common room lined with books. I noticed most were devoted to the region's ethnography, geography, and history.

"If you need anything," she said at my door, "don't hesitate to ask." I thanked her, more grateful than ever to be in a good place. She parted, closing my door behind her. I dropped my pack, drank the rest of my water, and collapsed onto the bed, sleeping face down without budging for four hours.

When I woke, I had just enough energy to find a grocery store to purchase more bananas and fizzy water, plus yogurt, rice cakes, and a ginger homeopathic elixir the lady behind the counter swore on for settling a disturbed digestive tract. I returned to my room and collapsed once again. Three hours later, I woke feeling stronger. It was now early evening. This time I went out to see the town that would be my home for a few days, and I strolled deeper into the historic town and walked west along the banks of the Ebro. Soon a sign appeared, reading, "Nacimiento del Ebro," birthplace of the Ebro, which pointed farther west, indicating the underground source from which the first waters of the mythic river that gave its name to Iberia emerged. The waters first pool, then flow east through Reinosa to a manmade reservoir used for water, irrigation, and leisure sports. From the reservoir, the river flows into a serpentine form that slips southeast toward Logroño, the river's midway point, and onward to the Mediterranean. As it goes, it grows larger and larger into a formidable river. Where the washerwoman pulled out Our Lady of the Ebro in Logroño, it is over 150 meters (492 feet) wide.

Some two thousand years ago, Pliny the Elder, in his *Natural Histories* (Book III), wrote about the native Cantabri and the Roman administrative town of Julióbriga, the people who once occupied the place where I now was. Recent excavations on the banks of Reinosa's manmade reservoir unearthed Julióbriga, which Pliny noted was just a stone's throw from the *Fontes Iberis*, the source of the Iberis, and which over time gave its name to Iberia and Ebro, peninsula and river.

This setting reminded me of a similar site in France, the source of the Seine, the great river that eventually flows through Paris but is born in Burgundy. There, the waters also emerge from underground, in a stand of mossy rocks and dense woods, and there, archaeologists found a bronze sculpture in the water. It was of Sequana, the Gallic goddess of the river, standing in a duck-shaped boat. Might there be such a goddess and river connection here too? As I crossed the river on a small footbridge, two ducks below paddled about and made me laugh. They could easily be the same ones who had almost clipped my crown in Burgos.

The road led to the small village of Fontibre, on the outskirts of Reinosa, set in a small oak, maple, and beech forest. Near its chapel was a watery cul-de-sac, and there the Ebro flowed forth from underground. Rising above and hovering over the surface of the water was Nuestra Señora del Pilar, patroness of all Spain, depicted just as she originally appeared to Saint James around AD 44, Mother Mary standing atop a Roman-style pillar. That original miracle had occurred in Zaragoza, site of El Pilar's main sanctuary in Spain and also another historic city through which the Ebro flows. In Zaragoza, it was the second time Mary had come to James. The first time she had visited him in Muxía in Galicia. Both times she came to lift his spirits as he made efforts to evangelize Christianity in Spain. And here she was, like Sequana, in the quiet shimmering pool of Spain's most legendary river and marking out traditional territories—rivers, streams, caves, and mountains—of the older Iberian goddesses who had once roamed here as well. Once again, the new and old were acting as protectors of wellness, justice, innocence, and the earth.

This discovery was worth the effort, though my energy was flagging once more. I turned back toward my hotel, and on the way stopped at a newspaper kiosk to buy a topographical map of the region to aid me in exploring the Ebro and the best footpath to Cervatos and its ancient Romanesque church. I was surprised to see a scallop shell on the map marking the Way. Had I really left the Camino? Seeing the shell bolstered my spirits just as Mary of the Pillar had done for Saint James.

The young innkeeper was closing up for the night when I stepped in. I asked her about the medieval churches of the area and the Ebro and its legacy. She grew excited and showed me a framed map in the vestibule that marked all of the Romanesque churches of the area. "We have a rich medieval history and many legends," she said. She next led me to the common room and pulled several books off the shelves, stacking them in my open arms. "Read these while you are here." She then gave me a peck on my cheek, bidding me a good night as she might a dear aunt. She reminded me that there was a kettle and tea bags in the common room, free for guests to use. I made myself a cup of mint tea, sat at the table, and began reading.

I learned that the Romanesque churches in this part of Cantabria had a different look, where the central moral or Biblical themes common on churches in urban settings were more likely to be interspersed with folkloric ideas from the local and rural world. Here, acrobats and musicians did not necessarily mean only temptation or sin but were also about the real pleasures of the countryside. Gluttony and greed, sins more likely to unfold in urban settings, were less represented here, but lust was amped up. Nearby churches here had more than the usual proportion of erotic scenes, the most famous being the one in Cervatos, a Kama Sutra in stone. I learned that two other churches nearby offered similar lessons, each a few kilometers away. I marked them all on my new topographical map.

I also discovered that the folklore here had older roots, like its neighbors in Basque Country and Asturias and remote parts of Castile, León, and Galicia. Here, too, was the fierce feminine divinity, the Asturian *xana* and the Basque Mari and lamia, known as the *anjana* in Cantabria. Anjanas also are believed to dwell in springs—like the Mary at the Ebro's source, and caves, like Nájera's Madonna, all protecting innocence, justice, and nature.

I took the books with me to my bedside, and after a little more reading, drifted off into deep sleep—that is, until my gut woke me with a renewed rush to the bathroom.

MISTRESS OF ANIMALS

BEFORE ONE OF those mad rushes, I awoke in the midst of a vivid dream: I was walking to the *nacimiento del Ebro* and stood before the statue of El Pilar. My eyes followed the lines of her long hair and robe down to her feet, which I discovered were goose shaped, like La Reine Pédauque's. Another mad rush in the middle of the night caught me in the midst of another memorable dream: I was back in Sarlat, walking in the central square, my pannier in hand as I shopped for the week's food at the Saturday market. I ran into my friend Cédric from Biarritz, and he gave me a beautiful, lacy, floppy hat to protect me from the sun. "To keep you safe and well," his dream persona said.

As the sun cracked through the shades, I rose feeling a little stronger than the day before, and I even felt up for breakfast. The butter and milk, which came from my hostess's farm, was a pleasure to eat and felt more nourishing than usual. After breakfast, I left to find the closest church marked on my map, that of Bolmir, an easy stroll just east of Reinosa on the way to the Ebro reservoir. I left paved roads for dirt lanes, where I was surprised and delighted to feel that familiar underground thrumming of leyline energy pulsing up into my feet from the soft earth.

The Bolmir church was wrapped on all sides by ancient oaks that parted to reveal walls on which folkloric sculptures seemed to tumble: sculpted, coiling snakes; magical frogs; cavorting lions; grinning boars; horses and bird messengers; and a few unabashed Sheila-na-gigs showing their privates. Originally this was not considered an obscene gesture—that's a modern reading—but was a reminder of Mother Earth's womb, from which we all come.

I felt good and pressed on, climbing up a slope and farther east, entering the grounds of the ongoing archaeological excavations at Julióbriga. It was an Iron Age Cantabri settlement over two thousand years ago and a Roman settlement from the first century AD. The Romans abandoned Julióbriga in the fifth century. In the Middle Ages, locals used stones from Roman structures to build the small church of Santa María de Retortillo, devoted to Mary, in the midst of the old Roman town. By the time I reached the church, I was privy to a view of a large blue body of water extending beyond it, the Ebro's reservoir.

A sturdy and steep stone stairway led up the outer wall to the church's bell tower. I climbed it for the best views of the territory, to see the velvety green mountains folding around the blue lake and giving form to the snaking river entering and exiting the larger body of water. A herd of thick-maned horses were running along the lakeside. Below my feet, all around the base of the tower and radiating outward from the church, were the skeletal remains of Julióbriga, pushing their contours up from under moss cover and topsoil. Far beyond the water rose the higher peaks of the Cantabrian range, crisscrossing layers of blue mountains capped in snow.

I climbed down and walked around Santa María de Retortillo. Its western entrance held a commanding and robust Mary as the Queen of Heaven, not too unlike the regional *anjana* who similarly protects and defends important water sources. On the eastern apse side, among the sculptures just beneath the roofline, was a stone goose, standing on upright legs, puffing out her belly and flapping her wings and beak. From both the east and the west, this place had its divine protection.

I traced my way back to Reinosa, stopping for a refreshment in Bolmir's village café, where two of the four tables were taken by boisterous locals playing a competitive card game. Their shouting and laughter stopped as I stepped in, and all eyes turned to me.

"We saw you pass on the way up," the bartender said. "We

hoped you'd stop in for a drink to tell us who you are. Are you a pilgrim? We don't see too many pass this way."

"What do you mean?" I asked. "Is this a pilgrim route?"

"Of course!" exclaimed one of the card players, a woman with fiery red hennaed hair. "There are many ways to Santiago de Compostela, and the one you are on right now is the Camino route from Santander that passes through Bolmir, Reinosa, and Cervatos and continues south to Frómista to join the Camino Francés."

"It has been so since around the tenth century," piped in a bald man wearing an oversized cardigan as a woman with spiky, gray, short-cropped hair nodded. In a few words, leaving out the sordid parts, I told them my tale, from Saint-Jean-Pied-de-Port to landing here, and my interest to visit Cervatos the next day to see its enigmatic images. I saw them cast glances at each other, then they all returned their eyes on me.

"You have to realize," said the fourth card player, a woman in a bright purple jogging suit with jet black hair, "that people in the Middle Ages didn't see the world as we do today. Don't judge the images in Cervatos from the modern mind's notions. Today, people see those stones as titillating pornography, but they are not, they are more complex than that, and more honest." Their advice delivered, the group returned to their cards. I finished my mineral water, and with enthusiastic *buen Caminos* in my wake, wove back to Reinosa.

It was time to check email. Before departing from Frómista, I had sent a quick message to my family about my new direction, and now I wanted to assure them I had landed in a good place and was getting better. Because my inn didn't have WiFi, I searched for a café. Not only did I find one with connectivity, but it also had a wonderful chef who made me a fragrant and reviving chicken noodle soup. I settled in, and with a hot bowl pulsing steam laced with the scent of paprika and garlic before me, I pulled out my tablet to find two new messages.

"Shortly after you wrote about turning north," Miles wrote, "I was already seeing a sort of egg-shaped route under your feet." He was right: after my research in Spain's north was completed, I would be looping back to Sarlat, and the whole loop looked like an egg. Miles got the goose humor in addition to having total faith in me. Reading his words was better than my chicken soup.

The other email was from my agent: I now had two firm contracts, one for each book. It was time to get cracking. I sat back, stunned at the timing. Both joy and relief flooded my bones. I was glad I was in Reinosa, courtesy of Camino timing and grace, however rough.

That night was less traumatic but still testing. I woke several times, once again, but didn't have to rush quite so desperately to the porcelain. This time, though, I was drenched in sweat, and my dreams, still vivid, were also unsettling. After a breakfast of toast and tea, feeling somewhat patched together, I filled my water bottles and stuffed rice crackers, yogurt, and a banana in my pack, along with my topographical map and compass, and stepped south to Cervatos. Reinosa's industrial outskirts released me onto a dirt path into a narrow and lush green valley. Birds flew across the path, trilling with song. Horses grazed in the small meadows, many of them with newborn foals on spindly legs nuzzling their mothers for milk. To my surprise, the yellow arrows of the Camino appeared. I saw no people. An hour later, I walked over a footbridge into the tiny hillside hamlet of Cervatos, its church visible on its highest point. The houses surrounding it were all pretty, made of stone, with well-tended kitchen gardens. Wildflowers swayed in any uncultivated fields. The whole setting made me feel as if I had stepped into a Brothers Grimm fairytale.

I climbed up to the church. Just opposite the apse and across the small street were a grandmother and grandson seated on their terrace in rocking chairs facing the church. I greeted them and they lifted their hands in silent welcome. Then I turned toward the apse and had to stop myself from gasping aloud. Every corbel and capital was like a chapter in a medieval sex manual, offering up carvings of every possible position. Many showed men with the burden of such large penises that they could not stand. Others, to balance things out with the opposite gender, were labia-fanning Sheila-na-gigs. I looked sheepishly over my shoulder toward the grandmother and grandson to see that they were ignoring the whole spectacle—both me and the church. It was all too familiar, too ho-hum, too natural for them to give a hoot. They rocked back and forth and stared into a space somewhere beyond the church and me. I adjusted my attitude and walked around, trying to look at the images as a person of a thousand years ago might have, as the card player of Bolmir had advised.

I began to see a bigger picture, and the setting as being one for the herders and farmers of the day, for whom these facts of life were evident in nearly everything they did. Turning the corner to the west entrance, I found a figure that was bigger than any of the other engravings on the wall around it: a large, winged woman at whose breasts two hybrid creatures—part eagle, rabbit, and lion—nursed. The sculpture could have just as easily been from an ancient Greek temple as from medieval Spain, for here was Potnia Theron, Artemis, the Mistress of Animals, and the goddess of the wild and the innocent.

Art historian Tessa Garton, specialist of the Romanesque on the Camino routes to Santiago de Compostela, especially those in this region, has written that often the messages in the stones are mixed and can be a befuddling blend of official Catholic Church-approved and local and unofficial (read: profane, sacred with strong pagan interpretation, folkloric). In this way I could see how the Mistress of Animals survived as Mother Earth, who created us and who now feeds us from her breast. Later, Mary became that vessel, most pointedly when she appeared as Nuestra Señora de la Leche, suckling the baby Jesus. That image rose in the Middle Ages with the growing cult of Mary in Europe, which gained momentum just as the Church was clamping down on people's lives and controlling every aspect of it, snuffing out the old forms of worship, especially when it came to nature spirits and goddesses. But people found another way in, through Mary. She still gave her breast to feed us, with the official Church interpretation of that being that we mortals receive divine grace through her mother's milk. It all sounds pretty syncretic to me, and like a move on the Church's part to hold the tenuous gains it had maneuvered.

This Mistress of the Animals in Cervatos was made sometime in that earlier transition period, when symbols were still migrating and had footholds in both old and new ideas. I looked more closely at the western gate, studying its arches and corbels, and noticed that there were yet more engraved images set between the corbels, acting as square spacing tiles. One, almost directly above the Potnia Theron image, showed a woman with two snakes suckling at both breasts. She seemed to smile at me, as if to say, *Good, I'm glad you didn't miss this snake and goose-footed clue.*

I checked the dates of the church's construction. It had been built in two periods, in 1129 and 1199, dates that bracketed the period of migration of this image moving from that of mother goddess to Eve and sin. The church in Cervatos preserved the twelfth-century dynamic of old to new and kept alive a time and place where the new idea had not yet been fully written in stone, even as it usurped an older image. It occurred to me that, like Oô at the source of the Garonne and Sequana at the source of the Seine, here, too, was the mother goddess persisting at yet another river source—the Ebro. The serpent was not only the life force born of the goddess and a leyline of energy mapped on the earth but was also a river.

I came back to the front of the church to find the grandmother and grandson still sitting in their chairs but now fast asleep. Disproportional fatigue hit me for the short distance I'd walked. Just as I wondered how I would manage to walk back, an older man passed me, and called out, "*¡Ánimo y fé y buen Camino, peregrina!*" It was all I needed to rally to Reinosa.

PREHISTORIC PILGRIMS

AS THE DUCKS of Burgos fly, El Sidrón cave and its forty-nine-thousand-year-old Neandertal residents were a straight flight northwest from where I was. On land, reaching the center of the mountains of Cantabria's neighbor, Asturias, required two trains, one north and the second west. I made an early start, feeling rested and stronger than I had in several days, and I was even optimistic, though I was heading out without reservations. I remained positive—so happy to be upright and to have slept through the night—even when I learned it was a holiday weekend, that of Corpus Christi. Though a religious affair, I knew Spaniards well enough to know that celebrating the transubstantiation of Christ's body and blood into bread and wine still meant a party.

I slipped west on the second train along the northern edge of the Picos de Europa, the steepest and highest slopes of the Cantabrian mountains and got off in Villamayor, El Sidrón's nearest habitable neighbor, a bucolic traditional village of stone and timber houses with jutting wood balconies built along the south bank of the Piloña River.

Two trout fisherman were casting their lines into the river as families set up picnics along the waterfront. The air was crisp with pine scent and the smell of grilling meat, and several men were busily setting up festival tents at the nearby campground. As I left the train platform I asked the first local I met about a place to stay. He wrinkled his brow: every place was booked. But he began contacting the village grapevine and quickly someone heard of a neighbor whose holiday renters had just canceled. Within moments, a woman met me, eager to offer a good price for two nights. As we walked to her apartment, she suggested we stop to let me do grocery shopping at the village store, which was about to close.

"The only places open this weekend will be the village bar and the campground, which is going to hold a big music festival with open-fire grilled meats, and lots of *sidra*," she said, referring to the hard cider that is a specialty of Asturias, which boasts ample apple orchards.

Stomach-friendly groceries in hand, I followed my host down a narrow, hedge-rowed lane away from the village center, past grazing sheep in a tiny meadow, to a little stone cottage surrounded by massive purple hydrangeas and more sheep. Though no longer in Castile or Cantabria, I was still in the realm of northern folklore. Here, the anjana, lamia, and Mari were called *xanas*, female bird-footed spirits who inhabited rivers, springs, and caves and acted the same on behalf of nature and justice. I wondered if one inhabited the ancient El Sidrón Cave or the Piloña River.

My hostess left me to unpack after I assured her I would call if I needed anything. I couldn't believe my luck as I went from room to room: I had my own cozy cottage with a full kitchen, dining room, bedroom, and large bath. I squealed with delight when I saw the washing machine, and put all my clothes in it. Having wrapped myself in two plush towels, I made myself a pot of soup and sank with relief into the pleasure of safe shelter and good food. I hung my clothes on the line and burrowed in for a good nap.

Later, as the festivities amped up, I dressed in clean clothes and walked back into the village to the twelfth-century Romanesque church in its center on the main square. As I admired its corbels, almost all of them featuring the heads of dragons, some spewing water, others swallowing creatures that looked either like squid or humans, a local passing by told me that the church was built both for local worship and to receive pilgrims on their way to Santiago de Compostela. Once again, I was on a tributary of the Camino, one that joined the Camino del Norte up north and the Camino Francés to the south. Why had I ever worried about leaving the Camino? It was impossible! I grinned with joy as I wandered the settlement and visited the campground for a glass of refreshing frothy cider. A man poured it for me, holding the bottle in one hand over his head and a glass in the other at his thigh, letting loose a lightning bolt of golden liquid arching over his head and shooting into the vessel. This is the traditional way Asturians aerate their effervescent elixir—not an easy feat. I happily took the proffered glass and gathered with others around a drum flickering with a warming fire. The society was idyllic and welcoming, but my energy waned all too quickly. I finished my glass and returned to my little cottage for soup and sleep.

Festivities went on all night—music, drums, fireworks—and I slept through it all until a procession of bagpipers blasted me out of bed in the morning as they passed along the lane. I threw open my window in time to find the whole village trailing behind them. I dressed and ate breakfast while studying a tourist map my hostess had given me of the mountainside. It lacked the details of a good survey map but showed that El Sidrón was a few kilometers away, easily accessed through a nearby mountain settlement. I slipped a water bottle into my shoulder bag with the map, threw on a sweater and my rain parka, and followed the last remaining villager to the campground. The pipers were there, still sending up a cacophonous song. I took the small bridge to the other bank of the Piloña, waving to the trout fishermen I'd seen the day before as they were casting their lines once more in a state of deep concentration and bliss.

As soon as I was on the other side, the bank steepened, the forest closed in, and all sounds of song and chatter evaporated. It was as if I had slipped through a veil to another world, one not too different from when Neandertals lived there fifty thousand years earlier.

It felt strange to be there and even stranger to hike without the reassuring weight of my pack. I climbed higher and began to realize that the lines marking roads and distances on the map were all wrong. I followed the mountain road I'd stepped onto and used my compass to confirm that it made switchbacks that veered away, not toward, the cave site located at the foot of the hill on the other side of the valley once I summited this hill. When I finally arrived at the village that I believed to be the one on the map, there were no paths leading from it down the valley. All was fenced off and wild pasture. The village seemed abandoned, dashing my hopes to find a local to ask for guidance. Thick gray clouds blotted out the sun, adding to the heavy mood of the day and place I was hoping to visit.

In 1994, spelunkers exploring the limestone passages of the hillside that I wanted to reach had entered a narrow cul-de-sac in the subterranean rock and seen a human skullcap on the cavern's surface. They left it untouched and quickly reported it to authorities, everyone thinking these were yet more remains of victims of the Spanish Civil War who had been taken to remote places and shot by Franco's thugs. It was an unfortunately recurring theme across Spain, especially in Asturias, a region known for resisting the fascists, where many members of the resistance also hid in caves and tragically, at times were discovered by the enemy and dispatched on the spot. Palpable relief came when investigators discovered that the bones were from some forty-nine-thousand years ago—too old for modern mayhem.

As paleoanthropologists and paleogeneticists puzzled through the many bone fragments unearthed at El Sidrón cave and conducted successful genetic analysis of the DNA fragments they were able to recover from the bones, they found they were handling the remains of thirteen people, seven adults and six children, all Neandertals. The genetics also informed them that many in the small group were related. Furthermore, based on regular and repeated cut marks on the bones, it appeared their bodies had been butchered, either for food or for some sort of burial ritual involving defleshing the bones. Whether for ritual or for survival, cannibalism seemed to be the best explanation. It turned out that their fates were as grim as the deaths of those who were murdered by Franco.

The sun remained obscured. The now insidious fatigue returned, and I was not sure how far I had to go and how I would get back. I panicked when I felt a wave of nausea.

Suddenly, there was a sign of life: A couple emerged from one of the three houses clustered before me in the settlement. Both looked as if they had partied all night in the campground below, worse for wear, but they were alive. I ran over to them, explaining my mission and asking if there was a footpath behind their house that would let me climb down the meadow and over the ridge to the cave. They looked at me as if I were mad.

"You're near as a bird flies," the woman said, "but there's no direct path from here." I would need to take a small road, which she pointed toward, off to the side, which would lead away, and then, after several kilometers, pass a trailhead marking a footpath to the cave, another kilometer beyond.

My day was quickly turning into a forty-kilometer roundtrip, a tough distance even when I was in better form. My energy was plummeting. I saw that my water was almost gone, and it was not a good time to tempt dehydration. What a fool I was. I must have looked pathetic because the woman offered a solution.

"My husband is about to head up to our pasture to feed the horses," she said. "He can drop you off at the trailhead." He didn't seem thrilled, but he acquiesced. I wasn't all too thrilled, either, taking in his grizzled and unwelcoming expression. I cast a quick glance at my phone; it still received a signal. I accepted.

We trundled up the hill on a single lane dirt road in a beat-up Fiat. The man spoke in monosyllables but managed to call into question my sanity. A middle-aged woman. Alone hiking. To a Neandertal cave. On Corpus Christi. I couldn't resist the irony of his statement and cast caution to the wind.

"Why not?" I said. "Both Corpus Christi and El Sidrón concern a kind of cannibalism."

Rather than snarl, he let out a chuckle, the downturned frown turning into a slightly upturned smile. When he dropped me off at the trailhead, he gave me clear instructions in more than monosyllables, not only for getting to the cave but back to Villamayor.

As his car disappeared around the bend, I descended onto a bramble- and vine-covered path into impenetrable oak woods. Thorny vines blocked the passage at several points, making it necessary to find another way around while keeping my eye on the nearly invisible track. After several misleads and dead ends, I finally stood at a rock face deep in the dark valley, looking at the cave entrance, itself well secured and covered with more vines and brambles after having been closed at the end of the last excavation. But still, the whole point had been to stand there, see what this place was like, feel its contours and landscape firsthand with my own senses and understand the context of a 49,000-year-old dinner party. I closed my eyes. I smelled damp mineral, musty oak leaves decaying, and an oppressively heavy weight, perhaps my own state of being or my overactive imagination. When I opened my eyes, I saw extraordinarily beautiful and pure nature wrapping around me like a velvet cape. The sun was coming out. My mood and my sense of hope rose. I gulped my last drop of water and climbed out of the valley, moving as fast as I could to reach water and shelter before nightfall, a maneuver that was better than any other to make me feel compassion for those who had gone before, both Neandertals and medieval pilgrims trusting all around them to see them through.

The sun was setting by the time I crossed the bridge and the campground's welcoming festive fairy lights and campfires appeared before me and the sound of song and laughter rushed at me. Desperately thirsty and hungry, but not for meat tonight, I bypassed the grilling meats on the open flame and went to the village bar for a large bottle of mineral water and a piping hot bowl of vegetable soup.

Returning to my little cottage, I collapsed. In the middle of the night, once again, I found myself in the repeated rush to and fro from the bathroom for the rest of the night. I was now seriously worried. The next morning, I was back at the train platform, this time heading east and toward Sarlat. That day, listless and foggy, I hoped to get as far as Santander, find a pharmacy, and work out how to return to France from there.

The train came. I boarded and slumped into an empty seat before bothering to take off my pack. A kind woman across the seat from mine helped me wriggle out of it. She spoke only French, a pilgrim too, she told me, having seen the scallop shell attached to my bag. *"Merci,"* I squeaked.

Two men—one small and compact, the other tall and round—watched from across the aisle, pilgrims also. "Hello *peregrina*," the wiry one said. "I am Jesús. This is Guillermo. We're schoolteachers from Gijón!" Leaving the many joining tributaries, I had now joined another main route of the Camino, the Camino del Norte, the northern coastal route that followed the Atlantic coastline to Santiago de Compostela. The two men were all questions. I had mine, too: why were these three pilgrims all looking rather fresh as if they were just starting out, heading east and not west?

"We are beginning this year's stretch of the Camino del Norte from Santander," said Jesús. "We'll then walk west to our home in Gijón," he chirped. Guillermo nodded and smiled. The two had already walked the other routes of the Camino. After they completed the Norte, they planned to tackle the routes in France and Portugal.

"And you?" I asked the Frenchwoman. Talking with my fellows was helping me feel a little better.

"I'm finished for now," she answered. "I will return next year to continue. I ended earlier than I planned; I just couldn't take the crowds. I'm returning home now."

"Where is home?"

"Toulouse. But I'm stopping first to see my cousin in Basque Country." The three then asked about my Camino. I explained my circuitous pilgrimage, leaving out the food poisoning, then half-jokingly said that I was looking for the next sign to guide my way.

"That is precisely why we are so addicted to the Camino!" Jesús exclaimed.

"You never know what will happen," Guillermo added.

"And what gifts await you around the next bend," finished his friend.

"Or ordeals," I threw in my two cents as my insides rumbled.

"But even ordeals become gifts," Jesús insisted.

Sí. He was right. I knew this, and I was often the one who said it. I rallied. Maybe this conversation was the gift. We arrived in Santander, wished each other *buen Camino,* and dispersed like the wind before I could ask the Frenchwoman where in Basque Country her cousin lived.

NIRVANA

I **HAVE LITTLE** recollection of how I managed to navigate my way through Santander's busy harbor. All I remember was walking into the first hotel I saw—a luxury accommodation, outside my usual pilgrim budget—already digging out my credit card for emergency use. The kind woman at the reception desk cheerfully checked me in, offering me an unexpected and reduced pilgrim price. She must have sensed my need because she accompanied me to the elevator, handing me a bottle of mineral water, and punched in my floor number when the doors opened. Six floors up, posh guests entered the elevator as I exited, vast views of the harbor opened below from large windows. I found my room, closed the door, dropped everything, stripped down to my underwear, and, forcing myself to drink all the water in the bottle in my hand, crawled under the lush, comforting covers and slept for hours, waking only once to rush to the bathroom.

When I woke, I pulled myself together and found the neighborhood pharmacist, telling her everything about my symptoms. She asked numerous astute questions that narrowed it down to the most likely source of the food poisoning and offered me a probiotic designed to tackle my particular ailment. I would have kissed her were it not for the wide countertop between us. After a stop in the grocery next door for more bananas, rice cakes, and sparkling water, I returned to my room, took the probiotic, and went back to sleep.

When I woke early the next morning after an uninterrupted night, I knew I had turned the corner. I also knew it was time to get back to Sarlat as soon as possible, that very day, because there I could affect a full recovery and then get to the remaining research for the Neandertal book, which was only possible from there.

But the train and bus schedules had a different trajectory. A bus could get me as far as Hendaye by early afternoon, and from there I would have to patch my way, via several trains, to Sarlat. I considered breaking the journey in Biarritz, hoping to see Cédric. He had offered to let me stay at his place, but I knew it was small and didn't want to impose, especially in my present state. I decided I would call him after I checked into a hotel. I slept most of the bus ride to Irún and Hendaye at the border between Spain and France, but as we neared it I jolted awake to a familiar feeling, that strange but electrifying magnetic pull I'd felt in 1986, the first time I'd crossed there. I only now realized that I had managed to keep my promise to myself to come back and find out what this geography was all about; in fact, I was thick in the very mission of doing so.

The bus came to a stop near a bridge and dropped me off, with the driver indicating I just needed to cross the bridge and the road would go straight to Hendaye's train station. Not with a little irony did I see the bridge's name: the Pont Saint-Jacques, Saint James Bridge. I was just stepping across it when I heard someone calling to me. It was the woman from Toulouse.

"What are you doing here?" I exclaimed.

"Visiting my cousin who lives here," she said, "and now I'm heading home." Her pace picked up as we reached the peak of the bridge's arch, and I could feel she was in a hurry to catch her train. I matched her pace but then slowed as my phone came to life and began vibrating. It felt alien: no one had called me for weeks. I wished the woman *bon retour* and took the call.

"Beebe?"

"*Oui*? Cédric?"

"Tell me, is that you walking across the Pont Saint-Jacques?"

"What?"

"Shouldn't you be halfway across Castile by now?"

"But how do you know this?"

"Look down." There he was, standing on the rails below the

bridge. *How on earth?* He explained. His work for the rail company often sent him to the surrounding areas from where he lived to repair and maintain the rails, and he had just been assigned to work for several days here in Hendaye. "Imagine how strange, on my first day here, there you are, walking across the bridge. I saw you only because I stopped to take a break and happened to look up."

"Strange indeed," I said. Trail magic, I thought.

Continuing to talk to him from the bridge, I told Cédric my story, with all the details. He insisted I stay with him.

"You shouldn't be traveling with food poisoning or staying in hotels," he said emphatically. "Besides, though it is only Wednesday, all the hotels within a hundred-kilometer radius of Biarritz are fully booked for this weekend's annual festival, Waves & Wheels. The bikers are already arriving." I had never heard of the festival but quickly learned that hundreds of motorcyclists from all across Europe and Asia would be descending on the town for a long weekend of music, drinking, surfing, and motoring around, showing off their rigs to each other. I was about to resist Cédric's invitation, but he insisted. He said he was already planning on cooking plain rice and chicken for me and added that it was his duty given how hard the universe had worked to cross our paths. In deep gratitude—and disbelief—I accepted.

There was more trail magic: two mutual friends of Cédric's and mine from Sarlat were coming to the festival that weekend and could drive me home with them. I agreed to take the short train ride to Biarritz and wait for Cédric at the station. He would finish his last hour of work and meet me to show me the way to his home.

"Maybe this will teach you not to go on any more spiritual journeys," he joked before we hung up.

"And yet, of all of the Saint James bridges in all of the towns in France and on all of the routes of the Camino, I had to walk across yours?" I could see him laughing down below the bridge. It was surreal and wonderful.

SA'DI'S DAUGHTER

OVER THE NEXT few days, with Cédric's ministrations, probiotics, rest, fresh sea air, and the albergue nostalgia-inducing atmosphere of eight motorcyclists sleeping on Cédric's living room floor—the two mutual friends from Sarlat and six other strays Cédric's big heart had invited in—I mended well. As soon as I was settled in the apartment, I sent Nadiya a text, letting her know about my expected return to Sarlat and asking if Le Chardon would be available two weeks earlier than I had planned to arrive. I had reserved the weeks I expected to be there ahead of time, but now, with the summer season heating up, I knew the chances of open spots were slim. This was reinforced when I heard nothing back.

While Cédric was at work, I set off on my own, discovering the outlying region was among the ones with the highest concentration of medieval chapels and churches depicting *femmes aux serpents*. Most harkened from the early twelfth century and showed their originating roots more from the Mistress of Animals than from sin. I took local trains and took paths that radiated out to visit several of them, each one reinforcing everything I had learned on the Camino and from historians about the appropriation of deities and symbols by the new incoming faith, as well as how old stories still find a way to take root in new creations. Returning to Biarritz from my last excursion into the countryside, I found that our friends from Sarlat had just arrived. As soon as I opened the door to Cédric's apartment, they rushed me with hugs of joy and demanded to know how I had landed there. They, too, were sure

I would be somewhere near León by then. When I told them my story, they marveled at the timing on the Pont Saint-Jacques and agreed that it was the doing of the Camino. "This is your right path," declared the one who was also a former pilgrim to Santiago de Compostela.

We decided to go out to dinner in celebration. Just before heading out the door I checked my email messages and found one from my mother.

"The way you journey," she wrote, "you are Sa'di's daughter." This was unexpected; tears pricked my eyes. "A lot of Sa'di's poetry," my mother elaborated, "is about his experience on the pilgrimage road. He did not take the straight path either, and ended up seeing a lot of off-the-route places. You are his daughter in spirit." It was high praise for my mother to equate me in any way with her favorite thirteenth-century poet from Shiraz. It also told me that she fully supported the life I had chosen, however much it had caused her to worry in the past. I was becoming who I had always wanted to be, a full-time writer, a part-time nomad, and now, I was heading back to my spiritual home of Sarlat, from where I would do all the research that I needed to complete the writing of the second contracted book.

Feeling outrageous joy and unfathomable luck, I went to dinner with my friends. As Auch had been my last pilgrimage's holy destination on this goose-footed journey, so Biarritz became this one's. Next time, I vowed, it would be Santiago de Compostela. Again, I had no idea how I would pull that off, but I now trusted that the means and the way would arrive with perfect timing.

Just before turning in that night, my phone pinged, and I saw an incoming text message from Nadiya. By some miracle, she wrote, the couple who had reserved Le Chardon for the next two weeks had just cancelled. The place was mine. The Camino's personal event planner had struck again. There was another ping. "P.S." she wrote, "I have a surprise. Will tell you when you get here."

OUR LADY OF SARLAT

TWO DAYS LATER, I piled into the back of my friends' car. Before we rolled out toward Sarlat, I thanked Cédric for manifesting Nirvana on earth and his care and good cooking. He was still chuckling as we drove away. After four hours on winding country roads through rolling river and hill country, with the fields overtaken with sunflowers and radiating grapevines, we arrived in Sarlat. It had been thirty-five days since I'd landed in Toulouse and met Our Lady of Oô. Again, it felt like a lifetime. Nadiya had instructed me to pick up Le Chardon's keys from the shopkeeper across the small path from the apartment. I called her when I had let myself in.

"And the surprise?" I cut to the chase.

"You have arrived in time for my wedding celebration."

It was to take place in a few days, on the summer solstice. "Now that you are here for it, I could use your help."

"Anything," I chirped excitedly. We agreed to meet later to catch up and go over details. I hung up, elated to be home and overjoyed by my friend's good news; she had been through a lot in recent years and had found happiness once again. And thanks to how things had played out for me, I got to be there to share in her joy. Not only does the Camino guide and provide, but it also orchestrates schedules, even if it takes ice storms, food poisoning, cancelled reservations, book deals, and friends standing under bridges to do so.

I looked around the studio and hugged myself. Nadiya had left loving touches here and there—hand milled lavender soap in the bathroom, roses in a vase on the dining room table, a big bowl of local walnuts on the kitchen counter—to fully welcome me home. In more perfect timing, Saint Sacerdos cathedral next door began ringing out the seven o'clock bells, their deep, brassy resonance bouncing pleasingly off the amber-toned limestone walls.

Early the next morning, the familiar ice-shoveling sound from the fishmonger below my window rustled me from bed. Market day dawned, and I dressed quickly. The fishmonger was laying out glistening trout and flats of oysters when I pushed open the door to the street.

"*Bonjour, madame*! Welcome back," the fishmonger called. I bought a dozen oysters from her to share with Nadiya. Next, I visited the goat cheese seller from Rocamadour who was arraying pungent white disks of soft *cabécou*. I acquired some, then moved on to the baker, sausage maker, and wine merchant, and filled my pannier. All the aforementioned then gathered at the baker's table for their traditional market day breakfast, pooling their cheese, sausage, rustic bread, and red wine, and tucking in. I felt with pleasure my familiarity with this kind world and being back in it. Then came a sudden thump on my leg.

"Mr. Stripes!" She meowed loudly, in complaint, as if to say, "Where have you been?"

"I'm back for a whole glorious month," I told her while rubbing her ears and stroking her back. Seemingly appeased, she purred à bientôt in her wake as she sauntered off toward the breakfast club and sidled up to the sausage seller.

I made a beeline to Petrus and Jean's olive and spice table in the neighboring square. Petrus settled me onto a stool behind the stand and plied me with hot tea, walnut cake, and questions, wanting to hear everything. She bagged olives and spices for customers who also began to listen to my tale and chimed in on the potent magic of the Way of Saint James. Several of my listeners had also walked it. Before I knew it, the hour had arrived for me to meet Bernadette at the market café. She was already there, having secured a table in the dappled sun next to a colorful produce stand. We hugged and kissed, ordered *grand crèmes,* and picked up where we'd left off since her last letter.

"I've been reading a lot about the lives of Jesus, the Buddha, and Mohammad," she began. "And I've been thinking a lot about death."

Our mutual friend, Vivienne, who had been Bernadette's nearest and dearest friend since arriving in Sarlat decades earlier, had recently passed away. Despite Bernadette being self-sufficient and solitary, the loss had left her lonelier than she expected.

"I've realized that it is really hard to achieve liberation in the way of the Buddhists," she said. "I feel as if I am already in a bardo state, stuck here, and it troubles me. I am neither of this world nor of the next, and even though I believe all is one and divine, I am being tested and am troubled." She took a sip of her coffee, looking pensively into the cup.

My rock was rocking. Bernadette, too, had been on pilgrimage. I listened and let her talk.

"This is where I think the Muslims got it right," she continued, returning to her books. "They say that to submit, really submit, to God's will, you just have to relax into it." She laughed. "You and I probably won't achieve the ability to pass through all the bardos the way the Tibetans do, but if we just relax and submit, and love and be in it, but not of it, we'll probably come out pretty well, even as we must keep on traveling." Not only did she read the lives of the prophets and sages, but she found a way to elegantly merge their messages into one spiritual practice.

"On to a new Chemin," I said and raised my cup.

"On to a new and glorious Chemin," she said, picking up her cup and gently tapping mine. "Now, tell me about the goose."

I told her about Oô, about not resisting, about the ice storm and Hemingway, the emerging book deals, about Ismael and the crown-strafing ducks of Burgos, about resisting, about food poisoning and Rohan, about Neandertals and Nirvana, and about arriving in Sarlat in time to celebrate a friend's wedding. I told her that I understood the walk was about me wondering if I could make it as a writer and getting a resounding yes, but that the walk, still, as she had said, had only just begun. I marveled at how once one accepted the possible metaphor and symbolism of the ancient goose and duck in European lore, that they uncannily showed up with special messages made just for each of us.

"Come have lunch with me," she said as I finished. "I've already planned it—a lunch to celebrate your return. My table is set for you and Petrus. Just bring something to drink that goes well with Moroccan olive and lemon chicken tajine." I knew immediately what to bring: a dry Breton cider, Vivienne's favorite drink.

After our coffee and before lunch, I returned to the market and wandered the clothing stalls until I found a few threads to purchase that were appropriate for a wedding party. I then wandered more widely and took in the whole town, reacquainting myself with every stone, garden, and living being. I stopped at a wine merchant on the edge of town for a bottle of cider. I passed the movie theatre while returning to the town center to find its marquee lit up with the name of a new film, *Compostelle, Le Chemin de la Vie*—Compostela, the Road of Life—a film by Freddy Mouchard. The next viewing was that evening.

At Bernadette's, Petrus was already there, unwinding after a demanding market day. I popped the cork on the cider and poured it into three champagne flutes. We toasted to Vivienne and to friendship and to the Chemin. Bernadette handed me a book, *L'oiseau et sa symbolique*, by French art historian Marie-Madeleine Davy, on the art and symbolism of birds. A gift.

"I think it speaks to the *Chemin* you just made," she said without further elaboration. We ate and fêted and laughed through the afternoon.

Back at my studio, I made a pot of herb tea and sat at the open window overlooking the square, listening to the laughter and clinking glasses bubbling up from the early evening revelers at the café below. I opened the book and began to read.

Davy wrote about the shared symbolic meanings of birds all across Eurasia, in both art and sacred beliefs and practices. She had found that among the diverse peoples across this massive land mass, birds have long been held as messengers from other realms and also as the ultimate shamanic creatures who can easily traverse all three realms of water, earth, and sky. The book included a whole chapter on birds and snakes, and I knew why Bernadette had given this to me. The connection between the two creatures was real and went back deep in time. As I read, the sun set. I switched from tea to wine, still glued to the book and seated by the open window. The café below was now serving dinner and its outdoor tables were lit with candles.

Birds and serpents, Davy noted, have a common reptile ancestor. One branch of its descendants evolved limbs, feathers, wings, and the ability to fly and swim just about anywhere. The other evolved scales, strong belly muscles, and the ability to shimmy and swim, also just about anywhere. They both lay eggs and have seasonal patterns, molting feathers or shedding skin, migrating or hibernating, disappearing and reappearing. Both creatures—and this stopped me in my tracks—were used to depict the divine Mother Earth, the Mistress of Animals. The goose and *femme aux serpents* on medieval church walls were indeed based on an alchemy older than the Bible or any other Abrahamic text.

I called Bernadette, Our Lady of Sarlat, and thanked her for the book.

"Never forget," she replied, "you're *always* on the Chemin. I wonder where it will take you next?"

After we said goodbye, I realized that the new Camino movie began in ten minutes. I grabbed my wallet, keys, and a sweater and booked it to the theater. I arrived just as the lights dimmed and the film started to roll. The filmmaker Mouchard launched viewers into an esoteric mystery tour, beginning with the chapel of Eunate, the octagonal chapel in Navarra with its outer ring of arches, which he called a spiral meditation, confirming my own theories about the place. He next asserted that the whole Camino was a spiral labyrinth meditation and that this was precisely what the Game of the Goose was: a massive labyrinth-like walking quest on the Camino. The whole purpose of this is to walk a path of spiritual liberation, which has been made possible by walking in and with nature; nature heals us when we open to *her* and commune with *her*. I got goose bumps as I watched, as if the timing of this film and the filmmaker's vision were personal messages, telling me that what I had been tracing had also been tracked by others in similar ways.

The film ended. I stepped out into a dark night, the sky splattered with shimmering bright stars, my mind spinning as I headed back to the cathedral square. I walked past my building and kept going, climbing up the hill behind Saint Sacerdos to the wall that sits between it and the enigmatic twelfth-century tower, the *lanterne des morts*. I sat, dangling my legs, soaking up the golden glow of the cathedral and square below against the velvety night. The stained glass in the apse was fully illuminated by candlelight, revealing the form of Mother Mary standing on a crescent moon in a bright blue gown and ruby red cape. Whether her foot caresses the moon or a serpent, she felt to me exactly like the Mistress of Animals who brought protection, sustenance, and harmony to all on earth.

Mr. Stripes had sniffed me out and jumped up to join me, climbing into my lap. "Hello, Mr. Stripes," I said, rubbing her ears. She meowed and leaned in. My heart burst, overflowing with so much joy, almost too much, all of it delivered in an unbroken flow of remarkable synchronistic days. I suddenly understood better, deeper, what Bernadette and the Camino had been telling me all along: why does it matter, all this worry over being successful? You *are*, simply by doing and being, stepping forward and trusting, learning and expanding. One cycle ends, and another begins. *You're always on the Chemin. I wonder where it will take you next.*

Me, too.

THE SPORT OF JOY

THE MONTH FLEW by. I helped with Nadiya's wedding festivities and visited numerous Neandertal sites, conducted interviews with archaeologists, and spent long hours in libraries and museums. In a blink, the day arrived to return to Toulouse and fly home. I packed my small pack, cleaned Le Chardon, and went to wait at the post office, where a friend was picking me up to take me to the train bound for Toulouse. From there, I would fly to London and change planes for Philadelphia.

Nadiya joined me outside the post office to see me off. When my ride approached, I gave Nadiya a big hug. I could feel one of her one-liners bubbling up. Since I'd first met her years earlier, she was known for spontaneous one-liners erupting from her heart and soul, always potent. Neither she nor I ever knew when they might appear.

"There's only one sport on the planet," she said, "and we're here to do it."

Sometimes, like dreams, Nadiya's one-liners require interpreting.

"Sport?" I asked.

"Yes, sport. One little sport is to be sad, but the biggest and best is to be happy. The sport of joy."

In London my flight to Philadelphia was cancelled, but if I ran fast, a flight to Boston was departing soon from another terminal. I ran. As I went, I pushed away the rising anxiety and decided instead to cultivate the sport of joy. I would roll with the outcome either way. I made the flight with five minutes to spare and landed in Boston late at night. Courtesy of the airline, I had three hours of sleep in an airport hotel before rising to catch the early morning commuter flight to Philadelphia. Bleary-eyed, I took my seat and promptly drifted off to sleep until a woman flopped heavily into the empty seat next to me.

"I can't believe I made it," she sputtered. "My nonstop flight was just canceled and this is my best option for getting to Atlanta this afternoon for a funeral."

"There must be something in the air," I said. "I had a similar experience getting here from London."

"What took you to London?" she asked.

I gave her a brief account of my egg-shaped pilgrimage.

"I know the Camino well," she said. "I'm a spiritual counselor and lead sacred tours."

"To the Camino?" I asked.

"No, on the Inca Trail, to Machu Pichu."

My heart skidded momentarily to a stop. I'd written off the last premonition the long-haired Australian woman had shared with me, about something from this Camino connecting to the Inca Trail. I was sure it was the one thing she'd gotten wrong that night we had dined together in Villafranca Montes de Oca. But no, she'd nailed it and had a perfect batting record. "No kidding," I managed. "Tell me more."

"What I offer on the Inca Trail is very similar to what spiritual guides do on the Camino," she said. "Rites of initiation, rites of transformation, holding the space for people on their journey, and offering counseling when things come up that they want to process through. Pilgrimage is very powerful and when walking in places with potent energy, such as the Camino or the Inca Trail, it can really change a person." She paused. "Death is like that too, the ultimate Camino." The funeral she was going to was that of a dear, lifelong friend. I offered her my condolences, but she waved her hand.

"It's sad, but death itself is nothing to fear. It's the human nervous system that's wired with fear, but once we slip out of fear, joy hits us and the universe expands."

"How do you slip out of the fear?" I asked.

"By meditating, by dancing, by doing anything that makes you fully present and in the here and now. If you bypass the nervous system and let the rest of the body speak, joy naturally replaces fear." *The sport of joy.*

Her words aligned perfectly with my goose-footed quest. I'd become clearer about what mattered to me and had released, I hoped, the outdated things that held me back. I'd sought right livelihood and was inching more and more toward living it in ways I couldn't have imagined. I'd walked in the footsteps of La Reine Pédauque and the Mistress of Animals engraved all along the Camino and had been initiated into deeper connections to life, nature, community, beauty, and the earth.

I also knew I had so much more to learn and to unearth about the goose and her metaphorical board game. I had hardly arrived on the final winning square. There was more searching and dice rolling up ahead. The quest was still unfolding. I had to return to the Camino. As usual, I had no idea how or when, just that I would.

PART III

THE SWAN

A PILGRIMAGE IN FRANCE AND SPAIN

RETURNING

"**THEY ARE ALREADY** heading south," Cécile said as we drove past a flock of wild geese resting in a farmer's just-plowed field, chowing down on bugs. My friend had just picked me up at the train station in Gourdon, a village south of Sarlat, to welcome me and take me home. "Winter is coming early this year," she added, looking at me and then at my svelte pack on the backseat through her rearview mirror. Despite her concern over whether I had packed enough warm clothes, I took this news about the geese as a sign that they were migrating at the time I also returned, nomadic once again. I was jetlagged, elated, but also feeling a foreboding I couldn't explain, plus disbelief that I was actually here again, less than two years since my last visit.

And what an epic two years it had been. The two books, courtesy of the ice storm and Hemingway's mojo, had demanded nearly all of my attention but now sat on bookstore shelves. I had also continued other work, pitching and writing, including new book projects. One had just come to fruition, a contract to research and write a new guidebook on the Camino, the main reason I was here.

Perhaps the foreboding was from the whirlwind of it all: the ink had only just dried on my new contract when I boarded the plane in late September for France. And perhaps it was the realization that I had last left the goose quest somewhere in the middle, perhaps at best along the two-thirds mark of the metaphorical Game of the Goose. When would this Game end? When, if at all, would I land on the final winning square? Either way, I was deep midstream on the path, and I knew from the board game that the final third was the most challenging section. Up ahead were squares 53, the Tower, and 58, Death. Both demanded the ultimate test of letting go, and both had the greatest potential to halt one, at worst, or transform and rebirth one, at best, if a person could rise to the challenge.

"Death itself is nothing to fear," said the spiritual counselor from Boston, whose words returned to me. What a strange, seemingly coincidental, meeting that had been, orchestrated through several flight cancellations to bring a calming message now as I crossed this threshold. Why then the foreboding?

I'd felt it ever since Miles had left me at the curb in Newark Airport. It had been the hardest goodbye of all my prior departures for research trips, and I didn't want to let him go. It had felt as if as soon as I released him, I would be tossed at sea. When I finally relinquished my grip around his waist and watched him get into the car and drive away, I willed myself to take a deep breath and get control over my monkey mind and edgy nerves.

Cécile took me right to Saint Sacerdos on the cathedral square. "We will have a celebration when you return, pilgrim," she said cheerfully. Soon after she drove off, Nadiya met me at the heavy blue door to let me in. She no longer owned the apartment; it had been sold to a new proprietor who was keeping it as a rental property. Nadiya had put me in touch with him to arrange the rental, but for old-time's sake, she had also offered to be the one to meet me with the keys to let me in. I was arriving late enough in autumn that Le Chardon was free, especially for the four short days that I would be there before departing for Saint-Jean-Pied-de-Port. I just needed to touch base, leave some nonpilgrim clothes for when I returned to inhabit the town more fully, and find my grounding again among my friends, especially Bernadette.

As we arrived on the third-floor landing and Nadiya opened the studio's door, I learned there was another reason she wanted to be the one meeting me and letting me in. Yet more news: Le Chardon was for sale again, now by the new owner. Though he had only recently come in possession of the building, his long-term plans had changed. There were already interested buyers eying it as a year-round home, willing to pay the asking price, which was beyond my reach. My four short days there suddenly felt more like saying goodbye than hello; by the time I returned from the Camino, Le Chardon could be gone.

Nadiya left to run an errand, and we agreed to meet for a glass of wine in the early evening. I dropped my pack and walked to the middle of Le Chardon's one big room to stand on the spot where, nearly ten years earlier, the day I'd first stepped into this place, I had experienced, in no exaggerated terms, a rebirth. Every leg of that first journey a decade ago to get here and something about the place itself had begun to loosen unfinished business that for most of my life I'd hidden, carried, and worn like armor. Something about this place had unlocked memories ripe for release and affected a strong catharsis. But it was the land, too, its ancient humanity that somehow had reached out to me as I arrived and had told me that I walked on the shoulders of ancestors and was more than I had imagined, that we all were. On this spot a decade earlier, I had dropped the armor, released the pieces of the past that didn't serve me, and fallen deeply in love with this place that seemed to love me back as fervently. I'd never felt so free, light, open, trusting, naked, or alive. A shiver ran through me, as if the apartment held the somatic memory of that day too.

I had known all along that the possibility might arrive one day that Le Chardon would sell and no longer be open for renting. I had to let it go. I knew that my home was not the apartment but was the place and people, the land, the ancestry, and the beauty of this corner of France. In answer and providing perfect closure, Saint Sacerdos began ringing her resonant bells announcing that it was seven o'clock. I let the vibrations roll over me and do their magic, and then I set off for the large market square to meet Nadiya for a glass of wine. As I reached the plaza, the setting sun was casting rose-orange rays across its ochre stones, making them glow like fire.

After Nadiya and I parted, I wandered a while through the narrow, golden, medieval streets, smelling the rose blooms on the vines growing up the side of limestone walls, greeting the familiar faces of people passing me on the cobblestones. Eventually I wound up at the hill behind the cathedral to take a seat on the wall between the cone-shaped *lanterne des morts* and the church. The sky was now dark-blue velvet, lit with the evening star and crescent moon. As much as I hoped she would, Mr. Stripes did not appear, but the resident *rouge-gorge* was in full voice, perched in the solitary pear tree on the hill and belting out a Queen of the Night-worthy staccato.

I slept so hard that night that even the fishmonger's early morning ice-shoveling did not wake me. By the time I finally stirred, the market was in full swing. I dressed quickly and rushed down the stairs. The moment I opened the blue door, a French tour group passed, led by a guide, heading up the hill to the *lanterne des morts*. "Some think the tower was built and devoted to the pilgrims going to Santiago de Compostela," the tour guide said. The dice were rolled, and the goose game had resumed. I greeted the fishmonger, then ran to catch up with the group. Just then, someone came bounding toward me and bumped demandingly into my legs. Mr. Stripes! I stooped and greeted her just as the tour guide was explaining that tombs had been found around the *lanterne des morts* that may have belonged to pilgrims: Sarlat had been on a tributary route to Compostela, and many pilgrims came here to visit the cathedral and its other sites. That these were the first words I heard as I left Le Chardon, a place perched next to the *lanterne des morts*, felt auspicious.

The group continued on up to another historic site. Mr. Stripes took off to hunt. I returned downhill to the market and plunged in, visiting with familiar faces and purchasing food for my four days. I then wended the way to Petrus and Jean's olive and spice stand for a visit until my appointed hour with Bernadette at the market café. She was already there when I arrived.

"I am reading more on and studying death these days," Bernadette said with a gleeful smile, diving right in, no preliminary chitchat. I felt the skin on my forearms prick. "And resurrection," she added, smiling even more broadly. I sat down and we ordered coffee.

"Tell me more," I said, waiting for the next throw of dice.

42

THE ALCHEMICAL JOURNEY

"**I'VE BEEN WATCHING** this Belgian series," Bernadette began, "*Le Voyage Alchimique*. A part of it is about the Chemin de Saint-Jacques, the Camino de Santiago, not only to Santiago de Compostela but also onward to the ocean. You should watch it before you leave. It will prepare you," she said. "The film delves more deeply into the metaphor of alchemy, that each person is the master alchemist of his or her own life, and that everything is connected." She sat back, pleased. "Just as the Game of the Goose is a metaphor, so is alchemy, both leading the initiate to be transformed through walking and seeking, to become a spiritual master, where the goose becomes the swan.

"What does this have to do with death?"

"And resurrection," she clarified. "Death *and* resurrection. Death is never the end."

"How long have you been waiting to tell me this?"

"A while, but its timing had to be when you returned to walk again. I think a lot about this goose walk of yours. I think this is the next piece to launch your next journey."

We finished our coffee, and Bernadette had more shopping to do. "Come over for tea this afternoon, and we'll watch *The Alchemical Journey* together."

Four hours later I climbed up the wooden stairs to Bernadette's fourth-floor apartment. The door was ajar, and she called to me to let myself in. Her windows offered an expansive rooftop vista of the medieval town, including a bird's-eye view of Saint-Sacerdos cathedral, its bell tower anchoring everything around it. Beyond were the chaotic oak-covered hills with hard-to-pin-down, maze-like contours that wrapped around the town in its craggy protective valley. Bernadette stood at her kitchen counter pouring hot water over bundles of fresh mint and spoonfuls of gunpowder green tea that she had stuffed into a large silver Moroccan teapot with a swan's-neck spout—one of the habits she brought back with her from southern Morocco after living among the Chleuh for two years.

Her tablet was set up in her living room next to two overstuffed chairs. When the tea was ready, we took our cups and settled in. Bernadette hit *play*. Enter the Belgian mystic Patrick Burensteinas, narrator and alchemist, leading the viewer in a seven-part film series. The fifth part, which we were watching, was entirely devoted to the Camino. It began in Brussels and journeyed to Chartres, then Mont-Saint-Michel, Rocamadour, and finally, all across the north of Spain on the Camino Francés and onward, not only to Finisterre but also to other key sites on Galicia's coast. The film concluded in Paris, always a good idea. Burensteinas's itinerary followed the footsteps of the fourteenth-century Parisian scribe, manuscript merchant, and celebrated alchemist Nicolas Flamel on his historic pilgrimage to Santiago de Compostela.

Legend recounts that Flamel found an esoteric Hebrew manuscript and made the pilgrimage to Compostela to find someone who could translate it. In León, he met a doctor who was a *converso*, a Jew who had been forced to convert to Christianity, who could translate the document. Alas, the doctor died before he completed the task, but nevertheless, what he did translate was enough to unlock two alchemical secrets: how to convert iron to gold, and how to create the philosopher's stone, a magical mineral that imparted immortality.

I poured Bernadette and myself each a second cup of tea, and we waded into the film more deeply.

Not unlike the Game of the Goose squares, the alchemical voyage featured and connected sacred places on the Camino in France and Spain that were encoded with spiritual and transformative messages. These were found engraved in church stones and sculptures as well as through the locations' orientations on the landscape. The initiated student seeking esoteric wisdom could learn how to walk, seek, see these messages, and connect the dots from one place to the next. In so doing, he or she would be guided in unlocking the secret of turning heavy base metals, like iron, into more luminous and valuable metals, like silver and gold.

Alchemy has had a long association with blacksmiths—people who, in the ancient world, were considered as not only special but also possessing magical skills like the ability to turn metal ore into stunning and useful forms, such as chalices and cauldrons. Their craft was also a spiritual metaphor for burning off the impurities of one's base mortal and ego aspects to reveal one's eternal and luminous soul hidden within.

Pilgrimage, Burensteinas suggested, stimulates the natural process of this burning-off of the accumulated detritus of our lives and our egos. Arriving in Santiago de Compostela, and later on at the ocean, offers a process to strip away the impurities and reveal the true, numinous being underneath—a soul shining with the brilliance of gold. It is the same alchemy implied in the Game of the Goose: the spiritual seeker takes up the journey and handles ordeals and receives gifts while shedding unnecessary baggage and lightening up. The ultimate and final test, the real alchemy, takes place on the death square, with the full and final release of base metal—base ego—toward becoming fully reborn, transformed, iron to gold, goose to swan, mortal ego to eternal spirit.

"Voilà," Bernadette said as the film ended. By now we had finished the tea and had also polished off a bottle of cider. "This is the great transformation I see for you on this Chemin: never before have you been so ready to die to your old self and to be reborn to who and what awaits you in the second half of your life."

Can one *voluntarily* die to his or her old self, and can one control that by walking? I didn't think so, and in that moment I put my finger on the source of my foreboding. When or how it all happened was an uncontrollable mystery. I thought of Le Chardon being for sale, which was a manifestation right there of my dying self, but it was happening before my resurrected being showed up. I was truly liminal, betwixt and between. The pilgrimage had begun.

Back outside, stragglers from the market lingered in the late afternoon as merchants packed up their vans. I made my way to the cathedral square and then up the hill behind it to the *lanterne des morts*, thinking of the medieval pilgrims who had come to this place, some of whom were possibly still there, buried under the hill. The tower's door was unlocked and wide open. I went inside and stood under the conical dome in the center. It was like being in Eunate or Torres del Río—a place of acoustic perfection. I sang to hear my ordinary voice alchemically become almost angelic. I could almost watch the sound waves bounce along the windows and walls. That was when I saw that the high ledges of the Romanesque windows were arrayed with offerings and prayers. Usually empty, they had been turned into altars cluttered with piles of acorns, an apple, a handful of autumn tree leaves, snippets of grapevines, a feather, some herbs, numerous little polished rocks, a color post-card of Venus and another of Mother Mary, and many notes and prayers—everything tucked here and there. I even could make out where a splash of red wine, a libation offering perhaps, had dried into a streak along the ledge. In the center of it all, propped up against the glass of the window, was a scallop shell. I had no idea who had left these eclectic offerings, but I knew it was done as a spontaneous and sacred ritual. I reached into my pocket to feel for the small scallop shell I'd brought back with me from Galicia years ago, after my first pilgrimage. I had planned to take it with me on the Camino this time, but instead set it next to the other shell, wanting to join in the ritual at this sacred spot. I whispered the petition and prayer for my pilgrimage and my return.

I heard a meow. Mr. Stripes stood at the doorway, calling plaintively. I went with her to the wall, and we sat and listened to the rouge-gorge in the pear tree launching into her melodic evening song. The tree branches bowed low, heavy with fruit, marking another amazing autumn that I was so blessed to be present to witness. We listened closely, adding our own notes to the bird and tree night music before turning in.

Though I had a lot of base-metal-burning ahead of me, I savored every moment in Sarlat, taking walks, visiting with Bernadette, and spending long moments pacing about Le Chardon, caressing the stone and wood, the Buddha on the mantle, and the windows looking out onto Saint Sacerdos and sixteenth-century humanist writer La Boétie's house. I soaked in the studio's energy and life-changing generosity and thanked it wholeheartedly for all it had given me. I finally came to accept the reality that we both now moved in new directions.

On my last night in Sarlat, I had just finished cleaning the studio, set my pack at the door, and turned down the covers, when Bernadette called. We had already said goodbye that afternoon.

"I just needed to tell you that I think this time on the Camino is going to be a bigger deal than all the other walks you've made before."

"Because I am writing a guidebook on it?" I ventured, though I knew she meant more. My foreboding returned.

"*Non*," she said, patiently, "because you have already been initiated into its deeper levels and know they exist, but you are still discovering what it's all about." She paused. "I also wanted you to know that I'll be with you every step of the way. I am especially thinking of you tonight because you are stepping through a major threshold."

Over lunch we had talked about many thresholds, all rushing together toward the same gate. To arrive here, I had said a lot of goodbyes, more than usual, in a short span of time. I had visited my family in Colorado and felt the weight of saying goodbye, even if temporarily, to my birthplace and my aging parents. I had returned to intense last weeks in New Jersey preparing for this trip, saying goodbye to close friends, and then saying goodbye to Miles, all of which had made my departure more painful than any other for reasons that still eluded me. And now, after my intense relatively few days here, I was saying goodbye again, with the added wildcard of Le Chardon compounding the weight. It had been an intense succession of goodbyes, releases, and see-you-laters laced with uncertainty about my return. My departures this time came close to what medieval pilgrims might have felt after putting all their affairs in order and heading out, knowing their return was a fifty-fifty proposition. And now, I was launching headfirst into a massively demanding project, a dream-come-true no less, but one that would occupy the next two years of my life to fully manifest. Guidebooks were blood and tears, flesh and sinew, and for me, more demanding to write than any other work of nonfiction because of the many truths, sources, and experiences they have to gather and fluidly bind.

"Those aren't the only thresholds you are going through," Bernadette said. "You are also saying goodbye to your youth; you are now firmly on the path of the second half of your life. Trust me, that's quite the doorway to walk through." And there it was, the root source of my foreboding: I'd never before felt so liminal or vulnerable in my life. As usual, Our Lady of Sarlat had seen it clearly before I could even sniff it out.

Early the next morning, I closed the door to Le Chardon and went slowly down the uneven wooden stairs. I caressed the heavy wooden blue door before pulling it open, then listened as the bolt clicked smoothly into the iron socket when it closed and locked. I pushed open the mailbox flap in the door, inhaling and hoping to find that first scent that had wedded me to this place years earlier from that same flap. It was there—the soft, comforting perfume of my grandmother's house, of linen closets, fresh paint, lilacs, and sun-warmed stones. Right as I was feeling that it had all been a dream, there came a thump. "How is it that you always know when to show up and make me so happy?" I rubbed Mr. Stripes' back and ears and listened to her purr.

Nadiya arrived seconds later to see me off too. I reached in my pocket for the keys to Le Chardon and felt there also three rocks. One came from the mountains of my birth in Colorado, one came from the beach of my present life in New Jersey, and the third from my home of homes, the dirt path here leading to the wall between the tower and the cathedral. These small stones would accompany me across southwestern France and northern Spain to the highest summit of the Camino at Monte Irago. There, I would leave them, along with a small cross a friend had given me for this journey, at the foot of the huge, towering iron cross, the Cruz de Ferro. The small gift cross was tied to my pack with a small scallop shell as talismans.

I handed Nadiya the keys and gave her a big hug.

"Whatever is set upon the path for you or for me," she said softly, a classic one-liner bubbling forth from her prophetic lips, "we are strong."

"Thank you," I said, smiling from ear to ear. "À bientôt,"

"À bientôt, she replied, "*et bonne route.*"

THE GIFT

I BOARDED THE train in Sarlat, happy it was running on time and hadn't been turned into a last-minute bus, took my seat and watched with emotion as it pulled out and along the Dordogne, slipping past ancient limestone ridges, deep green forests, and clifftop castles all reflected in the waters of the wide river. The train conductor greeted me. I gave him my ticket. He looked at it and wrinkled his brow.

"Where are you going?"

"To Bordeaux and then to Saint-Jean-Pied-de-Port," I said, and pointed to those same words printed on the ticket.

"I can see," he said.

"Then I don't understand."

"The train numbers, times, and price of your ticket don't match. These aren't trains to Saint-Jean."

But I had bought the ticket from his colleague, I explained, and again, the ticket was printed with the correct names. None of this mattered, it seemed, the numbers were wrong. He grew impervious to my reasoning, as if I somehow had the power to wrangle a hot mess with computer-printed numbers on the ticket, and he began to tell me that I had to get off the train in Bergerac and go to the ticket window there and sort things out, but then his eyes fell onto my backpack and the scallop shell attached to it.

"You are a pilgrim?" he said, interrupting himself mid-sentence.

"I am."

"Give me a few minutes." He left with my ticket. He still had not returned when the train pulled into Bergerac. I stayed where I was. The train left Bergerac, still no conductor or ticket. Only when we approached the sea of vineyards radiating around Bordeaux did he reappear, his grim face replaced with a grin. He explained that the computer system had been down that morning and though it came online when I'd bought my ticket, the updated numbers had not yet loaded. He'd sorted it all out. "*Bon chemin,*" he said, handing me a new ticket. It is likely that had I not been a pilgrim, I would be back at the ticket office in Bergerac.

In Bordeaux the train for Bayonne was already there. I booked to the platform. A conductor stood near the door and asked to see my ticket, scanned it, and frowned.

"You have no seat reservation here," he said. "No seat, no boarding." He pushed my ticket back at me.

By now my French was skimming on the edges of its capability—I had no vocabulary for this ordeal. I did my best to explain the ticket's history. The train whistle blew announcing the last call to board. Another conductor came over to listen to my tale. The two wrinkled their brows and looked at me dubiously. But then, the first conductor's eye went to my pack, which now rested at my feet, and the scallop shell.

"You are a pilgrim?" I nodded. They looked at each other and back at me. "Get on," he said, "we'll sort you out. For now, go sit in the café car." Lord praise Saint James. I gathered my pack in relief and joy and from the corner of my eye noticed their smiles that spoke of their own pleasure in aiding a pilgrim to Compostela—a deep part of French history given the routes through the hexagon, not to mention all the Franks who built and inhabited the Camino Francés, French Road, in Spain. I felt as if my journey had been blessed by the Pope.

As I clambered aboard, just behind me, a young woman rushed on with a huge pack, a massive scallop shell swinging from the lid. She saw mine and in English said, "Pilgrim? Camino?"

"Yes," I said, "and yes."

She laughed and seemed relieved to meet another wayfaring stranger on an even stranger journey for the modern era. "Where are you sitting?" she asked.

"Until I get sorted out," I said, "in the café car."

The train began moving. She disappeared deeper into the train to locate her assigned seat. I went to the café and ordered a coffee and settled at one of four tiny seats in the narrow space. Several times during the journey the two conductors walked through, looked at me, smiled, and kept going. I thought I had been sorted out. Midway, the other pilgrim found me and joined me for a coffee. A financial advisor from Oregon, she had lived and studied in Poitou for a year as a college student. This was her first time back in France since then. She had gone to Poitou to see old friends and now was here on this new adventure, one that arose out of her interest in both this part of the world as well as from being an avid mountaineer. We discovered we were both staying at the same pilgrim's inn in Saint-Jean-Pied-de-Port.

"So is another American woman," she said, "from Tampa. I know her from a pilgrim's network but have never met her face to face. She's meeting me at the station."

I thought of Luke, then of the jetlagged Korean grandmother sleeping on my shoulder, then of Cédric, not too far away now, and his inordinate kindness and timing. The train neared Bayonne. One of the conductors came over. "Disembark here for your connection to Saint-Jean. Your ticket will be fine." That train had two small cars and no reserved seats. "*Bon chemin*," she said, and winked.

We made our train connection and sat next to each other on the tiny, crowded, pilgrim-packed train to Saint-Jean, looking around to see the same wonder and anxiety written on everyone's faces. Leaving the flat landscape for curving hills, the train tracks slipped into the natural groove of an alpine river valley formed by the Nive River. Mountains steepened and grew with each kilometer. We followed the contours of the Nive and with it flowed into Saint-Jean.

The woman from Tampa was there, calm, cheerful, and welcoming. She had arrived the day before to sleep off jetlag and to recalibrate after having just come from evacuating from a hurricane that had ravaged her area of Florida. Despite the chaos at home, she had decided not to cancel or postpone her Camino, a journey she had planned for a long time.

At the pilgrim gîte, our host showed us our bunks and told us our evening communal dinner would convene in three hours. I left my gear and went along the old cobblestones to the pilgrim's welcome office on the middle of the hill in the middle of the medieval walled town. A man with a long curly white beard like Saint Nicholas, who moments before had been telling lighthearted jokes, gestured to me to sit before him on the other side of the table. He handed me an altitude map of the full 800 kilometers (500 miles) ahead, then began to tell me about the first day's crossing via the Napoleon route, the high path over the mountains, the one I had completed during that epic ice storm a year and a half earlier. An old Roman route named after the area's most recent invader, it was the preferred route during the Middle Ages for pilgrims who wanted to avoid being ambushed by bandits on the more sinuous Valcarlos valley route along a tributary of the Nive River toward Roncesvalles. That valley path was also named for an invader, Charlemagne, and his largely failed military campaign in Spain in AD 778. Although banditry no longer poses a threat, the Napoleon route remains the most popular route, both for its spectacular views and the bragging rights trekkers like to claim after ascending it successfully. Today the route is opened only in good weather and the warm season. My guide marked the places on the Napoleon route in red ink, showing me where I needed to be extra careful.

"Actually, I'll be taking the Valcarlos route," I said. He looked surprised. The next day's weather forecast was for a perfect sunny day with warm temperatures; everyone else was taking the high route. But I needed to take the Valcarlos route for the guidebook, to be reminded of how the path worked its way across the valley. After my most recent—and more intimate than usual—experience with the high path, I knew its every mountain-hugging inch.

My guide grabbed another map from a shelf behind him. "Be

careful there too," he said. "Many people think the Napoleon route is hard and the Valcarlos is easy, but that is an illusion. The Valcarlos is also difficult in its own way." He marked the second map with red ink at the especially dangerous spots. "The route has sheer climbs, especially at the end, but also narrow and slippery trails. In some stretches there is no room for a trail, so you have to walk on the edge of the mountain highway through the narrow pass and its roadside margins are almost nonexistent. Watch for cars, but also be careful with your footing so you don't slip down the slope toward the river." He smiled brightly, as if he had just told me Santa Claus was going to give me exactly what I wanted on my wish list. He then took up a fresh accordion-folded pilgrim's passport and stamped the first square with the form of a medieval pilgrim in cape, hat, and staff. Hearing the punch and seeing the still wet ink of the image made the visceral reality of where I was flood through me: I was indeed back on the way of the wild goose. Moreover, with guidebook contract ink now fully dried, I knew that even if the tower square or the death square of the Game of the Goose undid me, I had to finish this walk no matter what and take it all the way to the earth's end at Finisterre, noting every detail as I went. A bomb of joy went off inside me: this was the life I most wanted to live.

I thanked the volunteer and wandered along the ancient cobblestones of medieval Saint-Jean-Pied-de-Port, the town now my familiar friend. Once again, I felt the energy of the millions of prior pilgrims' footsteps pulsing underfoot. I climbed to the citadel and then stopped by to say hello to the innkeeper and his sweetheart at the place where I'd stayed on the last two treks. I kept going, retracing the path Sarah and I had taken five years earlier, the one that had launched this whole wild goose chase. When I reached the chapel of Mary Magdalene in Saint-Jean-Le-Vieux, my French flip-top phone, newly reactivated in Sarlat, rang.

"*Bonne route et bonne chance*," Cédric said when I picked up. "On your return to France, for old time's sake, consider breaking the journey here in Biarritz, food poisoning not required." I laughed. I was touched by his kindness and comforted by knowing that many weeks from now I had a midway point on my return to Sarlat. Who would I be by then? A duck, a goose, a swan? On the winning square? Or sent all the way back to the beginning?

I returned to the gîte. The young woman from Oregon ran up to me as soon as I stepped through the door.

"I've been looking for you. Here!" She exuberantly extended her hands toward me, in them, a solid hand-spun wooden pen. "My father made it. He gave me a few to give as gifts as I feel inspired by people I meet on the Camino. I just knew you had to have the first pen; not only are you the first pilgrim I met on this trek, but you are also a writer." It was a magical gift. I took the beautiful instrument gingerly, deeply moved to tears. My angel seemed pleased. "I hope it serves you well," she said. There could be no more perfect talisman than this for a writer hellbent on making a living as just that. I thanked and hugged her and slipped the precious cargo into the side pocket of my trekking pants, right next to the small journalist's notebook, ever ready to be pulled out and flipped open for notes and insights in service of the guidebook as much as the quest.

Seventeen pilgrims gathered in the stone and timber kitchen and began to set the long wooden table in the center. We hailed from Germany, Denmark, Italy, Ireland, England, Switzerland, France, Canada, and the USA, a mix of men and women ages nineteen to eighty. With the table set, our host stood at its head and offered us an aperitif of sweet wine. We raised our glasses. I could hear through the open windows the shuffle on the cobblestones of more pilgrims arriving from the evening train and the medieval bells downhill from Sainte-Marie's church. I felt both excited and queasy. I could see my companions felt the same. We clinked and drank.

"Before we begin to eat," our host said, "I want to ask you each to share what is the theme of your Camino were you to reduce it to five words. Think of it as a film or a book title, and don't think too hard," he added, "just say what comes."

Many uttered themes about finding purpose and clarity for their lives. Others expressed the hope to endure well the physical challenge of five weeks of nonstop trekking. Some had just retired, others had lost a loved one, some were changing careers or domiciles, yet others simply needed a break from everyday life and a long walk to hit the reset button. When it came to my turn, I heard myself blurt, "Lightening up while going deeper." Quick, honest, unexpected. I touched the wooden pen in my pocket and felt light already, knowing I had been given the ultimate tool of my calling to launch the adventure ahead.

THE VALLEY WAY

SLEPT IN fits and starts, adjusting to the sounds of the dorm that ranged from late-arriving pilgrims dropping their packs on the floor near my head to the expected cacophony of snores and other bodily eruptions. The morning dawned bright and clear but, true to the unpredictable weather in this mountain pass, rain clouds were moving in and would arrive by afternoon. I felt the taut nervous energy of pilgrims on the precipice. I felt it inside, too, despite having done this before. As I stuffed my sleeping bag into my pack a young, athletically built man near me asked, "Which route are you taking?"

"The Valcarlos," I replied.

"Ah, the easy route," he said, so easily, it stung. My ego screamed inside. Why was this a competition?! *Lighten up and go deeper,* I reminded myself and offered him a tight Cheshire cat grin. If the Napoleon route was the route of the ego, I considered, offering its surmounters bragging rights on the other side, then the Valcarlos route was the route of ego-tempering. What had happened to that mantra I was supposed to master? *What's possible if it doesn't matter what others think?* Was I thus to always be a work-in-progress? I was among the last to depart. Oregon and Tampa had long gone. I hoped I would see them on the other side of the mountains.

Just before crossing the bridge over the river, I stopped to visit the church of Sainte Marie du Bout du Pont, Saint Mary of the End of the Bridge. I petitioned her for safe passage for me and my companions as well as for my loved ones all around the world wherever their paths took them. After lighting a candle and taking a few centering breaths, I crossed the bridge and began the climb. My companions had gone left, launching directly onto a sheer ascent. I went right and followed a branch of the Nive, the Nive d'Arnéguy, heading into its valley on a gentler uphill slope. After lush, sweeping, open meadows, the landscape took a narrow and steep turn, and the path led me up as the river descended farther below and disappeared. Mountains gathered and jutted toothily all around me like a gathering of giants looking for something good to eat.

I aimed to stop overnight midway in the mountain crossing at Valcarlos, where Charlemagne camped twelve hundred years ago. As a last act of thumbing his nose at the Iberians who had rejected him, he sacked Pamplona before riding to this pass and camping there. Little did he know, groups of outraged Navarrese and Basques tracked his retreat. As he unsaddled and set up camp, they caught up to his rear guard, commanded by Roland, one of his trusted officers, and attacked. Roland and his men were swiftly dispatched, and Charlemagne woke to learn his grave mistake. Yes, this was the ego-snuffing route. I considered this history as I passed a herd of grazing black-and-tan Manex sheep, many with phys-ics-defying spiraling horns jutting horizontally from their faces. I preferred their peaceful company to war-mongering imperialists. I found the valley way as stunning as the other route; each had its own distinct and remarkable beauty.

I climbed further, then descended some, climbed a lot, then descended a little, each time more steeply, both up and down, head-ing deeper into the V-shaped funnel of mountains ahead. Dense chestnut and beech woods hugged both sides of the trail, and in this season, the trees dropped spiky leather-skinned nuts the size of tennis balls onto the narrow footpath. I stepped carefully not to slip or twist an ankle, stopping at times to pick up a nut, peel off its sea-urchin skin, and pocket the glossy mahogany nut inside. It began to drizzle and the trail started to feel slippery. A starch-white egret flashed overhead while lifting off from upper branches and flying high, then diving low into the tight gully of the invisible river below full of trout. I stopped and heard the rouge-gorge deep in the woods, his song similar to that of his cousin who had sung to me from the pear tree in Sarlat.

Late that morning, I heard fast-approaching footsteps, the first all day. Four young people appeared, two brothers from South Carolina and a just-married couple from Florida. No sooner had we exchanged the basic details then another merry group of pilgrims arrived—a family of five from North Carolina, first a young man in his early twenties, followed by his aunt, uncle, and parents. The young man called in a cinematic tone back to his father coming up at the end.

"We must find our staff, our mystical friend and support that will walk with us all the way to Santiago de Compostela!" He grinned, adding, "Though, dear pilgrim, it is the staff that picks the walker." He stuck out his hand and shook mine vigorously. "I'm Brady."

We ten walked together for a few kilometers, with everyone's stories tumbling out as Brady spread wit and sunshine at every turn while he and his father wove this way and that looking for their magical fallen tree branch.

The South Carolina brothers were taking a gap year from their lives. One was finishing school and the other was in between jobs but apprenticing as a physical trainer. He made his brother stop every hour to stretch and hydrate—a devoted coach. They each said that they hoped the Camino would give them more direction in what to do with their lives. The North Carolinians had a business together and had lived next door to each other and their work, but weeks earlier, wildfires had consumed everything, making them both homeless and jobless. They walked to give thanks for their lives being spared, and said they hoped that by the time they walked into Santiago they would have a plan for what to do next. Rather than wallow in loss, they celebrated being together and alive.

"It's actually freeing to own very little," Brady chimed in, "having no possessions to weigh you down." He suddenly swerved into the forest, seeing a promising stick, his father following close behind. I fell into step with the just-married couple. The husband had recently finished his tour of duty as a Marine. Soon after, he had returned home to marry his sweetheart; he had suggested that for their honeymoon they walk the Camino.

"Why the Camino?"

"Ever since I read Paolo Coelho's *The Pilgrimage* years ago, I've wanted to walk this trail, but my work made it seem as if I may not make it."

"Might not make the pilgrimage?"

"No, might not make it, period," he answered softly. "It was dangerous work. I was deployed to Iraq many times and there were many times, too many, where I could have been killed."

We walked several paces in silence. "I also connected to the movie *The Way*," he continued, "maybe because it came out when I was still serving, and it hit a raw nerve: I worried that my father might have to be like the father in the movie and carry my ashes."

His wife said little, just listened. I could see she was putting all her energy into the steep slope and the newness of the heavy pack on her back. It was clear she would do whatever it took for her husband to heal and for their marriage to succeed. When her husband asked what had brought me to the Camino, I gave the more straightforward answer, that I was writing a guidebook.

"You're Jack from Ireland!" he exclaimed, suddenly animated and chipper, referring to one of the four main characters, the travel writer, in *The Way*. He had watched the film numerous times and knew each character's lines by heart.

"I just wish I had some of his editorial contacts," I half jested. Jack's fictitious life as a travel writer was somewhat more perfect than the reality.

We reached the village of Arnéguy on the border with France and Spain. The drizzle turned to rain. We all stopped to pull out ponchos and help each other stretch them over our packs. The newlyweds and the brothers then kept going, intending to reach Roncesvalles before heavier rain moved in. The North Carolina family had fallen back somewhere, perhaps for a magical staff. I stayed in Arnéguy to take in the village, visit its lodging options, cafés, and trail markings, then enjoy the warm company of its single café, where I heard Basque, Spanish, and French from the five men gathered at the bar. Leaving the village, I went slowly along the river, once again visible, enjoying the colors of the kitchen gardens I passed, all staked with green beans, kale, carrot, and onions. The trail returned to thick forest and sloped the rest of the way up to Valcarlos, with spiky chestnuts and slick wet leaves underfoot all the way.

Valcarlos was quiet, not a soul about. Most of the pilgrim places had closed, but near the village center I came upon an older man chatting with a young woman in the doorway of the town hall. The woman ran the small Valcarlos tourist office.

"The municipal albergue is open and is clean and comfortable, but there also is a small studio with its own kitchen that the owner wants to rent for almost the same price as the albergue." A gift of the Camino. I took it. I went a few paces further down the same road to meet the studio's owner in front of a row of bungalows. She opened the door to the first one and welcomed me home. Her place was next door, she pointed out, if I needed anything. She left me to settle in. I was deeply touched when I saw that, in the few moments between getting the phone call from the tourist office to meeting me, she had gathered and arranged a wildflower and herb bouquet on the kitchen counter next to a few things for my breakfast.

I stripped off my pack and my clothes down to my undergarments and crawled under the beckoning cozy bedcovers, falling instantly asleep. Two hours later I jolted awake, fully disoriented, and shouting, "Why am I here?" It all rushed back. I was back on the Camino, at the beginning. The road never felt so long as in that moment. I took a reviving hot shower, stretched my stiff limbs, and went out to explore. Unlike the wild meadow it had been in Charlemagne's time, the area today is a roadside village straddling two sides of a mountain valley funneling toward Roncesvalles, with a handful of houses, inns, a bakery and grocery, and one lively bar that also serves as a restaurant and second grocery store. I found the municipal albergue off the town square, and inside, found the North Carolina family, all fast asleep on their bunks. Two other pilgrims from Mexico City hung out on the balcony.

Disasters, natural and human, seemed to be the theme of this year's walk, with the tolls and urgency of global warming never having been so pressing or obvious as they were now, from the hurricane in Florida's Gulf Coast to the fires in North Carolina, the atrocities of war in Iraq. And now I learned that these two men from Mexico City had come straight to the Camino from clearing the debris from the earthquake that had devastated their neighborhood, city, and country.

"Our families and friends are okay," one of the men said, "but we will all have to rebuild. We stayed long enough to help clear the destruction, but then the two of us decided to keep to our plan, many years in the making, to make this pilgrimage. Rebuilding can wait. Who knows, maybe by the end of this long walk, what we want to rebuild will change. You know?" I was thinking as he spoke that this was what our beloved Earth was asking all of us to do right now.

I continued my investigation of other places in town, speaking with the few locals I encountered. At the church of Santiago, set high on the upper slope of the village, I stopped at an elaborate mural on the stone wall below it. It was of a Basque festival with people in traditional costume dancing around a bonfire, along with a Goya-inspired, bull-horned sorcerer. The pagan elements of communing with nature seemed more celebrated than demonized. The Pyrenees, both a frontier and a remote terrain, has preserved old ideas longer than most of its neighbors farther in France or Spain.

I stopped at the combination bar, restaurant, and grocery store managed by three commanding and cheerful women. One manned the bar and grocery store, going from stirring dry martinis behind one counter to weighing zucchinis behind another. The other two worked in the steam and sizzle of the kitchen, churning out mouthwatering dishes. I purchased food for the trail, ordered a glass of wine, and stayed for dinner. As evening descended, the bar gathered nearly every villager and a few road trippers, including a large group of motorbikers, their black leather and tattoos harmoniously merging with the townsfolks' cardigans and silk scarves. I looked around me to see people from many corners of the globe and all walks of life. They all pulled me in, the one pilgrim who'd come out that night. I found myself in a remote village in the Pyrenees that was paradoxically a dynamic international gateway.

The chefs feted us with creamy asparagus soup, salad, fried trout stuffed with cured ham, and homemade honey custard. All the tables around me filled and everyone at intervals raised their glasses to each other. I returned to my studio in pitch dark but seeing clearly: if we could all live together like this, our world would be fine. Back under the warm covers, I knew, in that moment between wakefulness and sleep, that what I was experiencing was the whole point of Mother Goose, Mother Goddess.

THE ELEVENTH GOOSE

SLEPT DEEP and long in Charlemagne's valley, and the next day I returned to the narrow up-and-down trail and the company of the Nive d'Arnéguy River, located once again far below at the bottom of a steep ravine. Most of the trail hugged the edge of the mountain highway or was carved into the mountainside, more goat path than footpath. Dew and fallen chestnut leaves and nuts continued to make it slow going. After many undulations, the path took but one direction: upward, into the sheerest final climb through a primordial beech forest, until landing in the pass where Roland and his men had fallen just before Roncesvalles.

A chill ran up my spine as I left the forest and arrived at the summit, surrounded by rippling meadows of white, yellow, and orange flowers mingled with pink and purple heathers and pale green grass. I visited the marker honoring both Roland and Our Lady of Roncesvalles, and then, as swiftly as I had arrived, I slipped into another oak and beech forest, this one inhabited by mysterious shaggy brown horses who grazed on undergrowth in the maze of tight trees. One horse, seeming to take umbrage at my thinking that he and his team were cute and funny, came to the trail's edge, stretched out his neck, reared his head, and let out a heckling, mocking neigh while shaking his head and baring his teeth. Thus humbled, I walked into Roncesvalles.

I researched every inch of Roncesvalles, taking copious notes, before taking myself, free of the day's demands, to sit once more before Our Lady of Roncesvalles. Her chapel and her image on the altar held the same magnetism and energy as the ethereal beech forest, meadows, and mountains outside. I felt new energy pulse in my limbs. I didn't want to stop walking just yet. Calculating that the late Spanish lunch hour was near at hand, I jumped up and returned to the trail, hoping to make it to Burguete in time for a good lunch and return to Hemingway's good-luck hotel. I stepped quickly, excited by the thought of staying once again in that magical spot, and passed through the enchanted forest, visiting the memorial to the witches' coven, and out into the open fields on the edge of Burguete.

Unlike the day of my prior arrival in Burguete, this autumn day fell on both a weekend and during hunting season. I found the hotel booked full and every table in the café packed with lunchtime revelers. The owner shrugged his shoulders apologetically and simply wished me luck before rushing off to deliver more plates to waiting tables. I went down the central street to find, at each door I knocked on, that all rooms and tables were full. Midway down, thinking I needed to keep walking to the next village, I heard a woman call to me. It was one of the waitresses I had seen serving lunch in the last accommodation. She directed me to a doorway not clearly marked, and indicated that it also was an inn. I knocked and waited. Moments passed in silence before a woman in her sixties, wearing a blue apron, opened the door. The intoxicating smell of fried potatoes, grilled lamb, roasted peppers, and saffron flowed tantalizingly toward me. It came from a kitchen deep inside the house, past the grand and deep foyer and large ornate dining room I could now discern.

"Hola, *niña*," Sainte B of Burguete said warmly. She had a room and led me to it, up a massive staircase to the upper floor. The room was spotless, a simple monk's cell, but it was arrayed with centuries-old, hand-hewn and -carved oak furniture—an armoire, desk, bed, and nightstand. A Russian Orthodox painted icon of Mother Mary sat on the bedside, the only work of art. A cross hung on the wall above the bed which was covered in a starched white linen bedspread, and the window looked out over sweeping green hills. Once again, I had lucked out. For lunch, however, I was on my own. Today, Sainte B cooked only for her family.

I kicked off my shoes, showered, and made a picnic with my provisions from Valcarlos, all the while staring out the window at the verdant hills. I spent the rest of the afternoon investigating every nook and corner of Burguete with my notebook in hand, feeling again the support of Hemingway's spirit, my notebook filling and my new pen flowing and fitting in my hand already as a dear old friend. When I returned to my lodging, Sainte B of Burguete came out to stamp my pilgrim's passport and collect the fee for my room. I learned that her house had been in her family for centuries. "This is a happy place," she said. "You will rest well tonight."

I had sweet dreams, all of family and childhood. I woke early, refreshed and pulsing to go. I quietly slipped down the stairs and out through the heavy wooden door. After a coffee in the café in the center of town, I headed back onto the trail and into the rolling and forested countryside, its meadows swaying with wildflowers. I thought of the angel and the saint, Gabriel and Santiago, whom I had met there nearly two years earlier. In that moment, I heard someone call my name and was suddenly joined by Brady and his family, he and his father brandishing the walking sticks they had gathered in the forest just before Roncesvalles. Brady had already begun whittling symbols of the trek into his.

Three French pilgrims from Provence joined us as we walked. Like a pendulum, I found myself swinging back and forth between conversations with the Carolinians and the Provençals all the way to Zubiri. We continued like this the next day, all the way to Pamplona, after which the city scattered us like the wind. For the Carolinians, this was where they planned to rest, rethink their gear, and perhaps make a day trip to nearby sites. The Provençals pressed on, keeping to a more regimented schedule, what with having houses and jobs to return to. For me, the demands of guidebook research in a big city were daunting: hundreds of visits, conversations, notes, and photos. By the time I was finished, anyone I had met since Saint-Jean-Pied-de-Port was long gone. Though I missed their camaraderie, I had rich encounters with others—both locals and the next wave of pilgrims.

Early on the morning of my departure from Pamplona, I found breakfast in a rare bar open at that hour. I saw a light and heard the sound of an espresso machine and followed these signs down a narrow street to a café where an angel was churning out hot egg sandwiches and strong coffee. I sat down and ate while reading the daily newspaper that was lying on the bar counter. It forecast sunny and mild temperatures. On the same page as the weather report was the daily horoscope. I read under my sign: "The lines of your personal development are already drawn, but now is an auspicious time to manifest them and put them into practice: it is a time when you can pick a hard path"—word for word: *un camino difícil*—"because you have the wind at your back." I quickly flipped the paper shut. Enough already. Even with the wind at my back this time, I felt done with hard paths. I felt for the pen in my pocket that reminded me why I did what I did. I paid for breakfast and left. By then, the only word that stuck with me from the newspaper was *camino*. It was just a silly horoscope.

But for good measure, just to be sure, before leaving the medieval folds of the city, I stopped at the San Lorenzo church to utter a prayer at the altar of San Fermin, Pamplona's patron saint, for safe and easeful passage. There, a priest with cheerful countenance walked past. "*Peregrina*, would you like a stamp for your credential?" A sign.

"*Por favor*," I said and went with him through the open door to the sacristy where he pulled a stamp and inkpad from a cabinet. After he inked and dated a grand image of the church in which we stood, he placed his hand on my head and recited a benediction for pilgrims. When he was finished, he flashed his warm, bright smile again. "Don't worry, *peregrina*, you will have many sunny and good days ahead of you. Your Camino is blessed." Here, too, was the lucky goose. I thanked him and stepped out into the bright sunshine, feeling hopeful and stronger this time than I had on my last walk. I left the old city, passed through the university's spacious green campus, and took the gravel path into the countryside.

SAINT MARTIN'S GOOSE

THE PRIEST'S BLESSING, like the gift pen, worked as a talisman, propelling me forward. I focused on being present in the work of each day and trusting the path ahead. Many good but mild days of sun unfolded from Pamplona all the way to Burgos, as if the padre had orchestrated the weather. Walking and working—for both the guidebook and other ongoing writing work—made for long days and squeezed out every ounce of my energy. I fell into my bunk or bed each night and fell promptly to sleep, recalling no dreams, and waking early to repeat the cycle. Any pilgrims I met each day, I did not see again; they walked a straight line to Santiago de Compostela as I walked in circling spirals around each place to document every nuance and talk to locals. It was both a hard but truly blessed path: the priest's and the horoscope's words held true.

And though this walk wasn't as spontaneous as my prior Caminos, I could still feel the Camino working its magic on me, the long days of walking on a sacred leyline slipped through my skin, changed my cell tissue, and brought on unexpected rushes of insights, including the intense dreams that eventually emerged because of the long trek. They returned with their familiar processing themes: jumbles of scenes merging places and times, of walking; working; being with family members and friends, both alive and deceased; and at times, forcing a reckoning with my own mortality.

But the goose? Certainly, as I retraced my footsteps through Navarra and La Rioja, the leyline hummed and the places I had visited before with goose associations still held their special clues and magic. But no new signs or hunches arose, not even in Logroño with its inlaid Game of the Goose square. The guidebook progressed, I followed the path and the stars, but the goose slumbered.

Then, after Logroño, somewhere near Ventosa and the village's hilltop church surrounded by swirling red earth and radiating vines, a feeling of being rewoven hit me. It was as if the yarn of my being was both being unraveled then reknit simultaneously. This strange sensation persisted into Nájera and the town's cliffside monastery, guarding in its deep-red rock cave the miraculous Mary that King Garcia III had seen in 1044, surrounded by her birds, lilies, bell, and candlelight. The same feeling rambled with me to Santo Domingo de la Calzada with its hen and rooster miracle and the grace bestowed there by the town's namesake sainted engineer. And on, through San Juan de Ortega, with the scent of roses and honeybees still in the air, and across the scintillating ancient limestone landscape of Atapuerca, whose 1.2-million-year-old human presence still sent spine-tingling chills through my limbs. After all my heady communion with wilder terrains, the urban energy of Burgos hit me like water breaking a dam wall and bowling me down. I had to quickly close the wide-open sensory doorways. A sense of foreboding, not felt since Pamplona, also rushed in.

More cautiously, I approached Frómista, knowing the source of my anxiety. My gut tightened at the memory of my last time there. Vulnerability was at the root of my foreboding, and it had been at the root of all the thresholds I had walked through of late, facing the risk of illness while homeless, being so far from those I loved, and, as Bernadette had called out, crossing into the second half of life. I reminded myself that earlier pilgrims of all ages had walked this way without emergency medicine or all the supports we have today, let alone three-digit phone numbers bringing aid right to you—and I took a deep breath and marched into town.

Seeing Frómista's Romanesque church of San Martín's honeycomb body, sculpted with so many stories in stone, dispelled any remaining angst. It was too beautiful, and it was splendid to be back here again. Swept into the church's beauty, I noticed again I was not alone in my reverie, that swallows were there too, flying energetic laps around the upper towers. I joined the scene and revisited the three waterfowl sculptures but still found no clue as to why they were there—until I went inside. How had I missed this before? Saint Martin stood on the altar, across from Saint James and on the other side of the crucified Christ in the center. The church's name was the biggest clue.

Medievalist scholar Philippe Walter recounts that Saint Martin was one of the most popular saints in France. Stories of his frequent appearances on various routes of the Camino came from Frankish pilgrims and settlers in the Middle Ages. He was associated with two animals, a donkey and a goose—one a creature serving Christ and the other a familiar of the goddess. On his feast day, November 11, the traditional festival food is roasted goose. Saint Martin represents the merging of old and new, of pagan and Christian.

The most famous story about Saint Martin, who was fabled to be generous, concerned a poor and shivering soldier he came upon in winter who had no cloak. Martin immediately cut his own cloak in half to share with the man. Such giving made him akin to a golden goose, an old mythic idea in Europe that equated this animal with abundance and endless wealth. In the story of Saint Martin's cloak, the poor man is considered Jesus in disguise, and Saint Martin's gesture is the ultimate submission to God. But it turns out, this story has an older, pre-Christian version in which a mortal meets a poor old woman and shares what he has with her. She is later revealed as the mother goddess who tests character, guards nature, and exacts balance and justice in human affairs. Over time, the goddess became a powerful forest fairy, but her animal of choice remained the goose. Saint Martin's character and generosity merged with this older story, Walter explains, and associated him with a connection to the divine ancient realm of hybrid bird-women, who were also known as mother goddesses among the Celts. Walter even adds that this symbolism shows up in the Game of the Goose, where a sacred bird acts as a guide to the player on an initiatory journey. The goose here is privy to secrets in the eternal spiritual realm, which it can impart to the astute seeker.

Could these three ducks and geese on Saint Martin's church, each holding its own side of the building, be guardians and guides to sacred secrets? Did they not guard the treasure—spiritual truth—as did the web-footed mother goddess of southern France and northern Spain, seated in her cave, or the geese of the Game of the Goose?

Early the next morning, the hospitalera in my albergue told me to fill all of my water bottles before setting off, that the day's forecast called for unseasonably hot and record-breaking temperatures for mid-October. Instead of winter coming early, it seemed summer was extending its reach. But geese usually don't get things wrong, recalling what Cécile had said. They seem to know things the rest of us can't see, even other birds.

I passed Saint Martin's geese, representing the ancient goddess who worked her magic through a charitable and devoted saint, and strode deeper into the *meseta* on a flat and flax-toned path, feeling light and free of anxiety. Thresholds are a given, and at each the goose kept telling me I would find guidance. I relaxed, and with my senses freed of fear and wide open again, I began to pick up on something else there walking with me, something intangible, something I didn't think I had ever felt before. It seemed to walk with me, thickening at times in the air as if slowly manifesting energy into matter. I felt only benevolence. I shook my head, tried to clear it. Either I was working too hard, going loopy, or something extraordinary was about to happen.

THE FORK IN THE ROAD

NO SOONER HAD the sun cleared the horizon and risen did the dry sizzle and heat begin to finger into the exposed high plateau. The low, rippling hills and huddled tree groves of the meseta before Frómista gave way to a nearly treeless, flat, and wide horizon that showed more baldly the effects of a two-year drought that still had not broken. The cropped wheat fields looked less like a giant crewcut and more like a dust bowl. The Ucieza River that I paralleled was bone dry, its reed grasses brown and stiff, the poplars lining its banks making rasping noises each time the wind rustled their brittle leaves. My sweat seemed to be the only source of water within kilometers, and thus drew swarms of thirsty flies landing on my exposed arms and face, and most maddening, my mouth and my nostrils. Whatever that intangible benevolent energy had been, it had evaporated more quickly than the Ucieza. I flailed and waved my arms and tried to calm the creepy shiver that wiggled across my skin with the relentless insect invaders, but rather than help me, this only seemed to draw more flies, until I began to run like *una loca*. "Why am I doing this?" I screamed at the hot blue sky. I forgot the guidebook. I forgot the goose. I forgot myself. I was almost out of water.

Was it a mirage, or was that really a village growing closer as I kicked up a dust storm? Yes, it was, and there was a cluster of green, refreshing trees skirting its edge. I ran faster. But upon reaching the settlement, I found no one, neither local nor pilgrim. Everything stood closed, and there was no sign of a shop or café. I went to the trees, but the flies came with me. This was surely hell. I jumped back onto the dirt road to jet to the next settlement, many kilometers away. Only when I realized I hadn't seen any trail markers for some time did I stop at a fork in the road and try to reason out my next steps.

A woman suddenly appeared, walking briskly toward me. She had to be an illusion. In this heat, she wore a sweatshirt over a flannel shirt and wool tweed skirt with wool kneesocks and white running shoes. An empty canvas bag swung on one arm as the other tapped with steady rhythm a gnarly walking stick made from a fallen branch. I blinked. She was still there and walked right up to me.

"*Buen Camino, hija,*" she said kindly and touched my arm like a loving grandmother. "When I saw you by the river, I picked up my pace to tell you that the water in our village fountain is safe to drink; you should be sure to fill up. It's going to be a killer of a day."

I turned to see the fountain to which she pointed. It sat on the edge of the trees from which I'd just bolted. Surely this was a fairy godmother, or Mother Goose herself. She had to be: who dressed like this in such heat and seemed not to sweat? And hold on, the flies had also dispersed.

"How long has it had been this dry?" I asked.

She shook her head. "In all my eighty years, I've never seen a spring like this year's. It did not rain once. Not once. Nor did it rain this summer. The aquifers are empty, and the rivers are dust. And we have only ourselves to blame," she added. "We've altered the world too much: How can anyone deny this? Anyone who has lived on the land all their life has seen this." And anyone, I thought to myself, completing her unspoken logic, who has not lived directly on the land, has been in a fog of denial.

"Are you from this village?" I pointed to the settlement behind me.

"I was born on this very earth," she said, "on a farmstead near here, where I still live. I grew up here, I raised my family here, and here I am, still, even after my husband passed away several years ago and my children have all gone on to their own lives in the cities. But I love living here, near this small village, with my roots deep in the earth."

"Even now, with the drought?"

"Yes, *niña*, especially now, for the land needs love and attention."

A soft wind picked up and rustled the empty cloth sack hanging on her arm. I turned and walked with her toward the village. She told me she took walks with her dogs in the afternoon, but right now she was heading to the village for bread and milk.

"But I didn't see any shops."

"No need," she replied. "I get my milk from the local dairy farmer, and I get my bread from the baker. Everyone knows where to find both. There's no need to hang a sign. For the rest, I grow all my vegetables and I raise chickens." We arrived at the fountain. "After you get water," the wise woman advised, "go straight along the riverside to the small hermitage, a special place devoted to Nuestra Señora del Río, Our Lady of the River. There is a fountain there, too, but soon after, you will get to Villalcazar de Sirga, another special place. Be sure to stop and visit La Virgen Blanca." I filled my bottles. She hugged me and set off into the village. As soon as she left, the flies returned. I distracted myself by heading toward the path along the river and trying to pull up from memory all that I knew about La Blanca.

She was perhaps the most famous and the most potent of the Marys on the Camino. She had performed so many remarkable healing miracles that the thirteenth-century poet king Alfonso X devoted numerous songs to her in his *Cantigas de Santa Maria*. The most frequent miracle she performed was curing many from blindness, both physical and metaphorical, opening eyes to both vision and divine presence. Before I knew it, I arrived at the riverside chapel.

Though locked, it had an open vestibule that offered refreshing shade. I took off my pack, removed my shoes, peeled off my socks, and pressed my feet with delight against the cool pavement. Miraculously, the flies seemed to draw a line at the chapel, as with the wise woman, and once again disappeared. An information poster mounted to the wall recounted that in the twelfth century, after a flood locals found an icon of Mary floating down the Ucieza. It floated ashore here, marking the spot where people honored her and built a church. Centuries later, in 1650 villagers in the area formed the brotherhood of the Most Holy Lady of the River, and ever since then, each year on Pentecost Sunday they hold celebrations in her honor.

I sat there a long time, contemplating this millennium-old devotion to Mary along the lands of the Camino. More than Jesus or James, she was the most common divine figure, with every settlement having a chapel or church devoted to her more often than to anyone else. Her cult was present in Christianity from the beginning, and some scholars have found evidence that Mary often took the place of Artemis in populations that worshiped the latter. The Benedictine Order under Cluny also encouraged and amplified Marian devotions. Even the Templars, the military religious order founded in 1119 to protect pilgrims to the Holy Land and later to Rome and Santiago de Compostela, had among their top practices a strong dedication to Our Lady. Curious that she should appear so often in rivers, caves, and on hilltops.

In the cool and respite, I fell asleep to wake some time later to dried socks and late afternoon. I reshod and walked to Villalcazar de Sirga, one of the most famous Templar settlements on the Camino after Ponferrada. I passed low hills that were manmade mounds, bodegas built into hillsides with ornate doors leading to subterranean tunnels and chambers where villagers stored their harvested food and homemade cheeses, sausages, and wine. Entering the village, I noticed that, in high contrast, a soaring fortress-like tower and church overshadowed everything else around it. It was the only surviving structure of a Templar compound that had once offered pilgrim lodging and other support structures for the Camino. La Blanca still resided here in the heart of the church fortress.

I arrived as the caretaker was beginning to lock the doors for the day and rushed up the steep stairs. At the top, I passed a young woman seated on the first step, deeply engrossed in writing in her journal. She glanced perfunctorily at me as I flitted past, and in that split second, I felt as if I had just caught sight of myself half a lifetime ago.

The caretaker let me slip inside for a quick glance at La Blanca but nothing more. She was modest and lovely but my pleasure was muted by my short visit. Disappointed, I went back outside. The young woman was gone, evaporating as deftly as the wise woman on the road had. I began to wonder if I was prone to mirage-like hallucinations now that I was on the hot meseta. It was time to stop for the day. The hot sun shone in one last blinding blaze of glory before sinking below the horizon and pouring its concentrated yellow rays like liquid gold down the two village streets that ran east to west. It seemed those two streets had been aligned that way for the singular reason I now witnessed: a molten spotlight of the last of the sun's rays highlighted every detail of the church's western wall, which was now lit like red volcanic stone.

Only then did I notice the central engraved figure over the entrance: La Blanca in all her glory. Unlike the more modest figure inside, this one was a fiery eternal queen holding court while seated on a throne made of two standing lions. It was a medieval replica of the Classical style common in the ancient Mediterranean which depicts the ancient mother goddess as creator and sustainer of all life. A thousand years ago, someone had planned this placement and image so that she would be revealed and revered by the setting sun casting daily light onto her magnificence and her miracle working powers to those of us below.

Then I looked even more closely. La Blanca's feet rested on the back of a docile serpent dragon. In her right hand, she held an orb, and in her left, now empty, it looked as if she once held a scepter, or as easily, a spindle. A happy baby Jesus nestled in her left arm, reaching his hand for her breast, for the mother's milk that nourishes and sustains us all.

As the sun departed, I climbed down the steep steps. I felt disoriented from the intensity of the day, but then the grounding scent of aniseed, butter, and sugar wafted down the same street that had just channeled the sun. I inhaled and followed it to its source, a small bakery selling crispy aniseed cakes. I was famished, and the cakes hit the spot. I turned back to the center to secure a bed and find dinner. On my way, I passed a small flyer pasted to an outer wall announcing a new book on the Camino, *El Juego Templario de la Oca en el Camino de Santiago* by Fernando Lalanda. I jotted the title down, planning to look it up later and see if it added any insights to the increasingly popular theory that the Game of the Goose was a Templar creation. More often than not espoused by male pilgrims, this theory cast the Templars as the creators of the Game of the Goose, claiming it was really a map that hid treasures and esoteric truths on the Camino in such places as here. The treasures in question, like the metaphor of vision, were both material and spiritual. Associated with all this was the golden goose, a magical creature that the Templars possessed. It may have been their most precious treasure, which offered endless gold as well as spiritual wealth. As much as the goose was a survivor of ancient European traditions connected to the divine feminine, here it had migrated to also being a source of wealth for male romantics devoted to monk knights protecting pilgrims and treasure. The goose was what each seeker made it.

There was a third possibility, one I saw as merging the two views: Since the Templar Knights were also fervently devoted to Mary, could she be their true golden goose?

Right across from the church I found an inn that offered me both a bed and a pilgrim dinner in the bar. Many locals were already gathered there, crowding around the counter to enjoy conversation and an early evening drink. The bartender took me to a table; I seemed to be the only pilgrim there. But as the bartender returned with my garden salad, grilled hake, roasted potatoes, and carafe of wine, the young woman I'd seen at the top of the church steps entered the bar. She looked my way and smiled. She joined me and we fell into easy conversation.

She had just graduated from college in Oregon with a degree in social sciences. Taking a break between school and job hunting, she hoped the Camino would galvanize her direction. "What I really want to be is a writer," she confessed hesitantly, almost as if this might sound silly. I hadn't yet told her about my own walk-of-life.

I also recognized the tone in her voice for I too had once had it, having too often heard how people responded to that very wish with critique or by outright writing it off as a pipe dream. "I saw you running up the steps," she said before I could reply to her confession, "and thought it would be fun to talk with you, and here you are."

"I saw you too," I said, "and thought the same. I also loved seeing how intensely you were writing in your journal. It's clear you love to write."

She beamed. "I do. I really want to be a writer. I'm hoping this walk will give me the courage to give it a chance." Like me, I knew that she could not *not* write. It was as essential as breathing. "What brings you to the Camino?" she asked quickly, again, as if feeling she'd said too much.

I leaned forward as if to share a great secret. "I'm a writer and am researching and writing a new guidebook on the Camino."

"For an actual publisher?"

"Yes."

She began to laugh and couldn't stop. It was infectious. We picked up our wine glasses and clinked. "I can't believe it," she said. "In all the villages in all of the Camino, you happened to walk into mine." We laughed more and clinked again. "Do you mind if I ask you how you pulled it off?"

"Truthfully, I feel like I'm still pulling it off, but I now have more traction and tread and a thicker skin. It's definitely not a straight road and certainly not a well understood one, but if your heart calls you to follow it, it's worth answering the call to find out what's possible." I smiled, hearing myself merge Miles' words with Sarah's.

We cut the crap then, and talked craft over dinner, lingering long afterward to finish the wine in the carafe. When we said goodnight, we hugged a hug of kinship and encouragement. I wrote in my notebook just before turning in that on that day I had experienced the full force of the triple goddess—maid, mother, and crone: the young woman setting off onto her life path was the maid; I, the woman in the middle, deeply on my path but still both daughter and mother; and the wise woman at the fork of the road who had walked long enough to know that even in a drought she could be strong and self-sufficient and help the likes of me find water and my way. Out on the sunbaked, fly-riddled meseta, we three formed an interconnected, flowing, sacred circle.

I departed Villalcazar de Sirga early the next morning. No one else was visible on the trail. The sun rose on a vast, flat expanse of straw-colored fields. Songbirds flitted around tall stocks of wheat that had escaped the harvest as olive green lizards scurried across the path to find the next patch of weeds. Sometimes, from nearly dry waterholes I heard frogs grumble, hoping for rain. And with the rising sun and fresh sweat, the flies returned, sticking to my skin, and swarming near my mouth and nose. I forgot the triple goddess and La Blanca and swatted away at them, finally rushing into the protective arms of the town of Carrion de los Condes, where the flies halted at the gates and the weekly market unfolded within. This was the Camino, with its alternating ordeals and gifts, often like a massive series of mood swings. On the upswing, I passed colorful tables arraying from the Plaza de Santa María, all of them piled high with produce, farmhouse cheeses, sausages, breads, piles of clothing, household goods, and kitchen gadgets. The square's church of the same name offered a medieval backdrop to a scene that would have been familiar to a pilgrim arriving there centuries earlier when the town, like now, was both a market center and a pilgrim stop. I let the time-travel effect take hold of me and folded into the scene, soaking up the town, visiting its churches, alber- gues, hotels, and cafes. But while I absorbed many things, goose signs were not among them. I parted the town, passing on the outskirts the tenth-century monastery of San Zoilo with its thick Renaissance embellishments. As I crossed the Carrion River upon leaving, I saw ducks below, swimming in place against the river's current. On a whim, I counted them: fourteen, the full number of waterfowl on the goose game. Coincidence, duck humor, or a sign? I had little chance to consider it. As soon as I traversed the bridge and passed the monastery, the flies returned with a vengeance. I could hear their wings now, slicing the air with a subtle metallic rattle.

I booked it to Terradillos de los Templarios, arriving numb, hot, and thirsty, and sought refuge in the shade of the hamlet's thirteenth-century, red brick Mudéjar bell tower built by Iberian Muslim masons in Castile. The church was closed. Not a soul stirred in the hamlet. The albergue I aimed for, named for the last Templar Knight, the grand master Jacques de Molay, who was murdered in 1314, following all his brothers, was quiet, though the gate was wide open.

The hamlet, as the name implied, was associated with the Templars, the same ones who had built up Villalcazar de Sirga. It was here, fables recount, that these monk-knights may have hidden the golden goose, the magical bird who lay golden eggs and was the purported source of the Templars' wealth. With Jacques de Molay's death, knowledge of the whereabouts of the bird was lost. Or was it? Recalling serpent symbolism studying New Testament scholar James H. Charlesworth's admonition that the modern mind has lost its ability to think symbolically, I felt that it seemed foolish to put a literal interpretation on a medieval fable. Rather than an actual golden goose, this bird had to be a metaphor, like Mother Goose, for a divine presence. My mind returned again to Mary. She was certainly there, a magnificent golden presence as La Blanca in Villalcazar, where each day she was revealed in glory by the setting sun, herself a bright eternal sun, a golden egg, showering us all with love and light, the ultimate wealth.

Or what if the golden goose is within? Could that be what the Game of the Goose guides us toward, finding our own golden goose through a path of inner spiritual transformation? That by walking, or playing, we are initiated and awakened to the greater possibilities within ourselves and begin to shed the literalist and material ideas of life, trading yellow gold for spirit gold? Here again, was Bernadette's alchemical journey.

I waited and looked around and still saw no one stir. A new surge of energy rose within me, and I refilled my bottle at the village fountain and propelled forward. As soon as I did, the flies bore down on me with their disco-ball eyes, rattling their metallic wings. Midway to the red brick village of Moratinos, I found a marker identifying the medieval monastery of Villaoreja that once stood on the left of the trail and offered hospitality to pilgrims. Locals had built a stone labyrinth in the center of a grove of trees and installed benches, creating an energetic marker for a once vibrant place and a reminder of the spiral form of the Game of the Goose and the quest. The path of enlightenment is not a straight line but a layered and spiraling effort.

I passed into Moratinos to its village square, which was covered in colorful crocheted tapestries hanging from trees and banners strung across the plaza and church. A third wind of energy pushed me on to the next hamlet of San Nicolás del Real Camino. When I arrived, the fragrant roasting meat, blistering red peppers, and free flowing red wine pulled me toward a café on the trail's edge. There, two splendors unfolded at once: first, I was drawn into a late lunch and celebration of the sixtieth anniversary of a local couple; and next, my tablet pinged with a message that childhood friends from Colorado, who were on a driving tour of Italy, France, and Spain, were somewhere west of Burgos. Was there any chance they could intersect with me on the Camino? I gave them my coordinates and fifteen minutes later, friends from over fifty years of my life walked through the door of the café. Villagers plied them with the same exuberant warmth, food, and wine. We had landed firmly on a golden goose square, or at the very least, on one of its golden eggs.

CYGNUS

AFTER LUNCH, MY friends and I called and booked three rooms at a family inn in Sahagún, eight kilometers (five miles) farther ahead. Then I hopped into my friends' rental car, riding the wind of this unexpected coincidence. After we checked in, we wandered the town, visiting the remarkable red brick and geometric-patterned Mudéjar churches, the signature style of the structures in Sahagún and its surrounding areas, where stone was scarce, but red-brick baked earth was plentiful and stunning. Iberian Muslim masons developed the aesthetic and constructed such Mudéjar churches, mosques, and synagogues across medieval Spain. Sahagún boasts at least four such holy structures, and we talked and walked and visited each one, winding down for tapas in Sahagún's Plaza Mayor, which was throbbing with the town's local life. I told them about the guidebook, and I told them about the goose.

I also had a history with Sahagún and now I was sharing it with people with whom I had an even deeper history, and the merging of these two streams both dispelled fatigue and flies and brought on deep contentment. Years back, I had spent a few weeks in Sahagún visiting friends who generously let me stay with them and pulled me into the rich community, especially with one native family headed by a matriarchal powerhouse whom we all called La Paca, not merely Paca. La Paca had sought me out every day I was there and taught me something new about life on the meseta. From her I learned the secret to making the best *tortilla española,* Spanish potato and onion omelet. When it came time to set a plate over the frittata-like mass and turn it to cook on the other side, La Paca had said, "You must flip it with confidence. Confidence is everything." I also learned from her and her family how to make wine as I joined their annual *vendimia*, harvesting, destemming, and pressing countless kilos of both white and red grapes, then storing the result in large vats in their underground bodega for the first fermentation. La Paca's son-in-law had sealed that door and set a lit candle on the floor on the outside. "If the flame goes out," La Paca explained, "it means the gases are strong and to stay away because it can suffocate you." Then we all went upstairs to a massive feast prepared from foods grown in the garden and came close to finishing what remained of the prior year's wine. For the first time, I had fully grasped the labors of the year engraved on so many medieval Romanesque churches in France and Spain, showing each month's work in the agrarian calendar. September was always the *vendimia*. It was a mythic September in Sahagún.

Perhaps the apex of my heady time in Sahagún was when La Paca took my friends and me to help her clean and prim the Érmita de Nuestra Señora del Puente, Our Lady of the Bridge, on the bank of the tiny Río Valderaduey, right on the Camino, where it crossed a medieval stone bridge on the outskirts of town. For generations La Paca's family was the caretaker of the hermitage and greeted pilgrims on their way into Sahagún. The hermitage also marked the midway point of the Camino for those who had begun walking from Saint-Jean-Pied-de-Port.

Early the next morning, my friends set off. I walked with them to their rental car. As we hugged goodbye, one, a scientist with a strong background in biology, said, "I've been thinking about what you told us last night about the Game of the Goose, the flight of geese, and the path of the Milky Way. Since geese, swans, and ducks are so closely related, you ought to look into Cygnus, the swan constellation in the Via Lactea. Navigators often locate Cygnus in the sky," she added, "to identify the location of the Via Lactea. It's like a gateway to that part of the galaxy."

I watched them drive away, my head abuzz with what she'd just said. I recalled an article I'd written on an archaeologist working in North America who had told me that among many Native American traditions, Cygnus guarded the gateway to the land of souls toward which the recently deceased traveled via the Milky Way. Merging this idea with the one that holds that the Camino was a terrestrial map mirroring the celestial one of stars in the sky, the Game of the Goose could be seen as a map for both heaven and earth. The game maps onto the earth-packed road below the celestial events—gateways, thresholds, meetings, departures, transformations in motion—unfolding in the Via Lactea far above. Moreover, that way is marked by tradition with clues and hunches, guarded and guided by swans, ducks, and geese who lead the pilgrim on the ultimate journey and destination: meeting oneself at the soul level.

I recalled the many geese and ducks I'd met standing at thresholds, such as the twenty-six ducks of Morlaàs in Aquitaine. It was they who first taught me that ducks and geese are gatekeepers, guides, and guardians to hidden worlds right before our eyes. And now, here was the alchemical process that transforms us from duck and goose to swan, Cygnus, the final threshold, the winning sixty-third square of the game.

I retraced my steps back to San Nicolás del Real Camino and then turned and walked back to Sahagún. I saved time to linger at the hermitage of Mary of the Bridge on my return, slowing and savoring the full feeling of being a pilgrim to Santiago de Compostela as I crossed the stone footbridge to the chapel. Only then did I connect the dots: here was yet another river Mary, another watery divinity on the Camino protecting passage.

The hermitage's red brick Mudéjar horseshoe arches, now half sunk into the earth, held the same roughshod beauty that had moved me twenty years earlier. I could still hear La Paca turning the heavy lock and pushing open the thick wooden arched door while handing me a broom. We had swept the floor, dusted the surfaces, and replaced old flowers within large vases on the altar with new, fresh cut from La Paca's garden. Back then, the altar held the image of La Virgen del Puente, but now it was kept in a church in town during the cooler months and only brought here in summer. I learned that today La Paca's granddaughter carried on her care of the chapel, which this day was locked. I wish I had known to check all those years ago to look at Mary's feet for telltale webbed feet.

I savored the cool morning air and poplar tree shade of the hermitage and ran my hands along the sunken horseshoe arch of the outside wall, thinking of La Paca and her generosity and that of the friends who had invited me here. Though La Paca had passed away a few years earlier, I could still feel her spirit.

I walked briskly back to Sahagún, wrapped in these warm memories plus revelations from my Colorado friend about Cygnus. All this—meeting all these friends in Sahagún, two streams of personal history merging into one—felt like goose timing.

SAINT JAMES'S DICE

STAYED ON in Sahagún another day to catch up with work and take a rest day. It was then, while doing some research on the internet, that I discovered that a local parish priest in Logroño, Rafael Ojeda Bermejo, had been the main influence and force behind the inlaid Game of the Goose boardgame on the Plaza de Santiago in that city, now 250 kilometers behind me. But if I could find him and talk to him, I would stop back in Logroño on my return to France in a few weeks' time. I dug some more: Ojeda had passed away the year before. As I read more, I saw that he left a legacy consisting of his good works and kindness as a beloved member of his community, as well as some writing and a series of sketches of the Game of the Goose. A regional magazine had published one of his articles, containing his ideas about the goose and the symbolism of the game. I excitedly tracked down the editor but my every effort to secure a copy hit dead ends. It felt as if I stood before a locked door behind which I knew there was real treasure. The existence of Ojeda's article was like that piece of folded paper in the young man from Köln's pocket, only now I could legitimately have a look, if only I could find a copy. It tortured me, but I had to let it go.

On the eve of my departure from Sahagún, I saved for last a visit to La Peregrina, a thirteenth-century church and monastery overlooking the western skyline that housed on its altar a statue of Mary dressed as a pilgrim. The sun was just skimming the horizon's treetops when I passed through the Gothic-Mudéjar horseshoe-arched entrance. King Alfonso X, in his *Cantigas,* wrote about this place, telling the story of pilgrims who arrived in Sahagún in the pitch black of night, unable to see where to go or how to find shelter, when a mysterious woman carrying a luminous staff approached them and led them to food and lodging. She was La Peregrina, none other than Mary appearing as a pilgrim herself.

A young woman greeted me enthusiastically at the monastery's entrance and asked to see my pilgrim's credential. When she saw that I had journeyed from Saint-Jean-Pied-de-Port, she asked if she could hold on to my credential in order to fill out a certificate acknowledging I arrived at this halfway point on the Camino. I had forgotten this was where I could get this and happily left my pilgrim's passport with her and went to visit the monastery's church. On the altar stood Mother Mary, dressed in a medieval traveling cape and hat adorned with scallop shells. A sturdy wooden staff in her right hand carried a water gourd. In her left arm, she embraced her cheerful and chubby Son, his only attire three rays of gold radiating out from his crown to form the triple-spired pattern of the Trinity, or in my new way of seeing, the goose's footprint. Otherwise, he was buck naked and didn't care.

I uttered prayers of gratitude at La Peregrina's feet, then visited the restored monastery, now a remarkable archaeological site. Over two decades earlier, restorers had removed coats of plain white plaster from the walls to find, to their surprise, older and more ornate plaster work underneath that appeared like the elegantly sculpted and painted geometric patterns found on the walls and ceilings of the Alhambra palace of Granada in southern Spain. In the Middle Ages, when Sahagún was one of the most powerful Benedictine centers in Spain and Europe, the town's religious buildings had all looked like this, a mixed style that resulted from their being created by builders from Iberia's many communities, Jewish, Muslim, and Christian.

Back at the entrance, the woman stood from behind her desk, and with ritual formality and blessings presented me with my credential and a parchment illuminated with medieval-style dragons and floral patterns. In the calligraphic text I found my name. Tears pricked my eyes with unexpected emotion. The woman

congratulated me and hugged me warmly. When I stepped outside, the sun was inking intense rays of strong pink, orange, cherry,
and violet across the horizon. I watched until the psychedelic sky
turned dark blue, and the milky star road came out.

The next morning, back on the trail, the same strong sun bore
down in relentless hot spears, more flies than ever hounding my
way. I pushed myself to pick up my pace in a futile effort to outrun
them. I tried to squeeze into the bit of shade offered by scrawny
rows of young poplar trees lining the path. I saw few pilgrims.
Many had decided to ditch the meseta and its unprecedented
drought and take the bus to León. But I had thrown my dice,
gambled on walking this whole trail, noting every nuance of it,
and now forgetting my own name, let alone why I was here. The
flies and heat pushed me past a point of tolerance than I could
handle in the moment, and I felt oddly unanchored, drifting away
from both body and mind.

It wasn't just the absurd heat and flies, it was also the miles and
miles of unbroken, straw-toned, and flat terrain whose monotony
magnified the unease of my body, and worse, the noise in my head.
What constant chatter arose in my mind; I seemed to be thinking
of every single thing that had happened in my past, both resolved
and unresolved. Why was I back there, again? Hadn't I finished
going over this, and this, and this? I actually began to run, trying
to outpace both the flies and myself, seeking to reach the next refuge as quickly as possible. I spiraled and kicked and squirmed, and
the last thread that held me in my body suddenly snapped, and I
hovered over my crown, seeing what a spectacle I had become. I
found a bench near the emaciated poplars and forced myself to
stop, take a deep breath, and an even deeper glug of water, and
forced myself to hold focus on the bottom of my feet and my solar
plexus and ignore the increasing swarm of flies moving in for a
kill. I then willed one foot forward, then the next, doing my best
to hold my focus on my feet and plexus. Remarkably, it worked.
The more steps I took, the more I reclaimed body and mind. The
flies, I chanted aloud, were temporary. And so was the heat. Did
not the Camino guide and provide? I recalled the miracles and gifts

MARY'S DICE

THE NEXT TWO days, dust and drought persisted and flies came and went, but I was different. I practiced a new way of walking, focusing on where my feet touched the earth, knowing I was not alone. I reached León, passing through the city's remaining thick Roman walls and into its medieval heart, stopping first at an uneven square known by three names: Plaza del Grano, Plaza del Mercado, Plaza de Santa Maria del Camino—plaza of grain, of market, of Mary. There was a lot going on there. The plaza had been the old grain and bread market square, but it also is on the Camino and holds a Marian miracle within its broad and uneven cobblestones, which have been polished to a shiny gloss from nearly two millennia of foot and cart traffic. It stands outside the first walls of Roman León and within the broader medieval walls that fortified and enclosed both the original city and today's city center.

In the sixth century, a shepherd boy spied something hiding in a bush and approached it to find an icon of Mary. Locals built a chapel, Iglesia de Santa María del Mercado, in Mary's honor near that spot, a place that had already been erected by the time a first historical reference was made to it in 1092. City excavations also found the locale contains old Roman stones and inscriptions, suggesting it was already a holy site in pre-Christian times.

I walked around the early Romanesque chapel, finding rich, mixed, and several saucy images on the corbels and capitals, a gathering of both pagan and Biblical characters existing in harmony. It was clear the building had been early enough for the migration of symbols from one sacred system to another to still be in process but not yet fully appropriated by the Church.

Inside, the chapel was uncluttered and serene, focused wholly on Mary on the altar, who surprised me. I had expected to find a more archaic Mary, such as the ones I'd seen all along the Camino, which also had appeared via natural channels, such as rivers, apple trees, or caves. But this bush Mary was a *pietà*, the suffering mother who held her son when he was brought down from the cross. In this sculpture, which dates to the sixteenth century, Mary cradles Jesus in her arms in deep shock and grief. Her son is draped across her lap with his face up and his head falling back, his chin pointing to the sky.

Only when I turned to go did I spot the icon more likely to be the one the shepherd had seen. Set on the side near the back stood a solitary Mary looking much like a guide one might meet on the path, her arms relaxed and hanging at her sides. Face death courageously, she seemed to be saying—addressing my question as to why the pietà, and not this image, was front and center—for after it, there is resurrection. *Ánimo y fe*, as the woman in Estella had called to me months back, *have courage and faith*.

I walked deeper into León, where all roads lead to the Gothic cathedral of Santa María, so fine and lacey that it seemed to be made more of stained glass than of stone. The Gothic cathedral was built over three older churches, the first one built by Visigoths over the old Roman baths. The cathedral was devoted to La Blanca, the White Virgin, the celebrated Mary of great miracles and of the golden setting sun, whom I had met in Villalcazar de Sirga. I found her image standing at the western entrance, the baby Jesus in her arm, welcoming the visitor to step inside. Though La Blanca held her son, her posture seemed to me to be similar to that of the solo Mary I'd just seen at the side chapel in the church of Santa María del Mercado. Once I found a place to stay and could leave my pack, I would take La Blanca up on her invitation and make a proper visit to her temple.

Deeper into León's old Roman heart I went, heading to where Mercury's temple once stood and now sits the Basilica of San

Isidoro, an eleventh-century Romanesque church. I found pilgrim accommodations on the square across from the church, then rushed to the basilica before it closed for the afternoon. The dusty heat from outside gave way to fresh cool air and incense. I began in the back and wandered along the nave, looking at each sculpture on the capitals and all the stonemasons' marks on the pillars. These marks were individual signatures, identifying who worked on what stone, a way to keep track and pay each artisan for his labor. It also was a way the masons could encode into the stones sacred symbolism and special symbols personally meaningful to them, their craft, and their society of itinerant artisans.

One of the marks was an arrow, a symbol I had thought of as more modern than medieval, for it has come to represent the Camino through the yellow arrows that were painted all along the trail in the 1980s by O Cebreiro's parish priest, Elías Valiña Sampedro. But now, as I looked at the medieval arrow, I saw it in reverse, forming a goose's footprint. I heard footsteps approaching and turned to see a priest. He welcomed me enthusiastically and asked where my pilgrimage had begun. I wanted to give him the whole story, the many pilgrimages, even the lure of the quest, but a group of pilgrims arrived in that moment, making a beeline toward the small table the priest had just abandoned, set with stamp and ink pad, so I went for brevity.

"In Saint-Jean-Pied-de-Port."

He looked at me quizzically, then invited me to walk with him to the table. "That is a long way," he said, "and you have come far, but I think it always begins even before those first steps on the trail."

"I began in 1986," I fessed up, "when I first heard about the Camino." He smiled. "It always works that way," he said. He took my passport, stamped it, and handed it back. "The Camino calls and that is the starting point. But we are always given signs, signs only we can read and interpret." Had he seen me lingering on that stone-etched goosefoot? Was he giving me a green light that I was on the right track? I'd like to think so, but I never had a chance to ask. The line grew longer behind me, and he gently took my

hand and recited the pilgrim's prayer, asking that my way be protected and blessed. He then made the sign of the cross over me.
The way he invoked this benediction, with the melodic kindness
in his voice, made me cry.

"*Tranquila hija, todo esta bien*," he said, concerned. "Don't
worry, daughter, all is well."

"It's just very touching to receive such a blessing," I offered.
I wanted to talk to him about how Saint James had appeared by
my side, about how I was looking for the goose, about how he
reminded me of my grandfather, who had been a kind and intuitive man like him. Instead, I thanked him and let the others behind
me have their turn. "Remember, *hija, todo esta bien,*" he repeated
as I walked away.

As I sought lunch I took stock of the rollercoaster of beauty
roiling inside me. After lunch, I went back to the cathedral and
stepped through La Blanca's western gate and into a forest of intricate and richly toned stained glass lining all sides of the spacious
nave and towering columns. It all led the eye to the altar on the east
side, the direction not only of the rising sun but also in Christian
sacred architecture the direction of the ideal and celestial city of
the heavenly Jerusalem. I was so overtaken by the kaleidoscope of
color and glass that I stood a while in front of a doorway on the
north arm of the cathedral before I noticed the stonework there,
which centered on another image of Mary. Her posture mirrored
that of La Blanca's on the western entrance, strong and regal. In her
left arm, she held the baby Jesus, and in her right hand, a flower.
She was known as La Virgen del Dado, Our Lady of the Dice.
Apparently, inside the stone flower in her hand, was hidden a pair
of dice. *Dice?*

According to a legend, sometime in the late Middle Ages, local
gamblers would come here and sacrilegiously use the cloister for
their gaming. One day, having seen the purse of a visiting pilgrim
in the cloister, the gamblers enticed him to join their game. The
more the gullible pilgrim played, the more he lost. In frustration,
he threw the dice hard toward the cloister's doorway where they

struck the baby Jesus. To everyone's shock, the stone sculpture began to bleed. Ever since, his mother has been called Mary of the Dice. It is said that she tucked away the dice inside her flower for safekeeping and to teach the pilgrim a lesson about giving in to foolish temptation.

Spanish writer Juan Atienza notes in his book, *Leyendas del Camino de Santiago,* that this legend is told from a stonemason's point of view: the dice represent the cube form in sacred geometry, which in turn, with its square solidity, represents the sacred, grounded earth. Here are merged heaven and earth and mother and son in a threshold space where the divine is made incarnate, earth-bound, through the mother who gave birth to the Son of God. The legend warns the visitor not to cast one's dice with mortal gamblers but with the divine. And Mary, who is often cast as the guardian to the earthly places where we can connect to heaven, she is our guide into the deeper wisdom encoded on earth, hidden in a place where one must seek it mindfully, as in a walking meditation, be it in a cloister, within a labyrinth, or on the Camino. Rolling her dice was a win. Atienza calls this dice Mary a Black Madonna for her connection to the rich, dark earth; for her role as the bridge between heaven and earth; and for her role in taking us deeper into spiritual devotion in the center of the cathedral after her sister, La Blanca, in the light of the sun, the yang to her yin, invited us in.

I looked more closely at her. She seemed to hide more than dice but wore a facial expression that, though commanding, felt more approachable than that of her sister on the western gate. I wasn't alone in my impression. In 1915, when art historian Georgiana Goddard King, who famously documented the whole of the Camino Francés's medieval art, stood here, she noted that of all the Madonnas in León, this dice Virgin appeared to her eye as the most human and the most regal.

I rolled my dice and entered the cloister, the enclosed garden, *hortus conclusus,* the deeper heart and womb of the cathedral. It all overlayed perfectly with the form of the Game of the Goose, with its goose goddess guardians, its labyrinth-shaped game board, its dice, its gifts and ordeals, and the paradise in the final square and center.

I spent another day in León, walking as much as I did on a typical day on the trail, if not more, to cover all the aspects of the city. That night, past sheer exhaustion, I skipped dinner and fell into bed, sleeping without waking or dreaming. It felt like a miracle when I woke early, fully restored and anxious to be back on the trail. I left the city at dawn.

Over seven kilometers (4.4 miles) later, I came upon another shrine to Santa María del Camino, the same Mary who had come to a shepherd in the sixth century at the site of the Plaza del Grano on the east side of León. A thousand years later she appeared to another shepherd whose name we know, Alvar Simón. In 1505, Mary approached Alvar with a rock in her hand. She threw the stone and the two watched it roll and grow and grow until it became a massive boulder. Mary told Alvar to return with the authorities and show them the place where the rock had landed and have them build her a church there. He did, and it took little convincing in this boulder-free area for the authorities to accept the shepherd's vision. They quickly built a chapel. That sixteenth-century chapel had been entirely rebuilt in 1961, but the figure inside the modern building was the original icon from the first chapel.

With its modern architectural ingenuity, the rectangular form and angle of the structure, even from the street level, drew my eye through its doors to the tunnel of light that flowed down the nave to a luminous being seated in a grotto on the altar. In parallel imagery to the Mary of the Camino on the east side of the city, this one also had Mary's image on the altar in the form of a pietà, but it was altered in a curious way: Jesus lay face down across his mother's lap with his chin and gaze facing the earth, and his legs looked primed to step off the platform and onto the road.

From bush to boulder, separated by a thousand years, came the two visions of the same Madonna on either side of the city and on the Camino, both connecting Mary to nature as much as to being our guardian and guide on the earth. The two formed a perfect bracket around León, an east-to-west line in whose center sat the cathedral with two other Marys, La Blanca and the Black Madonna. Moreover, in the first pietà on the east side of León, Jesus had faced the sky, and his legs had been fully immobile. But here, he seemed to be saying, "Remember the earth as you unify heaven and earth, and more, I'm ready to walk with you as you press on." It all tumbled into place, with the four Marys of León forming a massive labyrinth that covered the whole town and its suburbs. The first, on the market square outside old León, welcomes us in, reminding us of life's sacrifice and divine will with Jesus looking up to his mother and the sky. The second, La Blanca, welcomes us into the center as her sister, and the third, the Black Virgin, takes us deeper, to the sacred earth's center and hidden truths. The fourth one is seen upon leaving the city, exiting the labyrinth, and she reminds us to take the deeper wisdom gained here back out onto the trail, into the world, and more, that we are not alone in this walk: Jesus joins us on hallowed earth.

The whole of León and the Camino was indeed a hidden map with special squares and, like on the Game of the Goose, the map contains hidden messages that can catapult one's journey toward a deeper inner and outer awareness of all things, most especially, of one's own essence. Stunned, and exhilarated by this realization, I resumed the westward walk solo, but I was certainly not alone. And not long after leaving, another pilgrim joined me, an upbeat man from Vancouver. He loved everything about the Camino, and especially its history, which was one reason why he was walking.

"Are you a historian?"

"Oh, no, I'm an accountant," he laughed. "But I love my work. I love helping people fulfill their dreams." A financial advisor, he managed client wealth, investments, and retirement plans. I liked him, but I grew reticent. I was a financial advisor's worst idea of sound financial planning, having invested everything I earned back into my writing. I hoped he wouldn't ask me what I did.

"And what do you do?" he asked.

I hemmed and hawed and finally blurted out, "I'm a writer, and I've probably done everything you advise your clients not to do." I regretted saying it as soon as it blew past my lips.

"Are you happy?" he asked.

"I couldn't be happier," I confessed. "I love what I do."

"Then you *are* wealthy," he said. "By living as you do, life has given you pockets full of joy."

"Pockets full of joy," I repeated, "what a beautiful thing to say."

"It's true," he said. "You have a wealth one cannot cultivate without risk. I've found that people who aren't happy in life need investments and retirement plans more because they *don't* have pockets full of joy to propel them into more fruitful lives. You live a life of contentment, no matter your financial status. And," he added with a warm smile, "you make the world a better place because you are doing what you are called to do, not what is expected of you by social norms." I felt a surge of extra joy exceeding the size of my pockets, as I realized that I was indeed living my right livelihood, which had been my goal all along, and following my soul's calling. To be told this by an accountant from Vancouver was as potent as the first time a local had called me a pilgrim. I fully relaxed and thoroughly soaked up the financial advisor's sunshine, patting my pockets to feel the golden joy. We returned to talking about history, and time and distance flew past. The dusty ochre road began to turn reddish yellow then rusty from the increasing iron-rich earth and our growing nearness to the mountains of León. In Villadangos del Páramo, the Canadian declared he was done for the day. I thanked him for his good company and perspective and continued on for a few more kilometers, hoping fate would put him in my path again. With my pockets full of joy, I arrived in the village of San Martín del Camino and was drawn toward an open door and a friendly woman standing there.

She welcomed me to her albergue. Passing in through the large kitchen, with its counters overflowing with piles of peppers, squashes, and gourds next to wheels of cheese and arrays of wine, I declared this my halt for the day. The hospitalera checked me in and showed me to my dorm room. "Dinner is at seven," she said, "and everything is made from ingredients from my daughter's farm."

By the time I returned from taking a shower and handwashing my clothes, other pilgrims had claimed most of the beds in the room. There was a couple from Sicily, a quiet young man from Korea, a shy young woman from Mexico who had just graduated from college, an older businessman from Madrid, a honeymooning couple from Seville, and an actress from Finland. For days, because of the demands of my work, I had been missing the camaraderie of other pilgrims, but that day amply made up for it. My joy was untarnished even when a group of haughty cyclists from Milan arrived and dominated the other dorm room and communal spaces, filling the albergue with lycra and testosterone. That is, until two Californians arrived, women of a certain age who were fit, tall, and muscular, with sparkling eyes and bright smiles. We learned they were police officers celebrating their recent retirement by walking the Camino.

"We hope we'll each get the answer for what to do next with our lives before we finish walking," one of the women said.

"Have you gotten any hints yet?" I asked.

"Not a one," the other chimed in, "but a lot of stuff comes up, stuff you have to slough off. Maybe we have to shed what doesn't serve us anymore before gaining answers for our next steps."

We were all helping to set the table, and everyone—except the gawking men from Milan—nodded in accord. We all were going through the same thing. Earlier that day, I had fretted over my financial status but was gifted with pockets full of joy, pockets I'd had all along but had not seen as wealth. We sat down for dinner as fragrant savory dishes came out of the kitchen: pumpkin soup, garden salad, grilled smoky paprika chicken, baked root vegetables and caramelized onions, chocolate pudding, and copious local red wine. We all bonded further through food and drink, so after dinner, when one of the Sicilians picked up a guitar and began to sing, we all joined in, even the bikers, as one big happy family. The next morning, we all hugged, and one by one, we set off into the gray drizzle that had gathered overnight.

The dirt path turned a deeper iron-rich, blood-orange red with each step. It magnified the beauty of several cream and black spiral-patterned snails that crept slowly across the track, coming out in droves on the lush, wet day. I stepped carefully around them as I passed corn, wheat, and beet fields. A cottony mist hovered six feet above the ground. As I left the meseta and neared the mountains, the land rippled into hide-and-seek hills. One crease opened to reveal a thirteenth-century, nineteen-arched stone bridge leading with fanfare into Hospital de Órbigo. The bridge had been the scene of a fifteenth-century jousting match over the unrequited love of a lady. The heartbroken challenger won against dozens of competitors and finally made the pilgrimage to Santiago de Compostela to let go of his romantic longing at Saint James's feet; thereafter he was a free man. May that he found his own pockets full of joy.

Soon after Hospital de Órbigo, I continued to walk alone. No one else was visible on the trail as I neared a van parked to the side of the dirt road where two men worked in a ditch. One said "*buenos días*," to me when I was within ear shot. I returned the greeting and felt from him the usual goodwill many locals offered passing pilgrims. But his companion straightened up from his work and gave me a bone-chilling up-and-down scan and, without preliminaries, said, "Aren't you afraid to be out here all alone?" His tone was challenging and cold. Everything about him sent off alarms. I hastened my pace.

"He didn't mean it," I heard the first man call after me, apologizing for his friend. Whether he did or didn't was not the issue. I flew along the trail, adrenaline, fear, and anger propelling me forward.

51

HOUSE OF THE GODS

SCANNED THE terrain as I went, seeing that it was still just me out there, and them. I sent out a silent prayer for protection. "*Todo esta bien*," I heard the words of the priest in León echo back at me in my head. I also heard another voice, someone from behind, calling my name along with the sound of rapidly approaching feet. It was the accountant. How had he materialized from thin air? With gratitude and shaking knees, I waited for him to catch up.

"I saw you back there when I came up over a rise and I got a bad feeling," he told me. "Do you mind if I walk with you?"

"You have no idea," I said. "Or maybe you do?"

He confessed that something about one of the men by the van had set off his own inner alarm.

The Camino guides and provides. What a dear man.

Slowly, my adrenaline rush dissipated and my heart rate returned to normal. We kept a steady pace forward and by the next village had fallen back into easy conversation, picking up where we'd left off the day before. Midway to Astorga, we arrived at a ruin of partially crumbling red-earth clay walls, some covered with tarps and outfitted with benches covered in cotton Indian-ink prints. Along the earth, polished river rocks formed a large labyrinth. Other stone structures formed hearts. Someone had planted rose bushes here and there. One bloomed with a rare dusty lavender rose that perfumed the air with the scent of honeycomb and lilacs. A food cart near the trail offered baked goods, boiled eggs, fruit, granola bars, and yogurt next to a small donation box. On it was painted the words, *La Casa de los Dioses*—the House of the Gods.

David, the oasis's founder and host, greeted us and invited us to rest and enjoy a cup of tea. The Canadian accountant and I gladly accepted—it had been an overcast and chilly morning—and went inside the tent shelter, which was centered on a steaming teakettle, the wall arrayed with myriad herbal teas. Inside sat the Finn, her cold hands wrapped around a hot cup of tea. The night before I had told her of my worry over losing my parents and she said that she had just lost hers, which was the main reason why she was walking. "Be comforted, though," she had offered, "they remain with us. I feel them with me all the time. They walk with me now." I had looked up to see the young Mexican pilgrim across the dining table had also been listening, a tear rolling down her cheek. Losing her parents, it turned out, was her worry too. "Isn't it curious we three sit together tonight?" she had said. I now hugged the Finn like an old friend. We all sat down with David and learned that he lived out there among the ruined walls and had no running water or electricity but nevertheless was committed to offering generous hospitality to passing pilgrims in this forgotten place where there were no cafes or albergues.

"Why *dioses*?" I asked David.

"I want to honor everyone's beliefs," he answered. "Whatever god or gods—or even goddesses—people believe in, this is a place of complete acceptance, peace, and wellness, open to all who need it." His was an expression of the true face of God, whether we put one or many faces to it. After we finished our tea and thanked our host, the Canadian and I continued to Astorga. The Finn lingered, in no hurry to leave the warmth of the tent.

As the terrain rose, the earth darkened even more, with rainbow-hued, mineral-dense stones scattered across the crimson path. A soft rain began to fall, saturating the vibrant colors. Near Astorga, the waft of honey cakes and chocolate—two celebrated local confections—issued tauntingly from bakeries and factories on the outskirts of town. Once an Iron-Age hilltop fortress, Astorga was conquered in 19 BCE by the Romans, who turned the settlement into an administrative center for mining and transport. Several roads intersected there, including a route from the south, the Via de la Plata, or Silver Route, which, by the Middle Ages, like the Camino Francés, turned the old Roman stones into a pilgrimage road to Santiago de Compostela. We climbed along those very cobbles up and into the walled town. Midway in, the Canadian and I parted, he for his hotel and I to complete my day's research and search for a bed.

After the Romans left, Astorga remained important as a hub connecting the Galician coast on the other side of the mountains to Spain's interior, with the region's muleteers using their donkeys to transport goods over the difficult mountain passes. Following the age of colonial expansion into the New World, Astorga became a transport hub for shiploads of cacao, which were carried by mule over the mountains to Castile and transformed to chocolate. Smart locals, realizing Astorga's dry and cool climate was perfect for choc-olate-making, began perfecting the craft, and soon Astorga was famous for its chocolates. Several families still made chocolate and preserved centuries-old secrets, one reason why wherever I explored, the city seemed to be paved with cacao.

In Astorga, I studied sacred chapels, Roman remains, cafes, and accommodations, and of course did the essential research of sam-pling chocolates, but I encountered nothing pertaining to geese, at least not directly. In the cathedral, as in Santo Domingo de la Calzada, I found a special exhibit of medieval sculptures of Mary, which reminded me that she remained the most prominent and abundant holy personage on the whole route, even more so than Jesus and the Camino's namesake of Santiago. Thinking about this, I later came upon a curious historical note from the Galician parish priest of O Cebreiro, Elias Valiña Sampedro, the same man who had painted the Camino with yellow arrows. He wrote that some of the earlier medieval sculptures of Mary had shown her alone, and only centuries later did people insert the baby Jesus into her arms. One of these augmented Marys was a favorite of mine, Our Lady of the Ebro in Logroño. When she was originally found in the Ebro River by a washerwoman, she had been traveling solo.

Visiting an excavated open-air Roman home in the middle of Astorga, which was sheltered with plexiglass floors and roofing, I came upon an intriguing possibility. The vestibule had a partially preserved mosaic of Orpheus in the center, playing his calming lyre. Surrounding him on the edges were grapevines, birds, and a bear. Scholars have interpreted the lyre—a gift from the god Apollo—as representing the soul, and the animals and grapes as symbolizing the body and the seasons. I remembered meeting the wild and divine man of the forest that I encountered in the bear form of Hartza in Oloron-Sainte-Marie in the Pyrenees years earlier, and thought of the birds, like geese, as extensions of the wild divine feminine. Together, they animated both body and spirit.

Intrigued but thoroughly exhausted, I found a small, family-run inn on the western edge of town, where I enjoyed a simple dinner and a good hot shower. Before I knew it, I fell into a deep sleep and did not stir until morning.

52

THE GANDER

THE PATH OUT of Astorga led through wild, open sky and knobby, rolling terrain covered in heather and brush growing over dark-red soil and rainbow mineral stones, deep into the territory known as the Maragatería, named for the native peoples, the Maragatos, who live there. On this outer edge of Spain's central plateau, purple- and slate-tone mountains rose and drew near. The tallest peak, Monte Teleno, was considered a sacred mountain for thousands of years, and scattered all around its skirt and plains are prehistoric petroglyphs whose spiraling forms align to the rising and setting sun. Geese rule here too, if one were to take up the name of the approaching small hamlet of El Ganso, or the Gander.

In 1142, El Ganso was an important village, with a Benedictine church and pilgrim hospital. Today, like its church, it is a tiny, quiet, serene place. But it seemed to me to hold a mystery: no one I asked knew why it was called "the Gander," except those French and Spanish seekers hot on the goose trail who insisted it was a hidden clue. More intriguing to me was that up until then, all the references to waterfowl that I had encountered on the Camino had been to female geese. What did the gander mean, then, and why a gander out in the middle of seemingly nowhere?

But the first thing that struck me when I began speaking with a local family was that I had framed my question wrong: the town isn't in the middle of seemingly nowhere. It is indeed another threshold, a place of transition, of shifting, of connecting two realms—be it heaven meeting earth or plateau meeting mountains and of pilgrims going deeper and higher. Perhaps the gander is a reminder to the seeker, at this place of dramatic transition, to merge the wild divine female and the wild divine male into a harmonious whole? Warming to this idea after seeing Orpheus's bear and bird mosaic in Astorga, I took a rest and had some mineral water at the funky, Western-inspired Cowboy Bar in this Maragato herder, muleteer, and farmer settlement; then I went to explore the tiny village church, devoted to Santiago, of course, the Camino's wild divine man. Surely, here was the gander?

The church's stark, whitewashed interior contained few embellishments other than a bold altar holding the crucified Christ before a painting of a heavenly Jerusalem. I did not see Santiago. Was Christ the gander? Feeling no more the wiser, I was turning to exit when my eye caught a graffiti-like etching on the back of the wooden entrance door of a very clearly delineated ladder. However modern or ancient it might be, the etching felt like a message to remember the mystical journey represented by Jacob's ladder, the vehicle of ascent to heaven. It was the perfect message for a threshold place between plain and mountain, male and female, and mortal pilgrim and divine presence. Before me was a major ascent, both physical and spiritual.

As I left El Ganso, the mountains rushed to meet me. The trail twisted onto rocky and uneven earth and led toward the first mountain and into the village of Rabanal del Camino. I arrived there early. As much as I loved the town, I felt pulled to continue so I could sleep that night deeper in the mountains, perhaps in Foncebadón. I wandered for a while, researching and visiting accommodations, cafes, and the church, speaking with locals as I explored. By mid-afternoon, and after a snack of nuts and fruit on the outer wall on the way out of Rabanal, I continued higher into León's mountains. They fanned out all around me in infinite blue-green layers, carpeted in pink and purple heather, feathery green ferns, and scrubby oak and pine forests. Entering Foncebadón, once a dirt-road hamlet famous for wild dogs and no human inhabitants, I felt a sudden contrast, given that the newly laid concrete road felt more like a highway than a mountain path and seemed wider than the ancient settlement itself. It nestled two kilometers below the Camino's apex, the Cruz de Ferro; despite the modern meddling, an energy emanated from the mountain that no amount of human folly could blunt. It was alive.

I knew I needed to spend the night there. I walked into the center, passing another modern addition, this one with more elegant consideration to historical continuity—a round stone tavern with a thatched roof and mosaic inlaid floors, a medieval style sign identifying it as La Taberna de Gaia, Gaia's Tavern. Both the sign and the mosaic floor boasted a great white goose standing in the center of a red Templar cross.

I found a bed and wandered the town, taking in every stone, old and new, and soaking in the fresh, thinner, charged alpine air, which seemed to be oscillating with exhilarating electricity. This place felt good, in part because it reminded me—barring the new concrete road—of the Colorado mountain towns of my childhood, places where I'd spent idyllic summers with friends. It felt again as if my childhood in Colorado had a special wormhole connecting it to the Camino. As would happen with such a revelation, that night the dreams returned, and I was again walking the Camino while simultaneously revisiting my childhood and Colorado haunts and people, always with a pack on my back, the permanent pilgrim. I also again slept right on the Camino, with my head near a wall that lined the path. Intermittently, between dreams of high-altitude mountain towns and goose-footed beings, a persistent howling wind tore through Foncebadón, slamming shutters and banging doors without cease all night; this woke me at intervals, making it feel as if I had not slept at all.

53

THE TOWER

WHEN I COULDN'T fall back to sleep, I stared at the ceiling and tried to breathe. The banging outside and the soft snoring of a fellow pilgrim added to the strong feeling of anchorlessness and inbetweenness already brought on by sleeping so near the Camino's penultimate threshold place. I thought of all the thresholds I'd crossed, of what Bernadette had told me, that I was crossing my own life's crowning threshold from youth to older age. The only other frontier land more ominous than that was the final crossing, death, which I hoped was a goose square far-off in time.

I took some deep breaths and tried to sleep, wondering who I had been, who I was becoming, but having no answers for either. I finally fell into a light sleep that carried me to the dark hour just before the dawn. Then I rose quietly, grabbed my pack and sleeping bag in a bundle, and slipped out. I packed my gear in the vestibule and set off into the inky dark. The wind had brought with it an overnight rain that had soaked the trail and weighed down the feathery pink heather stalks into bow shapes pointing toward the wet earth. I splotched uphill through mud just as dawn's first rose fingers slipped over the slopes and lit up the eleventh-century ruin on Foncebadón's outskirts, once the medieval hermit Gaucelmo's refuge for pilgrims. Centuries later, it felt as if he were still there, despite the crumbling walls and toppled roof, guiding and protecting us. I could also feel the drought-tortured earth breathe in relief for the first time in months. Despite the cold air and my lack of sleep, I felt a warm calm radiate from my core. My uncertainty and anchorlessness dissolved.

I entered a pine forest filled with rowdy early morning titmice flying like trapeze artists from high branches. They careened over my head all the way up to the Cruz de Ferro, the iron cross on Monte Irago, fifteen-hundred meters above sea level.

The nearly two-meter medieval iron cross towered atop an over-five-meter-high oak trunk post planted in the center of a tall mound of stones, all offerings from passing pilgrims. In Roman times, these mountains were Mercury's domain, and people traveling there made stone offerings for safe passage. It is likely that Romans had taken over a native Iron Age tradition, transplanting a similar indigenous god with Mercury, to whom the locals also made stone offerings. And after the Romans left, natives and pilgrims alike, up to the present day, have carried on this tradition. Many pilgrims have released regrets, wounds, and sorrows with their stones, while others have expressed gratitude and given thanks.

I approached the high mound, ready to submit to the mountain gods, sky gods, and Santiago for grace and safe passage, not only on this physical threshold but on the more metaphysical one in my life. I undid the small cross tied to my pack and took out my three stones, then climbed the mound carefully. At the foot of the cross, I knelt and lay them down.

"Thank you for all that you have given me," I whispered, to the stones, to the hill, to the earth, to those I loved, to the Great Spirit that is in all things. A flood of deep gratitude washed through me as I realized how many people, how many places, had supported me on the Camino and in life. "Thank you," I continued, "for all who have come into my life and enriched it. Please bless them all." Tears filled my eyes. Frozen in place, still kneeling, unwilling to descend just yet, I watched as drops of water slid down my nose and dripped onto the stones. When I finally stood, I saw a young Argentine with long, dark, curly locks and deep-brown eyes who had arrived at the foot of the cross, midway through his own ritual. Upon finishing, he stood and looked at me and gave me a melancholy smile. Tears also streamed down his face.

"Now we can walk more lightly," he said. He took a deep breath to steady himself. "What a beautiful place. So much energy from all those who have done this before us."

"Yes," I said. That was it, he had nailed it. The energy of so much emotion of millions of travelers resonated there. He gave me his hand and the two of us climbed down the stone hill and sat on a bench near the edge of the pine forest. An unspoken kinship of support and humanity wrapped around us, and we spoke healing words without the need for speech. It felt as if the young man was my son and I his mother, each of us witnesses to the other's vulnerability and strength. He was the perfect witness for such a threshold as the one I stepped through.

We sat like that for a long while and then both stood up at the same time, ready to continue on. Before parting, he gave me a look of understanding. I was sure he had felt the same kinship, and I wondered what threshold he was now stepping through. I watched him return quietly to the trail, and I followed after a few minutes. All was quiet but for the titmice, who still swung and flew like otherworldly fairy folk in the towering trees.

Comparative mythologist Mircea Eliade wrote that a sacred place is a site where the divine careens into the mundane and where we experience, just by being there, something beyond the ordinary. Once a place is identified for its ethereal power, we humans always return to it, regardless of the era—prehistoric, Iron Age, Roman, medieval, or modern. We lay our own energy onto nature's natural resonance, building an even more potent sacred place. I began to understand that while this wild goose chase had its private goose footprint signs and clues, some places on the Camino had universal, meant-for-everyone footprints, markers that said, "This place here is directly connected to heaven and will change you." That was the case with the Cruz de Ferro—and with the whole trail of the Camino, its many sacred places strung like prayer beads into a unified strand, its serpent body decorated with trident-like footsteps of the mother.

Back on that numinous trail, I saw the young Argentine weave in and out of the meandering and steep path, which was surrounded on all sides with magnificent and silent purple-blue mountains. I arrived in the mountainside village of El Acebo to see the young man standing at the entrance, waiting for me. He flashed his beatific smile, affirming the something intangible and transcendent that we'd shared on the summit. He was continuing on. I decided to stay, not ready to leave the mountains and the magic they held. We said goodbye and I watched him disappear down the slope toward the large valley below.

I found a place to stay, dropped my pack near my bed, and went back out to walk along the edges of El Acebo and the mountain. I passed a wild raspberry patch, its branches extending toward me with three plump, globular berries. I plucked one and tasted slate, sunshine, kinship, and transcendence. I thought of the Argentine as I sat on a crumbling wall until after sunset, unable to take my eyes off the sweeping layers of darkening blue mountains all around me. Somewhere out there, I had a sacred son, and he, a spiritual mother. I knew I may never see him again but that in my heart he would always be there. I whispered a prayer of grace and blessings to guide and guard his every step and gratitude that we each had midwifed the other through that potent doorway.

54

THE DRAGONFLY

I PARTED EL Acebo as the sun rose. The trail was wild and empty, with just me. It remained that way all the way down the mountain, with the trail weaving through the untamable terrain of jagged rock outcroppings, narrow stony paths, and thick stands of chestnut, oak, and poplar forest free of human interference. The thrumming energy of Monte Irago went with me, and Mercury's mountains emitted their special pulse all the way to the bottom and into the pretty town of Molinaseca, where I entered the bowl of the Bierzo region. A great expansive and fertile valley with a culture unique to the area, El Bierzo possesses a special microclimate found only in its bowl, courtesy of the surrounding mountains and the moderating effect of the Atlantic nearby to both the north and west. Here, in contrast to the alpine world of the Maragatería, the valley nourishes apple, peach, apricot, plum, fig, and olive trees; an array of colorful vegetables grown year-round; and special wines made from grapes grown only here.

I felt as if I had crossed the threshold and entered Paradise, arriving in the small town of Molinaseca via a sturdy medieval stone bridge. Trout jumped in the Meruelo River below. Over the bridge, the Camino led me down the center of Molinaseca along a street that felt as if it had remained unchanged since the twelfth century. I wandered and wove in and out of the tiny side streets, each one inviting exploration with their stately stone homes whose walls were engraved with sculptures and embellishments, some of which appeared like protective talismans. One stone house especially stopped me, a thick-walled home with a wide-arched wooden door over which the lintel was engraved with an equal-armed cross, like a plus sign, set atop a triangle. The three free arms of the cross had small perpendicular bars capping each end. Did it represent the crucifixion on Calvary Hill? Or the Cruz de Ferro and its stone-offering mound?

Arriving around a corner, an elderly man pulled by an energetic and friendly Yorkshire terrier stopped next to me.

"*¡Buenos días, peregrina!*" he exclaimed.

"*¡Buenos días, señor!*" I replied as his small dog wagged his tail and demanded a greeting from me as well. I stooped down and pet the Yorkie while taking in the formal attire of his human: starched white shirt, dress trousers, tie, and a much-loved hand-knit cardigan.

"I see you're curious about the engraving on my door," the man said.

"This is your house?" I straightened up. "May I ask what the cross and triangle represent?"

"I will tell you what I know." He began at the beginning. "In 1969 I bought this old building. It was probably built in the twelfth century but had been restored in the eighteenth century when the owner set the door with a new stone frame. That was when this symbol was engraved. No one was able to tell me what it meant, so I figured it was the trinity and set there as a sign of protection. But then I spoke with several historians, and one of them, who was especially versed in Molinaseca's history of the 1700s, thought that this particular style of cross on a triangular base was how people indicated the home of a healer."

"A healer?"

"Yes, you know, traditional healers, *brujas*, witches, which really means *meigas* and *curanderas*." These were the terms for white witches and healers. "They were like local doctors, helping cure people of ailments both physical and spiritual. This was a long and old tradition here, before such knowledgeable people lost their standing as leaders and were demonized and persecuted, probably not too many decades after this lintel was set into place."

"It's pretty cool to live in healer's house," I said.

"It is!" he enthused. "It has a good feel to it, so I think there is truth to the symbol's meaning."

We stood for a few moments—man, dog, and me—gazing up at the door, another threshold place, this one leading into warm shelter and wellbeing. A third possibility struck me—the cross's three free arms also formed a goose's footprint. But I kept that idea to myself. I was about to continue on when the man turned toward me.

"Do you have a moment?"

You're a pilgrim, I heard the keeper of Torres del Río's church tell me, *you have all the time in the world.* "Of course," I replied.

He unlocked his door and went inside as the Yorkie stood and waited with me at the entrance. I peered inside the house, which retained its medieval character—a large, cavernous front room that had probably once housed farm animals on the first level, while the people lived on the floor above them, protecting the animals at night from cold and predators, and in turn letting the animals' body heat rise to warm the household. Now the cavern was full of carpentry and gardening tools and several workbenches—a builder's home.

The man was rummaging for something on a bench along the far back wall. A few moments later he returned, holding a dried water gourd made from a type of summer squash, the same shape and type so common in images of medieval pilgrims. He dusted it with a cloth and handed it to me.

"I grew, dried, and hollowed this myself," he said. "It weighs nothing and is a symbol of the pilgrim. I want you to have it." He helped me fasten it to my pack. I felt as if I had been knighted, as if Saint James himself was there, giving me this most potent and practical pilgrim emblem. In fact, I could feel him next to me, chuckling and petting the Yorkie.

"You should also know that the gourd here, in these mountains, is more than just a medieval pilgrim's water canister. Right up until the time I was a young man, miners and other laborers used these gourds to carry water to work. It still works, so remember this: if you need more water, fill the gourd. It's organic," he added with a laugh, jesting at the modern world's ways from a place that had never stopped being organic.

"This is indeed the home of a healer," I told him as I thanked him. We gave each other the formal cheek kiss Spaniards give each other, and I walked away, feeling as if I had said goodbye to my own grandfather. As I marched forward, I felt folded into a history that involved not only pilgrims but also healers, miners, builders, farmers, and a very kind man and his little dog. As if to deepen the wonder of the day, three times on the short plod from Molinaseca to Ponferrada, with its massive Templar castle on the hill, a large metallic blue-green dragonfly careened into my chest, tapping my heart before hovering, perhaps stunned, for a few moments at face level, then lifting up and flitting off. When I had experienced such magic out on the meseta with my first dragonfly tap, I had been sure it was a fluke, a rare occurrence that could never possibly happen again. "Message received," I called out, "and thank you." I practically skipped into town.

55

THE TWELFTH GOOSE

THE TEMPLAR CASTLE towered over Ponferrada and dominated every view of the town. I checked into a place to stay right at the feet of its thick outer walls, near the bank of the Sil River. I showered, handwashed some clothes, and set off to research the town and soak in its streets, foods, wines, churches, museums, and of course its formidable castle, which has been a key center of Templar activity since the twelfth century. The Tau cross engraved over its gate made the connection clear that this special cross belonged to the Templars as much as that of the Antonine Order, with their healing bread. Its possible association with the goose footprint kept me alert to look for signs for the quest.

Perhaps it was because of my good night's sleep on the mountain, my encounter with the builder in Molinaseca, or the dragonfly taps, but instead of exhaustion after a day of walking and research, I felt energized. I saved for last my favorite site in town, the Basilica de Nuestra Señora de la Encina, Our Lady of the Oak, on the central historic square near the castle. If there was any sure connection between the Templars as devotees of Mary, it was here, and again, that she made herself known through wild nature, the signature of La Reine Pédauque, Mistress of Animals, mother goddess.

According to legend, one day in the twelfth century, during the building of the castle and church, a Templar knight went into the surrounding oak forest to cut and haul wood for the construction. Deep in the forest, an oak stood out and drew him nearer. Inside the tree's trunk, the knight found a beautiful wood-carved image of Mary, La Encina. He took her back and installed her on the new church's altar, where she has remained.

I saw her now, resting in her cool stone cavern. Finding a pew in a dark and quiet corner to the side of the altar, I sat to bask in the light of the divine mother of the holy oak. She is one of the famous Black Madonnas on the Camino, an iconic figure some scholars believe represents the venerated pre-Christian mother goddess reincarnated as Mary.

I reveled in her radiance, sitting there in the church's shadows. An itinerant musician entered and approached her. He did not see me. Assuming the church was empty and that he had it all to himself, he took out his guitar, stood beneath the altar and Mary's feet, and launched into a soulful sung prayer composed on the spot. The music washed over me and electrified my skin, and I sat still, so as not to disturb the intimate communion before me. The musician finished, hung his head, wept a bit, then left, but the song oscillated in the air for many moments afterward and its sound waves seemed to concentrate into scent, for the church was now flooded with the butterscotch fragrance of tree resin. La Encina.

My head was spinning when I finally stood and left, not so much now from the work demands of the day as from the intense mysticism of it. The sun was beginning to set. The darkening, velvety blue sky accentuated the glow of the castle's and the church's pale yellow stones. I still needed to work off my high, so I kept walking, crossing a bridge over the Sil and heading south to the outskirts of town, where I passed a stone cottage whose chimney was emitting tufts of smoke. In the small garden in front, an elderly man was stooped, cutting kale leaves off a thick tree-like stem. Kale is a key ingredient in the regional specialty, *caldo del Bierzo* stew of onions, beans, pork, and potatoes, and I imagined a cast-iron cauldron inside the man's kitchen hanging over the cooking fire and already boiling away. The man stood up and greeted me, and he was the spitting image of my grandfather, someone I had lost when I was fourteen. My grandfather was a kindred spirit, a fellow explorer, a confidant, someone who had taught me to be who I was and not let being a girl get in the way—to fight for my rights and not be molded. He would, at the drop of the hat, be open to an adventure that led us across town, up the mountain, into the next village, inquiring and exploring as we went, letting a great uncharted adventure unfold. Or we would work side by side in his workshop, building and inventing contraptions in wood, metal, and plexiglass. He had told me golden words to live by— words I hoped to claim through my deeds—that being kind was more important than being successful. Instead of my walk working off my high and clearing things up, a new wave of head-spinning hit me.

"*Buen Camino, hija*," the man said. He'd guessed I had to be a pilgrim, given my trekking clothes and their handwashed appearance. He pointed the bundle of kale in his hand toward the sky. "It looks as if it will be overcast tomorrow but no rain."

"Good for walking," I offered.

"Yes, yes. But let us hope the sun returns, or better yet, that rain arrives soon. The earth is thirsty." He shook his kale leaves to free them of any small inhabitants and then wished me *buenas noches* and went inside. In that moment, I wanted to follow him, help him chop the greens, caramelize the onions, stir in the beans and pork and broth, and tuck into a warm bowl of stew by the roaring fire.

"*Buenas noches*," I called after him, and rolled back down to Ponferrada, thinking of my grandfather. I realized that today I had met two men like him. That night I dreamt I was riding my brother's old, white Peugeot ten-speed bike on the Camino. It was a bike he had carefully saved his money to buy when we were growing up, and I had watched him with admiration for both how he took excellent care of it and also how he would take it out for magnificent adventures, zipping across Colorado hills, mountains, and plains. In the dream, I knew the bike represented independence as much as the joy, love, and admiration I have for my brother. As I rode that emblematic bike along the Camino in my dream, I felt freedom and strength. I also discovered Templars who had returned to maintain and protect the path. One stopped me on the bike to offer advice. "You can do the Camino in short stages," he said, "there is no crime in that. Just enjoy it. Stop to eat a tortilla, take your time riding to the next place to sleep. Don't worry about the money," he added, "but be sure to oil the gears." I woke up chuckling, grabbed my notebook and jotted down the dream and its words of wisdom before they faded, considering the message.

The money part certainly was a theme that had been worrying me. Though I knew I was walking my path of right livelihood and that this was the one for me, it was still a financial tightrope. And there I was, nomadic, on an exceedingly tight budget, and just making it with all the peripatetic writing work, along with the guidebook research, moving my office and work with me as I stepped along. I suddenly couldn't stop laughing, because there I was, getting financial advice from a member of the Knights Templar, who are often called Europe's first bankers. They took vows of poverty but their practices had accrued for them inordinate wealth, such that it enabled them to build the castle and church standing just outside my window. I thought also of the Canadian accountant and wished I could tell him about my dream. He would understand. He had been like the Templar in my dream, telling me that my pockets were full of joy and not only assuring me that I was on my right path, but that I could also relax into it and trust the process. I devised a new practice, to utter gratitude anytime any worry or anxiety surged. *Oil the gears.* This made me bust out into another bout of laughter.

I packed, had a coffee and croissant on La Encina's square, crossed the great iron bridge—*pons ferrada*—over the Sil, and departed Ponferrada. The westward way took me across the fertile bowl of the Bierzo valley. I passed pear, apple, and apricot trees, and kitchen gardens overflowing with kale, staked tomatoes, and bright-red peppers with dark-emerald leaves.

I heeded the dream Templar's advice and took my time. I saw three people harvesting green olives from the trees around their village church and stopped to talk. One had spent her life as a migrant worker in Columbia and the USA. She told me that this year the olives were stingy because of the two-year drought. "All stone and little meat," she said, adding, "I've seen a lot of the world and I pray for it all the time. We have to pray for it. We are living on the precipice." She set down her bucket and put her hand on my shoulder. "*Buen Camino,* and please, pray for the world as you walk, and pray for us all when you hug the apostle. Will you do this?"

"I will."

We hugged. I carried the blessing and petition of the olive harvesters, along with the grandfathers and Sainte Bs, and many, many others, as I continued slowly over the rolling garden landscape. I pondered Bernadette's words about how this walk was more important for me than all the others, that this time it was especially going to be about death and rebirth, about crossing a threshold, about an alchemical journey that would burn the base metal to purify it to the higher vibration of silver and gold. Like the goose, it was all a metaphor for getting real and living authentically and taking care of the earth and everyone. About oiling the gears.

For centuries and millennia, we had sorely failed in this, taking too much from the earth and from each other. The foreboding, the death I had feared, was not necessarily my own but all of ours, all of this Earth's. This was the goose goddess speaking loud and clear, reminding us of justice and balance from her wild cave, riverside, tree trunk, and mountain. This was the urgency, to hear her. If only we could all but live like these people I'd met on the Camino—growing and harvesting, preparing and storing, keeping it simple and small scale, gathering around a fire with each other, telling stories, honing a craft for entertainment. I prayed, and prayed, and prayed, each footfall a petition.

Two-thirds of the way across the valley bowl, the orchards and kitchen gardens gave way to radiating striped seas of green vines turning autumn colors of pale yellow and deep red against the fertile earth of El Bierzo. Behind them, a backdrop of blue-purple mountains grew in size with each kilometer. They marked the final mountains I had to cross to get to Santiago de Compostela, the final steep ascent, the third-highest summit of the whole trail since Saint-Jean-Pied-de-Port.

I spent the night in the wine town of Cacabelos, surrounded by vines that gave a surreal calm, as if the rest of the world didn't exist or we were sheltered from its ruin. The next morning I walked through more vineyards and rolling hills, and it was even more beautiful than the day before. In a natural high, I sauntered into the sinuous riverside foothill town of Villafranca del Bierzo, a place where, in the Middle Ages, one would find forgiveness and redemption in case it was impossible to make it all the way to Compostela. The ritual site was right there, upon entry to the town, at the Romanesque church of Santiago's north gate, the Puerta de Perdón, or gate of pardon. All pilgrims needed to do was pass through this gate, and their sins were erased. I stood there and considered it: could I pass through it and ask for the whole world's redemption? A soft breeze blew, and a rouge-gorge alighted on a branch near me. Ever the optimist, I took the appearance of the bird as a resounding yes.

But the gate was locked. I touched it, hoping that would count, and then descended into the town that hugged the Burbia River on both sides in its steep and narrow valley. The main square was dappled with welcoming sunshine. I sat at an outdoor table and enjoyed a big lunch. After thorough research and notetaking, I still wanted to keep moving, so I journeyed up and out over the Burbia River and into the steep mountain folds. It was nearly five in the afternoon when I arrived in the next settlement, the hamlet of Pereje, but still I wanted to walk.

I arrived on the margins of Trabadelo just as the sun slipped behind the narrow slopes, filtering through the upper branches of an ancient chestnut grove. It quickly disappeared but cast enough lingering light in the sky for me to see the trees's wide, gnarly trunks and their spirited branches reaching to the sky like holy dancers, the spiny encased orbs strewn everywhere on the forest floor, and an older woman deep in the woods gathering nuts in a huge burlap sack, storing up for winter. *Winter is coming early,* Cécile had said.

I knew from friends in both Galicia and the Dordogne that chestnuts are sacred. They store well in barns and cellars and stave off starvation in thin times. Both places call chestnuts the "bread of the poor." When all other food sources fail, these nuts single-handedly have kept communities alive until spring. As the path took me into the heart of the tiny village, I wondered if the chestnuts were like the olives this year.

In the village, a hot, heavy perfume, both floral and sweet, infiltrated everything, billowing in thick clouds from a large pot on a single burner set in the street. The woman who was stirring the pot with a massive wooden spoon invited me to take a look inside. I saw a thick, dark, red jam and recognized the dense apple-like flesh of quince, which turns from white to claret when cooked. The woman was making her annual supply of *membrillo*, quince paste, from her own fruit trees. "Do you need a place to stay?" she asked. I nodded and she handed me the spoon and told me to stir.

She crossed to the other side of the street and went into a café, reemerging a few moments later with a key. Enlisting another pilgrim who was lounging at an outdoor table to take over the wooden spoon, she showed me to a pristine room with an inviting bed with fresh-pressed sheets and a hand-embroidered bed cover. The price was almost that of a dorm bed, though I had the space to myself. *Don't worry about money*, the Templar had said in my dream. After handing me the key, the woman went back to stirring the thickening fruit paste. Once in the room, I hugged myself as I looked out the large picture window to a grassy meadow speckled with autumn wildflowers of white, yellow, and purple. The Valcarce River bubbled at the other end of the meadow and filled the woods with a sweet lullaby.

That night I joined a communal dinner in the café run by the same woman, along with her husband and son. There were just a few pilgrims there: a young Spanish man walking as a spiritual retreat, who spoke little but smiled a lot; four middle-aged French cyclists who were having a reunion with each other and a two-week break from work; and a young German couple on their honeymoon. We ate fresh garden salads, grilled trout, and homemade yogurt custard for dessert. Instead of the traditional dollop of honey atop the custard, I asked if I could try the quince jam. The husband tried the combo too, and we declared it a divine pairing, a special seasonal custard. I asked him about that year's chestnut harvest, mentioning the woman I had seen gathering nuts as I walked into Trabadelo.

"People are going to need the nuts this year," he said, hinting at the economic downturn everyone had been feeling was coming, "but the drought has made for a meager harvest. Not all the nuts are good. We'll see if they get us through." I felt the edge, that ancient worry humans still have encoded in their bones from surviving millennia by farming and herding to assuage the fickle hunt. But the truth also was that nature used to deliver more abundance to us before we knocked the balance off-kilter. The drought was human-caused through imbalanced activities. The earth was telling us in no uncertain terms to awaken from our illusions and live more simply and gracefully on her body.

I retired to my room and opened the window to let the soft murmuring of the Valcarce River lull me away from worry and into sleep. At midnight I woke to a soft light—the stars and splash of the Milky Way, so potent out there, far from the artificial light of cities and towns. A soft wind carried the scent of fallen chestnut leaves and lingering quince jam. I fell asleep again and dreamed I had gone back with my parents to my childhood home. The poplar trees that we had planted together had grown well. In the dream, we gathered with friends and neighbors under their branches and celebrated. Only then did I notice that I was wearing my backpack and needed to return to the trail. It was so hard to say goodbye.

56

THE CASTLE

EARLY THE NEXT morning, under blanketing mists I walked out of Trabadelo along the narrow Valcarce River valley, which strings along tiny villages with terraced gardens hugging the riverbank. In one village, Vega de Valcarce, the small granite church of Mary Magdalene, Apostle of the Apostles, was open. I went in. Midway down the nave was a wooden statue of Saint James as pilgrim, and below him was a small table with an inkpad and stamp. I pulled out my passport and stamped it, then walked to the altar with its gilded retable, in whose center stood the Magdalene surrounded by the core holy family of Jesus, Mother Mary, and Saint Anne, the Virgin Mary's mother.

The keystone over the sacristy door to the left caught my eye: it had a perfect goose's footprint carved into the stone. Why was it there? I went outside to find someone to ask. A few paces away on the street stood a man in an open doorway, with a small table before him set with pamphlets. A sign over the door read *Camino Castle Project*, the "t" in castle graphically shaped into a Tau cross, the symbol I'd found on the Camino associated with both the Antonine Order and the Knights Templar. A great white-and-red flag with the more familiar Templar equal-armed red cross with flaring ends told me that the man was more connected to the latter. Surely, I thought, he would know about the sacristy's goosefoot. But before I could ask him, he asked me a question in greeting.

"Have you visited the castle on the hilltop?" He pointed to the tree-shrouded hill behind me. I'd never known there was a castle there. He invited me into the vestibule and told me his story and mission. Attila was originally from Hungary but based in Belgium, and he had walked the Camino a few years earlier. When he arrived in Vege de Valcarce, he had such a profound experience in the castle on the hill that he decided to return there to live. Another man appeared down an interior stairway. An architect from Vega de Valcarce, Fidel had joined efforts with Attila to restore the castle and open it as a pilgrim refuge in the Templar spirit of service and hospitality. Fidel had grown up right next door to the castle ruin— it was where he had played as a boy—and he knew it was a special place. The two were raising funds to restore the ruin and turn it into a special albergue for pilgrims. Known as Castillo de Sarracín, it was most likely first founded in the ninth century, but then rebuilt in the fourteenth, though the men before me were sure that between those two centuries in the twelfth century, Templars had also occupied the castle.

"How do you know?" I asked.

"The signs are there," Attila elaborated, "but we are still looking for historical documentation to tell us more."

"Signs?"

"Its location, its later additions that date to the peak of the time of the Templars, and the fact that they would have been active here," he offered. But it was the experience he'd had there that told him it was a special place. Soon after, he heard other pilgrims report similar experiences. Fidel nodded in agreement with everything Attila said.

"What about the goose's footprint in the church?"

Attila studied me for a moment. "Yes," he finally said, "near the altar." I nodded. He gave me an impish smile but said no more— just like the young man from Köln in Burgos who had initiated me into this whole goose mystery years back. Each person had to find out for himself or herself. This was, after all, a quest.

I thanked the men and made for the castle. Everything about its location imbued it with power, and its thick and broken walls hugged tightly to the high perch of a narrow and steep crest overlooking the tight green valley below. It looked like a ship balancing on the tip of a wave. I could definitely feel something there but couldn't discern if it was the castle or the stunningly beautiful location. Perhaps I didn't linger there long enough because I was anxious to make the taxing ascent up O Cebreiro's imposing mountain looming before me, but I failed to gain any further insight into either castle or the engraved goose footprint in the church.

I pushed onward and upward through a few more pretty valley village settlements before the path veered left and entered a rocky, narrow, and sheer passage through an ancient chestnut forest. Nuts coated the jagged stone trail, making my progress painfully slow.

Centuries earlier, during an extreme snowstorm, a single villager climbed up a similar slope, intent on arriving in time for mass at the church of Santa Maria of O Cebreiro. No one else ventured out that day, and once inside the church the villager found that the priest really didn't want to perform the Eucharist, having recently begun to doubt its mystical power. The priest viewed the villager as a simpleton for braving the weather for something in which he himself had little belief, but he reluctantly went through the motions of performing the mass. To his astonishment, as the priest blessed the host and wine, the wafer turned to flesh and the wine turned to blood. The priest understood in that moment that the faith of the villager had been so great that it brought about a miracle, which taught him a lesson about the power of faith and renewed his own devotion. To this day, the church retains a vile filled with the miraculous blood from that momentous mass, along with the original chalice and plate used that day. Local legend also recounts that at the moment of transubstantiation—at the consecration during the mass, when the wine normally only symbolically turns to blood and bread to flesh—the wooden statue of Mary to the right of the altar tilted her head slightly and smiled. Her head still angles slightly toward the altar from where she sits in the church at the top of the mountain, a ninth-century place sheltering messages of alchemical rebirth. I felt Bernadette at my side in anticipation as I climbed.

At last, after what felt like an eternal effort, the dark gray granite walls of the church appeared and then so did the village. Behind me, the entirety of the mountains of León lay at my feet in layers of purple and forest green.

"*Bienvenida, peregrina,*" the priest called out as I stepped inside the church. Behind him, the statue of Mary peered from the wall, smiling the same grin she had given the day of the miracle. The priest invited me to a table where he stamped my passport and invited me to return later for the evening mass.

I lingered. First, I stood before Mary, a nine-hundred-year-old wooden sculpture that looked ancient and vibrant at once. Then I stopped before a protective case containing the chalice, paten, and small vials of blood from that miraculous snowy day centuries earlier and its miracle of transfiguration. Just as holy, to me, was a side chapel devoted to Saint James and pilgrims, which contained the tomb of O Cebreiro's parish priest, Elías Valiña Sampedro, who had practically single-handedly mapped, marked, and resurrected the medieval Camino in modern times, from the 1960s to 1980s, driving across the north and splashing bright yellow arrows on the rocks, posts, and walls of the historic route. Everything about this place was about resurrection and transubstantiation. As I turned to go, I wondered what miracles, if any, I might encounter.

Before exiting, I bought three postcards on sale at the church entrance. One was of the wooden sculpture of Mary and Child. The other two were by Franciscan friar Miguel Castellanos Sotos, wildly free-flowing psychedelic paintings merging the Mary of O Cebreiro image with what looked like a chess board and a montage over a human form that itself looked lit up by the seven chakras from seat to crown. In one of the postcards, Santiago de Compostela's cathedral sat on the top of the human form's head like a royal crown. That same figure held the chalice and wafer, O Cebreiro's miracle, over the throat, the fifth chakra, the center of will and expression. I had no idea what these images meant and why they were for sale there, but I was excited that they were created by a man of the Church, much like the inlaid Game of the Goose square in Logroño had been designed by a parish priest. What was certain was that these images and ideas were about intimate spiritual experience. It was exciting to think that the modern Catholic Church, in these contexts, was open to both interfaith images and also to the ideas of personal and direct paths to the sacred.

I left the church, found a place to stay for the night, and then performed my daily pilgrim rituals: washing and resting and finding fellows to share a glass of celebratory wine. When the sun was just beginning to descend behind the mountains, I returned to the church for the evening mass.

The same priest who had welcomed me that afternoon, full of faith and pure kindness, performed the Eucharist. I felt a crescendo of energy and wholeness wrap around all of us present, pulling us together into a community in union, a true communion. I felt blessed and peaceful but had no visions or insights except that I liked being there and felt that it was a place of power, a goose place, for sure.

I slept in fits—my bunkmate crooned Italian love songs during his after-dinner shower and then flopped into bed and snored the rest of the night—and rose early. Through the dark and misty hamlet, I joined fellow pilgrims out on the lookout point of the mountain to witness the sunrise over the peaks we'd climbed up the day before. Infinite layers of dark purple and velvety blue gave over to psychedelic oranges, reds, and pinks—almost like the ones in the friar Sotos's postcards—almost pulling me over the ledge and into the infinite swirl.

THE CASTRO

THE SOFT DIRT trail carried me and my fellow pilgrims deeper west into more layered mountains, through oak, pine, chestnut, beech, holly, and birch forests that wove thickly over both valley and slope. Soon, the group I had started my day with began to spread out, as if everyone felt the need for solitude after the potent mountaintop slumber and sunrise. The peace and wholeness of the mass, communion, mountain, and Mary filled me. So did the scintillating thrill of freedom that rippled through my limbs and spine from the sheer joy of just being out there walking, with everything I needed on my back. I could hear the mythic call of the goose from the depths of the earth and felt her divine grace supporting each footfall.

Then, it happened again: a large metallic blue and green dragonfly, this one the size of a lollipop, flew right at me and thumped my chest right over my heart. This had first happened on the meseta, then near Ponferrada, and now here, on O Cebreiro mountain. How could something so unusual as this happen not just once, but three times? Was the dragonfly's appearance like a fairytale, where things occur in triplicate to deliver the message in full? As before, the creature hovered before me for a few stunned seconds, perhaps wondering the same thing—and then as suddenly flitted over my shoulder and flew deep into the woods. Perhaps it was simply saying, *yes, I heard you, quack, honk, quack.* I think this was my miracle on O Cebreiro mountain.

When I arrived in the village of Triacastela, many hotels were closed and nearly all the albergues were full. I found a bed in a place with only four spots left. Five minutes later, others claimed the remaining beds. What was happening? Then I remembered. We were a day's walk from Sarria, the main starting point for many pilgrims to Santiago de Compostela. This was because the Church gave certificates of pilgrimage only to those pilgrims who completed the final one hundred kilometers to Santiago de Compostela no matter where they had started from. I knew that the next day, in Sarria, the swell of arriving pilgrims would be even greater, but knowing this did not prepare me for the shock and shift. It became more challenging to walk, and I needed often to step aside for high-paced walkers with daypacks, bikers on holiday, and large groups singing and clapping. I also stopped seeing anyone I had met before Sarria; they seemed to disappear in the crowds. At the same time, the sense of camaraderie we'd all shared also disappeared, and the newcomers seemed to stick more fiercely to their own group. But this too was pilgrimage. I considered that if O Cebreiro was the fifth chakra of will and voice, and Santiago the seventh chakra of wisdom, according to Friar Soto's postcards, then this stretch was the sixth chakra, where I had an opportunity to develop my vision and understanding.

Although throughout the next day more pilgrims wove past me on the path, the Camino still held its magic, undulating through hills held closely together with heavy mist and dark green forests. Anchored here and there were tiny granite- and slate-roofed hamlets tucked into the folds of valleys and creeks, and birdsong filled the branches and the airwaves. Cows also began using the trail as much as humans, sauntering from one pasture to the next. I heard a bull deep in the forest call out, perhaps to his heifers or simply to the splendor of creation. Village gardens all along the way burst with towering, prehistoric-looking stalks of collard and mustard greens.

Arriving in Sarria, the town's famous monthly herding and produce market gave it the feel of a hardworking agrarian town as much as a popular pilgrim starting point. It took several tries before I found a free bed in a place located high on a hill capped by castle ruins and Romanesque church.

That night in the streets of old Sarria, a party mood descended on the pilgrim community, which by now was packed with fresh faces and bodies adorned with new shoes, clothes, and packs. I felt almost underdressed, even ragged. I calculated that I had been on the trail for six demanding weeks of walking, researching, and writing. When I walked along the Sarria river to clear my head, I found my cure: eight geese picking the earth for bugs along the riverbank like there was no tomorrow.

The next morning, mists shrouded the town and hill as I slipped past Sarria's castle and the pilgrim hospice and monastery on the town's edge devoted to Mary Magdalene. Crossing the medieval Ponte Áspera bridge, I plunged again into primordial oak forest. The terrain ascended steadily, then spit me out onto a plateau coated in meadow grasses dotted with yellow and pink flowers. The land descended again, plunging into the deep and wide river valley of the Miño, taking me into the riverside town of Portomarín, which had been rebuilt in the 1960s higher on its hill to allow for a new dam that gathered the waters of the river into a reservoir far below, flooding the old town whose outlines I could just make out under the water.

I stopped in Portomarín to scour the town for research. At the twelfth-century San Nícolas church, I discovered half-bird and half-human characters carved into the walls that spoke of humans in possession of magical powers granted to them by the animal with which they merged. One was a goose woman, the spitting image of Mother Goose were we to pull her from the storybooks, right down to the babushka-like scarf tied carefully around her grandmotherly human face and her fat goose body. The albergues were filled to bursting, but an innkeeper gave me a basement room in his drafty riverfront inn.

The next day I departed from Portomarín's river valley on a switchback path before rising out of the mists and valley into rippling green hill country. On the outskirts of Castromaior, a village named for its "large castro," a twenty-four-hundred-year-old Celtic hilltop fortress a few hundred meters away from the modern village, I saw an elderly man seated on a low wall in an orchard.

His basset hound was sniffing back and forth around the grounds, until he saw me, at which point he let loose eruptive short howls and then launched into an impressive run with his short legs and long body, his ears flying like propellers, right up to me, demanding my full attention. It made the man laugh out loud with pleasure, and I was delighted for the company.

"Does your dog hunt?" I asked the man as I approached him with his dog.

"In his own way," he joked. "It's wild boar, deer, and pheasant season, and though he's trained for the hunt, he seems more interested in fallen apples and chestnuts. I think he might be a vegetarian." I sat on the wall next to the man, the dog between us, still insisting to be the center of attention.

"My ancestral home is here," the man said, pointing toward a house and garden, "but most of the year, I live in Lugo." That was the large city nearby, to the north. "But now that I am retired, I come here on weekends to keep the house in good repair, and because I love it here. It's just that it's hard to make a living off the land anymore—yet, life, real life, is here. You know?"

"I do."

"We used to live just fine from just the land for so long. I'm not sure where we lost the touch."

You mean since the time of the castro?" I asked.

"Yes, and you must be sure to visit it. It's easy to miss. After you leave the village, follow the signs, except the last one, which is vague. When you see that sign, look instead for a large information board tucked off the trail on the other side, under the trees to the left. Look carefully and you will see a little footpath near it. It will take you there."

He stood and walked with me to the center of the village. "We are the modern residents of Castromaior," he said, "but we never forget the ancestors of this land, or that this earth is precious." We stopped in front of the village church, a tiny twelfth-century chapel of pale yellow limestone. "Take your time at the castro," he advised. "It has several concentric walls that encircle the hilltop settlement, like onion layers around a core. Though not all of the rings have been excavated, you can see their contours out-lined under the green grass and rolling earth." He wished me *buen Camino* and walked back with his dog to the orchard wall.

I followed his advice and found the elusive footpath. Within moments I stood in the center of the millennia-old, onion-shaped settlement. The innermost circle had a gateway that required stepping through, and then upward to arrive at a world that was hidden on high until the last moment, entirely invisible from the ground below. The wind suddenly came from nowhere and began to push at me, howling and swirling as it went. I went to the center and took in a three-hundred-sixty-degree view of the plum and blue mountains across the east, north, and south, and the silky, rolling green lowlands thick with forests and rivers to the west. I also could see pilgrims passing two hundred meters away on the trail, entirely oblivious of me or the castro. I called to them, but they did not hear. What a perfect place the ancient people had chosen for a protective settlement.

Archaeologists had excavated a part of the central settlement, revealing below a section of the original round and square homes with adjoining walls. Some still had their large mill stones for grain on the hut floors, ready for the cook to return to prepare the por-ridge or bread. Others had stone basins in their walls, places they may have stored food and water. Across the large, enclosed hilltop circle I saw a cluster of trees on which someone had hung a dream catcher, and to its right, a yellow arrow that pointed to a small, notched opening on the opposite wall. It marked the way back, after traveling through deep time to the more recent Camino. In the very center of the castro was grass and knobby contours, which spoke of as yet unexcavated forms underneath.

I could hardly pull myself away, and remained there for two hours, pacing around and taking in the remarkable remains. Part of the draw of the place was the hilltop itself, which held a pure and magnetic energy, like drinking crystal clear glacier water. I circled and paced and sat, each time noticing something new. It would earn me a beet-red face and arms, but in the moment, I didn't care. I finally walked to the center of the hill, dropped my pack, lay down, closed my eyes, and just let the wind wash over me. As it did, a strange feeling also blew through me, as if I were lying where the village well had once been, as if maybe a water source was under this hill. I was tempted to pull out my pendulum, which a friend had given me after I told her I was learning to dowse with farmers in the Dordogne, a traditional way of sussing out water, but I didn't try dowsing on the hill because I knew that the wind was too strong to detect a subtle movement from a hanging drop of brass. I closed my eyes again and got another impression, that people watched the sunset from where I lay. I opened my eyes and stood up, facing the southwest. There, a dip in the wall looked as if it would cup the setting sun like a Eucharist host dipped in a chalice of wine. The day grew late, and although I knew I would again be the last to arrive in town and have to hunt for a bed, I stayed a while more. This fairy-dusted place of enchantment outside of time was worth the uncertainty.

When at last I pried myself away and resumed walking, I realized how dehydrated and hungry I had become. Heat radiated from my skin, the kind of heat that promised sunburn, but still, I didn't care. I walked on air, gliding through tiny hamlets and craggy country lanes, passing a massive, ancient, granite cross and next to it an even more massive and ancient oak, its trunk so wide it would take two people touching fingertips to wrap their arms around it. I craned my head to take in the reach of its branches into the heavens as its gnarled roots did the same into the earth— the oldest merging of heaven and earth, long before humans built temples.

At sunset, I arrived in Eirexe, a hamlet with a handful of houses, a small church off in the field, and an inn, albergue, and café. Only four other pilgrims were staying there. After performing my daily rituals and catching up on my notes, I went across the small road to enjoy a beer with the locals gathered in the café. The café owner was filling drink orders and then moving around the room with a plate full of homemade cheese puffs, fresh from the oven, insisting everyone take a few. Many of those gathered were villagers, plus a few visiting hunters just back from pursuing venison and boar.

Two tables were full of card players, and in the back, three tables were set for pilgrims taking an early dinner. I took my beer and approached. Two tables were fully taken, one with four French pilgrims who were cycling together, and the other with a young Galician couple, a boyfriend and girlfriend with eyes only for each other. The third table held one person—a large, matter-of-fact, and confidence-exuding woman about my age.

"Care to join me?" she asked before I could inquire. I detected a slight German accent in her perfect English.

"I'd love to."

"I'm Susanna," she said as I took the seat across from her. She extended a beefy, welcoming hand. "I'm originally from Frankfurt, but I'm now living in Alaska."

"How did that happen?" I asked.

"The green card lottery," she said, and laughed loudly, but even this was drowned out by the now boisterous bar as yet more villagers arrived for an early evening drink. Our hostess came to our tables to describe the three-course pilgrim menu: a large garden salad, grilled chicken and potatoes, and homemade custard. As Susanna spoke to our host, I noticed that her Spanish was almost as good as her English. Her work in Alaska was seasonal, in fishing, I guessed, and she worked five months and was able to save enough to live on for the next seven. Every year, she walked a route of the Camino. This year, she had started in Oloron-Sainte-Marie and crossed into Spain over the Somport Pass on the Camino Aragonés, then joined the Camino Francés when the Aragonés Route ended in Puente la Reina.

"I absolutely love the freedom as a woman on my own," she said, referring both to her pilgrimage and to her work. "The only thing that I don't like is how some of the old guys on this trail think that we solitary women are only looking for hooking up. They miss the point, don't they?"

I'd had similar experiences so I shared a few with Susanna, such as the recent proposition from an old codger in O Cebreiro, and the attempted grope from someone whose wayward hand I'd struck back in Agès in Castile. I told her I'd also found that retired men who had been CEOs were the worst, not as perverts but as dictators, bossing everyone else around. Like the German executive who insisted I was handwashing my clothes all wrong. Or worse, the fellow who recently had actually yelled at me in Villafranca del Bierzo as I was leaving in the late afternoon, heading for Pereje, "It's too late and there is nothing in Pereje," he screamed after me when I ignored his insistence to stay in the same albergue as him. He'd stood in flipflops at the door looking like a rooster looking to order about hens. "Tell Pereje that," I had managed over my shoulder, seething with indignation. Had I listened to the little autocrat, I would have missed the chestnut forest and the woman stirring jam in Trabadelo, not to mention my self-respect. I didn't tell Susanna about the man and the van before Astorga. That had been an aberration, an anomaly—the Camino still remained safer than the smallest town in America.

Susanna snorted into her wine. "They just can't fathom that for some of us this hike is about freedom and the quest to be outside in nature and self-sufficient. In fact," she added, leaning in so closely that she nearly toppled her roast chicken into her lap, "this walk gives women a break from living in a man's world—work, home, and social life—it's all designed and made for men. Those jerks don't get it that maybe some women love this Camino thing because it's damn freeing."

We clinked wine glasses, finished dinner, and walked back to our pilgrim lodging. The next day, I hoped to see Susanna again, perhaps walk with her and hear more of her cutting and refreshing opinions, but when I awoke, she and the others were already gone. How had I slept through all the sounds—the snoring, the rustling, the walking stick clanging? I was sure it had to do with my sunburn and the time I'd spent on the castro hilltop. I had slept hard and deep, and my dreams had been vivid and filmic, one especially. In it, I descended down into the earth on a labyrinthine-shaped stairway carved into ochre-toned limestone. I had on my pack as I descended. Midway down, I learned that this was a Templar place and that my descent was a test, an ordeal, and also a treasure hunt. I was entering the ordeal, unable to see the path, not knowing what was around or before me, walking deeper into darkness, which I understood in that weird dreamlike knowing to be the valley of death. I had to cross it to gain the treasure.

No wonder I hadn't heard the others leave. I found myself desiring coffee more than I had on any other morning on the Camino.

58

DEATH

COFFEE, LIKE THE treasure implied in the dream, was long in coming. I walked throughout the morning over remote terrain, the heavy dream weighing on my uncaffeinated head as dense mist clung to everything. Was the treasure worth the walk into darkness?

The fog, inner and outer, persisted all morning until I entered Palas de Rei, a town famous for its cattle and farm fairs and its creamy herb-rich cheese. There, the sun at last muscled its warming rays through the clouds and burned off the thick morning mist just as I arrived at the church of San Tirso, built on the upper edge of Palas de Rei. The church door was open. I went in.

In the vestibule, staring at me at eye level, was a spiraling labyrinth, very much like the one in my dream. The labyrinth was the lower part of a tall wooden sculpture of Mary, who, rather than standing on a snake as usual, instead stood on a three-dimensional serpentine spiral. She towered over me—the mother goddess without a doubt—her feet resting on her beloved creation, the earth pulsing with energy, which she watched over and protected.

I looked over my shoulder through the door and into the church courtyard to see if anyone else was around to talk to, and saw another sculpture of Mary in native gray granite but identical to the one inside: the same mother holding her son standing on a throbbing spiral. I went deeper inside the church and saw two men seated at a table with an inkpad and stamp at the back of the nave. They waved me over.

"I couldn't help notice that Mary here is shown standing on a spiral, not a snake," I almost shouted.

"Did you read the banner hanging next to her?" one of the men said as he took my credential to stamp. I went back and read. *María, peregrina de dios, camina conmigo*, Mary, pilgrim of God, walk with me. This time I also noticed that the baby Jesus in her arms had lost his right sandal, which dangled by a strap from his bare foot. I peeked outside to see the same on the stone image. This was Our Lady of Perpetual Help. The sculptures were based on a story about when Jesus was still a child. He was outside playing in the garden when angels came to him and showed him his last days and the means of his death. Terrified, he fled inside and into his mother's comforting arms. As he ran, his shoe came undone. The theme of the story was that even *He,* God, had sought comfort in his mother's arms. It didn't explain the spiral, except that it seemed to represent the leyline, the earth energy, more than the vilified snake. I returned to the table. One of the men handed me back my stamped passport.

"She walks with us?" I ventured. "On the spiraling path of life?" The two men smiled and gestured for me to continue. "And the spiral, like the serpent, is the earth we walk along, a living energy, much like the Camino?" *Or the Game of the Goose. Or creation at large.*

Their smiles widened. A lightning bolt of excitement shot through me. I no longer needed coffee. *Buen Camino* was all they added. I thanked them and continued, arriving in a few kilometers at the hamlet of Leboreiro. As I entered the village's church square, an elderly man walked across the path in front of me, tipping his pancake-sized black beret in welcome. "Be sure to visit our special church devoted to Santa María," he said, pointing to the small chapel and cemetery.

"Is it open?"

"Oh, no, it only opens on feast days and in the summer. But you can still see the tympanum, which is truly something to behold."

The tympanum was an imposing image of Mary flanked by two angels swinging incense burners. She held a standing baby Jesus steady on her knee with both hands. Dating to the twelfth century, the image was the result of a mystical occurrence in Leboreiro that took place in that century, when the town was a popular stop for pilgrims.

One night, villagers saw an ethereal light glowing from the depths of a local spring. They dug down and found a hidden sculpture of Mary, which they immediately set in the place of honor on the altar of their little church.

But the next night, the light appeared once again from the depths of the fountain. To their astonishment, Mary had taken herself back to bathe in the waters. The villagers returned her to the altar, only to find Mary back at the fountain again on the following night. This dance repeated itself over several nights until a stonemason proposed carving her image on the church tympanum. This, he reasoned, would honor her more publicly, letting all who passed by to see her and know that this was her abode. It worked. Once the mason completed the tympanum, the fountain image of Mary remained on the altar, though this didn't stop her, at times, from leaving to go for a plunge. As recently as the 1960s, some Leboreirans reported seeing Mary bathing in the fountain at night. Some even claimed she was combing her hair, a curious continuity with the habits of the pagan northern Iberian earth goddesses living near water sources and dealing out justice and harmony. I was sure that if I could just lift the stone skirt over Mary's feet, I would find webbed feet.

I left Leboreiro by crossing a small stone bridge, stopping midway across to wonder if the stream below was the original water source where villagers had discovered Leboreiro's Mary. As if in answer, two ducks paddled into view from underneath the bridge. Perhaps this was what my strange dream had meant: that I would walk along a hidden spiral path, through the types of visions of death that caused the Christ child to lose his shoe, and then out to receive greater illumination about the many manifestations of Mary, the mother of us all, and find a treasure therein.

After a few more kilometers, I reached the outskirts of the large town of Melide. Like a guardian met at the fork in a road, Susanna appeared in the garden of a private home, seated at a patio table, sipping a frothy beer. She saw me first and called out. We hugged as she explained she was renting a room there. She had just come back from the town center where she had enjoyed a late lunch sampling Melide's culinary specialty, *pulpo á feira,* boiled octopus seasoned with smokey paprika, sea salt, and olive oil.

"You must be sure to have it," she advised, "but most importantly, you must walk your walk," referring back to our prior evening's conversation. "And hold the path meant for you," she called as I walked on, "not anyone else." I turned to see her grin. I had found my treasure today, indeed.

I decided on a private room, like Susanna, to catch up on work and to recover from too many nights with snoring companions, perhaps myself one of them. I went out into the town, doing research and enjoying a dinner of *pulpo á feira* and sautéed little green Padrón peppers. Then I returned to my room and worked long into the night, waking with a start, still dressed but now draped over the desk, my face pressed into my notebook. I had been dreaming and bawling like a colicky baby, drenching the pages in tears. It was four o'clock in the morning. I had no memory of falling asleep.

I went to the washroom and splashed water on my face, capturing the quickly dissolving threads of the nightmare that had woken me up. In it, I had finished the Camino and returned directly home to New Jersey without stopping in Sarlat. When I had realized this, I'd broken out into inconsolable tears: I had so much to do in Sarlat, so many friends to see, and so much more research still to conduct before returning to the States. Worse yet, in the dream I also learned that Miles had gone to Sarlat to meet me, for it was a place he too hoped one day to call home. But we had missed each other, and there I was, alone in New Jersey. That's when the tears turned on.

I dried my face and looked in the mirror. A haggard person looked back at me, a crease running across my left cheek from the notebook's seam. I looked and felt like a wreck, the result of weeks of chronic fatigue from walking, working, homelessness, living out of a backpack, and wearing the same grungy, handwashed clothes every day. I also felt the suffocating grief that, any day now, Le Chardon could be sold and that I did not have the means to buy it. I reminded myself again that it was just an apartment, and that Sarlat—its land and people—remained my true home, not a building. Why then did the sickening scent of death, grief, regret, and mourning hang over me? As soon as I asked this question, the answer came.

Le Chardon was symbolic of something bigger, that change is inevitable, and I had to let the old Sarlat and the old me die, in order to make room for new versions of both. Deep in all this was the deepest mourning of all, that time marched on, that I was no longer young, that I was inevitably getting older but was so unprepared for it, that time was no longer infinite but precious and limited. I wanted more desperately to run back to Sarlat to confirm not only that Le Chardon was still there for me, but mostly, that my friends of the market, fields, caves, and forests were there, that Bernadette was waiting with her ever-generous wisdom, that Mr. Stripes would find me on the wall, that my family so far away were well, and most of all, to hold Miles in my arms and tell him how much I had missed him.

I could not go back to sleep, so I gathered my pages, packed, and left.

59

THE THIRTEENTH GOOSE

MELIDE WAS PITCH dark, not a soul stirred. Coffee was all I could think of as I entered a tiny settlement outside the town and crossed a small square. No one was about, but I soon stood before a gorgeous medieval Romanesque church dedicated to Santa María de Melide. If only it were open. As if I had said, *Open Sesame*, the door creaked open, the smell of coffee wafted out, and a handsome young man with curly black hair and vibrant dark eyes pushed the heavy wooden door all the way open and offered me an exuberant smile. Surely, I was still dreaming.

"*Bienvenida*," he said. "Would you like a cup of coffee?"

There *is* a god.

He poured hot coffee from a thermos into two paper cups while explaining he was not an apparition but a volunteer caretaker of the church. His day job was in community service in Melide. On his days off, he came here to care for and offer tours of the church. He added that he was a modern-day Templar and deeply devoted to the energy of this locale, which he was sure, as sure as Attila was about the castle in Vega de Valcarce, that this was a Templar place.

"Why?" I asked, for he, too, had not yet found historical documents to confirm the idea.

"The geology and the energy," he said without hesitation. He then offered to give me a tour. I passed inside and saw for the first time two different drawings of the Game of the Goose taped to the inside of the church door.

"The Game of the Goose?" I blurted. My guide was already at the other end of the nave.

"Do you know it?" he asked. I nodded. "Then you are an initiate."

"I'd like to hear more." I said, undeterred by the sidestep at which he and so many of his brothers were so adept.

"First, let me first explain the church," he said. I joined him to get my first view of polychrome frescoes that covered the walls and dome of the apse, dating from the eleventh to fourteenth centuries. Below them, a huge stone slab that looked to be older than the church formed the altar.

"The church of Santa Maria de Melide dates to the eleventh century," my goose guide began, "but the church had an older foundation. The first church built here was from the eighth century, built by Visigoths. But before them, this location was holy to the Celtic people, who inhabited this part of Galicia. One indication of this is that there is a good source of underground water here. Another," he lowered his voice dramatically while pointing to the altar, "is there." During recent restoration work on the church, workers had lifted the altar stones—which probably dated to the Visigothic church—to find a large obsidian stone underneath, one that had been set there most likely during the Iron Age, well over two millennia ago.

Midway along the nave I saw a beautiful wooden statue of Mary. "Our Lady of Melide?" I asked.

"And of the Snows," he said. "She is very important."

"The Goose, possibly?" I ventured, hoping to nudge the conversation in that direction. He smiled but did not take the bait: it was for the initiate to work out the signs, clues, and hunches, not to be told the answers.

"Tell me more about the goose," I begged shamelessly, ignoring his cues to say nothing.

"Soon, soon," he humored, "but first, let me show you the baptismal font."

We went into the small sacristy to the left of the altar. In the center was a large limestone font that looked like a massive cauldron. My guide pulled a pendulum from his pocket and was about to explain why when three pilgrims from Madrid stepped inside the church. The three men in their fifties were all friends walking to Santiago de Compostela and had begun in Sarria. All three wore small wooden Tau crosses around their necks and I guessed that they, too, were neoTemplars.

Our host caught them up to speed on the tour and we all returned to the sacristy, where he held his pendulum over the center of the font and waited. Within a few seconds, the crystal teardrop tip began to move, slowly at first, then faster, turning in wider and wider circles over the bowl until it whirred around like a dog on a racetrack.

"This is where the underground waterway flows," our guide explained, "right under the font. This is why the church brothers placed this holy water vessel here. And it flows from here to the altar, under the black stone hidden there." To my surprise, I watched the other three pull out pendulums from their own pockets and replicate the experiment. They looked at me, wondering if I understood any of this, assuming I was a newbie, seemingly also implying that because I was a woman, it was unlikely that I understood. One of the men even began to treat me the way Susanna and I absolutely despised. Another started to walk around the room and followed the way the pendulum swung to determine his next steps. I ignored his friend and paid attention to his movement from sacristy to the altar, mapping the underground flow of water our guide had detailed. When at last all three were busy with this sudden druidic workshop, entirely ignoring me, I stepped back into the now empty sacristy and pulled out my own pendulum. Though my hand was stock still, the pendulum began turning immediately, in full circles, over the font. Then, I sensed a strong magnetic pull and became so fully engrossed in the experience that I didn't notice when things went quiet in the next room. The four men stood in the doorway, three of them with their mouths agape, as the pushiest of the Madrileños said, "I've never seen a woman, let alone an American, do this." How many clichés can one utter in a single breath?

"One reason the pendulum swings so vibrantly in this church," our host said quickly to deflect the tension, "is not only because of the underground water and the obsidian stone, but also because the whole rock bed is rich in quartz. This is precisely why this church was built here. The three together magnify a remarkable energy."

I still could feel the buzz in my hand and arm, and I knew what he said was true. The other three engaged him in further conversation and I took my chance to slip out. Before I fully left, knowing my goose question would not be answered, I wanted at least to look at Mary of the Snows again in the nave, a Gothic image with a Galician woman's features, dark hair, and pale skin.

"This is a Templar place!" the bossy Madrileño declared loudly just as I stopped before Our Lady. What did he mean by that? No women allowed?

"Why just Templar?" I shot back before I could stop the words. "This place has been many things to many people before the Templars existed."

"And you should not walk alone!" he said, ignoring me entirely, and then, most bizarrely, he switched messaging and tone. "Lucky for you, we modern Templars do not take vows of celibacy." Then, as Goddess is my witness, he winked at me. *Get me the hell out of here.* Fortunately, the caretaker saw the exchange and came to my rescue.

"This place is many things, has many layers, and in all, is a holy place," he said, ever the diplomat. "Come," he gestured to us all to exit the church, making sure the three men went ahead first, and holding back in the doorway to speak just with me.

"I know you want to know about the goose," he said quietly, "but that is for each person to discover. But I can say this much, she, *ella,* is here, all around, as I am sure you already know." He gestured toward the Madonna behind us, and we shared a conspiratorial smile. I thanked him, dropped a couple of coins into the donation box, and slipped away just as the controlling Madrileño maneuvered to make another effort to clip my freedom. Glancing back over my shoulder, I saw that our guide had blocked and detained the problematic man, telling him he had so much more to show him before he left. God/dess bless the guardian of Santa María de Melide.

I flapped my wings fast, flying swiftly down the trail. Rather than feeling anger, I was filled with glee, for I had just acquired both liberation and goose knowledge. I had also felt something scintillating and enchanting in that church, despite the attempted patriarchal takeover. My enchantment extended onto the path, which headed through a whole new terrain rich in both quartz and subterranean water, oscillating and energizing my flight into a lush forest brimming with birdsong, pine scent, and dappled shade.

After an hour of flying solo, I came upon a large group of Japanese pilgrims, most of whom were over seventy. Though journeying together, they spread out and respectfully gave each other the space and quiet to walk in his or her own way. Like a drop of water into a stream, I entered the group, savoring their flow, grace, and generous company on a magical ramble through green countryside—a very pleasant contrast to the pushy neoTemplar and his macho chest-pounding. Occasionally, one of my Japanese companions would pause at a stream, tree, rock, or flower and ring a delicate fairy bell. I began to understand that he or she had felt something especially strong there and had paused to honor its spirit. Here again was the goose.

As we approached the medieval stone bridge over the Iso River into the tiny hamlet of Ribadiso da Baixo, three of the grandmothers invited me to pause at the riverbank for an impromptu picnic. Before sitting down, they walked around, caressing the grasses, the stones, the air, the bubbling river water—all acts of reverence. We then sat and broke bread as they fussed over me like an adopted daughter. They were staying the night in Ribadiso, but I was continuing to Arzua. They stood and sent me on my way with intoned blessings for me and the beloved Earth.

The long street entry into Arzua took me into a large town with cheerful residents and a famous reputation for a nutty and floral cow's milk cheese to which the town gave its name. I found a place to stay, dropped my pack, took my notebook out, and launched into research, scouting, exploring, and interviewing, as well as the necessary work of sampling cheese. It only dawned on me as my head hit the pillow that in two days I would be walking into Santiago de Compostela. Though I'd done this before, it felt like the first time, and I had no idea what to expect.

60

ARRIVING

OVER THE NEXT two days, I took my time walking through the mosaic of villages, oak, eucalyptus, and pine forests. I passed tiny forest chapels, holy hills, and traveling herds of cows that pushed me to the edge of the trail—almost all of them guided by an older matriarch dressed in black and carrying a large staff. European robins sang all day long, lovely songs of forest and field. If I'd had a few of those ethereal Shinto fairy bells, I would have rung them at every turn.

On my last morning on the trail, I woke in the dark and began walking early. The sun slowly rose behind me, its light blocked by rainclouds but its warmth releasing eucalyptus and pine scent, which energized and increased my pace. Rain came in starts and stops, shrouding the approach to Monte del Gozo—Mont Joie, or Mount Joy—which was the shout uttered out by French pilgrims who arrived there to see the cathedral spires for the first time after a long arduous walk. Mist hid all of Santiago de Compostela. In the final five kilometers (3 miles), I did not see the cathedral spires until I was about to walk into the Plaza de Obradoiro, the cathedral's main square. I tried to slow down for my last kilometers, but the rain and anticipation sped me up. As I crossed into the city proper, I felt that familiar and strange mix of joy, accomplishment, and gratitude with disorientation and anchorlessness.

Because of new security measures that did not allow pilgrims to walk into the cathedral with their packs, I lingered on the square long enough to find the kilometer zero stone in the center with its scallop shell to touch and confirm I was really there. All around me, tour groups, vacationing families, and couples dressed in smart heels and fresh fashions rubbed shoulders with grubby, crying, laughing, and suddenly directionless pilgrims. The more people I saw run to each other and hug, the more alone I felt, seeing no one I knew. I felt utterly invisible to the locals, visitors, and pilgrims alike. My heart sank. This seemingly simple ritual of arriving always failed to be entirely gratifying.

I finally took myself on an aimless wandering across the ancient, rainbow-colored stones of the medieval town, which actually slowly lifted my spirit through its beauty and the slow realization that millions had walked these cobble streets before me, and many were walking now with me. Once again, I did not walk alone. I methodically visited all the accommodations on my path, noting details in my notebook even as I found them all to be booked full. After I had researched nearly every accommodation in the old town and worked a spiral back out to the old town's edge, I came upon a three-story townhouse of gray granite with pale yellow shutters on its windows. It was run by a mother and daughter who greeted me and cheered my pilgrim's arrival.

"Do you have a room?" I asked.

"We were booked full but just had a cancellation," the daughter replied.

"Is it possible to have it for four days?"

"So curious," she smiled with a quizzical brow. "The cancelled reservation was for four days."

"Not curious," her septuagenarian mother said, pointing a finger toward the sky. "It's the Camino." It was the same strange magic that I'd experienced several times both on the Camino and with Le Chardon and Nadiya. I felt lucky but also a pang of sadness—that door to Le Chardon and its particular magic was soon closing. But surely, just as it was here in Santiago de Compostela, this magic would continue. The joy of this moment dissolved any sadness I had carried from the cathedral square.

The daughter showed me to a pretty little room with pale yellow bedspread, thick granite walls, and a glass-enclosed balcony overlooking the medieval town. A single yellow rose in a crystal vase sat at the bedside. It reminded me of my mother, who would set a rose cut from the garden on my bedside table on early summer mornings to gently awaken me from sleep.

I shed my rain-sodden shoes and clothes and set them out on the sunny balcony to dry, enjoying, as I did this, a view of the whole medieval city below me. "Mont joie!" I cried. I put on dry, warm, and clean clothes and set off downhill to deliver the promised hug, prayers, and blessings to Saint James in the cathedral.

When my turn came, I stepped up the stairway behind the altar and stood behind the silver, gold, and gem-encrusted James and gave him a bear hug. I could feel the raised gold scallop shell on his back press into me. Everyone was suddenly there—everyone I'd met on the road and everyone I loved. First came Miles and his "just go and find out" explorer's outlook. Then came my parents and my brother and his family and their unwavering belief in me. Next, Bernadette, with her alchemical journey, and Nadiya, with her attitude of "Life is better when you float." Then, Petrus and Jean and their endless generosity, the Canadian accountant and his pockets full of joy, Sarah and what's possible, Cédric and his healing touch, and all the friends and family in the USA, France, and Spain who had rallied and cheered and never questioned the sanity of all this. Then came the folks I had met on this three-part goose quest—all the pilgrims and all the locals. All who had wished me a *buen Camino* and trusted I would deliver their prayers. The man with the gold sneakers in Pamplona. The olive harvesters outside of Ponferrada. The quince jam maker of Trabadelo, and the woman in the forest gathering chestnuts. The Sainte Bs of France and Spain. The angel and the saint from Buenos Aires. The hospitaleros tending to our physical and spiritual needs every day for little in return. The women from their balconies calling out "¡Ánimo y fé!" The birds, the animals, the trees, the flowers, the rocks, hills, mountains, rivers, and streams—all infused with the presence of the wild divine, feminine and masculine, the goose and gander, the Marys, Jameses, and Jesuses. And Susanna from Alaska, the seer from Australia, the Templar knights of Melide and Vega de Valcarce, and Mr. Stripes and her way of always finding me. I was overwhelmed by how they could all be here, and in a split-second announce each individual presence as distinctively as the aspects of a multifaceted diamond hitting the light.

I held Santiago's bejeweled shoulders a moment longer, finally releasing him as tears of real joy and amazement streamed down my face. I stepped down and followed the next set of arrows, the final arrows, that led at last to the tomb of the apostle. Whether his bones truly lay there or not, it didn't matter. He was here, everywhere, and now for weeks had walked with me, an ethereal presence I now knew was as real as the dirt path. *How does it feel to be visiting your tomb,* I asked him. *No big deal when you have transcended time and space,* he answered without pause.

I knelt before the crypt that held Santiago's ornate silver reliquary embossed with the chi-ro, the original symbol of Christ, the six-armed star, a replica of the more ancient seed of life that represents the union of heaven and earth. Funny that it also looked like two goose footprints joined at the heel. This had to be the sixty-third square, the center of the Game of the Goose and the final and winning move. How was it then, I wondered as I stepped back out into the nave and circumambulated throughout the whole cathedral, that it still didn't quite feel finished?

Perhaps it was a practical matter, that I still had another hundred-plus kilometers (62-plus miles) to walk to the Atlantic Coast, a pilgrimage in its own right. In the Middle Ages, Finisterre, Land's End, was considered to be the end of the world. It was not officially a part of the Camino Francés, but for many it feels like the natural end, most likely because the arrival at the sea creates a natural barrier and end to any further walking. Though I would walk it in the name of practical research for the guidebook, I also hungered for the ocean's natural threshold and felt it had something just for me, something to reveal about this nutty quest of mine.

I left the church and walked to the pilgrim's welcome office to gather my *Compostela*, the certificate acknowledging that I had completed this sacred walk as a pilgrim to Santiago de Compostela. Like concentrated trail magic, as soon as I walked in, there in the waiting line for their certificates were nearly all the people I'd met separately all along the length of the Camino, from Saint-Jean-Pied-de-Port to last night's outpost. How had the Camino orchestrated that? I saw the woman from Tampa, both women from Oregon—the one who had gifted me the pen and the aspiring writer just out of college, the young Argentine from the Cruz de Ferro, the poetry reciting couple from Dublin, young South Koreans I'd met in Pamplona, a French couple I'd walked with from Ponferrada to O Cebreiro, the merry band of pilgrims in San Martin del Camino, a fellow Coloradan I'd met in Triacastela, and so many more. Missing only were the Canadian accountant and Susanna from Alaska, the two who perhaps more than any on this trek knew about the deeper goose walk I was on.

After we received our certificates, several of us gathered and went for a celebratory meal in the medieval town. We hugged and said goodbye, knowing many of us were leaving the next day and that we would likely never see each other again.

I happily spent my four days in Santiago de Compostela before setting off west again. As a city I'd first come to well over two decades earlier and visited often since, it never failed to show me something hidden and new. On my last evening, I wandered along its ancient, cobbled streets, letting my feet decide where to turn next, and found myself on one of the cathedral's four squares, standing in front of a pilgrim information center and small shop. I went in. On the customer side of the counter was a thickly built and heavily bearded man standing in stocking feet. His boots were on the floor next to him, the soles completely blown out, as if they had been in an explosion. He had been studying a map the man on the other side of the counter had just spread out. The two turned toward me and smiled.

"Care to have a tarot reading?" the burly man asked. For any amount I wished to donate, I could have a reading, he added. Sure, why not. It seemed innocent enough.

"I've been walking the Camino perpetually for over two years," the tarot reader told me. "I'm Otto, from Brazil." We shook hands. He had walked four Caminos so far, one after the other, the Francés, Portugués, Aragonés, and Camino Mozárabe from Granada. "I'm now thinking of walking the Camino del Norte, as soon as I can afford a new pair of shoes." He laughed. I looked at his stocking feet and decided he may need new socks, too. I lay down five euros to help the cause and Otto reached in the large side pocket of his cargo pants and pulled out a tiny deck of tarot cards. He shuffled the cards and set them down on the open map. "Split the deck."

I split the cards. He drew and turned over the top three, laying them side by side: Four of Cups, Death, and Nine of Cups. "Your past, present, and future," Otto said. All I could see was my present: Death. Ugh. I should have said no to the reading. Otto saw where my eyes focused and said, "Don't worry, it ends well: your future is represented by the Nine of Cups, the card of harmonious relationship, with another as well as with yourself. But to get there," his face grew theatrically somber, "you have to fully process the past—Four of Cups—which is about worrying too much about what others think and wanting to be accepted by others." Hello, Sarah. *What's possible if you have nothing to prove to anyone?* "And then, of course, the present, but it's a metaphoric death, not an actual one. Death here is about letting go of the things from your life that are now dead, that have no life any longer. It is also about honoring the central place they once held in your life. You need to honor, mourn, then release these things before moving forward."

I tried to think about what it was I needed to release and recalled the tear-soaked dream I'd had in Melide about all the things I'd missed and needed to let go—places, people, youth, immortality. It was still true—I still needed to take the time to honor what had been and mourn it before moving forward. I understood why walking to the Atlantic Ocean made so much sense to so many: it offered this last leg to do just that, to reflect and reach a resolution by the time the trail ran out and there was no more land on which to walk. The ocean forced a confrontation, a meeting with the infinite that also had a definitive, finite end.

"It's a process," Otto continued. "It always will be, and it will cycle around, more death and more rebirth." He laughed. "Why do you think I'm addicted to walking?" Me, too, I realized. Bernadette would like him.

"So, here in Compostela," I said to Otto, "where I expected rebirth, I get death?" This was the fifty-eighth square, the tomb. I still had to throw the exact number on the dice to land on the winning square.

"It's the Camino's humor," Otto answered. "Why not draw some more cards to get to the bottom of this? No extra charge." The man behind the counter had by now become as fixated on the outcome as I had. Otto shuffled the cards again, I split the deck, and he drew out the top ten, laying them in the Celtic Cross pattern. Among them was the Nine of Cups, again, "which is good," Otto assured me, along with the Hermit and the Tower. Great. Ugh. The card of solitary life followed by the card of all known things toppling to dust. I should have stopped at the three-card reading.

"Don't worry," cooed Otto. "Instead of Death, which, recall, is your present moment, your current Santiago, these cards define the next few months, maybe year, where you will spend a lot of time working alone and where all the old ways will crumble but also where you will begin to build a new life, one that better suits and supports you."

Huh. That was exactly the year I had ahead of me, writing a new book, one that would require long hours in solitude and changing a lot about my daily life in order to pull it off, and also one on which I placed a lot of hope and desire for a long future engagement. "It's perfect, really," Otto was saying as I pondered all this. "Death clears things and frees you to go forth into the wilderness and discover the best way to build your life." I thanked Otto and wished him good luck too, for his next leg in life. When I turned to go, I saw a line had grown behind me. I was sure Otto would have new boots by the time the shop closed for the night.

As soon as I stepped outside, I ran into the Coloradan I'd met in Triacastela, a woman fifteen years older than me, who had also walked the Camino solo. We went to a nearby café. Over wine, I told her about my Melide dream and Otto's reading.

"Maybe getting older is simply learning to embrace this fact and let each victory, each glass of wine, be more pleasurable and joyous for the fact that it will all be over in a blink of an eye," she said. She had walked the pilgrimage, I learned, to give thanks and celebrate overcoming an aggressive cancer and gaining precious more years to live. We clinked glasses and I let her wisdom sink in. In the sweet air of a soft and gentle evening, we walked together to the kilometer zero stone in the main cathedral square, touched it for good luck, and hugged goodbye. Early the next day I was a nomad again, heading for the fishing village of Muxía ninety kilometers away, and then from there to Finisterre. I was excited for movement once again and for the electricity of the open trail.

THE LAMIA

TORRENTIAL RAINS MARKED the way to Muxía, creating a strangely claustrophobic experience of misty closed forests that hid until the last moment the approaching nearness of the open and expansive ocean. It also added focusing drama when I passed through a village on whose central square was a large fountain in which stood a towering nude woman carved from white stone. She had long flowing hair and her feet, immersed in the shallow water were clearly webbed and goose-like. Thus I came face to face with a lamia, that water fairy and affiliate of the mother goddess with goose feet and goose ways who worked fiercely with the mother to defend nature and protect justice. The lamia appeared in folklore all across northern Spain and into southwestern France, and though her signs were all across that territory, it took arriving in the far northwest for me to meet her in the full, literal form detailed in legends. The far outposts of rural and remote Europe, like this part of Galicia, were among the last to be fully Christianized, and the old stories survived longer in such places, and the fact that the lamia still held pride of place in the heart of this village told me that the people living there weren't shy about that history either. The web-footed goddess had survived and was once again celebrated in a place that still cultivated the earth, kept waterways healthy, and lived by the seasons.

The way to Muxía was a constant reminder of this, with chapels, shrines, and a monastery all built in places of ancient power associated with nature spirits and grace. It was also a walk done entirely in solitude, even more so than what I had experienced on the trek from Saint-Jean-Pied-de-Port to Santiago de Compostela. The silence allowed for a remarkable amount of processing, sorting, and putting into perspective. When I neared the coast and the fishing village of Muxía, I felt near the end, close to the winning square. The weather had shifted and everywhere was sunshine, yet the ocean was still hidden from view due to the tight hills and dense forests.

I picked up my pace, hoping to reach Muxía in time for the sunset, and dove into pine forest with a dense tapestry of fern undergrowth and lavender autumn crocuses pushing up against the dark brown forest floor. Only at the very last minute did the trees pull aside their theatrical curtain to reveal a crescent-moon-shaped beach and endless azure waters. I stepped through the curtain, so to speak, with an overwhelming rush of freedom surging through me as if I had just passed through Mother Earth's birth canal into a world of limitless possibilities. The ground underfoot shifted from spongy moss to soft sand. At the far end of the curved beach clustered the colorful village of Muxía on a narrow finger of land, with one side surrounded by its fishing boats in a protected harbor side and on the other exposed to the open ocean. There, where wind and waves have whipped since the Middle Ages, I saw the shrine of Nuestra Señora del Barco, Our Lady of the Boat, the site of many miracles.

Local legend claimed that the church's location was where nearly two thousand years ago Mary arrived from the Holy Land in a stone boat at the same time that, according to legend, Saint James was there evangelizing. It was during a low point in his ministry, when he was gaining few converts, that Mary came to him to tell him that his work was planting seeds whose growth he might not witness in his own lifetime. Encouraged, James watched her depart, leaving the stone boat behind as proof of her visit.

An hour later, I arrived at that tip of land where several massive stones, looking very much like a prow, stern, and sail, lay below the shrine built in Mary's honor. But those boulders were also attached to even older folklore that claimed them as magical healing stones for centuries, maybe even millennia, before Saint James's arrival.

The stone shaped like a sail, twice my height, was folded over in a concave curve, like a giant potato chip with its opposite tips resting on the ground and a passage opening beneath the peak of its arch. Traditionally, and still today during special festivals, people have crawled through that portal to ask for healing, forgiveness, grace, and cures for anything that ails them in body, mind, and spirit.

I took off my pack and crawled through, whispering a prayer for grace to heal whatever might need healing in order to make me stronger and more whole. Perhaps I imagined it, but I could feel an effervescent energy, like dancing fingers, pulling fatigue, pain, negativity, and old residues of past events out and away from me. I felt lighter on the other side.

I went into town and found a place to stay. The pilgrims there were all new acquaintances, people I had never seen on the trail across northern Spain. After having a rest and handwashing my clothes, I returned to the sacred rocks just as the sun hit the ocean's horizon, infusing the water and land with flaming dark orange, red, and rose. The waves crashed with rhythmic booms onto the polished stones, which were now bathed in fiery hues. I sat for a long time, letting the colors and tide wash away any remaining psychic cobwebs and grit. Only when the sky turned a deep velvety blue and the stars began to flicker did I pick my way over the rocky landscape and back to the village that was built so elegantly on a strip of land between forest, bay, and ocean. At the local café, I was quickly folded into local life. Everywhere in this place spoke of the goose, of humans existing in harmony with nature, of people in harmony with each other, of insiders and outsiders all being welcome.

My albergue faced the ocean, with a kind mother and daughter at its helm, running it like a well-captained ship. The few pilgrims there—a Canadian couple, three Spaniards, an Argentine, two Koreans, a German, and me—gathered in the kitchen and cooked dinner together. We were like lost children, wondering what to do next, now that there was no more road left to walk. Go home, turn around and walk back, stay here? I knew my answer: to walk south to Finisterre. I still had thirty-two kilometers (20 miles) of road left and I was happy, for I was in no hurry to be done, even though I felt I'd performed every ritual of closure, from hugging the apostle to experiencing the infinite ocean swallowing the sun.

I awoke before dawn and returned to the polished stones where I'd witnessed the sunset the night before. This time I faced east and waited. Slowly, light grew over the green forest canopy and hills, splashing soft pink, lavender, and tangerine across the land and sky. I could feel the colors run their fingertips though my hair as they worked their way over my shoulder and onto the ocean, tumbling across its slate blue surface and weaving together earth, air, water, and fire. Once the sun was up, I set off on the final leg of the way of the wild goose.

62

BETWEEN THE SETTING SUN
AND THE NORTH STAR

N O SOONER HAD I return to the trail than the rain returned as well. With it came whipping winds that tangled my poncho and drenched my pack, boots, and clothes. Shivering in the cool morning air, I gave up and submitted, letting this be a final baptism on my quest. I trudged laboriously up the steep and rocky side of a small mountain. I could smell but not see the ocean because of the dense growth of pine all around me, but courtesy of the cleansing rain, I saw dusty rocks being washed clean, their surfaces sparkling with crystals in white, rose, and lavender. Recalling the neoTemplar of Melide's mention of Galicia's quartz-rich earth, I held my focus on the glimmering earth and reached the summit energized. The sun came out. The wind stopped. I descended again into a lush wet forest. On my way down, a young man walked toward me on his way up, the first person I'd seen since leaving Muxía. He wore a baseball cap over long dreadlocks that swung with each step. Into his cap he had stuck several foot-long feathers, Musketeer style. He was a vision with his billowing, striped pajama pants, thin t-shirt worn under a handwoven Ecuadorian hoodie, and bare feet, and with his sandals swinging from a tiny backpack that was even thinner than Luke's. I said hello to him. He smiled in return but gestured that he had taken a vow of silence.

"Are you walking to Muxía?" I asked.

He rocked his hand from side to side. Not quite. With air drawings and wide arm movements he indicated that he had already been to Muxía and was now walking back from Finisterre; from there, he was walking back to Santiago de Compostela and then back and back and back, all the way to Saint-Jean-Pied-de-Port where he had begun. He next drew in the air the classic Camino arrow we all followed, looking at me to see if I understood so far. I nodded. He then reverse-drew the arrow and looked at me, waiting.

No way.

"You're following the arrows in reverse, the footprint of the goose?"

He smiled enthusiastically and bobbed his head vigorously. He placed his hand over his heart and then held both his hands in prayer position, bowed slightly, waved, and walked on. Having completed the novice's journey of spiritual initiation he was now making the journey back home as the initiate, mastering his deeper spiritual path and deepening it further with a vow of silence. I watched him vanish up the slope, swallowed by the trees. Of all the people for me to meet on my last leg of the Camino, it was a barefoot initiate following the goose?

Without knowing it, wasn't this what Sarah and I had done? I laughed at the irony: my first pilgrimage following the goose had actually been in reverse and yet, way back at the start, I missed the whole message of the way of the goose; to go deeper, to see beyond conventional arrow views. I had worried about what others thought, about the arrow view, and had not claimed my right livelihood fully, the goose view. *Why was I so dense?*

That was the question, all the more so, given that I had read many books on Camino lore by modern French and Spanish authors who stated that the walk west was a walk of initiating the novice to the spiritual path, and that the walk east, returning, was the walk of the just-initiated going deeper and mastering the newly acquired spiritual knowledge. West opened the eyes; east deepened the vision. Arrow vision was surface vision; goose footprint vision was seeing past limitations and illusions. Arrow vision was dust-covered rocks; goose footprint vision was rain-washed, multicolored crystal quartz.

The sun had burned off the hovering mist and dried my skin

and clothes by the time I climbed the last hill to Finisterre and could see the ocean once again. A serpentine path led me into the narrow town, which, like Muxía, was huddled on a jutting finger of land surrounded by water, this one a rocky crest like a spiky dragon's spine. It ran north-south, creating a perfect east- and west-facing ridge from which to watch both the rising and the setting sun, a natural landscape ideally suited to witnessing cyclical births, deaths, and rebirths. No wonder it had been a destination since prehistory and was considered by medieval Europe to be the end of the world.

Fishing boats bobbed calmly far below in the protective harbor near which I found a place to stay. Free of my pack, I climbed the final three kilometers to the southernmost tip of land, to the lighthouse on the precipice. There I sat on large, wind-polished boulders below the lighthouse, dangling my feet over the open ocean. I watched again as the sun lowered, kissed the water's sur- face, and then, like a fish coming to the surface to claim a delec- table morsel, the ocean swallowed the sun whole. Awe over such beauty, gratitude, love, and an unexpected sense of accomplish- ment overwhelmed me much as the ocean had the sun. Utter con- tentment and perfection exceeding words nailed me to where I sat. Communion and total trust flooded my cells. I understood better why many people need to keep walking from Santiago de Compostela to Finisterre. In Santiago, I had arrived, but my arrival didn't feel like the swan of the sixty-third square. It was more death than rebirth. But here, the whole orientation of land and ocean enacted and repeated the full cycle. One walked hundreds of kilo- meters to die and be reborn. Santiago de Compostela was the tomb, Finisterre the womb.

I stayed there a few days. I walked to a crescent-moon-shaped beach and found a sea-worn scallop shell to symbolize my journey to the end of the earth. Its cracks, chips, barnacles, and grooves made an honest and perfect symbol for my imperfect self—how long had it taken me to piece all this together?—taking an abso- lutely perfect journey. Like seeing the arrows in reverse, I could now see my life better along with the choices I'd made. Arrow

vision, representing surface conventions, called me a writer seeking
success, a wife, a daughter, a member of this club or that party.
Goose-footprint vision lifted the lid and revealed below the surface the authentic workings, so that I was inspired to write the
deeper stories, sink into the earth's lessons, and be a seeker of inner
and outer truths—a devotee of beauty; a devoted partner and best
friend; a loving and dedicated daughter, sister, aunt, explorer, and
pilgrim. Arrow view had everything to do with others' opinions;
goose view had everything to do with what best served my actual
walk-in-life. Arrow view flattened the narrative, goose view showed
every topographical possibility. Going from arrows to goose footprints was what launched and unfolded the alchemical journey.

Three days later, I caught the bus to Santiago de Compostela,
and after two more days there, I boarded trains for León, then
Pamplona, then Hendaye, Biarritz, Bordeaux, and at last, Sarlat.
Two French pilgrims sat in the same car as mine as our train
departed Santiago. One was returning to his home in Versailles,
and the other, to Paris.

"How do you feel about going back?" the man from Versailles
asked, his tone melancholy.

"I feel both sadness and happiness," I replied. "Sad to leave this
simple life and sense of adventure; happy to be returning to family
and friends."

"Me, too," he said, forcing a smile.

"Not me," said the Parisian. "I feel only sadness that after this
great adventure, I am going back to normal."

It hit me then: the key was not letting one's vision close down
again. The key was to keep the quest vision open, alive, and not
let life get routinized and "normal" again. Stay alert, awake, and
fully alive.

In Biarritz, I paused the journey for two days to rest and visit
Cédric. He picked me up at the station. "Did you find Nirvana?"

"This time I think I did. The key is to hold on to it once you
find it."

Two days later Nadiya met me at the train in Sarlat. "Le
Chardon still has not sold. It's waiting for you," she said with a

wide grin. I felt a flood of relief and joy. The nightmare I'd had in Melide was only that, a bad dream, and here I was, coming full circle after a massive three-part journey between the setting sun and the north star. And now I had three weeks to inhabit my home of homes, complete my research for the book while still in Europe, and then board the flight home to Miles's open arms and a life striving to hold onto goose vision and keep it open against arrow vision's pressure and habit.

63

THE SWAN

A FEW MORNINGS later, I dangled my legs over the stone wall above Saint Sacerdos cathedral in the sunshine as its Sunday mid-morning bells pealed uphill and vibrated every cell of my being. I'd just come from the tower behind me, the *lanterne des morts*, where the door had been open, and happily discovered that the shell I'd left there before beginning my Camino trek was still there. Someone had filled it with wine and surrounded it with polished pebbles, herbs, flowers, and notes, apparently using the shell as the center of a blessing ritual. It warmed my heart to know that as I'd walked the Camino, I was a part of a sacred act back in Sarlat. I closed my eyes, soaking up the warm sun, hoping Mr. Stripes would appear. I had not yet seen her since my return. I also reflected on how good it felt to be in Le Chardon one last time, which was allowing me to enjoy it but also fully let it go. In a sense, the new owner who was selling it had helped in this process. While I was gone, he had set to modernizing and refurbishing the place in order to make it more sellable. When I returned, it was in the midst of renovation, so he had offered me a reduced rent for the trouble. Little did I know that with the owner's frequent absence at the property, I had become an unofficial general contractor, letting the parade of plumbers, electricians, masons, city gas and water personnel in each day and conveying their questions by phone to the owner. Le Chardon ceased to feel like my space or smell like my grandmothers' homes; it felt more like Grand Central Station. No matter how beautiful and soulful my time there had been in the past, this last time was weaning me off my attachment. When the toilet stopped flushing and the gas was disconnected, I snipped the last thread.

But pilgrim life and the goose journey helped me adapt. I cooked my meals on a single electric burner, and I took bucket-and-sponge cavalry baths like horseback soldiers on the march or pilgrims in rough digs. I also was unexpectedly learning French construction and engineering terms, a skill that would come in handy at some as yet unknown time in the future when I could afford to buy a home in the Dordogne—a dream that had intensified, not diminished. I still savored the early-morning market-day sounds of the fishmonger's ice shoveling and the banter of the cheese, sausage, bread, walnut oil, and wine merchants setting up in the small square under my window. I especially knew to drink it all up now, for the next time I returned to Sarlat, access to this precious third-floor perch would be no more.

I also delved deeply into why I was really there: to soak up the energy and depth of land, culture, and people and to be with beloved friends, savor the market days, and do research in the local library with its rich collection of publications on the Camino. I thought of Otto the Brazilian tarot reader and tipped my cap to him. Le Chardon was a sinking ship, but in the vast ocean of the Périgord, other, more appropriate vessels awaited.

As if in affirmation of this resolution, I felt a soft bump and opened my eyes to the meows and demands of Mr. Stripes. The soft Sunday morning and its calm had brought her out. During the week, all the contractors' comings and goings in the building and on the street below, she explained, had put her off. My heart swelled. The Sarlat I loved was now complete.

In the afternoon, I set off across town for my date with my other mystic friend. Bernadette had already brewed her potent gunpowder-green-and-mint Moroccan tea and was pouring it into delicate Limoges teacups when I walked through her door. With a sideways glance, she said, picking up the thread of conversation from two months earlier, "Incidentally, the cycle always begins again. It's never done. You've just finished one cycle, one that took three pilgrimages to puzzle through. You are now beginning a new one, like a spiraling coil, going ever deeper." She set my teacup before me and smiled triumphantly. I hugged her and sat down.

"So from goose to swan and back to goose again?"

"We must go through death to get to rebirth," she replied. "And on and on, birth, death, and rebirth are constant companions. *That* is the alchemical journey. *That* is the way of the wild goose and of all the earth." She gave me a sly smile, "You, I think, will keep walking the Chemin, perhaps for the rest of your life. That is how you restart each cycle and take your journey deeper each time."

"I hope so."

"We're all on the Chemin in some fashion or another. Of course, most people aren't even aware of it, which is why I prefer my books." Goose vision over arrow.

The Advent season began when I still had a week left in Sarlat. Everyone in town was busy decorating the shops, chapels, houses, and streets with blue, white, and silver ornaments and lights. A large Christmas tree appeared in the cathedral square, giving off a pleasing pine and candle-wax scent. A crèche appeared near the altar in the cathedral, its manger created from lean-to tree branches, dried grass, and heather. It sheltered figurines of Mary and Joseph gathered around an empty cradle, awaiting the arrival of the Christchild on December 25. With them in the inner circle were a ceramic donkey and a sheep, but another, outer circle arrayed more witnesses to the miracle about to occur: a Périgord farmwoman with geese and a Périgord huntsman, dressed like mushroom hunters I knew in the region, holding a loaf of bread. As everyone awaited Jesus's birth—and then the shepherds and the wise men, pilgrims all—the mother goddess and the sacred wild man kept company with the holy couple and protected them, sustaining them and waiting to help in midwifing the celestial birth and eventual rebirth of light in the world.

A week later, at the airport and just before boarding my plane for the States, I called Nadiya to thank her one more time for my homecoming and her friendship.

"From here, it is going to be easier for you," she uttered into the receiver. I hadn't expected a one-liner this time, and it caught my breath. The past few years had been tough, but the ordeals, gifts, and this triple pilgrimage had given me a lot to work with and had also strengthened my walk on the path of my best right livelihood.

"That would be nice," I whispered.

Like a wild goose, I flew to my winter roost, sad to leave Spain and France, but joyous to reunite with Miles, family, and friends. I settled back into the familiar windy and gray ocean landscape, not entirely the same person I had been, yet more of whom I really was. True to Otto's prediction, it was a Hermit year, but one full of Nine of Cups connections. I worked hard to create the new book. I cultivated the deeper connections my walk had forged with those whom I love and with Mother Earth. I had become goosefooted. My pockets were stuffed with joy. I felt infinite gratitude for all the blessings of this life of right and vibrant meaning and livelihood. I also felt the stirrings, as geese do in late winter, to fly again and return to an ancient path which, no matter how many times one flies along it, is always new and fresh with new stories to share and new clues, geese, and hunches to impart. There is no end to goose vision. I learned at the end of my walk what had been before me all along since the beginning. It ends at the beginning and begins at the end. It is all about the journey in between, it turns out, and now it starts anew.

So much of the folklore and iconography I encountered on this route reaffirmed over and over the idea that the goose is the lost feminine divine, half of the equation to wholeness in any spiritual or social tradition. If one half is oppressed, ignored, or put down, then society is half-baked, unhealthy, and unwhole. The goose holds that space until the time we can turn this tide and expand back into both our halves, which includes healing not only our families, communities, and nations, but also the very earth from which we are created, receive our sustenance, and to which we return. Deep in the core of all of this is the goose, Mother Earth, and her wisdom can make us whole. In return, we must cherish and protect her too.

MEETING THE GOOSE, AGAIN

N THAT HERMIT year, long after I had given up on trying to acquire a copy of Father Rafael Ojeda's article on the Game of the Goose design inlaid on the Plaza de Santiago of Logroño in La Rioja, I received a golden goose. A fellow pilgrim and writer who was also curious about the Game of the Goose and had written about it—who was in fact my original source for learning about Ojeda's manuscript—said he was happy to let me have a look at his copy of Ojeda's essay. I held my breath as I carefully read the essay, as if I had rolled the perfect number and was about to land on the sixty-third square. *What might happen?* I hoped fiercely for illumination but was afraid the manuscript would reveal nothing.

Ojeda created many classic designs for the Game of the Goose boardgame, calling it from the start a mystical journey where you could learn only by stepping in and playing. He set it in its historical lineage, which he traced to a game in ancient Greece that was reintroduced into Europe by German bible sellers—a game that already had sixty-three squares featuring goose guardians, dice, bridges, a well, labyrinth, jail, and death. For Ojeda, the game was a metaphor for the development of our human souls: First, the soul is asleep and is unaware of itself, then the soul awakens and not only becomes aware of itself as a soul but discovers it is on a human journey. This awakening occurs through playing the game, through setting onto the road through life that it lays out. The Camino can be one such soul-path, and that is why it and the game are fused together.

But Ojeda also did something that no one else had done: He created a design for the board game that became the template for the the layout of the game inlaid in stone in the Plaza de Santiago in Logroño. This design divides sixty-three into seven rows with nine squares each and shows that on the path one must pass through and ascend all seven levels before reaching the square of transformation, goose to swan, pilgrim to Saint James. This is no accident—it is the path of the soul's ascent, and Ojeda's board design is a map writ large of our bodies' seven chakras.

The Game of the Goose's first layer, containing the first nine squares, aligns with the first chakra at the base of the spine, where all our grounding on earth and our earthly concerns are rooted. This includes our five senses and our ability to navigate the world outside. On the Camino, in the modern era, the journey begins in Saint-Jean-Pied-de-Port, but for medieval pilgrims the first leg of the journey started from their own front door. The second layer and second set of nine squares represents the second chakra, which has to do with relationships, creativity, and sexuality. The third layer and chakra, the solar plexus, is about self-empowerment, individu-ation, and confidence. The fourth layer represents the heart chakra, where we learn and express compassion, kindness, and universal love. The heart chakra is located at the center of the seven layers, merging the lower chakras with the higher—yet another earth-and-heaven marriage. The fifth layer of nine squares is the throat chakra, where we learn to use our voice and our will with respect and for upliftment. The sixth, the head chakra, including the third eye, is where true vision, perception, and knowledge arise. And the seventh layer of squares, landing at last in the winning square, is the crown chakra, the place of wisdom and universal communion, union and oneness with all that is.

Ojeda wrote that the placement of geese in each of the squares throughout is also not an accident. If you were to line up the Game of the Goose along these seven tiers of nine squares—exactly as the inlaid game in Logroño's Santiago square does—you will find that a goose leads you to the next level and meets you again in the middle of each level, a constant guide and guardian. The goose's transformation into a swan in the final square completes the full alchemical journey of transfiguration, moving from matter to spirit, the means through which full communion takes place with both ourselves and the Great Spirit of all that is.

Only after reading the article did I remember the two postcards I'd bought in O Cebreiro of modernist, psychedelic paintings by the Franciscan friar depicting the Camino de Santiago and O Cebreiro. I dug the cards out. One showed a painting of a seated person in meditation, his crown—again, the site of wisdom and union—capped with the cathedral of Santiago de Compostela, and his throat—the site of will and voice—overlayed with the chalice and host of O Cebreiro's miracle of transubstantiation. The heart, merging heaven and earth in the middle, was more abstract, holding two birds in a Valentine's heart, leaving it to the viewer to fill in. To me, it had to be the Marian labyrinth that embraced León with its four Marys guiding one in, then back out. The first chakra, again, to me, was Saint-Jean-Pied-de-Port; the second, Eunate; the third, Logroño; and the sixth? Where had a shift of perception come for me? It could have been in Palas de Rei's San Tirso church with the statue depicting Mary standing on a pulsating, spiraling Earth, or in Leboreiro with its goose-goddess fountain, or in Melide's church of Santa María and its telluric and underground water sources.

And why nine squares per row? Completing this connection and revelation, Ojeda also answered this question. Demeter, he wrote, who represents the fertile earth, travels for nine days looking for her daughter. Once she finds her, the cycle of life starts anew. Mother Earth works in cycles: Her daughter, Persephone—the animated and cyclical aspect of the Mother—must spend four months of the year separate from her mother in the underground, the declining and dormant seasons of late autumn and winter. She then returns to the surface to spend the eight months of the birth and growing seasons—spring, summer, and early autumn—with her mother. And the cycle repeats itself, four months underground and eight months above, over and over, birth, growth, decline, death, rebirth. As all life requires cycles, so does the soul, whose stages of initiation occur in seven levels, each one with a meta-phoric nine-day cycle of birth, death, and rebirth, and each one guided by the Mother Goose goddess guardian, who helps us fulfill our growth and complete our passage.

Ojeda helped me see that by walking a sacred path with intention, our spirit awakens one layer at a time, adding more enlightenment and wisdom as we proceed. By the time we reach the winning square, we cannot help but see more fully and be more transformed, earning our swan wings, even if only partially. Then the cycle begins again, ever deepening, but now with seventh-chakra goose vision rather than five-senses, first-chakra arrow vision.

There is a common saying on the Camino: the first third of the path tests the body; the second third, the mind; and the final third, the spirit. This too is the Game of the Goose and the mystical path of the pilgrim as he or she walks and awakens to the energy centers in his or her own body as well as those of the earth.

The path is there for all. Some engage it by seated meditation and prayer, others by a labyrinth walk inlaid like Ojeda's Game of the Goose on a patch of earth in their community, while still others, like me, who are perhaps less talented, need to walk it long and far.

I looked at the other postcard from O Cebreiro, with its similar psychedelic painting of a seated person in mediation, his chakras once again clearly marked, only this time in more abstract and explosive colors and lines, with no explicit overlay of forms as on the other postcard. But on this second postcard, next to the med-itator I saw a clear guardian and guide, none other than the icon of O Cebreiro's Mary: the lucky goose, leading, protecting, and championing the individual's earthly walk and awakening.

Holy mother of God and Goddess Divine.

However it comes, this goose view, this seeing below the dusty surface into a marvelous, interconnected luminescence, is what the Game of the Goose, and life, and the Camino, and any good long walk or good sit-down meditation initiates us to, over and over, as our seeing more deeply goes from challenge to practice to devotion. And once you land on the winning square, as Bernadette constantly tells me, the cycle begins again. It is an ongoing and deepening process, this practicing of goose vision over arrow vision. And goose vision brings with it contentment, harmony, wholeness, and balance—all the things that sustain us and our magnificently beautiful Earth.

ACKNOWLEDGMENTS

Thank you, blessings, and grace to the many and countless beings who have influenced, helped, championed, and cheered these efforts and this work: my publisher, editor, and agent; the many generous locals and pilgrims on the Camino; beloved family and friends on both sides of the Atlantic; Miles, always Miles, who so often reminds me that the only way to discover something is to "go and find out"; the Camino de Santiago and its leyline energy; and above all, the goose goddess herself, our Earth and Mother who creates, sustains, and inspires us every step of the way.

ABOUT THE AUTHOR

A Colorado native based in southern New Jersey, the award-winning travel writer and anthropologist Beebe Bahrami has devoted herself for over three decades to regular semi-nomadic treks, research, explorations, and excavations in France and Spain. In addition to *The Way of the Wild Goose*, she is the author of two travel memoirs set in France—*Café Oc: A Nomad's Tales of Finding Home in the Dordogne of Southwestern France* and *Café Neandertal: Excavating the Past in One of Europe's Most Ancient Places*—and several travel guides, including *Moon Camino de Santiago: Sacred Sites, Historic Villages, Local Food & Wine; The Spiritual Traveler Spain: A Guide to Sacred Sites and Pilgrim Routes*; and *Historic Walking Guides: Madrid*. Her essays and articles appear in *BBC Travel, Wine Enthusiast, Archaeology, Bon Vivant, The Bark, Pennsylvania Gazette, Fodors.com, Perceptive Travel*, and *National Geographic*, among others. Bahrami has walked over 5,000 miles/8,000 kilometers—and counting—on the trails of the Camino de Santiago since taking her first steps on it in 1995. She speaks French and Spanish and is working on Occitan. To learn more, visit beebebahrami.weebly.com.

CPSIA information can be obtained
at www.ICGtesting.com
Printed in the USA
JSHW051710130222
22767JS00003B/3